User and Task Analysis for Interface Design

JoAnn T. Hackos and Janice C. Redish

WILEY COMPUTER PUBLISHING

WILEY

John Wiley & Sons, Inc.

New York • Chichester • Weinheim • Brisbane • Singapore • Toronto

User and Task Analysis
for Interface Design

Publisher: Robert Ipsen
Editor: Theresa Hudson
Managing Editor: Micheline Frederick
Text Design & Composition: RDD Consultants, Inc.

Designations used by companies to distinguish their products are often claimed as trademarks. In all instances where John Wiley & Sons, Inc., is aware of a claim, the product names appear in initial capital or ALL CAPITAL LETTERS. Readers, however, should contact the appropriate companies for more complete information regarding trademarks and registration.

This book is printed on acid-free paper. ∞

Published by John Wiley & Sons, Inc.

Published simultaneously in Canada.

Library of Congress Cataloging-in-Publication Data:

Hackos, JoAnn T.
    User and task analysis for interface design / JoAnn T. Hackos and Janice C. Redish.
        p.   cm.
    Includes bibliographical references and index.
    ISBN 0-471-17831-4 (cloth : alk paper)
    1. User interfaces (Computer systems) I. Redish, Janice.
II Title.
QA76.9.U83H33   1998
004.2'1--dc21
                                    97-37932
                                       CIP

Printed in the United States of America.

10   9   8

Contents

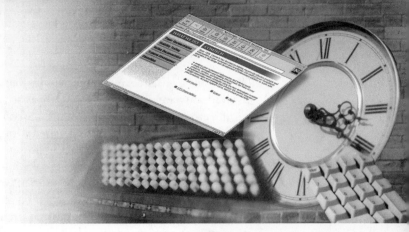

Preface

This book is the culmination of many years of practical experience and research in user interface design. Both of us have devoted our careers and our businesses to understanding people who use all types of products: documents by themselves, documentation as part of software and hardware products, software and hardware interfaces, and training. We came from document design, Ginny who founded the Document Design Center of the American Institutes for Research and JoAnn who founded Comtech Services, both in the late 1970s.

In our practices, we seemed to continually encounter frustrated users who found the interfaces of whatever products they were working with difficult to understand. In most cases, we discovered that the developers of those products—software, hardware, documents, or training materials—had spent almost no time understanding their users and how the users worked.

Particularly in the case of software, the developers seemed to spend most of their time describing the functional requirements of the new system and then programming the underlying structure. The interface was a last minute affair, tacked on at the end of the process with little or no thought given to its design as a coordinated and equally significant activity.

We needed to find a better way to produce high-quality, usable interfaces for products. And we each, independently, realized, as did many of our colleagues in documentation, human factors, and training, that the better way started in the field. Better interfaces came through observing and talking to users as they worked, making sense of what we learned from those encounters with users, and using that knowledge throughout design and development while continuing to work with users.

The first major user development activity that JoAnn's company engaged in involved software used by business-office specialists in Colorado hospitals. JoAnn's group was asked to find better ways to train and provide documentation to these specialists. What they negotiated with the company executives was two to three months of site visits to Colorado hospitals, following people through their daily routines, watching how they did their jobs and how they worked together to accomplish tasks. Only then did the team of writers and trainers work together to develop an integrated set of documentation and training materials to teach the business people how to use the new batch-oriented system of patient and hospital accounting. A year or so later, when the organization moved to terminals connected to mini-computers, the same team became leaders in the development of a new character-based user interface. Because the team had so much continuing interaction with users, the interface proved to be easier to use and learn than anyone had thought possible.

Ginny had the advantage of being part of the American Institutes for Research, where she was able to build on several decades of work and innovation in human factors, task analysis, and instructional systems design. When Ginny and her colleagues established the Document Design Center, Ginny set down a structured model of the process that the group would use on every project, a model that started with understanding your purposes for creating a product, the people who would use the product, what tasks they would use it to do, and where and how they would use it. It was surprising how often the idea of starting by making sure you understand these four issues, rather than just plunging into designing or writing, was a new for Ginny's clients.

But doing so paid off. One of the projects that Ginny's group did early on was to revise the employee benefits handbook for a major corporation. Although the client at first assumed that the professional writers in the Document Design Center would just take the book and redo it, Ginny's group insisted on doing site visits with users, and the client agreed. Ginny's colleague, Robbin Battison, led the project, observing and interviewing users in their offices, finding out when and why they did use the handbook, when and why they didn't use it, seeing how they fared when they tried to use it. Based on findings from the site visits, Ginny's group totally revamped the book. Because users went to the book with questions in mind, they made all the headings questions. Because users knew which type of benefit they were interested in, they made each type of benefit a major section and used icons to make the sections memorable—and this was before graphical user interfaces on the computer! The icons appeared with the section names in the table of contents and were the prominent feature of the running heads on every page. The new handbook was a great success. The client was happy. The users were happy. And the book won a major industry prize.

When personal computers started to appear on everyone's desk, a high level manager in a major computer company called on Ginny's group to help them communicate with this totally new group of users. The issues were identical to the ones that Ginny's group had dealt with in the stand-alone benefits handbook: understanding users who were different from the developers, understanding the tasks they were trying to do, understanding how the new way of working would fit into their environment, and designing to meet their needs.

By the mid-1980s, both of us were working primarily with companies producing software and hardware, and our focus on usability led to opening independent usability labs. Usability testing led to even more focus on the processes of user-centered design, including iterative design using informal and formal prototypes. We worked with many companies who not only wanted to improve the quality of their documents but also wanted to begin with the user interfaces of their products, from software of all types to complex medical equipment and other primarily hardware products that were beginning to add significant software interfaces to attract new customers.

This book, then, is the outcome of many years of experience working with users—visiting them on site, watching them in the usability lab, meeting with them to discuss initial design ideas, participating with them in interactive design exercises. The book is also, of course, the outcome of experience beyond our own. Many colleagues, both those we have worked with directly and those whose wisdom we have read or heard at conferences, have added to our understanding. Together we have all participated in a growing community of practicing professionals, researchers, and academics who are trying to understand users and find ways to bring sound user-centered and performance-centered techniques to the interface development process.

Some of the information in the book has its origins in presentations we and other colleagues have given at the annual meetings of organizations like the Society for Technical Communication (STC), the Usability Professionals' Association (UPA), and the Special Interest Group on Computer - Human Interaction (ACM SIGCHI). Our ideas have been honed by the responses of others to our presentations and by our responses to our colleagues' presentations.

We hope that you find the ideas, stories, and guidelines in this book stimulating. We hope that the techniques presented provide you with sufficient detail to get started on your own excursions into your users' world. We trust you will find it exciting and rewarding.

About the book

What is the book about?

This book is about doing field studies, going out on site visits to observe, listen to, and talk with the people who will be using your product. It is about seeing them being active at work or at home. It is about gathering information that will help you develop a product that they will want to use and be able to use easily and efficiently. It is also about taking what you learn during the site visits, making sense of the data, turning the data into useful information for design, and using it to develop prototypes of interface designs. Although our focus is largely on software and hardware, we make a strong point that every product has users who do tasks in definable environments, and every product has an interface. So whether you are designing a computer application, a fax machine, an oscilloscope, a user's manual, a web site, a help system, a benefits handbook, or anything else, this book is relevant to what you are doing.

How is the book organized?

User and Task Analysis for Interface Design is divided into an opening chapter and then four parts. In chapter 1, we introduce the concept of user and task analysis and its role in user-centered interface design. We also show you how user and task analysis draws on work in many disciplines and benefits from the varied backgrounds of the people who practice it.

In part 1, chapters 2 through 5, we introduce you to the fundamental reasons for going out on site visits and help you build a business case for doing so. To build a successful product you must understand the people who will use your product (users), the work they do (their goals and tasks), and the situations they work in (their physical, social, and cultural environments. Each chapter gives you ways of thinking about these critical factors and issues and questions that should shape your site visits): chapter 2 about users, chapter 3 about users' goals and tasks, and chapter 4 about environments. In chapter 5 on building the business case, we help you forestall objections that you may face if these techniques are not already being practiced in your company. We give you well-grounded information to counter possible objections.

Part 2, chapters 6 through 8, takes you into the details of how to get ready for your site visits. Chapter 6 introduces many techniques you can choose from to get good information for your interface design. It is not enough simply to meet with users and listen to their ideas about what they want in a product. To design an effective and usable interface means more—it means observing what users actually do, rather than what they tell you they do. We hope you come away from chapter 6 convinced that the depth of information you need for interface design comes primarily from actually going out to users, watching and listening to them as they work, and talking with them in the context of their work.

Chapters 7 and 8 help you plan for site visits by raising the topics to consider: your objectives, who will participate, where you will go, what you will do when you are there, how you will recruit participants, what materials you need to prepare, who should be on site visit teams, what kind of training those people need, and so on. You'll find lots of points to think about as well as tips for making decisions on these topics in many different situations.

We urge you to put down your planning decisions in a site visit plan, and we give you a sample site visit plan at the end of part 2. The outline of the plan is also available as a template in appendix A. Use the sample and the template to guide your own development of a plan for your site visits.

Part 3, chapters 9 and 10, is about actually conducting a site visit. Part 3 is filled with guidelines and tips. We want you to be confident that you are prepared to observe and listen carefully, to see and hear what users are really telling you both in their actions and their words, to probe beneath the surface of tasks for a deeper understanding of what users do and how they do it, and to do all that while being empathetic to the users so the experience is pleasant for both of you.

Part 4, chapters 11 through 14, helps you make sense of the information you have gathered and turn that information into interface designs. In chapter 11, you learn how to use a variety of techniques to analyze your data: workflow diagrams, task sequences, user/task matrixes, task scenarios, and many more. The techniques that you use will depend on the specifics of your situation: your objectives, where you are in the design process, how much experience your design team has with different types of data, and your role on the design team. We help you make those choices. All of the techniques serve the primary purpose of bringing the users home to the development team as real people doing real tasks and giving the team the information and motivation to focus at least as much attention on users and their needs as they have traditionally given to functionality.

In chapter 12, you make the transition from analysis to design. We help you think about qualitative and quantitative usability goals, about users' conceptual models and about metaphors for your design. We suggest several techniques for taking the analyses from chapter 11 and moving them to the design stage: from task scenarios to use scenarios, from workflows of the process users now do to streamlined and reengineered workflows that are even more logical and useful to users, and so on. You'll also see how to go from information to design through storyboards and sketches.

Chapter 13 is about prototyping and testing prototypes with users. We help you think about the advantages and disadvantages of different types of prototypes and different ways of evaluating prototypes. We show you how you can involve users deeply in the prototyping process, especially with paper prototyping sessions, which we describe in some detail.

Although detailed guidelines for designing screens are beyond the scope of this book, part 4 include tips for important aspects of design such as using grids and planning for specific elements of the design. We also point you to lots of resources to continue the design process beyond this book.

We close the book with chapter 14 about doing user and task analysis for documentation and training. Chapter 14 is addressed both to those with responsibility for documentation and training and to all others on design teams. User and task analysis is just as relevant to the design of effective documentation and training as it is to interface design. We help you think about the specific observations and questions you might want to do during user and task analysis so that you make wise decisions about the types of communication in products, what they should look like, how they should be organized, what they should say. We show you how the boundaries among documentation, training, and user interfaces have blurred so much that they must all be designed together. And we discuss the relevance of user and task analysis for different media and forms of communication, from user's manuals and online help to electronic performance support systems, web sites, and new ideas in computer-based training.

What else is in the book?

The chapters contain many stories, case studies, and examples designed to help you relate the discussion to your own experiences. Some of the stories come from published articles and books; we cite the sources for these. Some come from colleagues who have shared them. Where they have wanted their names used, we tell you who they are. Where they have wanted to be anonymous, we respected that choice.

Other stories come from our own experience in over 40 combined years of trying to understand users and tasks and applying that understanding to design interfaces, documentation, and training. Others are stories come from events that actually happened but are changed enough to avoid embarrassing the original participants. When the stories are not specifically identified, realize that they have slightly modified antecedents in real events. We have chosen not to identify the real events out of respect for the people involved, whether the stories have a positive or negative slant.

At the end of each chapter, you will find suggestions for further reading. Some of these articles and books are specifically referred to in the chapter; others are simply our suggestions about well-written work that will help you expand your knowledge of user-centered design.

Note also that the book contains three appendices. Appendix A is a detailed, annotated template of a site visit plan. Please feel free to use the template in your own organization, either as is or modified to meet your own needs. Appendix B is a list of companies that provide audio and video equipment that may assist you during user site visits or usability tests. This list is not meant to be exhaustive but to provide you with access to some organizations we have worked with. Appendix C offers a checklist for reviewing interfaces for usability.

Who should read this book?

If you are a software designer, interface designer, usability specialist, human factors specialist, instructional designer, or technical communicator, this book is especially designed for you. We introduce you to the techniques of user and task analysis so that you can use them to inform your design activities.

If you are an interface design or human factors specialist, you will find that the techniques we advocate in this book require the close attention to users in their actual work environments. You will find much here to use in training your team members or introducing user-centered design to the software developers you work with.

If you are a product manager, you will find much food for thought in this book. If you are contemplating including visits to your users' sites as an essential part of the pre-design activities for your product, we recommend that you begin with part 1. The chapters in part 1 will give you a good idea of why user and task analysis will be significant to the success of your product interface design.

If you are a manager of training or documentation, we recommend that you read through part 1 and chapter 14 and then direct your staff members to the details of parts 2 and 3. That will give them the information they need to get started with adding user information to the process of designing and developing documentation and training.

If you are a marketing director, a development manager, or anyone else in the organization who is responsible for ensuring that the products you develop are usable, then this book is also for you. We find that many people responsible for the development of products do not have much information about how products should be developed to ensure their usability.

If you are a business manager concerned about the usability of systems that your staff must use to accomplish their work, you also will be interested in the techniques that developers should be using in their interactions with you. It will be especially important to realize that you must give system developers, usability specialists, and others working on design, access to your staff members, not just to you or your managers if they are to design systems that will be genuinely usable.

If you are an instructor of software and product development, interface design, documentation, or instructional design, we recommend using this book to teach pre-design and front-end analysis. You will easily be able to apply the techniques taught in parts 2, 3, and 4 to your classroom activities.

How should you read or use this book?

If you are new to the concepts of user and task analysis, we recommend that you begin at the beginning. The introduction in chapter 1 and the foundations in part 1 will provide a solid starting point to learning why user and task analysis has a fundamental role to play in product and interface design. You will be able to use the information in these chapters to convince others on your development team and among your management that it is worth devoting the resources to gathering data by actually going out to users' sites and observing and listening to them as they work.

If you have already convinced yourself and others that user and task analysis is essential to your design process, you may want to go directly to part 2. In part 2, you go through the steps of planning site visits. After you have the visits planned, you can move into part 3 which explains how to observe and interview so that you get the information you need for a sound interface design.

If you have completed the first stages of your user site visits and need to begin to organize your information and present it to your development team, you may want to move into part 4. Here you will go through these essential steps: analyzing the data you have collected, turning your analysis into an interface design, and prototyping the interface and testing the prototype with your users.

Finally, if your task is to develop documentation and training, you may want to work through the foundations of part 1 and the techniques of parts 2 and 3. Then, review the perspective provided in chapter 14 before going back to chapters 11 through 13. Even though the details of the techniques in these chapters related to interface design, you will still find them relevant to designing user-centered information and training.

Acknowledgments

It is difficult to remember everyone who has contributed to work that encompasses two long careers. We apologize in advance to anyone we may have left out.

Much of our thinking has been influenced by work and conversations with colleagues at our companies. Ginny thanks Robbin Battison, Joseph Dumas, Ken Dye, Daniel Felker, Ken Keiser, Susan Kleimann, Marshall McClintock, Andrew Rose, and Jolanta Van Doren, as well as the many other colleagues who were and are part of the American Institutes for Research. Ginny also deeply appreciates more recent collaborations with Donna Mayo and Jean Scholtz, colleagues of Ginny's in work at Redish & Associates. JoAnn thanks colleagues at Comtech Services, especially Dawn Stevens and Bill Hackos. JoAnn also remembers with pleasure many conversations at the University of Colorado with David Jonassen and Martin Tessmer, two of the major contributors to task analysis in instructional systems design.

We want to also acknowledge the ways that working with and talking with others in the profession through professional societies like STC (Society for Technical Communication), UPA (Usability Professionals' Association), and SIGCHI (Special Interest Group in Computer-Human Interaction) has shaped our thinking. We would mention in particular our work or conversations with Fran Arble, Tom Dayton, Janice James, Michael Muller, Jakob Nielsen, Judy Ramey, Stephanie Rosenbaum, Karen Schriver, Ben Shneiderman, Patricia Wright, Chauncey Wilson, and Dennis Wixon, among many others.

We thank our clients for getting us involved in so many interesting, exciting, leading-edge, and, yes, sometimes frustrating, projects from which both we and they have learned so much.

Finally, we want to thank the people who directly contributed to putting this book together. First is our editor, Terri Hudson of John Wiley & Sons, Inc. We greatly appreciate her extreme patience with our schedule and her encouragement through the endeavor. We also thank Micheline Frederick and Sandy Bontemps for their help. We thank our reviewers, Judy Ramey of the University of Washington and Dennise Brown of Oracle Corporation. Their comments and criticisms have greatly improved what you read here.

We thank our book designers, Rodney Sauer and Jeff McLaughlin. Rodney developed the page design and the clean and useful look of the book, including the images that grace the part introductory pages. He transformed all the draft text and illustrations into camera-ready copy. Jeff contributed the wonderful original cartoons to the text. In addition, we greatly appreciate the contributions of Lori Maberry, Jeni Halingstad, and Donna Shephard at Comtech Services and Margot Steinberg at Redish & Associates in putting the drafts together, proofreading, compiling the bibliography, and generally keeping us organized.

Finally, our greatest thanks goes to our ever-understanding spouses, Joe Redish and Bill Hackos. Not only did they contribute ideas to the book, they also put up with weekends and evenings spent writing, editing, or on the telephone discussing ideas. They shopped, cooked, and took on other chores whenever necessary to pick up the slack from the busy writers. We love them both.

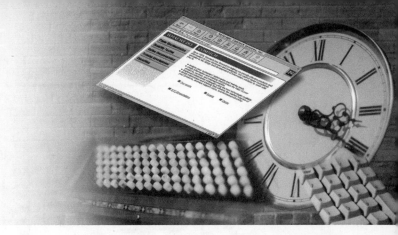

1

Introducing user and task analysis for interface design

The interface is what users see and work with to use a product. Interfaces can help or hinder, be effective or ineffective, as figure 1-1 shows. This book is about how to get and use the information you need to design helpful, effective interfaces.

Designing an effective interface doesn't happen by chance. Good design happens only when designers understand people as well as technology. Good design happens only when designers understand who will be using their product and the personal characteristics, habits of mind, physical capabilities, and limitations those users bring to their tasks. Good design happens only when designers understand what users are trying to accomplish—the users' goals and tasks—and how the users think about their tasks—the users' conceptual model of the work and the tools. Good design happens only when designers understand the circumstances under which users must work and how users as groups collaborate to accomplish a goal.

And good design is important. It makes users happy and productive, increasing customer satisfaction, one of the major goals for most companies. It increases efficiency and decreases support calls, thus making and saving money for companies.

Figure 1-1 Interfaces between product and user can help or hinder the user.

Cemex, a cement company in Guadalajara, Mexico, wanted to improve the speed and reliability of deliveries to improve customer satisfaction and internal efficiency. They set out to develop a new way for dispatchers to communicate with the drivers of cement trucks. Before they designed the new system, the designers held "conversations" with the dispatchers, and they watched the drivers. They learned what these people needed to do their jobs well and proudly. They then built those conversations into the design of the system and its interface. They succeeded. On-time deliveries of cement in Guadalajara, Mexico, went from 34.4% to 98.15% (Katel 1997).

When Federal Express wanted to redesign its ground operations manuals, JoAnn's team visited locations around the world, observing employees solving problems, using manuals on occasion, and often expressing frustration at how difficult it was for them to find the information they needed. The site visits led to a usability study to identify the details of the problems (organization, language, indexing, lack of examples, and so on). Following the predesign work, JoAnn's team and technical communicators at Federal Express reorganized and rewrote the manuals. They succeeded. Time to search for information in the manuals decreased by more than a third, resulting in a potential savings of more than $24 million per year in North America alone through reduced search times, better adherence to standards, and less need to call for help (Hackos 1995).

In both of our example stories, the design teams spent time observing and talking with users, listening to the people who actually did the work, watching how they worked, understanding how they performed tasks, and learning what the problems were by seeing them. They took that information back and analyzed it. They then created prototype designs and tested the prototypes with users until they met the usability goals of the projects. In fact, they used many of the techniques that we cover in this book.

Despite success stories like these, we all know that many products, especially software applications, are not easy to use. In large part, that's because the interfaces don't make sense to users who struggle to find what they need and to figure out what to do and how to do it. Tasks that were easy to do by hand or with older systems sometimes take more time and effort using a computer, a graphical user interface (GUI), or a new product design. As Tom Landauer (1995) has shown, productivity gains promised for computers in the workplace and the home have not been achieved.

There are many reasons for the problems that people have using interfaces. One is the pressure on designers to add more and more features. But the main reason for the problems is that products are too often developed with the focus on technology only and not on users. The heart of the problem is a lack of a firsthand, carefully considered understanding of the users, their tasks, and their environments.

Time and time again, each of us has been asked to rescue unusable designs, only to find that no one on the design team has ever observed a user doing the tasks for which they were designing. They were too busy to visit and observe users. Or if they did, they didn't know how to observe effectively or what questions to ask. Or they didn't know how to incorporate what they had learned into the design of the interface.

When designers visit users in their workplaces and homes to analyze who the users are, the work they do, and where they do it, the designs that result seem like magic. But it's not magic. It's hard work, good communication, analysis, and design techniques, and, yes, some vision and creativity, but vision and creativity based on knowledge.

What is this book about?

This book tells you how to get started, at the predesign stage, on the path toward designing a usable interface. We start out with the basics, explaining what you need to know about users, tasks, and environments. Then we take you through a step-by-step process for planning and conducting site visits. We include advice on how to be a good observer and listener and how to conduct an effective interview. Finally, we explain how to analyze the information you've gathered and turn it into interface designs. We help you move through basic design steps until you're ready to create and test design prototypes. We also discuss the importance of including strategies and designs for documentation and training as part of your interface.

We've deliberately taken an eclectic approach in this book, introducing you to many different techniques and variations on techniques for data gathering, for analysis, and for moving from analysis to design. What all of our techniques have in common is direct involvement with users and a focus on the work that users do. What they all have in common is that they are ways of doing user-centered design, by having this information before design and using it to keep everyone on the design team focused on the users and their work.

Other books and book chapters present their authors' particular methodologies only (for example, Beyer and Holtzblatt 1997; Dayton, McFarland, and Kramer 1998). We have included several of these techniques with credits to their authors among the many that we present for your consideration. We also discuss other techniques that we have used in both our practices as well as some that we have learned about from presentations at conferences and workshops.

We expect that you will adopt and adapt techniques from this book for your projects. You are likely to pick and choose from among the techniques and to formulate your own methods that are combinations of a number of useful techniques. [For example, that's what the Hiser Group, a consulting firm in Melbourne, Australia, did. They work with a methodology that they call the "Element Tool Kit." It is a collection of techniques, all of which are covered in this book, that they have selected for data gathering, analysis, design, and evaluation. They have found that the techniques they've incorporated into their methodology work well for their clients and the projects they deal with (Hiser 1997)].

You are also likely to find, as we have, that different techniques and combinations of techniques are needed on different projects. The circumstances may be different. The issues that you need to learn about may be different. The time you have to gather information, analyze it, and use it may be different. Some techniques may fit well with your company's corporate culture and others may not. We've tried throughout this book to suggest how to select appropriately among techniques for different situations. So take in the techniques we discuss in this book with a view not only to what you want to do now, but also with a view to what might be helpful in other projects in the future.

What we do not include in this book is information on how to do graphic design in the development of a GUI or how to apply the design standards promulgated by the operating system developers—Windows, Apple Macintosh, X-Windows, OS/2, and other standards. Good advice on design and books on these standards already exist. You'll find references for many resources on design and standards when you get to chapter 12, which is about turning analysis into design. In the appendixes, you'll find a checklist of design standards that JoAnn created as an amalgam of the platform-specific standards. But right now we hope you are ready to think about interfaces, not from the view of the operating system, but from the users' view of the work they need to do.

What is interface design?

All the products that we mention in this book involve interactions between humans and systems. The systems are sometimes computer based, sometimes document based. The first story we told in this chapter is about the interface to a software application for dispatching cement trucks. The second story we told is about the interface (organization and page layout) of a set of manuals that is currently delivered on paper but will eventually be delivered electronically. We could also tell stories, and we do, about employee benefits handbooks, cellular phones, hardware and software for home use, office software, online help, and many others. All of them involve designing effective interfaces to make the products usable.

Interfaces occur in everything you work with, including

- the controls on a hardware product

- the labels and signs on the hardware

- small liquid crystal displays on machines of all sorts

- the screens for software applications on mainframe terminals

- the screens for software applications on personal computers running operating systems such as Windows, OS/2, DOS, Macintosh, UNIX, and others

- the pages of a Web site

- help systems and online and paper manuals

- embedded tutorials and other types of performance support

- the page layouts of paper forms or other documents

An interface is the bridge between the world of the product or system and the world of the users. It is the means by which the users interact with the product to achieve their goals. It is the means by which the system reveals itself to the users and behaves in relation to the users' needs.

What makes an interface usable?

To be usable, an interface must let the people who use the product (users), working in their own physical, social, and cultural environments, accomplish their goals and tasks effectively and efficiently. To be usable, an interface must also be *perceived* as usable by those who must use it or choose to use it. They must be pleased, made comfortable, even amazed by how effectively their goals are supported by your design. In the best case, they will be oblivious to the design—it simply works so well that they don't notice it. The truly usable interface is transparent to the work the user is trying to accomplish. (See figure 1-2.)

Figure 1-2 A user interacting with a usable interface may be unaware that an interface is there at all.

Usable interfaces have certain characteristics in common:

- They reflect the workflows that are familiar or comfortable.

- They support the users' learning styles.

- They are compatible in the users' working environment.

- They encompass a design concept (a metaphor or idiom) that is familiar to the users.

- They have a consistency of presentation (layout, icons, interactions) that makes them appear reliable and easy to learn.

■ They use language and illustrations that are familiar to the users or easy to learn.

In short, usable interfaces fit in, simply and elegantly, with the users' life and work needs. If not immediately obvious to the users, they are quickly learnable. As we've said, such usable interfaces rarely happen by chance.

What is user and task analysis?

If we look at the history of successful designs, we often find designers who have developed remarkable insights into the way people work and learn. Those insights most often come from a close connection between designers and users. Designers who spend time with users, observing how they work, understanding who they are, testing design concepts and prototypes, are most likely to be successful in creating interfaces that are a delight to use.

The name we and others in the field of user-centered design give to these processes of interaction between designers and users is user and task analysis.

User and task analysis is the process of learning about ordinary users by observing them in action. It is different from asking them questions in focus groups outside the users' typical environments and away from their work. It is different from talking with expert users or managers who may claim to speak for ordinary users but often unknowingly misrepresent them. Such "user representatives" may know how users are supposed to work, or they remember how they did the work when they were users, but they often do not know what really happens in the users' world today.

In fact, experience has shown that users themselves do not know how to articulate what they do, especially if they are very familiar with the tasks they perform. If you invite users to focus groups or meet with them in conference rooms, they will tell you about what they do. But when you watch them performing their tasks, you will learn that their testimony is often incomplete and inaccurate. Users, like all of us, leave out activities that they don't even notice they're doing. They emphasize activities that they find difficult or boring or particularly exciting to the exclusion of ordinary activities. They report on what they believe to be true, not necessarily what is.

Only by observing users and by probing for more understanding in the context of their work will you get the information that will surprise you and make you rethink your design ideas. That means using site visits to do user and task analysis.

User and task analysis, as described here, focuses on understanding deeply how users perform their tasks today. That understanding includes

- what users' goals are; what they are trying to achieve

- what users actually do to achieve those goals

- what personal, social, and cultural characteristics the users bring to the tasks

- how users are influenced by their physical environment

- how users' previous knowledge and experience influence how they think about their work and the workflow they follow to perform their tasks

- what users value most that will make a new interface be a delight for them (speed? accuracy? help in recovering from errors? human contact? fun? a challenge?)

We have chosen to define user and task analysis broadly, encompassing some specific formal methods like constructing flowcharts or hierarchy diagrams of tasks, but primarily emphasizing the more qualitative and informal methods of watching, listening carefully, and probing for more understanding. User and task analysis of the sort we hope you will learn from this book requires gaining access to users or potential users of products from a wide variety of backgrounds and roles. It encourages the participation of many members of the development team, including those who decide what the software and hardware will allow users to do, those who create the software and hardware interfaces, those who write help systems and other documentation, those who design Web sites, and those who design instruction, whether delivered in the classroom or through electronic means.

Recent experience, especially in the design of application software, has shown that the qualitative methods emphasized in this book result in information that is most useful to interface design.

When should you do user and task analysis?

The major emphasis in this book is on user and task analysis before design begins, even before analysis begins. Successful design comes from a basis in direct observations of, not assumptions about, the users or potential users of your product. We have learned, and we hope we can impress on you that none of us, not even the most experienced designers among us, know enough about how particular users work and think to design using sheer analytical power alone. We have learned that interacting with users in their actual environments, and performing user and task analysis, is essential to designing usable products. That means we might as well start with the users rather than waste our creative energies on "neat" designs that don't and won't ever make sense to the users. It's amazing how many clever, and costly, designs have been thrown out during usability testing or, worse yet, shelved or completely redesigned after they've been released to the unwitting users.

We've also learned that, although there are some general guidelines for good design, such as "Speak the user's language," and "Be consistent," each product is unique. Although there is general knowledge about users, such as "They are not blank slates; they always bring the baggage of all their prior experiences," each set of users is different. Although doing user and task analysis for one product may give you insights that you can carry over to other projects, you cannot rely exclusively on prior work. For each new product, each new design, each new set of users, each expansion into another market or another culture, you have to do a new user and task analysis.

We do not preclude the thought that some user and task analysis often takes place later in the development life cycle to prepare documentation and training to support a new or redesigned interface. Nor do we preclude gathering user and task information later in the development life cycle through usability testing and alpha and beta site product introduction. If you continue to observe users during the development life cycle, you will continue to gather new information.

The only problem with these late-cycle activities is that they are less likely to influence the direction of the interface design. The later in the life cycle that fundamental design problems are recognized, the more time consuming and expensive the changes will be to make. In fact, we know that even when seemingly minor design flaws are recognized, they are often not corrected in order to meet a predetermined schedule or stay within a budget. So instead of making costly changes, or trying to patch up inadequate interface designs with help, documentation, and training, we urge you to do it right the first time. The information you learn later should be for minor refinements not major surprises.

A beta site visit or a usability test right before final product release should not be the first time that you observe users interacting with your interface design. Therefore, we recommend strongly that user and task analysis occur early, before design decisions have been made and so that they can be incorporated into early design ideas. Figure 1-3 is a flowchart showing the most effective placement of user and task analysis in the interface-design process.

By including user and task analysis in the predesign stages of the life cycle, you have the opportunity to create inexpensive design models and test them with users before you have spent much time implementing the design into the technical environment. You also have the opportunity to ensure that the design of the underlying structure of the software promotes the efficient interaction of users and interface objects.

User and task analysis also fits well into the whole system development life cycle, saving time even for those developing the database model or creating the underlying system objects. You will find this to be the case because user and task

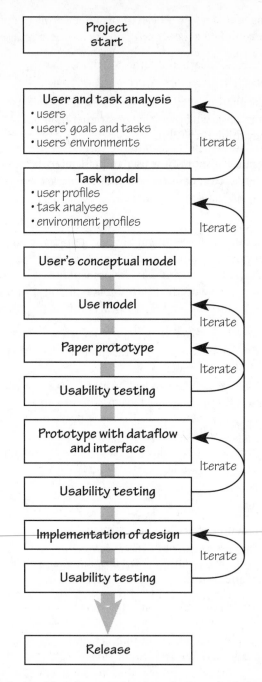

Figure 1-3 The relationship of user and task analysis to the interface-development life cycle.

analysis, as practiced following the methods in this book, will decrease the possibility that you will begin the underlying design of a system based on faulty information from users. We have all experienced the design delays and cost overruns that occur when we move forward with a design, only to have users tell us that the design represents "what they said" but not "what they meant." User and task analysis tells us that we have to gather information about what the users need from observing them at work, rather than only listening to their reports of what they think they want.

Figure 1-4 shows how user and task analysis figures into both the design of the interface and design of the underlying system.

Why do user and task analysis at all?

We recognize that user and task analysis has not been an integral part of interface design and product development. At the same time, we know that poor design takes an enormous toll on productivity and increases the cost of maintaining a product. Companies today pay double or more for poorly designed interfaces. First, they pay for the initial development costs; then they pay for the support costs when users call for help. They pay for field maintenance when users conclude that a usability problem is a product defect. They also pay the cost of making changes after the product is released.

Customer organizations also pay dearly for poorly designed interfaces. They pay when employees find new products difficult to learn. They pay when people make mistakes that have to be corrected. They pay when employees are unhappy and decide to quit rather than put up with a new interface. They pay when employees spend 20, 30, even 40% of their time asking each other how to do a task. They pay when all the employees settle on a method of performing the task that turns out to be inefficient, illegal, or just plain wrong.

Companies also pay for poor design in decreased sales. We know that it's relatively easy to sell to the early adopters, making initial sales to people who always buy the latest technology. But remember, no one ever had more than one pet rock. In the later stages of the sales cycle, customers rely increasingly on word-of-mouth recommendations. When the word-of-mouth is that your product is unusable or costs enormous sums for training and support, sales may be adversely affected.

User and task analysis, followed by other usability activities, can change all that, as the following story illustrates.

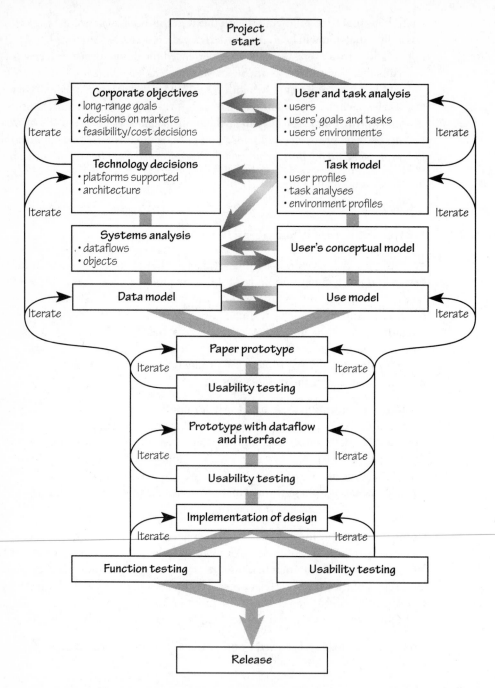

Figure 1-4 The relationship of user and task analysis to both the interface and the underlying system development.

The first version of Digital Equipment Corporation's RALLY software had disappointing sales. The company had to decide whether to scrap the idea or try again. The second time around they let the usability people take the lead. Dennis Wixon and colleagues observed and talked with users in the users' workplaces before doing any design. They used their techniques of contextual inquiry and affinity diagramming to do user and task analysis. They created prototypes and had users try them out as the design team observed and listened and talked with the users. They iterated the prototypes, taking into account what they'd learned from users, making changes, and having other users try out the changed version. When the second version of RALLY was released, it had excellent sales. Sales rose by 80%, some 30% to 60% above expectations (Wixon and Jones 1996).

Why isn't this done all the time already?

You, no doubt, have heard all the objections. You may even have voiced some of them yourself:

- Marketing already knows the users.

- The product is new—there aren't any users to observe.

- Our users are all too different—we can't possibly visit all of them.

- We don't have enough time in the schedule.

- We don't have enough money in the budget.

- One of the members of the development team was a user for 25 years.

- We really have some great design ideas already—we don't need users to question what we're doing.

- Users don't know anything about design.

- Designers should design, not users.

- We are users ourselves—we know what we need.

- We're reengineering the process anyway—what can the current users tell us?

- We've never done user and task analysis—we don't know how to do it.

- We've been holding focus groups and the users attend.

- We did a survey of the users and asked them what they wanted.

You will read more about these objections and how to counter them in chapter 5. However, remember that site visits can be scheduled and made quickly, that visiting a few users is infinitely better than visiting none, that a few pointed observations and quotations will often open the eyes of the most recalcitrant managers. The key, of course, is success. Try site visits and careful, effective observation on a small scale at first. See what you learn and how much it influences your thinking. Test your new design ideas with users and see what happens. And measure, measure, measure. Record the successes, calculate the cost savings, and analyze and redesign the failures.

Where does user and task analysis come from?

We don't claim to have invented any of the techniques that we present in this book. Some we have adapted and refined ourselves from work in other disciplines. Some we have learned, as we said earlier, from other usability specialists, and we've tried to give credit where due. Many of those techniques, we suspect, are also adapted and refined from other disciplines.

Usability is a relatively new field that has attracted people with a wide variety of backgrounds. People have come to it from anthropology and ethnography, cognitive psychology, computer programming, document design and technical communication, English and rhetoric, human factors, graphic design, instructional systems design, market research, scientific management, and systems engineering, as well as many other disciplines that we have not mentioned. Many of these disciplines have influenced the practice that we describe in this book. We should take a moment here to acknowledge some of the antecedents of the practice and also to explain how what we are talking about in this book differs from those antecedents.

Anthropology and ethnography

Anthropology is the study of people. Ethnography is the practice of immersing oneself in a culture in order to describe that culture. User and task analysis has borrowed from ethnography the methods of both unobtrusive observation (sitting quietly in the corner or like a fly on the wall) and participatory observation (learning about a culture by becoming part of it). Much of the philosophy of user and task analysis derives from ethnography, including respect for the people you are observing and the importance of paying attention to their language, their ways of working, and their environment and culture. It is from ethnography that we realize the importance of seeing who the people are and what they do in their own contexts (their workplace or home). User and task analysis, like ethnography, is about developing as rich an understanding as possible and, therefore, shares with ethnography the use of qualitative methods of analysis rather than quantitative.

A typical user and task analysis is, of course, not real ethnography. Ethnography usually means spending a year or two immersed in a different environment. Half a day with each user and a few weeks for the entire visiting time isn't the same. Ethnography, moreover, is usually only about describing the culture. A user and task analysis has a goal that goes beyond description. The point of user and task analysis is to design a product that may in fact change the culture being observed. So despite the titles of some papers in the field, we aren't really doing an ethnographic study of a set of users when we do user and task analysis. But we are making practical use of ethnographic philosophy and techniques, adapted to the goals of designing products and the constraints of product schedules and budgets.

Cognitive psychology

Cognitive psychology is the study of how people think and learn. It is from work in cognitive psychology over the last several decades that we have come to appreciate that we cannot just impose designs on users. People are active parts of the system, and because they are much less predictable and less well understood than the computers and other technological parts of the system, they require even greater study and understanding. Users come to any new product with preconceived ideas based on their prior experiences. They interpret what they see in an interface and draw their own conclusions about how it works that may be very different from the designers' intentions—and then they act on their conclusions, not on the designers' intentions. Cognitive psychology shows us that we must accept the users as reality because it is they and not the designers (nor their supervisors) who will in the end determine how the product is used (or not used).

Many of the techniques in user and task analysis and in other usability studies are also adapted from work in cognitive psychology. Think aloud protocols (asking users to talk aloud while working) are a cognitive psychology technique for understanding how users go about working, what they are thinking, and what hypotheses they come up with when things go wrong. And many of the techniques of usability testing derive from work in academic psychology. Once again, however, we have adapted these techniques to the practical realities of projects where the main goal is to design a product, not to do an academic experiment. Even when we are gathering quantitative data in usability studies, it is not to satisfy questions of statistical significance but to convince ourselves and others that we have discovered a problem that requires fixing. Experience has shown that with iterative small-scale usability evaluations, designers can meet the usability goals for products. That's a different use of the technique than is practiced in experimental cognitive psychology.

Document design and technical communication; English and rhetoric

Rhetoric is a discipline usually housed in English departments and is the background of many technical communicators. As Schriver (1997, 58) explains, classical rhetoric (in ancient Greece) was the art of persuasion. Today, it is the art of communicating with others through any medium. Schriver says that the three key ideas that rhetoric brings to practice in writing and graphic design (and thus to design of interfaces, too) are audience, invention, and heuristics. We can reinterpret that as understanding who you are communicating with (users), figuring out how to communicate with them (design), and having guidelines for doing so (heuristics).

Thus user and task analysis shares a focus on communication and users with rhetoric. However, in rhetorical studies, and in most English classes, as in most software and hardware development projects, writers (developers) don't actually go out and meet their audiences. They imagine them. They try to *think* of the users' relevant characteristics, using their own prior knowledge and analytic judgment. In that, user and task analysis in this book differs from traditional rhetoric and traditional software and hardware development. User and task analysis must be empirical, based on actual observations of actual users. Otherwise the chances are too high that the imagined audience will be just like the writer or developer.

Technical communication was done originally by engineers or scientists writing technical documents. Audience, but again usually an imagined audience, has always been part of the technical communication tradition. Then, in the late 1970s and 1980s, the discipline of document design developed, drawing on both traditional rhetoric and traditional technical communication as well as cognitive psychology and instructional systems design. The difference was that document design, as developed and practiced by Ginny and colleagues at the Document Design Center of the American Institutes for Research, as well as by JoAnn at Comtech Services and by Karen Schriver and others at Carnegie-Mellon University, was practical and empirical. Today, technical communication is primarily focused on documentation for software and hardware and follows the practical, empirical techniques of the document design methodology. And that starts with exactly the type of user and task analysis that this book is all about.

Instructional systems design

Instructional systems design (ISD) is a method for developing training. The methodology begins with doing needs analysis, understanding users and what they know, understanding the tasks they must learn to do, judging the gap between what they know and what they do not know, and then designing training to bridge that gap. Thus, user and task analysis has a long history in ISD, and ISD has great applicability to user and task analysis for new and improved product design.

However, there are differences in approach that both instructional designers and interface designers should understand and appreciate. ISD usually comes into play after the product for which training is needed has been designed. That means the procedures have already been developed and the understanding that instructional designers are seeking is how to get people who do not know the procedures to learn them. Thus, when they do needs analysis, they are looking at novices in the new system to see the need and at experts in the new system to see what the tasks are and how to do them.

This book is about doing user and task analysis when the procedures are not yet known. The goal of predesign user and task analysis is to figure out what procedures are needed and what they should look like. Thus it is much less focused than a typical ISD user and task analysis. The user part may be similar: to find out who is out there, what they know, and how they learn and work. But the task part is not similar. Instead of a neatly known task, in a predesign task analysis, the goal is to see the messy reality of how people really do work, with all the errors and problems that they have. So while the technique of drawing task flowcharts for procedures may be borrowed from ISD, in the type of task analysis we are discussing in this book, the flowcharts won't show just the one best way to do the task that you would want to teach someone. They show all the workarounds and ways that users actually do the tasks today.

Market research

Market research is about studying people as customers and consumers, especially their own views of their needs and desires, their preferences, and their reactions to new ideas. Marketing departments often have very useful information to aid in a user and task analysis. They may have data on size and composition of market segments; they may have demographic information about users as a group; they may have information on specific clients' installations. They may have excellent contacts, and individuals in marketing may know a lot about users and environments because they spend time in the field.

Market research shares the emphasis on people rather than technology that is the main theme of user and task analysis. However, the techniques for user and task analysis that we urge you to adopt differ from some of the more traditional techniques used in market research. Where market research tends to focus on attitudes and opinions, user and task analysis for interface design focuses on behavior. What users say they need may not be the best solution to the problems that are generating the statement of need. (Users may say they need faster computers when the problem is really network response time. The users, or the person representing the users in a focus group, may know only that the work goes more slowly than they want it to. A skilled observer watching the user working might see the real problem.)

Market research also tends to focus on customers or user representatives, not necessarily on the people who actually do the work. In doing user and task analysis for interface design, you must focus on the users themselves because they are the people who will actually interact with the design. You may also want to talk with supervisors and others, but only in addition to working with the users themselves.

Scientific management

User and task analysis is also indebted to the methods developed at the beginning of the 20th century by advocates of scientific management. Scientific management was a way to increase efficiency of work by doing detailed time-and-motion studies of the steps in a task and then reorganizing the task to save steps and time. The techniques of observing and timing people as they work, describing the tasks they do in detailed steps, and drawing elaborate flowcharts and other graphic presentations of task analyses come from this discipline.

Scientific management, however, was criticized for treating the human as a cog in a machine and not considering all the cognitive as well as physical steps that people take when they do work. Over the years, task analysis has moved beyond scientific management to acknowledge and include the decisions that users make as they work, the knowledge they bring to their tasks, and the ways they use that knowledge. Thus, as with the other disciplines that we have described in this section, the user and task analysis that we focus on in this book is informed by scientific management but moves beyond it in new directions.

Participatory design in the Scandinavian model

We close this chapter with one more antecedent, not a specific discipline, but a tradition of practice from which we draw both philosophy and technique. This is the Scandinavian experiences with participatory analysis and design. [Ehn (1993) is a good place to start for an overview.] For two decades, in Scandinavia, designers and workers have collaborated on understanding users and their tasks and on planning and designing new business practices and interfaces. Because of the power of workers' unions and legal requirements that workers be involved in decisions that will affect them, designers in Scandinavia have developed ways to encourage and realize collaborations between users and designers. Both the philosophy and techniques have influenced analysis and design ideas and methods outside of Scandinavia, including many that we discuss in this book.

References cited in the chapter

Beyer, Hugh and Holtzblatt, Karen, *Contextual Design: Defining Customer-Centered Systems*, San Francisco, CA: Morgan Kaufmann Publishers, 1997.

Dayton, Tom, McFarland, Al, and Kramer, Joseph, Bridging user needs to object oriented GUI prototype via task object design, in *User Interface Design: Bridging the Gap from User Requirements to Design*, edited by Larry E. Wood, Boca Raton, FL: CRC Press, 1998, 15–56.

Ehn, Pelle, Scandinavian design: On participation and skill, in *Participatory Design: Principles and Practices*, edited by Douglas Schuler and Aki Namioka, Hillsdale, NJ: Lawrence Erlbaum Associates, 1993, 41–77.

Hackos, JoAnn T., Finding out what users need and giving it to them: A case-study at Federal Express, *Technical Communication*, 42 (2), 1995: 322–327.

Hiser Group, *The Element Tool Kit*, Prahan, Victoria, Australia, 1997.

Katel, Peter, Bordering on chaos, *Wired Magazine*, July 1997: 98–107.

Landauer, Thomas, *The Trouble with Computers*, Cambridge, MA: MIT Press, 1995.

Schriver, Karen A., *Dynamics in Document Design*, NY: John Wiley & Sons, 1997.

Wixon, Dennis and Jones, Sandy, Usability for fun and profit: A case study of the design of DEC RALLY version 2, in *Human-Computer Interface Design: Success Stories, Emerging Methods, and Real-World Context*, edited by Marianne Rudisill, Clayton Lewis, Peter B. Polson, Timothy D. McKay, San Francisco, CA: Morgan Kaufmann Publishers, 1996, 3–35.

Other books and articles for further reading

Jonassen, David H, Hannum, Wallace H., and Tessmer, Martin, *Handbook of Task Analysis Procedures*, NY: Praeger, 1989.

Kirwan, Barry and Ainsworth, Les K., *A Guide to Task Analysis*, London: Taylor & Francis, 1992.

Moore, Geoffrey, *Crossing the Chasm: Marketing and Selling High-Tech Products to Mainstream Customers*, NY: Harper Business, 1995.

Norman, Donald A., *The Design of Everyday Things*, NY: Doubleday, 1988 (originally published as *The Psychology of Everyday Things*, hard cover published by Basic Books).

Rubinstein, Richard and Hersh, Harry, *The Human Factor: Designing Computer Systems for People*, Bedford, MA: Digital Equipment Corporation, 1984.

Shneiderman, Ben, *Designing the User Interface: Strategies for Human-Computer Interaction*, 3rd ed., Reading, MA: Addison-Wesley, 1998.

Wixon, Dennis and Ramey, Judith, Eds., *Field Methods Casebook for Software Design*, NY: John Wiley & Sons, 1996.

Wood, Larry E., The ethnographic interview in user-centered work/task analysis, in *Field Methods Casebook for Software Design*, edited by Dennis Wixon and Judith Ramey, NY: John Wiley & Sons, 1996, 35–56.

Zemke, Ron and Kramlinger, Tom, *Figuring Things Out: A Trainer's Guide to Needs and Task Analysis*, Reading, MA: Addison-Wesley, 1982.

PART 1

Understanding the context of user and task analysis

Part 1 introduces you to the three primary aspects of user and task analysis: the users, their tasks, and the environments in which they work. To design software and hardware interfaces that people will find easy to learn and will want to use requires that you understand what characteristics your users bring to their tasks, how they conceptualize those tasks before they begin interacting with your interface, and how the environment in which they use your interface may affect their ability to perform successfully.

To simplify the discussion and focus on one aspect of user and task analysis at a time, we have divided our initial presentation of the concepts into three chapters. However, it will soon become obvious as you read through these chapters that it is very difficult to maintain the distinction among users, tasks, and environments. They overlap and the edges blur. As we study users in order to design effective products for their use, we concentrate on people doing things and doing those things in particular places. We cannot study tasks or users, and certainly not their work environments, in isolation.

However, when you plan and conduct your field studies, you may want to gather information about users that is distinct from your understanding of the tasks they are performing. After reading chapter 2, you may discover that you want to learn more about your users' earlier experiences, how they prefer to learn, their facility for and interest in using instructional text, or their ability to understand and apply difficult concepts. Chapter 2 outlines the process to use with your design team to identify potential users, review assumptions about users, and formulate an initial matrix of users to study. You complete this information when you develop your site visit plan, which is discussed in detail in chapter 7.

After reading chapter 3, you may discover that you want to know more about your users as they perform specific tasks that your interface is designed to facilitate. You may want to know, for example, how they work with computers, what they know about applications, how much time they have spent doing this or similar jobs, how likely they are to move on to other jobs, and much more. You may want to know what goals they have, what tasks they do to reach those goals, and how frequent and critical each of those tasks is.

After reading chapter 4, you may discover that you want to know where your users work and under what conditions they are asked to perform the tasks that you are supporting. Are they likely to have clean, well-lit, and quiet office spaces? Or will they be working under crowded, noisy conditions? Will they be working in isolation or in conjunction with a group of coworkers? Will they be interacting with customers face to face or over the phone? Will they have easy access to information and training? You will be concerned about how these many aspects of your users' environments must influence your design.

In chapter 5, you learn how to make a case for user and task analysis in your organization. We introduce the typical objections to site visits that we hear over and over again in organizations reluctant to change their design processes, and we suggest responses. We offer suggestions for examining the assumptions your product development team may have by examining the problems that have occurred in many similar organizations. You'll find that questioning the common wisdom about users in your organization may lead to substantial cost savings both in development time and ultimately in meeting users' needs.

In addition, you learn to counter objections that your organization is already doing enough to understand users. These activities may include focus groups, marketing research, joint applications sessions with customer representatives, and others. In these overviews, we mention some of the shortcomings of several traditional data-gathering methods, especially when they are applied incorrectly.

The information in part 1 is designed to provide you with a framework for making wise decisions. With this framework, you will be able to decide which users and potential users to study and how to study them. By the time you have worked your way through part 1, you will be prepared to design user and task analyses to provide you with answers to key questions. The information that you acquire will move you more quickly to a successful interface design.

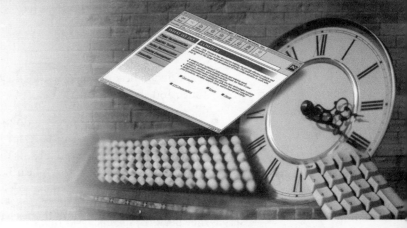

2

Thinking about users

In this chapter, you focus on learning about the people who will use the software or hardware interface, the documentation, or the training you intend to design and develop. You want to learn about the characteristics that may influence how people use your product, how they approach learning new tasks, how physical differences among them may affect your design decisions, and how motivated they are to change their ways of working. Some of these user characteristics will influence your design thinking, while others will prove interesting but irrelevant. But to decide that a user characteristic is irrelevant, you must first know that it exists and evaluate its impact on your work.

As you learn about your users, you will naturally investigate their characteristics in relation to the tasks they perform. However, it is important that you consider user characteristics independently of tasks. In focusing on users, you will want answers to questions like these:

- How do they think about their relationship to their work? Are they trained professionals? On a career path? Administrative or clerical workers? Simply putting in their eight hours? Working at home on their own time? For business or for leisure?

- Is what you are developing related to their primary work or something they use only occasionally? Do they want to invest a lot of time learning or will it be a minor part of what they do?

- What and how much do they know about the subject matter you are designing for? Are they already experts in the subject matter? Will they be

23

expected to become experts? Are they simply interested in doing a task once and walking away?

■ What experience have they had doing similar jobs or tasks? Have they been doing the same job or tasks for years? Are they moving to new jobs that are similar to their old jobs? Is the job or tasks you are designing for something they've never even heard of?

■ What tools do they know how to use? Are they expert typists or all thumbs? Do they surround themselves with the latest technology or flee from it? Are they used to filling out paper forms, or are they familiar with using computers for standard business or home activities?

■ What motivates them in doing their jobs? Are they doing their tasks for the money? Are they in the workplace for the social interactions? Are they trying to move into management or a profession?

■ What motivates them in using their personal time at home? What values do they place on learning?

■ What technical skills do they bring to performing their work? Are they skilled technicians who know how to fix anything they see? Have they ever used a mouse? A Windows application? A particular operating system?

■ How well do they read? Do they struggle with written information, preferring to learn by asking other people? Are they college graduates with experience using complex texts? Are they willing to read text when using products like yours?

■ What languages are they comfortable using? Do they use your language fluently, or do they speak only languages you are unfamiliar with? Do they have a special professional vocabulary, a vocabulary derived from their companies and their jobs, or the vocabulary of a social group that is relevant to your project?

■ Do they enjoy taking risks and exploring new ways of doing the same work? Do they avoid new experiences, preferring the "tried and true"? Do they learn by playing around with products? Do they want someone to show them how to do each step as they learn something new?

As you can see from these questions, it is difficult to separate people from the things they think and do, especially because, as interface and information designers, we are primarily interested in people in the context of their doing. Nonetheless, we believe that some separation in thinking about users, tasks, and environments will help you focus on important characteristics of each. Thus, in this chapter we focus on the users; in chapter 3 we focus on their tasks and in chapter 4 on their environments, even though we recognize that the three are intimately intertwined.

You may find that some of our questions and points are more relevant to your situation than others. You may be part of a group that is developing products for use within the company. You may be part of a group that develops "shrink wrap" products to be sold to the general public or to specific markets. Your products may be used primarily by individuals working alone or by people who work in groups. Your users may have no local support or considerable local support. We think that no matter which situation you are in, you will find useful information in these chapters. Select what applies to your product and your users.

Why study users?

We need to study users because users decide whether to use a product, not designers or writers. Even if the users' supervisors can dictate what they must use, the way people use products is self-determined. We also need to study users because the more we know about them, the better we can design for them. They are people with likes and dislikes, habits and skills, education and training that they bring into play whenever they work with a product. Donald A. Norman, in *The Design of Everyday Things* (1988), called this "information in the head." Users' prior knowledge and experience affect how they learn and use our products.

Designs that don't meet users' needs will often fail in the workplace or in the market, resulting in high costs in productivity, frustration, and errors that impact users and their organizations more than we can easily measure. But wait, you might argue. Plenty of products are developed by people who never met a user. Certainly products are designed by "ivory tower" engineers, programmers, information developers, and others—but what happens when these products are in competition with those designed by people who have taken the time to know their users? In case after case, we have learned that the more usable product is preferred. For example, in the modem market, products that users find impossible to install are returned to the store. At some companies, commercial software has to pass internal usability tests before it is approved for purchase. Software that fails to meet usability goals is considered too costly for the users and the organization.

JoAnn once met the man who designed the machine that painted the product labels on aluminum cans. She was writing a marketing piece for the company and was intrigued by the salesmen's insistence that their machine was the easiest in the industry to use—a contention that turned out to be completely accurate. She asked to interview the designer, who heartily agreed with the salesmen's claim. "How do you know it's the easiest to use?" she challenged. "I'm no 'ivory tower' engineer," he stated. "When I see the people on the floor having a problem with the machine, when it takes them too long to change out a part, when they have trouble making an adjustment, I watch and talk to them and go redesign the machine so that the problems are eliminated."

We study our users to discover answers to such questions as

- What are the individual characteristics that may affect their behavior with the software or information we design?

- What do they bring with them in their heads to perform the tasks that the job requires?

- What values do they bring to the job? Are they enthusiastic learners? Do they hope that their interaction with the interface will be fun, not boring? Are they interested in saving money, saving time, becoming expert, having an easy job to do?

- What do they know about the subject matter and the tools they use today or the ones we might present in a new interface?

- What is their prior experience using similar tools and interfaces?

- What are their actual jobs and tasks? What reasons do they have for using the product?

Sometimes during interface and information development, you wish that your users could function as blank slates, serving as passive input devices entering information into the database. But they can't. Unfortunately, and fortunately, your users bring a lot of baggage with them (see figure 2-1). The more you know about them and the stuffed suitcases in their heads, the more likely your design is to succeed.

Figure 2-1 Users bring a lot of baggage that affects the way they learn something new.

Users' prior knowledge and experience can work to their advantage. If your users are already familiar with one online help development tool, they will find it easier to learn the new one you are designing. If your users know how to operate one cellular telephone, they will be less likely to be confused by the buttons on one made by a different manufacturer. If they can use the previous version of the checkbook accounting program, they should be able to learn the new version's interface quickly and easily. Knowing what your users know will be invaluable to your design activities.

At the same time, of course, this prior knowledge and experience can get in the way of learning and using a new product. We often hear users say that the new product makes them do things differently than they are used to.

 One company decided to develop a new employee benefits handbook. They found that new employees quickly mastered using the handbook to find out about their benefits. Older employees, however, had considerable difficulty using the new handbook. They knew how to use handbooks and forms, and they knew they had to sign up for benefits every year by filling out the forms, but they did not know how to use this particular handbook and its forms. They were frustrated, confused, and antagonistic about the change.

People who upgraded to a new version of a popular software product were comfortable using the features and functions of the previous interface. The new interface, which changed the locations of those features and functions and altered the familiar graphic elements, was very frustrating for the experienced users to learn.

The transfer of old skills in these examples interfered with learning. As designers we need to know how much knowledge and experience will transfer to the users' benefit and how much will present challenges. The better we anticipate the challenges and take advantage of the benefits, the easier users will find our products to use. If you understand your users, you can often build solutions to help different user groups. For example, some software allows users to reconfigure menus and keyboard mappings to mimic older versions. Other software offers online help for specific groups of users.

Who are your users?

Before you can decide who to visit in your field studies, you need to decide who, in general, your users really are or who they are likely to be. Are your users the people who buy a product and take it home to use alone? Are they the people who make a decision to purchase but expect others to use the product? Are they experts who already know how to use similar products or novices who are faced with an entirely new responsibility? Are they department heads who supervise or the people who are being supervised? As you think about these examples of potential people to study, consider which ones are the actual users of the interface or information you are designing.

Many people who are presented as authorities about users are not users themselves. People who buy software for others to use are not users, although their perspectives are doubtless important to marketing and sales. Those who buy software for their own use are indeed actual users, but their behaviors as buyers may be substantially different than their behaviors as users. People who manage or supervise users are also not users themselves, although they may have been users in the past. Their perspectives on the users and the tasks they perform will enhance your understanding, but talking to managers or supervisors cannot substitute for interacting with actual users. Experts in the tasks you are studying may be users, but they may not be representative of the majority of your users. Former users, some of whom may be working for your organization as product analysts, may provide insight into users' behaviors, but their own distance in time and experience from actual users will make them unreliable spokespersons for the users.

Your focus must be on the people who actually use your interface or information. Depending on the product you develop, the users you want to study may include

- individuals who buy the software and use it without assistance or interaction with others, either at home or at their workplaces

- individuals who use the interface and information as part of the work they do, even though the product is purchased by someone else

- groups of people who use software and information as part of a larger business process

- those who administer the software so that others may use it successfully and who are themselves users of the administration interface

- individuals who repair products that are broken or who troubleshoot systems or processes that fail to work as intended and who are themselves users of maintenance interfaces and information

- those who install products for themselves and others and are themselves users of installation software and information

- customers of the users and others who are affected by users working with the interface and information

Each of these actual users can provide insights into your interface and information design.

Primary users

In this book, we define primary users as people who themselves use interfaces and information to perform tasks. These users perform tasks to achieve goals, goals which may be personal, individual, or an integral part of their jobs. A user who has just purchased a new oven wants to use the oven to cook dinner. A user who is reading a pamphlet from her insurance company wants to know which doctor she can go to. A user with a new cellular phone wants to receive a call from his office while he is awaiting a client meeting. A user who has to process a vendor invoice wants to ensure that it can be paid on time. Each of these users may be acting alone to achieve a particular goal.

Secondary users

Performing the task and achieving the goal indirectly affect others. If the new computer-like interface makes the oven difficult to operate, the entire family may go without dinner. If the insurance pamphlet is incomprehensible, the patient may choose the wrong doctor, adversely affecting the family's budget. If the salesperson doesn't get the call, the company may be affected by a missed business opportunity. If the accounts payable clerk does not understand how to use the software, the vendor's payment may be delayed. We define as secondary users those who are part of the larger community affected by the users' ability to perform the tasks.

Your particular users may be individuals interacting independently with the product interface and information you are designing. They may be part of a larger group of individuals who must interact with aspects of the product to accomplish a larger task. Their tasks may be affected by others outside and inside their organizations. To design effectively, you must understand both the individuals and their larger social and workplace communities.

You may also find secondary users who are affected by your product through their relationships to your primary users. Think of situations in which you are a secondary user of products that other people developed. For example, if you are working with a travel agent to plan a vacation, you will be affected by the travel agent's computer application. If it is slow and difficult for your agent to use, you may have to wait. If you are in line to pay for your groceries, you may have to wait longer if the cash register design causes the clerk to make mistakes. If you are trying to check out a book from the library, you may be frustrated if the librarian cannot easily and quickly perform the checkout function. If you are applying for a mortgage loan, you may be angry if the banker misinterprets the loan requirements. In these cases, the immediate user acts on behalf of secondary users.

As a designer and developer, you will want to understand the nature of the business or social interactions that occur between the primary user and others in the user's environment. You will want to meet the needs of the secondary users.

User communities

While users can be viewed from the perspective of their individual goals, characteristics, and behaviors, in most design environments, users are also part of a community. The community of users may include new learners and experts, teachers and students, those who administer and those who operate systems, those who use products and those who supervise the users, and those who repair products and those who break them. As a consequence of the diversity of users and the communities in which they interact, you must study them as individuals, classes, and interacting groups.

Users as buyers—a potential design conflict

Market research usually concentrates on the people who buy products or influence the decision to buy. In the design process, you need to concentrate on the people who perform tasks—the users. In some circumstances, especially among home office and small business users, the person who buys the product and the person who performs the tasks are the same. It is important, however, to distinguish carefully between the roles. A knowledge of user characteristics that may be important to the marketer may be insufficient to assist the designer in making the best design decisions, and vice versa. We have all had the experience of being an enthusiastic buyer of a new product and a confused and frustrated user.

It is not enough to understand the characteristics of buyers; designers must understand those who will actually perform the tasks with the product. In most business environments, you encounter many differences in goals, characteristics, and behaviors between buyers and users. New desktop publishing software may be purchased by a manager or purchasing agent but used by secretaries and clerks. The latest medical equipment may be selected by a committee of physicians and hospital administrators but used by technicians or nurses. The insurance policy may have been purchased by the owner of the company, but the pamphlet has to be understood by everyone who applies for benefits. Buyers and users often have very different skills, interests, and goals. Knowing one group provides little insight into knowing the other. You may want to talk to the buyers, but you definitely need to observe, listen to, and talk with the users.

Surrogate users

It is also not sufficient to interact with surrogate users. In some environments, managers and supervisors prefer to interact with product designers themselves. They guard the users from the designers, often in the mistaken belief that they can better represent what the users need. Supervisors want to tell you what their clerical staff do and what they need. Physicians want to tell you how the nurses perform their tasks. Expert technicians will inform you about how junior technicians are supposed to perform. Former application software users who have moved into management want to speak for current users. All of these surrogate users may have important roles to play in defining the functionality of a product. They do not, however, speak effectively for the product's users. In your field analyses, it is important to get past the surrogates and observe and talk to the people who will actually use your product.

Starting a user and task analysis

As you prepare for your user and task analysis, you must identify those who you believe will interact with your interface or information either directly or indirectly. The users may include technicians, operators, administrators, managers, clerks, customers, and many others who make up the entire community of people who will use aspects of the product you design. Here is one way to identify potential users to include in your analysis:

1.   Assemble a group of people in your organization who regularly interact with the users. The group might include people from customer service, training, and marketing.

2.   Brainstorm a preliminary list of users and potential users.

3.   Create a user/task matrix or a user/characteristic matrix to serve as an initial model of your community of users. Your field study should confirm or challenge this model. Note that a matrix is a table with different user types as the rows and different tasks or user characteristics as the columns. (See the example in figure 2-2.)

4.   Discuss the characteristics that you assume are typical of your user community.

5.   Decide how to test your assumptions.

Assemble a user profile team

You may either assemble a team to brainstorm a list of potential users, or you may call or contact those inside or outside your organization who know most about your users. In assembling your team, consider the following groups:

■   salespeople who call or visit buyers and users directly

■   sales engineering people who install and customize products at user sites

■   marketing professionals who have conducted research studies to identify the characteristics of those who buy and use the product

■   trainers who work with users in classroom settings or in the workplace

■   telephone support personnel who answer user questions

■   field support personnel who solve problems in the users' environments

■   consultants who study and advise on interactions with the user community

■   former users who now work for your organization

■ supervisors and human resources professionals who hire the users if the users are employees of the company

The role of this user profile team is not to tell you who the users are and what they are like but to suggest the list of users that will serve as a starting point for your study. Choose people for the user profile team who have direct interactions with the users, not those who simply have opinions about the users.

Brainstorm a preliminary list of users and create a matrix

Assemble the team members or contact them individually or as groups to discover what they know about the users you want to study. As you brainstorm with the team, begin to construct a list of possible users. Discuss differences that appear to exist among the users as you understand them, such as

■ experience in the job, educational level, background of training

■ age, gender, physical differences that may be significant

■ geographic locations, wage differences, culture and nationalities

■ language skills, terminology differences

■ job level, such as engineers versus technicians

The differences that you speculate about will be tested during your study. Some of the differences will lead you to determine which users you select to visit. For example, if you believe that the engineers who use your product are significantly different in skill level, need for information, and ability to troubleshoot problems than are the technicians, you may want to visit both groups as you design the next generation of the product.

As you discuss differences with your team, also consider the percentage of users in groups that you believe may be significantly different. For example, you may want to visit more engineers than technicians if you find that 80% of your market for the product is engineers. However, you may also learn that marketing intends to target more technician-level customers in the future, thus suggesting that you spend more effort studying the technicians than you might otherwise.

Create an initial user/task matrix

From these initial ideas, you create an initial user/task matrix that will form the basis of your study.

 JoAnn worked with a group developing a new product. The initial brainstorming session for the user and task analysis led to a user/task matrix similar to the following (see figure 2-2).

Users	Tasks likely to be performed				
	Getting comfortable with software	Basic software use	Advanced software use	Training the patients	Customizing the software
Patients	X	X			
Patient families	X	X	X		
Novice clinicians		X	X	X	
Expert clinicians		X	X	X	X

Figure 2-2 Initial user/task matrix for communication software.

The group discussed the potential characteristics of the patients and their families. The patients were stroke patients or patients with brain damage. They had lost their ability to communicate with language—neither understanding speech nor being able to speak. They were also likely to have lost their ability to read or write text. The group also identified a range of disabilities among the patients. The patients' families were likely, the group believed, to be primarily female and over the age of 65 with husbands who were stroke patients. The women were unlikely to have any experience with PCs and were likely to be experiencing significant stress. On the other hand, we speculated that the patients and their families would be highly motivated to find a solution to their severe communication problems and improve their life styles.

Discuss your assumptions about users

Remember that the intent of your field study is to confirm or challenge assumptions about the users. You may find that some of the differences your user profile team thought were significant are, in fact, not significant to your design. Other assumptions about similarities among users may end up pointing to significant differences that you had not anticipated (see figure 2-3). One design group, for example, found that in one of their markets, the pay scale was significantly lower than elsewhere. As a result, the users were not as experienced in the subject matter, had less education, had less computer experience, and experienced more frequent job turnover.

Figure 2-3 Gather a user profile team to discuss assumptions about users and to brainstorm a list of possible users to include in a field study.

In addition to discussing assumptions with your user profile team, you may want to extend the discussion to your development team. Hold a session in which you try to think about and define what designers, developers, technical communicators, and trainers consciously or unconsciously assume about the users. This exercise will help to emphasize the differences between assumptions and reality.

One development team discovered that the marketing people assumed that most of the users would be clerical workers unfamiliar with the new technology being planned; the programmers and engineers assumed that the users would be knowledgeable about the new technology and prepared to customize the software and troubleshoot the product. The field study was designed to uncover the characteristics of the real users so that the design of the interface and the product would be based on facts not assumptions.

Decide how to test your assumptions

Once you have developed a preliminary picture of the users and your assumptions about their characteristic differences, you can begin to think about techniques that you might use to discover if your assumptions are correct or incorrect. We'll talk more about assumptions and the importance of site visits to clarify your assumptions in chapter 5. In chapter 6, you'll find information on different techniques used during site visits. But first let's look in more detail at some of the issues you may want to focus on in your study of user characteristics.

What do you want to know about your users?

As you begin to plan your user study, consider the many different kinds of information that you may be able to obtain about users. You will want to study users according to three broad categories: (1) how they define themselves (jobs, tasks, tools, and mental models); (2) how they differ individually (personal, physical, and cultural characteristics, as well as motivation); and (3) how they use products over time and the choices they make about the levels of expertise they want or need to achieve (stages of use). We discuss the first two categories below. The third category is discussed in chapter 3 on analyzing user tasks and determining stages of use.

Jobs, tasks, tools, and mental models: How users define themselves

In planning your user study, you want to learn about how users define themselves in the workplace. By defining users in terms of their job titles, the tasks they perform, the tools they use, and the mental models of their workplace and tasks that they carry with them, you develop an initial model of how you think users might behave in relation to your product.

As a designer, you need to know where your particular users are in a continuum of knowledge and experience. If your users have always worked in a mainframe computing environment, they will be challenged to learn a product designed in Windows. If your users have always cooked on a stove, they may have difficulty learning to use a microwave. Many individuals and organizations have found that giving users many new things to learn simultaneously causes significant job attrition, loss of productivity, proclivity for inventing inefficient and troublesome workarounds, and more.

Users and their jobs

In the previous example, we initially defined our user community in terms of the roles they would likely play in relation to the software being designed. We saw them as patients, family members, and clinicians. These designations helped us organize our study but did not tell us anything about the individual characteristics of our users. In fact, these designations run the risk of becoming stereotypes that oversimplify user characteristics or distort them according to personal and cultural bias. For example, designers who assume that all nurses are female run the risk of alienating the males in their audience. Nevertheless, job roles may be useful in directing the course of your investigation, providing the opportunity for challenging the assumptions behind the stereotypes, as well as learning what characteristics of the job role are important to your design.

In JoAnn's study of nurses (both male and female), she learned that nurses are taught that nothing is official unless it is written down on paper. Nurses were extremely dubious about using a computer to record patient data, feeling, with some justification, that they might be accused of practicing poor medicine if the computer files were corrupted or lost.

Users do not exist in isolation from the work they do. Much of what you will learn about your users will be related to their workplace and the tasks they perform, issues covered in chapters 3 and 4. However, you will find that your users often define themselves in terms of their work. The individual characteristics they bring to the job, their motivation to learn and perform successfully, are influenced by the context in which they find themselves. For example, a financial specialist who finds herself responsible for evaluating her company's new plant site may become a very motivated learner of new decision-making software. The experienced clerical worker who believes that the company wants to replace him with lower paid employees may be unwilling to participate in a user analysis to support the design of new application software. A manager who performs a variety of jobs that require integrating diverse information and using it to make complex business decisions may be extremely frustrated by having to use many new tools that look and feel different and do not communicate with one another, even if the manager could easily learn each new software application in isolation.

Even strong cultural differences among users from many countries may disappear in the context of an individual's professional work. We find, for example, that engineers who operate high-tech equipment behave similarly not only because their professional education is similar but because they bring similar professional values to the task. Outside of work, the cultural distinctions may be very noticeable. At work, you may find more similarities among your users than differences. Culture may be critical to your product or may not be.

As you begin to think about the relationship of your users' personal characteristics and how these characteristics are affected by their task environments, you may want to focus initially on a concept we refer to as stages of use, discussed in chapter 3. The personal characteristics of your users will affect how much energy they choose to devote to learning and how they ultimately choose to interact with a product's interface, documentation, and training.

Issues to consider about jobs:

- Do the users all have the same job title? Despite the titles, do the jobs have the same content, responsibility, tasks?

- Do the users have different job titles that reflect wide differences in skills and responsibilities?

- Are the users professionals who have learned aspects of their jobs in school? Are they technical experts who have received extensive training in their jobs? Are they clerical workers who have learned their jobs in the workplace?

- Do your users consider their jobs to define their modes of behavior, including how they take responsibility for tasks, their relationships with colleagues and supervisors, or their interactions with customers?

- Do your users know a lot about their own functions but very little about those that come earlier or later in the workflow?

- Do your users have jobs that are defined by the organizations in which they work? Or are their jobs defined by their professional training or education?

Each of these questions, and many more that will relate to your particular areas of interest, will aid you in determining if there are likely to be significant differences among your users in terms of their job functions and how you will plan to gather information about these job functions during your site visits.

What they know about their tasks

Job roles do not, however, tell you everything you need to know about your users and how they define themselves. In relation to their jobs or the roles they assume for themselves, you need to know what your users already know about the tasks your design will support. For example, if you are a designer of ovens, you will want to know about your users' knowledge of using ovens for cooking. You will want to know about your users' knowledge of the task. For example, you may learn that they are experienced cooks and are familiar with using many other types of ovens with manual controls. However, because you are planning a computer-like interface for the oven controls, the knowledge that your users are familiar with manual oven controls and have little computer experience must affect how you frame your design (see figure 2-4). You may want to accommodate the actions of novice users by providing more performance support on screen than if your users were all experts.

If you are designing a computer-assisted design tool for architectural drawings, you may want to know how the architects learned to draw since drawing is a traditional part of an education in architecture. You may find it useful to your design to understand what skills the educational environment provides, especially when you must make assumptions about what individuals may or may not know how to do.

You may learn that your users have many years of education and experience in performing the tasks of their jobs. Or you may learn that their jobs are changing and they have never performed the tasks that they will be asked to perform in the future. Users experienced in the task domain will transfer all of their experience in

Figure 2-4 Users in the context of their task knowledge.

"doing things the old way" to the new environment, which may require that you provide a migration path from the old to the new.

Ginny worked with a company that was changing the business process for handling calls from customers. In the old process, calls from customers who wanted to order something came to one set of customer service representatives. Calls about billing came to a different set of customer service representatives. Calls about repairs came to a third set of representatives. In the new process, all customer service representatives would be expected to handle all types of calls. Everyone would be novices on the new software system. Representatives who were experts in one subject matter area would find themselves having to answer questions about other subject matter areas in which they knew little. The new system would have to be designed to support rapid learning of the new software and also rapid and correct responses to customers in areas in which the representatives were not yet experts.

Issues to consider about tasks:

- How did your users learn to perform the tasks that they do on their jobs?

- How long have they been doing these tasks? Have the tasks changed over time?

- Do they perform their tasks today in the same way they performed them in the past? Have the tasks changed?

- Do your users perform many varied tasks in a typical day or do they perform the same few tasks over and over again?

- Do your users teach others how to perform the same tasks? Do they supervise anyone's work?

- If your users have considerable experience, is there anyone you can observe in the organization who is new to the task?

- Which people in the organization are considered the experts? Who does everyone go to for help when something goes wrong?

With questions like these, you are trying to determine what information your users have about their tasks and how much experience they bring to task performance. You may be particularly interested in how they learned to perform their tasks, what they do habitually, how much depth of expertise they have, or whether they train and supervise others. You will want to know whether the people you visit consider themselves beginners or experts, problem solvers, or simply performers of mundane tasks.

What they know about the tools

In addition to understanding how your users define themselves in their jobs or roles and how they learn and think about the tasks they perform, you will also want to know about their knowledge and experience with the tools they use to perform their tasks. If you are designing ovens, you will want to know about your users' experience with other ovens. If they don't know anything about ovens, are they experienced users of roasting pits, a pretechnology method of baking. Do they have experience using the tools you are designing or redesigning, or are they experienced in doing the tasks in a completely different way than you anticipate supporting.

An experienced secretary, for example, may already know how to type a letter, how to use word processing software, and be familiar with PCs. Such a user may have prior knowledge about operating systems (PC, mainframe, Mac, workstation), prior knowledge about specific applications (MS Word, WordPerfect, WordPro), and prior knowledge about types of application software (word processing, spreadsheets, databases). With this wealth of information about prior knowledge and experience, you will be better prepared to take this knowledge and experience into account in planning your interface or information design.

In a study of the users of laboratory equipment, JoAnn learned that users, while knowledgeable about the equipment and how to use it in their work, were not willing to devote sufficient time to learning the tool to become experts. They used the tools infrequently, which meant they always approached difficult problems as beginners. Some of the users expressed frustration at the difficulty of using the old interface. They always felt that they were starting from the beginning and had to relearn everything in a short period of time, only to forget the details again. The new interface design needed to account for this pattern of recurring inexperience to help support the infrequent users in reaching their goals.

Although people have a goal and have been given a new product as a tool to reach that goal, they will discover alternatives if the product doesn't meet their needs for ease or efficiency of use. They will, for example, call a support desk rather than use an unintelligible manual. They will wash dishes by hand rather than learn to use a dishwasher with controls they don't understand. They will continue balancing their checkbook by hand rather than use a new check-balancing software if it requires that they act in a counterintuitive manner.

 Ginny worked on a project that was started in part because the company knew that even though users had software that enabled them to get information from the computer, many users were still using the telephone to get the information.

New users, people who have never performed similar tasks, may have an easier time learning a new process or product than people who have considerable prior experience. Knowing what percentage of your users are new and what percentage are likely to be experienced with the tools you are developing will affect how you think about your product design.

Issues to consider about tools:

■ What tools are your users using today to perform their tasks? Have they always used the same tools, or are they familiar with different versions of the tools, perhaps from different manufacturers?

■ How did they learn to use these tools? In school? In training? On the job? On their own?

■ How comfortable are they using the tools? Do they consider themselves experts or beginners?

■ Are your users familiar with technology that is similar to your intended design? Do they know PCs or mainframes? Windows or Macintosh? Mouse or keyboard?

■ To what extent do their tools define what they do? If the tools change, will their jobs also change significantly?

These and other questions about tools will help you understand the relationship between your users and their tools. Because you are in the business of designing technology tools like product and computer interfaces, the more you know about the tools your users interact with, the better you will understand how your design has to accommodate their current knowledge and experience.

Their mental models and vocabulary

The mental models that your users bring to a new product will emerge from the conversations you have with them. These conversations should help you understand how they apply their prior knowledge and experience to the tasks they perform. We refer to these internal pictures of how things work as mental models. Investigating your users' mental models of their tasks will help you discover metaphors that you can use to make your product design accessible and easily understandable to your users.

Mental model is a term from cognitive psychology that is difficult to define. It refers to a somewhat vague, amorphous, individual, and changeable collection of associations in people's minds. People use their mental models to make associations between information (words, pictures, sounds, smells) they are learning and information they already know. They use their mental models to predict the effects of their own behaviors and how they expect the world to behave in response (Carroll 1987; Stevens and Gentner 1983).

For example, when users first saw the picture of a trash can on the Macintosh desktop, they associated the picture with the function of physical trash cans— throwing something away. Thus users were able to understand using the trash can icon to "throw away" files they no longer needed. The pictorial object on the computer screen, representing the actual object, behaved in an expected way for the users. Knowing that most U.S. users had a similar mental model of what trash cans do, the Macintosh designers created a conceptual model of the trash can that included the behavior of throwing things away that we no longer want. They gave an analog of that behavior to the picture of the trash can on the screen.

Unfortunately, however, the analogy worked too well because the designers gave the trash can metaphor an additional function—ejecting a disk from the floppy disk drive (which has no eject button as PC drives do). Many users had difficulty associating the trash can with ejecting a disk and became confused and anxious because they thought they might be "throwing away" all the information on their floppy disks by dragging the picture of the disk into the trash can, as shown in figure 2-5. They called Apple customer service, apparently in substantial numbers, to assure themselves that the icon would indeed *not* work as their mental model led them to believe it would. The Macintosh designers had to go back and add another function to eject a disk.

Because of the power of another mental model, one drawn from experience with IBM-type personal computers, many users found themselves turning off their Power Macs because they misinterpreted the power button placed under the

Figure 2-5 Users did not want to "trash" their floppy disks by using the trash can icon to eject them from the drive.

floppy disk drive as the floppy disk eject button, as shown in figure 2-6. Designers who ignore the users' mental models or who are unaware of their existence may find that the designs they thought were obvious generate user mistakes that might have been avoided.

Figure 2-6 PowerPC users mistook the power button for the floppy disk eject button.

Mistakes occur when users bring their mental models to bear on what seems like an analogous situation. For example, one user had a garage door opener installed. When she came home from work, the installers had left the manual and the remote control on her kitchen table. As she read the manual she played with the remote control, pushing the button every once in a while. Her mental model of the task was based on a TV remote control—that is, with infrared technology; if you don't aim at the TV, the remote control doesn't do anything. But garage door openers use radio technology—no aiming. So while she was playing peacefully with the controller at her kitchen table, her new garage door was wildly flying up and down.

Mental models allow users to make sense of information on computer interfaces, machine controls, text and pictures in documents, and more. They interpret the information in terms of what they already know. If we better understand the mental models that users bring to the products we are trying to design, we are better able to create designs that are more immediately understandable and are easier to learn.

Figure 2-7 Users have powerful mental models that profoundly affect their behaviors with new technology.

We discuss mental models in more detail in chapter 11, where we explain how to analyze the data you have collected from your user studies and how to use the data in your interface design. The information you gather about your users' mental models will come from your field study observations and interviews as well as other interactions with users. Pay attention to how they talk about their jobs, tasks, and tools. Consider the vocabulary that they use to describe these functions. Focus on problems they have doing tasks. Mistakes often reveal what users expected to happen; their errors often come from applying mental models that do not match the conceptual model that the designer had in mind for the interface.

Individual differences

Interface designers and designers of information and training materials must consider a variety of possible differences among their users. Differences in personal characteristics, physical abilities, cultural assumptions, behavior and motivation in the workplace, expertise, education, and training all may affect how your users interact with your designs.

We call these *individual differences* because they are attributes that are intrinsic to the user. One individual may differ from the next. If you are developing a product, you should be concerned about how many people in your user population share these differences. For example, most users may be highly motivated to use your product. At the same time, you may find a significant number of users who are using the product because they have to. Your design must account for both.

Individual differences affect people's behavior in ways that you may need to take into account if they are likely to be present among your users to a significant extent. Or you may be required by law to take certain legally protected differences into account. Your sales and marketing strategy might affect your treatment of these differences. You may also decide that even though a difference may exist in a significant percentage of your population, you choose not to take it into account in the product interface design.

As you examine individual or group differences among your users, be aware of stereotyping. For example, we have encountered design teams that assume that female users are less skilled in computer use than male users. One design team decided to use pink colors on a product designed to be used primarily by women, assuming that women preferred the color pink.

Another design team assumed that the new computer users were as likely to be intrigued by clever animations as they were, so they included several animations as decorative elements in the interface. The users found the nonfunctional animations to be distracting annoyances while they were trying to perform complex start-up tasks with the software. In another case, adult users of the printer documentation considered the sophomoric attempts at humor in the text to be inappropriate for an adult audience.

Personal characteristics

When you examine personal differences among your users, you will be challenged to interpret their effects on your design. For example, we know that people have different learning styles. Some prefer to learn by reading and are willing to spend hours reviewing documentation before beginning a new task. They do not want to make mistakes or seem to be unskilled or stupid. Some prefer to learn by asking others how to do the tasks and watching them. Still others prefer to explore on their own and make mistakes in great number because they learn best from their own mistakes and from the processes they use to figure out solutions to problems. Still other users prefer formal training classes led by an instructor or lengthy and comprehensive self-paced tutorials and interactive multimedia instruction.

How people learn will affect your design decisions. You may want to provide instructor-led training if you have a substantial percentage of users who learn best in this way. For other users, you may want to provide comprehensive documentation in print, in online help, or on a Web site. For other users, a quick reference sheet or job aid they can pin to a wall is what will work best to get them going. Other users will never go to a tutorial or training class but want to learn just what they need to know exactly when they need it as they are working. For those users, built-in electronic performance aids like wizards, coaches, cue cards, and electronic assistants match their learning and working styles. In addition, you may notice similarities in learning style among your user population or differences that are influenced by national or corporate cultures.

You may need to pay particular attention to personality types among your users. JoAnn encountered one group of users that preferred working in a friendly, gregarious, talkative group. They were offended by training that required them to learn in isolation, sitting in front of a computer screen. Other users prefer to learn alone, quietly concentrating on their tasks without interference from others.

Users may have distinct tool preferences. For example, on the computer, proficient typists often prefer typing, keeping their hands on the keyboard, rather than having to move back and forth between keyboard and mouse. A design that requires frequent switches in tools may be uncomfortable and tedious for these users. Other users have memorized a significant number of commands and prefer to type them rapidly into command line interfaces rather than use a mouse to select items on menus or in dialog boxes. Users who perform tasks infrequently often prefer graphical interfaces in which they pick selections rather than having to memorize command syntax.

In one user study, Ginny found that current users preferred to use rote processes with little variation or flexibility. They were very unhappy when faced with a new interface that eliminated the routine and comfortable parts of their jobs.

The users working in a garment factory were used to having large work tables where several women cut patterns. The women's work was repetitive and tedious but the work environment allowed them to spend most of their time chatting with one another. They were able to pay sufficient attention to their tasks to do them accurately while focusing most of their attention on their social interactions. In such an environment, the imposition of equipment requiring complete attention, silence, and separation of the work group was not well received.

Other people may be most comfortable working alone or may prefer jobs that offer considerable variation in task performance. Your task is to learn what these personal preferences may be and how they will affect your design.

At the beginning of the book, we told the story of the cement company in Guadalajara, Mexico. In their design of a new system to help direct cement trucks to construction sites, the designers at Cemex found that the dispatchers could handle considerable flexibility in the decision-support system. Given accurate and timely information about truck location and the needs of construction customers, the users were empowered to use the system to make local and immediate decisions. As a result, in this otherwise chaotic business environment, on-time deliveries increased from about 30% to more than 98%, a phenomenal change. The system designers had engaged in extended conversations with the users throughout the delivery system to understand how things really had to work to be successful (Katel 1997).

In other cases, however, newly empowered employees may be seen as threats to the established management structure. In many instances, managers decline to give users access to technical documentation that tells them how to use aspects of the system that managers want to restrict to their own use.

Physical differences

In your field analyses, consider that some of your users may have physical challenges in using a particular design or interacting with an interface:

- physical disabilities that may restrict movement

- color blindness that may make objects of similar color completely invisible or virtually indistinguishable

- problems in distinguishing small objects or reading small type fonts, especially on computer screens, based on age or visual disabilities

A recent attractive and innovative stereo system is designed for optimal use at a distance from the listener. The stereo system also includes an alarm clock that users can set to wake them up. However, when the stereo is situated for good listening, some users who wear glasses have to find them first to see the number on the clock. They don't sleep with their glasses on.

A company decided to save money by ordering inexpensive keyboards for their new computer system. The keys, instead of being raised, were designed to be flat and even with the case. The keyboards were to be used primarily by men who unloaded heavy equipment from trucks. A user study revealed that most of the men using the new computers had very large hands, making it impossible for them to press only one key at a time.

Physical differences may be observed among individual users or they may be characteristic of a group of users, although not every member of the group will exhibit the same physical characteristics. For example, we know that individuals over the age of 40 are likely to have difficulty focusing their eyes on small close objects. They often find it difficult to read small fonts on paper or on a computer screen. While not every individual over 40 will have difficulty focusing, the condition is pervasive enough that interface designers should take it into account if they are likely to have many users in this age group. We know that very young children have difficulty with fine muscle control. An interface designed for them should not require fine motor control.

As you plan your user investigation, consider what you will observe so that you can discover relevant physical differences among your users. You may want to include a demographic questionnaire that carefully and sensitively asks about physical characteristics. Beware of asking questions that users may find insulting or intrusive. For example, questions about age should always be phrased in terms of age groups, such as 20–39, 40–59, and 60 or older. Be certain before asking such a question that you will actually make use of the information you obtain.

You may be able to observe physical differences in the workplace when you visit, but be careful not to introduce your own biases about physical challenges. Discuss with users what they are comfortable or uncomfortable doing rather than assuming that you know how a physical disability might affect your design.

Cultural differences

If your product is being sold globally, you know you need to attend to cultural differences. But cultural differences are associated not only with different countries but also with differences within a single country. In one case, products that were usable in the United States by people with an average height of 5'4" were unusable in Asian countries where many people are considerably shorter. The same product was also difficult to use in parts of the U.S. market which also includes shorter users.

Cultural differences may make some basic metaphors used in an interface design incomprehensible to some users. For example, an interface that assumes a left to right reading pattern may be difficult for people who read from right to left. Icons present particular problems because images that may be understandable in one culture may be unknown or obscene in other cultures. Language and literacy related to cultural differences may also present challenges to a good interface design. Language differences may result from educational differences or even from professional differences. In many cases, equally trained and skilled people from different industries use different terms for the same things. Each industry and profession may use specialized terms that interface designers must be aware of if they want people to use the interface effectively. Even within the same profession, you may find differences between experts and nonexperts in their use of terminology. Note, however, that you can learn the users' vocabulary only from the users. Don't assume they are all familiar with the language you use inside your design group or in your company.

Cultural differences may also be defined by age. The culture of children in the U.S. is markedly different from the culture of adults. These differences were made obvious in a touch-screen interface designed in the 1960s. Elementary school-age children were introduced to a computer-based learning environment and were asked to respond to questions on the computer screen by touching answers with a penlike stylus. The pens worked just fine at the beginning of the activity, but after several minutes the computer failed to respond to the stylus input. The researchers learned that the children had been putting the styluses in their ears. Enough earwax transferred to the screens to obscure the signals.

Corporate cultures may also affect how people learn and use products. For example, one major computer manufacturer did most of its user analyses with its own employees until they realized that their corporate culture created an atmosphere of learning and support that was not available to most of its customers. Some design firms have learned over the years that engineers who work for their customers lack the top-of-the-line equipment that is commonplace in their own environment, nor do customers have access to all the experts to troubleshoot problems and provide advice.

Motivational differences

Differences in motivation and attitude will also affect aspects of your interface and product design. Some people are willing to change and look forward to the challenge of learning a new process or a new tool. Others are openly hostile. Users who display hostility toward learning something new are often afraid of losing their jobs, losing prestige on the job, or being viewed by their peers as incompetent in situations where they had been the experts. Users who are not motivated or who are afraid of learning something new may need additional training, revised documentation, or even interfaces that promote ease of learning over ease of use. Just because the development team is highly motivated doesn't mean the users will be.

Motivation may also be related to learning styles. If people have sufficient time to learn in ways that are comfortable to them, some of their fear of a new tool may be dispelled. On the other hand, they may need a wizard-like interface that requires little learning curve to use.

To examine issues of motivation in your field analyses, you need to be attuned to comments from potential users, even to their body language. For example, if you are working on an inhouse product, you may want to find out about issues like these:

- Whose idea is the new design or the new tool?

- Is the new tool being imposed by management without user input?

- Is there obvious hostility among the people you observe and interview? Do they consider your questions to be naive because you don't understand that they believe they are powerless to affect their workplace?

■ Were the users involved in the decision making?

Good interview questions and general observations of the users' environments may provide the insights you need for the design process. Even if the interface design itself cannot anticipate all the motivation problems, you may be able to plan training, documentation, and customer support that will help reluctant users become successful.

The more you learn about differences and preferences among users, the more likely you are to consider their affect on your design problem. Of course, you may not be able to take all differences and preferences into account. In most cases, it is impossible to do so without making the interface design too complicated to learn and use. However, your understanding of your users' characteristics will help you handle the trade-offs more effectively.

What are the trade-offs?

As you consider how the information you gain about your users will affect your design, you will inevitably be faced with numerous conflicts. Users will exhibit individual differences that might easily lead to opposing design decisions. You may have users, for example, who have considerable familiarity with the most up-to-date software standards and others who are using obsolete equipment and operating systems. You will find users who want all the functions that you might be able to design and others who will only use your software in the most rudimentary way.

Many of the trade-offs you face will require consultation and collaborative decision making with others in your organization. The marketing people may need to investigate which of many different user types it would be most profitable to pursue. Your company's business strategy may lead you to design for the most sophisticated and innovative users or for those who are likely to prefer a new design that relies heavily on similarities with products they are already using.

Remember to ask about the long term. What about the users who will get the product two years from now? What if the company wants to introduce many other people to the new system in the future? What if you are selling into new markets? Decisions made now may constrain what you will be able to do for users later. Although you may have to make trade-offs, keeping the long term business strategy in mind may save you a great many usability problems in the future.

The decision-making process may be affected by legal requirements that demand accessibility for people with disabilities; require localization and translation of your interface, documentation, and training; or limit your options in presenting information. For example, medical software developers must be careful to refrain from practicing medicine without a license as they design software that assists medical professionals in providing patient care.

No matter where the complexity of users' personal characteristics may lead your design decisions, you should recognize that the more data you have to assist in your decision making, the more successful your decisions are likely to be. Too often designs are created based on assumptions about the users, assumptions that are frequently unrecognized and untested. User and task analysis lets you rely on data rather than assumptions in your design. Or at least, it assists you in examining your assumptions and recognizing their influence on your design decisions.

References cited in the chapter

Carroll, John M., Ed., *Interfacing Thought: Cognitive Aspects of Human-Computer Interaction.* Cambridge, MA: MIT Press, 1987.

Katel, Peter, Bordering on chaos, *Wired Magazine,* July 1997: 98–107.

Norman, Donald A., *The Design of Everyday Things,* NY: Doubleday, 1988 (originally published as *The Psychology of Everyday Things,* NY: Basic Books).

Stevens, Albert L. and Gentner, Dedre, Eds., *Mental Models,* Hillsdale, NJ: Lawrence Erlbaum Associates, 1983.

Other books and articles for further reading

Redish, Janice C., Understanding readers, in *Techniques for Technical Communicators,* edited by Carol M. Barnum and Saul Carliner, NY: Macmillan, 1993, 14–41.

Shneiderman, Ben, *Designing the User Interface: Strategies for Human-Computer Interaction,* 3rd ed., Reading, MA: Addison-Wesley, 1998.

3

Thinking about tasks

To build a successful interface and write successful documentation, you need not only to know about your users. You also need to know about your users' work. What do they do? What goals are they trying to accomplish? What tasks do they now do to meet those goals? What tasks will your product help them do?

How do they actually perform the tasks today? What problems do they have performing those tasks? Where can you see ways to simplify what users do so that they can accomplish their goals more easily? How do the tasks that one person does relate to tasks that others do to accomplish a given piece of work?

How do users differ in terms of the tasks they do or the way they use a product because of how long they've been using it, how often they use it, how comfortable they are with it—that is, what's the difference between novices and experts, and what other "stages of use" are there between those two?

To answer these questions, you need to do task analysis—and that's what we discuss in this chapter. We begin with the question "What is task analysis?" and go on to consider three main topics:

- starting with users' goals

- identifying different types and levels of task analysis

- thinking of users according to their stages of use

We describe the many types of task analysis that you should consider, including

- workflow analysis

- job analysis

- combining workflow analysis and job analysis

- task lists and task inventories

- process analysis, task sequences

- task hierarchies

- procedural analysis

What is task analysis?

If we are talking about goals and tasks, we are talking about task analysis. The point of any and all parts of a product—software, hardware, interface, documentation—is to help people do things. Usually we can think of those "things" as work. The work may be to

- admit a patient to the hospital

- find a customer's order in a database

- send a message to everyone on a project team

- put up a new Web site

- change payroll codes for an employee who has moved

- set up a new computer at home

Sometimes those "things" people do with what you are developing aren't "work" in the traditional sense of doing something that brings in money. The things people do with your product may be for personal benefit, leisure activities, or social interactions. For example, users may want to

- browse the Internet, looking for interesting sites

- take pictures of the children to make the grandparents happy

- cook a fancy dinner to impress a friend

- listen to a new recording while sipping wine with someone special

- record a program on the VCR to watch at a later time

Although these are leisure tasks, the users who are trying to do them still have goals (have fun, make others happy, impress that special someone) and are still doing tasks to meet those goals. Task analysis is as applicable to these leisure activities as it is to work activities.

Taking a broad view of task analysis

In this book we take a very broad view of task analysis. In addition to applying task analysis to both work and leisure, we also consider as types of task analysis all levels of generality and detail from people's goals to the lists of tasks they do to the specifics of the actions they take and the decisions they make. You may have heard the term "task analysis" used primarily to describe the most detailed level in which a task is decomposed into steps and decisions. We call this detailed level "procedural analysis" in this book.

However, we argue in this chapter that to build a successful product you must start by considering users' goals. In new designs, the list of tasks users do may change. The procedures (specific steps) they take to do those tasks may change. But users' goals are much less likely to change. If you don't understand the users' goals, you may well design a product with simple procedures that users have no interest in using. Task analysis includes understanding users' goals.

We also argue that, at the predesign stage, many types of task analysis are relevant and perhaps more relevant than the traditional view of task analysis as elaborating the procedural details. That's why we discuss a variety of types and levels of task analysis, including looking at workflow analysis covering the work of more than one user, looking at a single user's entire job, gathering task lists, and seeing processes at different levels of detail.

Understanding task analysis at the predesign stage

If you have come to this book with a background in documentation or training, you may already know about task analysis as an important step in understanding what to put in a manual or in training materials. But there is a critical and fundamental difference between the task analysis that we are talking about in this book and the task analysis that you might do later to know how to explain a procedure or train someone to work with a product.

Here the goal is to figure out how to design or redesign a product. The new product doesn't exist yet. You don't know what the procedures are. You are working with users and collecting data in order to decide what tasks the product should support and what procedures should be built into the product.

That means that you want to observe real users in all their messy reality. You want to observe, listen to, and talk with users at all stages of use, including novices and advanced beginners, not only competent users and experts. You want to see how these real users now do what they do, even if they don't do it efficiently, even if they make mistakes. In fact, you want to see all the errors, workarounds, and problems that they have. That's all information that can help you help them with your new design.

Documentation and training specialists have an important role in predesign task analysis, in part because they know about task analysis. They should be part of the team from the beginning because designing the interface must include decisions about where and how the product will communicate with users (from all the words and images in the interface to built-in performance and training aids to online help and tutorials to paper documents). Task analysis before design informs decisions about which types of communication are needed for which users and how to organize each type of communication.

However, many books on task analysis cover only the types of task analysis that documentation and training specialists typically do *after* the product is designed. At that point the new procedures are in place, and the goal of task analysis is to understand how to help someone who does not know the new procedures learn to do them. For that type of task analysis, you usually observe someone who knows the procedures and who doesn't make mistakes doing them. You are usually interested in the low-level details of each step that users take. You usually select the more expert performers to observe for your task analysis.

Task analysis for use in designing interfaces doesn't always lend itself to the straightforward flowcharts and neat lists that you can get after the product is designed. It's much messier, but it's a critical stage in successful product design.

Starting with users' goals

To do a task analysis, you should understand users' goals and how users move from goals to tasks to actions. For example, users inside a company may have goals like these:

- keeping my job

- getting done so I can go home on time

- making the boss happy so I get a good performance review

Users don't often talk about goals at this level. They usually focus on more specific work goals like "set up my calendar to be an effective planning tool." Nonetheless, users have goals and values like these. Products succeed when they help users meet their goals, and they don't succeed when they make the goals more difficult or impossible.

Companies also have goals for users doing tasks. Companies may have goals like these:

- increasing revenue

- increasing the number of applications that get processed in a day

- decreasing the cost of providing support

Sometimes the company's goals and the users' goals match. In the case of the three goals we just listed, we can make the argument that improving the usability of products will help the company meet those goals and also allow users to meet their goals that relate to doing a good job so as to get good performance reviews, etc.

However, in our experience, all too often products are designed only to meet company goals, or decisions about buying products from outside are made only in terms of company goals. The implementation makes it impossible for users to meet both their goals and the company's goals. Take the example of a company that puts into place a new computer-based, time tracking system in which employees are supposed to account for their work hours by charging each hour of each day to specific codes depending on what they actually do during that time. The company's goals are to stay out of trouble with the auditors, to have greater accountability, and to get better data to help with future strategic planning. The employees' goals are to get paid regularly, to go home on time, and to complete the substantive project work that is their primary responsibility.

If the computer-based system is difficult to use, employees can't meet both their goals and the company's goals. We've heard of systems in which employees don't put in the data that upper management expects to get out of the new system. It takes so much time to figure out how to do anything out of the ordinary that users assign all their work to the same code week after week. If they spent more time figuring out the system, they would work overtime for which they don't get paid. Time spent with the time tracking system is time not spent on doing their project work, but their performance ratings depend on how much project work they get done. Employees get their paychecks as long as they do fill out the computer worksheet every week, no matter what codes they put in. The employees are using the product in the ways that best meet their goals, but they aren't doing what management wants them to do. Because the developers didn't take users' goals into account in designing the new system, the company's goals aren't being met.

Successful products are designed by understanding both user goals and company goals (or parents' goals and children's goals or buyers' goals and sellers' goals). Goals give you users' values. Respecting those values when you design is the only way to make sure products succeed.

As we look at users' goals, we discuss these topics:

- relating goals to tasks to actions
- seeing how users choose tasks to meet goals
- seeing what happens when users have problems
- keeping goals as part of task analysis

Relating goals to tasks to actions

A task is what someone does to achieve a goal. As Donald Norman explains (1988, 46), "to get something done, you have to start with some notion of what is wanted—the goal that is to be achieved." It is true, as he also says (1988, 49), that we cannot always articulate our goals clearly, but when we do tasks we are working towards goals, such as

■ finishing this chapter before the deadline

■ getting dinner on the table before the hungry children complain

■ sending some information to a colleague in a different country quickly

Norman also gives us a picture of how people go about accomplishing their goals. Figure 3-1 shows his seven-stage action cycle, in which Norman takes us through the major steps that we all use in our interactions with all sorts of products from documentation to software to machines like stoves and overhead projectors to other types of objects like doors and lightbulbs. Every one of these products has an interface that people have to know how to use to do tasks and accomplish goals. The goal might be finding an answer (from the document) or communicating with a friend (through electronic mail software), making tea (by boiling water on the stove), providing information (by showing a viewgraph on the overhead projector), getting into a room (through the door), or having enough light to read this book (by using the light bulb). All of these products (document, electronic mail, stove, overhead projector, door, lightbulb) are either facilitators or obstacles for users who are trying to do tasks so they can meet their goals.

1. Forming the goal
2. Forming the intention
3. Specifying an action
4. Executing the action
5. Perceiving the state of the world
6. Interpreting the state of the world
7. Evaluating the outcome

Figure 3-1 Norman's seven-stage cycle of how people behave in terms of achieving goals and performing tasks.

Let's consider an example of a simple situation and follow it through Norman's seven stages, as shown in figure 3-2.

1. User forms goal.   Go outside to get some fresh air.

2. User forms intention (decides   Open the door.
   task).

3. User specifies action(s).   "It looks like I pull this handle here."

4. User does the action(s).   Pulls on the handle.

5. User perceives the state of   The door didn't open.
   the world.

6. User interprets the state of "Well. That didn't work. This handle sure looks like I should pull it.
   the world.   I guess it doesn't mean that. I guess I need to push it."

7. User evaluates the outcome.   Didn't get outside yet. (If the user still wants to meet the goal
                                 and still thinks this task is the best way to do it, the user goes
                                 through steps 3–7 again this time pushing on the door.)

Figure 3-2 Users go from goal to task to action to interpreting what happened.

Seeing how users choose tasks to meet goals

Norman's view of the action cycle is useful because it makes us realize that people
often have many options for the tasks they can do to achieve goals (see figure 3-3).
For example, to get dinner on the table before the hungry children complain, the
person responsible for dinner might use the stove, the microwave, the telephone
(to order carry-out), the car (to get the carry-out or to stop and pick up
something on the way home from work), or a combination of these options. What
that person chooses depends on how he or she weighs factors that are external to

how the task is done but that are an important part of a task analysis. These factors include time, cost, the person's skills and confidence in the different methods, the ease for that person of learning and using a particular method, and the value that person—and the customers, in this case, the hungry children—places on these and other factors, such as, in this case, taste and nutrition.

Figure 3-3 Users often have options of what tasks to do to reach their goal.

Take the example that brings us closer to our interest in software and documentation: To get information to a colleague in another country, the sender might be able to put it in electronic mail (e-mail) as an unformatted message, send it by e-mail as a formatted attachment, fax it through the computer, print it and send it through a separate fax machine, mail it, send it by overnight service, or get on a plane and hand-deliver it.

When the sender weighs cost and time, some of these options are clearly more favorable than others. Getting on a plane and hand-delivering a message to another country isn't a very feasible option for most of us. However, most of us are likely to factor in the time it takes to learn the tools required (hardware, software, and documentation) to use some of these methods if we don't already know them. For example, even though the sender's e-mail program allows attachments, if this is the first time the need for an attachment has come up, that user may decide that it's too much trouble to figure out how to send one and instead may just put the document into the message as unformatted text. The sender might spend a few minutes trying, but without quick success may give up and settle for a less-desirable but easier solution to reach the goal.

If you are designing a new e-mail program and want people to use it to send formatted attachments, you have to make learning that function easy enough to meet the typical user's self-imposed constraint on how much time it is worth to learn how to use the attachment function. You learn those users' constraints by observing them on the job doing similar tasks, if your product doesn't yet exist.

Both of these cases show that to design a product that people will use, you have to know the users' goals. You also have to know what matters most to both the decision makers who buy your product and the users who actually use it. That is, you have to know what they value (low cost, reliability, ease of learning, speed, etc.). You have to know what trade-offs they will make in deciding when and how to do different tasks to accomplish their goals. You also have to know about the people and environments on both ends of a process. For example, in our second case of getting a message quickly to someone in another country, you would also need to know about the technology that is available to the person who is receiving the message. All that should be part of a task analysis.

Seeing what happens when users have problems

Users may also change the task, change the goal, or give up. If users have problems getting through the action cycle, they may change the way they try to achieve the goal. A user who cannot quickly figure out how to use a computer fax program may change the task and print out the document for the fax machine instead. If no fax machine is available, the user may decide that the colleague doesn't need the information *immediately,* changing the goal to "getting information to the colleague in a few days when I can find someone who knows how to use the computer's fax program." The user who gets really frustrated may give up and decide that the colleague doesn't need the information after all.

Users decide when and how to use documents, software, and hardware. Understanding users' tolerances for time and effort for different tasks and different technologies is part of task analysis. It helps you set usability goals for design, which are discussed in chapter 12.

Keeping goals as part of task analysis

Some human-computer interaction (HCI) specialists suggest that task analysis must be *device dependent* (Benyon 1992). [See the reply by Diaper and Addison (1992)]. By "device," Benyon means the equipment, platform, tool, or product that will be used for the task. He suggests that a task analysis must be done within the context of a specific situation. The problem is one of definition, of which levels we accept as being part of a task analysis.

Benyon calls the goal level (Norman's first stage) the "external task," and he would exclude it from a task analysis. He would start the task analysis with what he calls the "internal task," which begins only after the user has formed the intention in Norman's terms.

However, if we start at Norman's second stage, we are missing a very important part of how users work. We are missing the essential connection between the users' goals and the specific ways of meeting those goals. If we start task analysis only with Norman's second stage, we run the risk of being device driven in the design rather than being user centered. Because users are goal oriented, the point of design must be to find the best device or program to help users achieve their goals.

In fact, in many cases, the problem that users have with products, and especially with documentation, is that the information is presented only at a very detailed, low level of the task. The user is looking for a way to meet a goal and the manual doesn't have any headings that relate to the user's goal. The documentation assumes that users know which tasks to do to reach their goals.

For example, if the product has a function for "grouping objects," the help is likely to have a topic on "grouping objects." For users who know about grouping, that's fine. But for users who don't already know that "grouping" is the way to move the parts of a picture together that may not be fine. They may not pick up on "grouping" as the task they want to do. Even if they see an icon, tool tip, or menu choice for "grouping, "they may not select it. Those users are looking for an entry on "keeping the parts of the picture together when I move it." The goal is to move the picture without having to move each piece and reposition it in relation to the other pieces. "Grouping objects" is a task the program makes users do in order to achieve the goal. The manual might have a section on "working with several objects or parts—grouping" that connects the novice's words with the program's name for the action. The index in the manual and the search list in help should have entries for "grouping" and also for perhaps "moving—part of the pictures together" or other phrases users look for. You find out if users have those problems by watching them do similar tasks and listening for their problems and their words for what they are trying to do. To design successful interfaces and plan successful documentation, you have to do task analysis on all levels from understanding the users' goals to knowing the tasks they do to achieve those goals to understanding how they now carry out those tasks.

Identifying different types and levels of task analysis

Goals are a critical part of task analysis. So is understanding what users do to meet those goals. In planning a task analysis, you might be interested in one or more of these variations on the theme, which we discuss in the next several sections of this chapter:

■ how work gets done when several people are involved (workflow analysis)

- what a single individual does throughout the day or week or month (job analysis)

- how workflow analysis interacts with job analysis

- what tasks are performed by all the people who might be using your product (task lists or task inventories)

- the order in which users do tasks (process analysis, task sequences)

- how a large task is made up of subtasks (task hierarchies)

- what steps and decisions users take to accomplish a task or part of a task (procedural analysis)

Workflow analysis

Early in a project, you may want to understand how a particular process is accomplished even if several people are involved in completing that work. This is "workflow analysis" or "business process analysis." Many companies are trying to simplify business processes. To do that you first have to understand the current process and then look for redundancies and unnecessary steps in that process.

Consider the process of getting a prescription refilled. At least two people are involved: the patient and the pharmacist. More people may be involved, including a relative, friend, or other caregiver of the patient; a clerk or pharmacist's assistant at the pharmacy; a receptionist at the doctor's office; and a doctor. In fact, if more refills are not already allowed on the prescription, the pharmacist must contact the doctor before refilling the prescription. A workflow analysis would reveal that, in a typical situation.

1. *The patient contacts the pharmacy.*

2. *The pharmacist or pharmacy clerk takes the information.*

3. *The pharmacist looks up the patient's prescription and realizes that approval is needed for a refill.*

4. *The pharmacist calls the doctor's office.*

5. *The doctor's receptionist sends the call to the doctor or takes a message for the doctor to call back.*

6. *The pharmacist waits for a call back.*

7. *After the call back, which the pharmacy clerk takes, the pharmacist fills the prescription or contacts the patient to say the prescription can no longer be filled.*

The work flows across people, and in this case across sites, as shown in figure 3-4.

Figure 3-4 You may want to see how work flows across people.

Workflow analysis is a very important type of task analysis because the situation in which different types of people are involved in the process is much more common than processes individuals do alone. The people involved in the process may be at different sites, as in our example of pharmacists and doctors. They may be in different divisions within a company. For example, getting an invoice paid may involve a technical person who receives the invoice, various levels of management who must sign off on it, the accounting clerk who now puts it into the computer, another clerk who pulls up all the invoices due to be paid on a certain date and prints the checks, and a mail room clerk who stuffs the checks into envelopes and puts on postage. Or all the people involved in a workflow may be in the same division or office.

If you do a task analysis by looking only at one part of a workflow process, you risk developing a product that will not be used because it is incompatible with the rest of the workflow.

To do a workflow analysis of getting a prescription refill approved, you would need to spend time in both pharmacies and doctors' offices. You would need to observe and talk with pharmacists and their clerks. You would need to observe and talk with doctors and their receptionists. You might also want to talk with patients and their relatives, friends, and other caregivers.

Interviews and observations with the people involved might reveal that up to 80% of the calls that come into a doctor's office in the course of a day are for approvals on prescription refills. They may also reveal that the calls interrupt what the receptionist and the doctor are doing and that the calls back to the pharmacist interrupt the pharmacy clerk and pharmacist. That's all part of the workflow analysis. You might conclude from the workflow analysis that the current process of getting approvals for refills wastes time that the people doing the work would rather spend doing other tasks: filling other prescriptions in the case of the pharmacist and seeing patients in the case of the doctor. You might conclude that opportunities exist for simplifying and streamlining the process. What if pharmacists and doctors could communicate by computer? Pharmacists could send messages and check for replies (from many doctors) at times convenient for them, and doctors could check for messages (from many pharmacists) and send replies at times convenient for them.

In most cases you will be doing site visits because you already suspect that a problem exists and you already have an idea for solving the problem. In gathering data for your workflow analysis, you need to focus on getting information that will help you decide on the probability that your idea will succeed with the users, help them meet their goals, and support their values. You want data that will tell you what you must do in the design to make your solution attractive to the users. You want data that will tell you about constraints that you need to take into account in your design.

In the example we've been using about getting prescription refills approved, part of your workflow analysis might be to find out who actually does the calling back and forth. If, as often happens in workflow analysis, the answer isn't "always person A," you should get information on frequencies. How often is it the pharmacist who calls? How often is it the clerk? How often is it the doctor who actually returns the information? How often is it the receptionist who actually talks to the pharmacy? Note that to get a good sense of these frequencies you would need to select the sites to visit to give you the best chance of observing the range of possibilities. That is, you would probably want to go to some small pharmacies and some large ones; some individual medical practices and some large practices with several doctors and a larger staff.

Why is knowing how the work flows today important? You might think that it is most likely that the person who now makes the calls will be the person who is most likely to put the information into the computer and that the person who now takes the calls is most likely to take the information from the computer. However, you might also be thinking about changing the tasks that people do or the roles that people play in the process, eliminating some and moving others from one person to another. As you do your workflow analysis, you should consider and make notes about each user's goals and values as well as the environment to help you decide if the changes you are contemplating are going to be acceptable to the users.

Q   In our pharmacy and doctor workflow example, if you are thinking of changing from using the telephone to the computer for refill approvals, you will need to consider issues like, Where are computers in doctors' offices and in pharmacies? What is the likelihood that the environment will change? Do you expect the doctor to use the computer? How likely is that?

Although we've separated our discussion into chapters on users, tasks, and environments, during a site visit you are considering all three at the same time.

Q   So even though the computer doesn't figure in the actual workflow of the current process in our example, if you were doing observations and interviews to gather data on the current process, you would also want to look at and ask about computer use: Do the people involved now use computers? What do they use them for? How comfortable are they on the computer? We know from other studies that doctors don't like to look as if they can't do something. So if the system you design isn't easy to learn and use, the doctor might not be the person who actually looks for and replies to requests for refill approvals. When the requests come over the computer, the receptionist might receive them and a paper system might develop between the receptionist and the doctor that they perceive as more cumbersome than the current system of phone calls. Your idea of changing the workflow might be defeated.

In a workflow analysis, you should also extend the workflow to look not only at the people who are involved in the actual work you want to change but at the people who are involved at the entry and exit points of the workflow. Their goals and values may impinge on what you can do to improve the workflow and on the way you design new processes.

Q   In our example about getting approvals for refilling prescriptions, you would also want to consider the patients' and caregivers' goals. How much time on average does it take in the current system to accomplish the task of getting the prescription refill approved no matter how much it interrupts or bothers the pharmacist and the doctor? If the patient needs the prescription quickly and the turnaround time in the new system is longer because doctors and pharmacists only check the system at intervals during the day, the patient may be less pleased and prefer a pharmacist and doctor who work in the old-fashioned but immediate response, phone call mode. If a typical scenario is that a caregiver comes to the pharmacy thinking the prescription can be refilled, finds out it can't, and now waits for the approval to come, the caregiver is likely to be extremely anxious about time. The caregiver may have left the patient at home and perhaps would find it very difficult to make another trip to get the prescription later. In designing a new system, you want to take these needs into account.

Workflow analysis shows who does what at each step of the process. In our view, however, workflow analysis is more than drawing flowcharts of the steps in the process and showing who does each step. It includes understanding the goals of all the people involved in the process (what they value). It includes understanding them as users, especially in relation to technology or other changes you are thinking of making to the workflow.

Job analysis

Another type of task analysis you might want to do early in a project is job analysis—understanding all the work that a person in a certain position does during the day or week or month. If workflow analysis is a horizontal picture of how work moves across people, job analysis is a vertical picture of all the types of work that flow through a particular person as shown in figure 3-5.

Figure 3-5 You may want to see all the work that a particular person does.

Job analysis can help you

- **find** new marketing and development opportunities
  (What are these people doing for which your company might develop new products that would make their jobs easier?)

- **understand** specific features to build into your product
  (If these people get interrupted a lot while working, you may need to consider how to help them get into, out of, and back into your product quickly and easily.)

■ **learn** what pressures they are under and what they value
(If typical users do the same task repeatedly, you will want to develop and test your product in a different way than if typical users do many different tasks or will only use your product occasionally.)

Although we've called this type of task analysis "job analysis," it really means what people are doing over a period of time and across different activities. You might, in fact, be interested in what people do at home, in their personal lives, or for leisure, instead of what you might have thought of as their "jobs." Susan Dray and Deborah Mraczek visited families in the United States, France, and Germany for Hewlett-Packard to understand how families use computers (Dray and Mraczek 1996a, 1996b). A Microsoft team visited families to "build a comprehensive understanding of home activities and how they are accomplished, systematically examine home activities for new software opportunities, and determine ways to improve usability and increase customer satisfaction with Microsoft's consumer software products" (Juhl 1996, 215).

To do a job analysis, you must work directly with the people in that job. Written job descriptions seldom give you a realistic view of what people in a job actually do during the day. Even managers telling you about the people they supervise may not give you the full picture of what these people actually do and how they accomplish their tasks.

You should actually observe and talk with the people as they do their jobs or have them keep track of what they do for you. Just talking to them outside of the context of the work (or leisure) may not be enough. People don't remember what they do all day. Away from the situation, their sense of how much time they spend doing something or how often they do it may not match reality.

The best way to do a job analysis is to spend time with people on the job. In different companies, this is called "shadowing," "walking in someone else's shoes," "walking a mile with someone," or "a day in the life of…" If you cannot spend time with users, you might have users keep a diary of what they do, writing something down every fifteen minutes or checking off items from a list you've built from previous observations. (See the section on the technique of "customer partnering" in chapter 6 for more ideas on having users keep track of what they do when you aren't observing them.)

In doing this type of task analysis, you might be interested not only in the list of tasks that people do in a given job, but also in factors such as

■ **Frequency.** How often do these people do each task?

■ **Criticality.** How important is each task to their job?

■ **Time to complete.** How time consuming is each task?

- **Difficulty**. How much of a problem is accomplishing this task?

- **Division of responsibility**. Do all the people in that job do this task? Do different people with the same job title do different tasks?

As with any type of task analysis, you want to watch, listen to, and talk with several users with varying degrees of experience and responsibility to get a good overall picture of the job you are interested in.

Combining workflow analysis and job analysis

An overall task analysis might include both workflow analysis and job analysis.

Let's say managers in your company complain about how much time their administrative assistants spend on the phone making arrangements. You do a job analysis, sitting with administrative assistants, talking with them, and having them keep diaries of what they do. You find that one of the most frequent, critical, and time-consuming tasks they do is arrange meetings. You then have several administrative assistants talk you through how they arrange meetings and you sit with one administrative assistant for an entire day. You find that first they get information on the times when all the potential participants are free. This usually requires several phone calls, often with time spent waiting for calls to be returned. Then they try to find a room for the best times by calling facilities management. That also requires at least one phone call, sometimes several. Based on this job analysis, you conclude that an automated scheduling program could make the administrative assistants' lives much easier and their bosses happier.

If you design a new program just for the one group you watched and talked with, however, it may not have as widespread use or as much value as it could. You should also ask: Who else in the company could use this program? You are really asking: Who else does a similar task? You are saying: What other job analyses should I do?

In our example, you would ask: Who else schedules meetings? Who else wants to use the rooms that the administrative assistants are booking for meetings? You would probably come up with several other types of people in the organization, from staff who do their own scheduling because they don't have administrative assistants to people in specific divisions who need large rooms for their work, such as trainers. You might now want to watch and talk with people in those other jobs. How do they schedule meetings and training sessions? Would they need different features in an automated scheduling program? What words do they use for the tasks they might do in the new program? What difficulties do they have with the way the task is done today that you could also overcome in a new program?

In addition to thinking about other people who do the same task, you should also think about the flow of work that is required to have the overall work you are concerned about go smoothly.

In our example of an automated scheduling program, you would now ask: Who else would have to put information into an automated scheduling program or get information out of it? You might think of facilities staff who are in charge of the rooms, audio-visual staff who are in charge of overhead projectors, VCRs, etc., and cafeteria staff who bring refreshments to meetings. (See figure 3-6.)

Within each of these groups, someone might be in charge of putting information about options that schedulers can select into the database and changing the information in the database when needed. For example, someone in facilities would probably be in charge of keeping the list of available rooms up to date, indicating for each how many people it holds and what different choices meeting schedulers can select for the physical arrangements of chairs and tables. Other people in each of these groups would need to be able to get information out of the program. For example, people in the cafeteria might use the program to know which meetings have arranged for refreshments, what refreshments, and what time to deliver them.

Figure 3-6 You may want to do both a workflow analysis and several job analyses with the people involved in the workflow.

If other users' tasks related to the work aren't considered and included in the program, the person whose job you were trying to improve might still have to do a lot of work in the old way.

In our example, if facilities, audio-visual, and cafeteria staff tasks aren't included as you design the automated scheduling program, the administrative assistants will still need to make many phone calls. If the tables aren't in the right place, if the overhead projectors aren't delivered, if the coffee service doesn't come on time because users in facilities, AV, and the cafeteria can't use the program easily, the entire project to automate scheduling might fail.

Workflow analysis helps you to find all the user groups you need to involve, and it helps you understand all the tasks that have to be included in the task list for the product. Even if you cannot put all these functions into the product right away, you can design to avoid conflict with them and you can design to phase them in later and have them fit smoothly into the product. If you know about all these users from the beginning, you can make design decisions that will work for them—even if the functions that focus on them aren't in the first release.

Task analysis to develop a task list or task inventory

Part of the predesign analysis you must do for any product is to develop a task list. A task list is an inventory of all the tasks that users want to accomplish within the overall area that your product will handle.

You might at this point ask the question "What is a task?" You might say, "I know it's what someone does. I know you've said it's what someone does to achieve a goal. But how do I know if I'm listing my tasks at the right level?" What you are really talking about is granularity: How big a task should you think of as a task? The question "What is a task?" came up on the listserve and one of the usability specialists on the listserve gave the following very clear and useful reply:

"I'd suggest a task is any observable, measurable action that has an observable beginning and an observable end. For the sake of consistency, you may want to agree among yourselves [a project or design team] about the level of granularity you'll use. For example, is the task "prepare dinner" or "peel the potatoes"? What you decide is a job, a task, or a step doesn't really matter, so long as you're consistent among yourselves. It probably would also be worthwhile to think about how long your list would be using whatever level of granularity you decide on: a list of five tasks or of five thousand tasks may not be helpful." (Dick Miller, listserve contribution, July 1997, used with the author's permission.)

When getting an initial task list to decide on a product's functionality, you might, in fact, want to start with a relatively short list of tasks: the ten to twenty major functions that users will want or need to do with the product you are designing. Figure 3-7 shows you at least part of such a list for an electronic mail program.

Partial task list for an e-mail program.

- Write a message.

- Send a message.

- Receive a message.

- Read a message that you received.

- Reply to a message.

- Save a message to look at it later.

- Forward a message to someone else.

- Send a formatted file with the message.

- Send the same message to several people.

- Keep an address book.

Figure 3-7 Part of a task list for an electronic mail program.

Later as you plan the design, you'll want to break those tasks down into smaller units at least until you get to the level that is likely to match the menu choices and icons of an interface, the titles of help topics, and the second or third levels of headings in a user's manual. For example the high-level task of "Keep an address book" might include lower-level tasks such as

- ◼ Start a new address book

- ◼ Add someone to the address book

- ◼ Change information about a person in the address book

- ◼ Delete someone from the address book

A task list does not tell you *how* the users will accomplish the task. It only indicates what the users have to be able to accomplish with your product. The *how* is your design problem. The goal of design is to figure out the best way to create a product that lets users easily and quickly do these tasks.

A useful task list is one that lists all the tasks that all the different types of users want to accomplish, and names the tasks from the users' point of view and in the users' words. Thus, in getting a task list for an e-mail program, you would probably have a task of "sending the same message to several people." Put it in your task list that way and not as "using the Group Distribution function."

This users' task list should drive decisions on the product's functionality. If the point of a product is to help people do work, the functionality of the product should come from understanding the overall work and the specific tasks that users need to accomplish—not just from the capabilities of the technology.

You may, of course, add tasks to the list that users don't do now or that they would not think to put on the list because they don't know that they will be able to do them. That's often the advantage that you get by introducing new technology— that users will be able to do tasks they can't do now. However, the new tasks must still meet goals and needs that users have.

In many cases, tasks that you think of as new aren't really. For example, you might think that "setting up a distribution list" and "sending the same message to several people" are new tasks for an e-mail program. In fact, people were doing these tasks before, just in different ways. They were putting distribution lists on memos, making many copies of them, and distributing the copies.

You get a task list by observing and listening to users doing similar work, by talking with users either individually or in groups about the work they do, and by collecting scenarios or stories of their work. As with job analysis, issues of frequency, criticality, time to complete, difficulty, and division of responsibility are relevant to gathering a task list.

Process analysis, task sequences

A task sequence is a series of tasks on the list that users must do or are likely to do in a certain order, as shown in figure 3-8.

In an e-mail program these sets of tasks have a natural sequence:

- Write a message.

comes before

- Send a message.

- Receive a message from someone else.

comes before

- Reply to a message, or
- Forward a message to someone else.

Figure 3-8 Two natural task sequences for an e-mail program.

The task sequence may be logically necessary: B cannot be done until A is complete. You cannot send a message until it is written. You cannot reply to a message or forward the message until you receive it.

However, the task sequences that you observe in site visits may not be logically necessary. Users may be doing tasks in a certain order just because they've always done them that way. If you find everyone doing a sequence of tasks in more or less the same order, it may be because the current version of the product leads them to do it that way, because management has imposed that order to achieve consistency across users in the way that things are done (standard operating procedures), or because users have been trained to do the tasks in that order.

You may also find that different users do the same tasks in a different order. Even if supervisors tell you that there is a prescribed task sequence and everyone does the tasks in the same way, you may find individual differences as you observe. Except in highly prescribed fields, usually where safety is a paramount issue and where users have extensive training, you will generally find many variations on task sequences even when supervisors tell you everyone is doing the same thing.

You can gather information for task sequences from observations and from interviews. Getting information on task sequences is a process analysis just like workflow analysis. The difference is that in workflow analysis you are getting information on how a process is done that involves different users at different points in the process. For the type of task sequence we are discussing in this section, you are getting information on how individual users each do a process, as shown in figure 3-9.

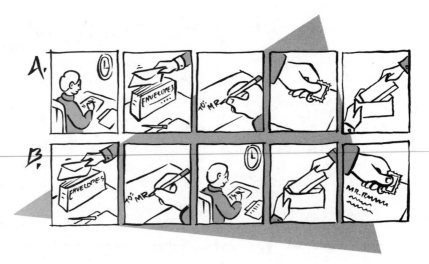

Figure 3-9 Doing a process analysis of two different people sending a letter to someone. Note the individual differences in the task sequences.

You can get information on task sequences with the same methods you use to get task lists. In particular, when you observe users, note the order in which they do the tasks to meet a goal. As you gather information about task sequences, try to find out if users always do the tasks in that order and why? If different users do the same tasks in different orders or if one user does it one way sometimes and another way at other times, try to understand how important that flexibility is to the users.

When you begin designing the new interface, make use of this information. Consider building in flexibility to meet individual differences. For example, if you find that users sometimes write messages before addressing them and sometimes address them first, don't create a software product that forces users to select an address before composing the message.

You may find that typical current task sequences aren't very efficient. Much of the work in reengineering business processes is changing task sequences to make them more efficient. That can help everyone, but you should also be aware that many users, especially users who have been doing the same task sequence over and over for a long time, will find it difficult to change. Don't arbitrarily change task sequences without good reason. When you do change task sequences, you should think about how you are going to help users make the transition to the new process.

Task hierarchies

Task analysis is hierarchical. We can take tasks at any level and decompose them—divide them up into pieces—to see the tasks at greater and greater levels of detail. We can take a job and divide it into the tasks that make up the job. We can take one large task and divide it into the smaller tasks that make up that task (see figure 3-10). We can take even a smaller task and show all the steps and decisions in it (see figure 3-11).

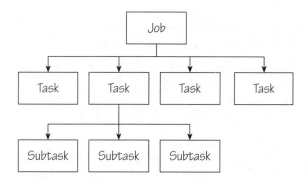

Figure 3-10 Task analysis is hierarchical. You can break up a job into tasks and each task into subtasks.

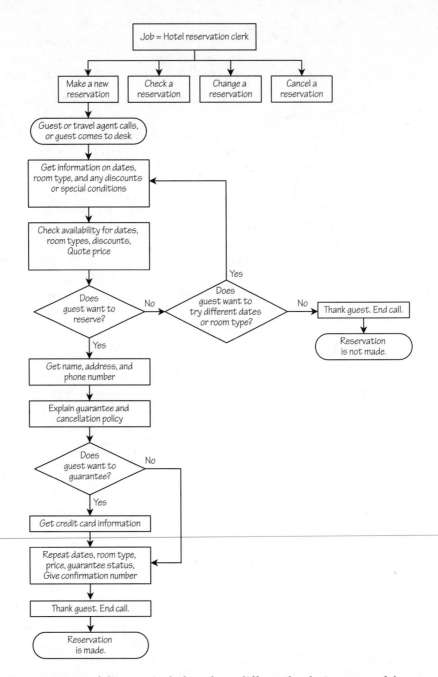

Figure 3-11 A task list may include tasks at different levels. Be aware of the relationships. This figure includes four tasks at the same level and then the procedure (subtasks and decisions) for one of the four main tasks.

That's the issue of granularity. As you think about task analysis and your predesign site visits, you need to decide what level or levels you are most interested in and how deeply you want to decompose each task. When you gather information in your site visits about users' tasks, you may find that you have put tasks at different levels of granularity into the same task list. You'll want to look through your list and perhaps group some of the tasks that belong together under the same larger task.

Procedural analysis

When we take one specific task and divide it into the steps and decisions that a user goes through in doing that task we are doing "procedural analysis" (see figures 3-11 and 3-12).

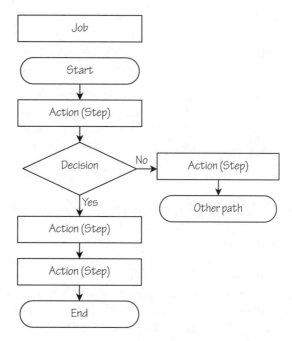

Figure 3-12 You can carry a task analysis down to the individual steps and decisions users make as they carry out the task.

The procedural level differs from the types of task analysis we have been talking about up to now because it always includes working within the constraints of a specific interface. You are seeing *how* users carry out their tasks with the tools they currently have.

You may be planning to entirely change the users' procedures. Nonetheless, it may be very important to get a detailed picture of just how users actually do the tasks today. A procedural analysis allows you to understand both the physical steps that users take and the mental decisions they make while doing a specific task. Doing a procedural analysis of users working in their current mode may give you important insights for your new design.

You do a procedural analysis by observing and listening to real users doing real tasks. Although you can do this in a usability laboratory, you get another dimension of reality by watching and listening to them in their real environment as you do in site visits.

Depending on your objectives, you can use your procedural analysis to create an idealized picture of the process that typical users typically follow. Or you can show an actual flowchart of the process as a particular user did it with all the errors the user made and the wrong paths and repeated loops that the user took as shown in figure 3-13. Procedural analyses of real users doing real work are often quite messy, but they are very informative. They show where current processes are difficult for users, thus providing opportunities to improve the process and to improve the software and documentation for doing the process.

To recap what we've covered, task analysis means understanding the work users do and how they do it. With your understanding of users' goals, you can look at work in many ways and at many levels, including workflow analysis, job analysis, combining workflow and job analyses, task lists, task sequences, task hierarchies, and procedural analysis.

Thinking of users according to their stages of use

In this last section, we relate what we covered in chapter 2 about users to what we covered in the first two parts of this chapter about goals and tasks. In addition to all the ways of characterizing users that we discussed in chapter 2, users differ in their interactions with a product because of the specific tasks they do and the frequency and expertise with which they use the product. As we think of users in terms of frequency and expertise, we can characterize them as being in different "stages of use," from novice to expert.

The model of characterizing users by stages of use was originally developed by Dreyfus and Dreyfus (1986) in *Minds over Machines*. We have expanded the model through observations that we and others have done during usability testing and site visits and through the work of Scandinavian researchers and others who have focused on the collaboration between users and designers for the development of software interfaces. (See, for example, Ehn 1989, 1993).

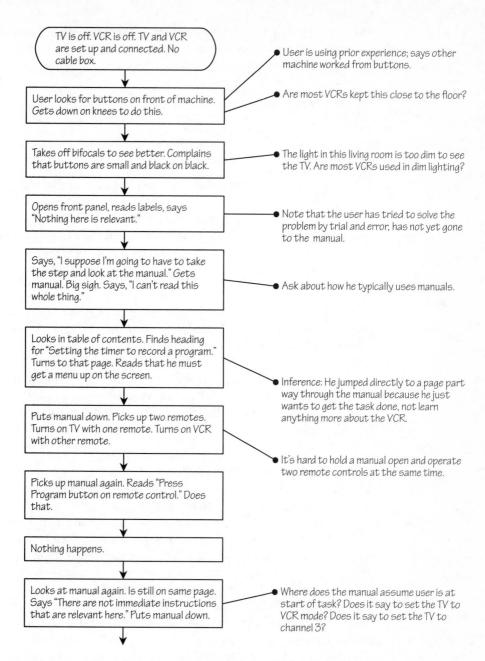

Figure 3-13 You can use a task analysis to show how a real user really does a task. This is a middle-aged man in his living room trying to program his VCR, a task he has once done with another VCR but has never tried with this one.

Any particular user at any particular moment in time with any particular product is at one of the four stages of use:

- novice

- advanced beginner

- competent performer

- expert

Although with any particular product you will find some users who progress through all the stages, most don't go all the way to expert performance. Nor do they need to. We cannot all be expert at everything. We all "satisfice" (Simon 1976) by trading off time and effort for the benefit of greater expertise. Depending on our need, we may remain more or less a novice with some products, be an advanced beginner with many, and be an expert in other aspects of our lives.

The stages of use provide a useful way of categorizing users whom we observe in field studies, as well as a model for thinking about interface and information designs. Some interfaces and information products, for example, are designed primarily for advanced beginners who will perform a few functions over and over again. Other interfaces and information products are focused more exclusively on the needs of competent to expert performers, those who have considerable previous experience with similar products and who want to use the new products as comprehensively as possible. Some must meet the needs of users over the entire range.

Users change over time

Although not everyone becomes an expert, one of the most important points that we gain from the stages of use model is the reminder that users do change over time. Although every user is a novice initially, most move on to being advanced beginners. Many may want to be competent performers. And some users, given sufficient motivation and time, transform themselves into experts. Facilitating movement through the stages should be one goal of design—giving users a product interface and information that supports their continued learning and experimentation. In fact, if we design an interface effectively enough, our most experienced users will find things to do and ways to do them that have never occurred to us.

Occasionally we hear developers argue that they need not study potential users because the users will change once they must interact with a new product. Certainly users change as they add skills and knowledge through their experiences with a product. However, products will succeed only if they facilitate users having successful first experiences, and only if they also allow for growth and learning and for a variety of patterns of use. To design those successful products, you must understand the users' starting points and how users learn and change over time.

Let's look at each of the four stages of use to understand the characteristics that are typical of users at each stage.

Novices

All new users of a product are novices at first—they do not know exactly what to do to use the interface or information. It may be similar to something they are already comfortable using, or it may be drastically different. It may do one or many things that they have been unable to do before, or at least not so easily or conveniently. Figure 3-14 highlights typical characteristics of novice users.

Novices are often faced with a great, and sometimes frightening, unknown. What will happen if they fail to learn and perform effectively? Do they risk embarrassment? Loss of a job? Frustration? Anger? Or simple annoyance? No one likes to look foolish, even to one's self.

- Fear of failure, fear of the unknown

- Focus on accomplishing real work

- Impatient with learning concepts rather than performing tasks

- Theoretical understanding only—no practical experience

Figure 3-14 Characteristics of novice users.

Luckily, in some instances, being a novice can be a short-lived experience. Sometimes the novice experience lasts only minutes or hours as the user becomes comfortable with the differences between the old known behaviors and the new unknown ones. Approaching a new product armed with prior knowledge of and experience with similar products doesn't eliminate novice behaviors or feelings, but it may considerably shorten their duration. The better the product is designed to account for users' prior knowledge and experience, the shorter and more pleasant the novice experience is likely to be.

However, in other situations, being a novice can be extremely unpleasant. If the product is poorly designed, novices may find themselves completely stumped, unable to succeed, frustrated at wasting precious time without achieving a goal. The new behaviors necessary to succeed in using the product may seem awkward or frustratingly different from previous experience. Novice users, faced with a poorly designed new product, one that does not accommodate their goals, may react with an extreme fear of looking stupid. They want to succeed, they want to perform some task successfully, they want to achieve a goal, but they are unable to do so. If they fail, they may put the product aside "for another time." They may give up and never use the product. They may even choose to leave their jobs if using the new product is an absolute requirement.

From observing many novices approaching new products, we can offer two critical generalizations to the designer:

- Novices are very goal and task oriented.

- Novices often do not want to learn, but simply to do.

Novices are often impatient to accomplish some task without taking time to learn or develop sound mental models of the new product. Novice users of an information kiosk in a museum are not interested in becoming skilled at using the kiosk interface. They want to browse the information or find a specific answer immediately. Novice users of a desktop publishing program want to start creating pages of text, not first become experts on the conceptual differences between word processing and desktop publishing.

All users will be novices with your new product when they first get it. But not all novices are the same. As we said in chapter 2, no user is a "blank slate." All are nonnovices in other ways. All bring their prior experiences and knowledge to their use of your new product. As you work with potential users on site visits, you need to find out about their prior knowledge and experience.

You need to gain a good sense of where users are in terms of subject matter or domain knowledge, experience with the technology, and experience with previous versions of the product. For example, if you are designing a new Windows version of a hotel reservation system that has existed as a DOS program, you want to know:

- How much do typical users know about making hotel reservations? (That is, subject matter or domain knowledge.)

- How familiar and comfortable are users with Windows? (That is, experience with the technology.)

- How much do users know about the old DOS-based hotel reservation program and how long have they used it? (That is, experience with previous versions of the products.)

Will there be users who have never made hotel reservations, who are unfamiliar with Windows, and who have never used the old program? If turnover in hotels is high, you may have people who are novices in all these ways. Will there be users who know about making hotel reservations and have used the old program but who will be new to Windows as well as your new version? They are novices in some ways but may be experts in the subject matter.

Novices who are subject-matter experts are likely to transfer their previous experience. If most new users will be transferring from an earlier way of doing the same process, even on paper, you must understand that current process and build the new program and information materials to facilitate the transfer. Consider how your design will accommodate these users' mental model of the tasks. Novices who are not subject-matter experts may not be loaded down with that previous knowledge and experience, but will then have to learn to make a hotel reservation while they are also learning a new program.

Novices who are competent or expert performers in their subject matter and already comfortable with the technology are more likely to move quickly from stage one (novice) to stage two (advanced beginner). When the subject matter is also new, however, even a well-structured interface may initially seem extraordinarily difficult to learn. Learning both a new technology (for example, Windows) and a new program (for example, a reservation system in which the order of doing tasks has been changed) at the same time can be overwhelming. If many users will be in that situation, consider including interface assistants (wizards, cue cards, coaches, and guides) and teaching tools, such as print manuals, tutorials (both paper and computer-based), and online help in your design.

You also need to evaluate how long most users are likely to remain as novices. How often will the same people use what you are developing? How much turnover will there be among users? How much do users want to invest in learning? Users of walk-up kiosks are nearly always novices. Some definitely gain experience, but kiosk designers should not count on having expert users as they design. On the other hand, computer programmers using a new version of a language compiler are likely to move quickly through the novice stage and prefer a product design that quickly accommodates higher stages of use.

In designing your site visits, consider the different types of novices you will find. You should observe some people who are new to the subject matter, the technology, *and* the product. You should observe some people who are transferring to your product, including a range of people who are at different stages of use with the technology and with older versions of the product. In many site visits, we make a particular effort to observe users who are novices at performing the tasks (subject-matter novices). We also make a particular effort to observe advanced beginners with the current process and product, not just experts who are usually far less typical users.

In your site visits, also pay particular attention to frequency of use. Infrequent users may always behave as novices. Frequent users are more likely to move quickly from novice to advanced beginner.

Advanced beginners

Once novices move beyond the fear of failure and begin performing the tasks that allow them to achieve their goals, they become advanced beginners. An advanced beginner is a user who is focused simply and exclusively on getting a job done as painlessly and quickly as possible. In most instances, advanced beginners use a particular product only incidentally and infrequently in their work or home lives. Very few of us, for example, choose to be any more than advanced beginners of our microwave ovens. We are content to heat leftovers, boil water, or use the built-in timer. The microwave allows us to perform many more exotic tasks which we have neither the inclination nor the time to learn. We learn to answer and make calls with the telephones on our desks; we may even become adept at forwarding calls or placing them on hold. But how many of us have to look up the instructions for arranging a conference call, or better yet, enlist the help of the local expert to do the arranging for us? We're not interested enough in the intricacies of the phone system to learn more than a few basic tasks.

Even in the workplace, people use many products, especially application software, only incidentally and infrequently as part of their jobs. They may use desktop publishing software to write an occasional letter or memo or a spreadsheet program to set up a small table and perform a calculation. They are quite content to learn a few tasks they use regularly, such as setting selected words in bold type or using the summation function to add rows and columns, but they're unlikely to learn about creating style sheets or using the spreadsheet to perform statistical analyses of data. Figure 3-15 highlights typical characteristics of advanced beginners.

- Focus on accomplishing real work
- Impatient with learning concepts rather than performing tasks
- Randomly access tasks
- By adding new and progressively more complicated tasks, begin to develop an empirically based mental model

Figure 3-15 Characteristics of advanced beginners.

Many users never learn to perform more than a few tasks with a product. In fact, up to 80% of the users of a typical software or hardware product never move beyond the advanced beginner stage of use. By definition, higher stages of use require experience with many tasks, often over longer periods of time. Thus users who are content with a few tasks remain advanced beginners.

Many advanced beginners, focused on performing the tasks they need, are content to ignore the rest of the interface. If, however, we have not, as designers, recognized the needs of advanced beginners and identified the most often performed functions, we may create an interface that is difficult for advanced beginners to navigate. For example, interfaces that provide too many alternative methods of performing the same function may confuse advanced beginners. Interfaces that emphasize exotic, and infrequently performed, functions may obscure frequently performed functions. Interfaces that fail to optimize the most commonly performed functions will be difficult for advanced beginners to learn and use.

Like novices, advanced beginners are often reluctant to spend precious task-oriented time learning concepts. They tell us that they don't have time to learn, only to get on with the job. However, as advanced beginners gradually increase the number of tasks they can perform, they begin to form a concept or mental model of how the software or hardware interface is organized. This mental model enables them to learn new tasks more easily, especially if the interface they are using is unswervingly consistent. For advanced beginners to learn effectively, a consistent interface is a necessity. Consistency allows users to plan how they might perform a new task based on their experience performing previous tasks. Their plan relies on their mental model of the task. If the interface has maintained consistency among tasks, the users' plan will work, and they will be successful in learning the new task.

Advanced beginners who are already skilled in the subject matter but not in the technology are most likely to be impatient learners. They will try to make sense of the interface to accomplish their goals without assistance from documentation, tutorials, or interface assistants. Only when they cannot make sense of the interface will they seek outside assistance from people who already know what to do, technical support services provided by the manufacturer, or the documentation, whether online or in print. They are also most willing to spend time learning to use the new product because they will see the greatest payoff from the time and effort. Subject-matter experts, or those who need or want to become experts, are likely to continue learning new tasks, moving into the next stage of use—competent performance.

On the other hand, advanced beginners just learning the subject matter are likely to concentrate on learning the few simple tasks that they need to perform at the moment. And advanced beginners who are infrequent users and who do not see themselves as ever becoming subject-matter experts are also likely to learn only the tasks they need to reach their immediate goals.

The difference between novices and advanced beginners is that the advanced beginners can perform several tasks well. The difference between advanced beginners and users at higher stages of use is in part the number and complexity of the tasks they have learned and, in part, the advanced beginners' difficulty in handling problems. Advanced beginners are usually not comfortable trying to diagnose and correct problems and are often unsuccessful at it. In your site visits, you might want to pay particular attention to signs of confusion and requests for assistance when advanced beginners encounter problems.

Differences in frequency of use, breadth of use, and subject-matter knowledge also distinguish advanced beginners from users at higher stages of use. Infrequent users of your products and information are unlikely to progress beyond the advanced beginner stage. Frequent users, even ones who work with the product all day every day, may remain advanced beginners if they only do one or two tasks repeatedly and have little understanding or interest in the broader domain that the product covers, and may remain uncomfortable with anything beyond the few tasks they know well. Users who lack subject-matter knowledge are likely to remain advanced beginners longer than those who are competent in the subject matter. As you plan your site visits, decide how you will identify the mix of advanced beginners and users at higher stages of use. Look for situations and users who differ in frequency of use, breadth of use, and subject-matter knowledge.

Don't rely on users characterizing themselves on scales in which you ask them to rate how comfortable or how knowledgeable they are with the subject matter, the technology, or the product. Advanced beginners are likely to rate themselves as more comfortable and more knowledgeable than users at higher stages of use. They are comfortable with what they do, and they don't know what they don't know. More competent performers are often more aware of their lack of knowledge.

Competent performers

In the stages-of-use model, competent performers are defined as those users who have learned a sufficient number of tasks that they have formed a sound mental model of the subject matter and the product. Competence, as a result, comes only with experience, not from first learning a conceptual framework for the tasks.

As competent users gain experience using a product to perform more tasks, they begin to understand how the various tasks fit into a whole. As a consequence, they become better at foreseeing how an interface will behave and planning how they will perform a new task. They also increase in their ability to diagnose and correct problems. Novices and advanced beginners are often completely stymied by unexpected results of their actions. They have few, if any, resources to trace back what they have done and recognize actions that did not produce the results they wanted. Competent performers, because of their increased experience using the interface, become much more skilled at recognizing an incorrect series of actions and finding ways to trace back and correct them. Figure 3-16 highlights the typical characteristics of competent performers.

- Focus on performing more complex tasks that require many coordinated actions
- Ability to plan how to perform a complex series of tasks to achieve a goal
- Willingness to learn how tasks fit into a consistent mental model of the interface as a whole
- Interest in solving simple problems by applying a conceptual framework to diagnose and correct errors

Figure 3-16 Characteristics of competent performers.

In a usability test, JoAnn watched two users struggle with setting up the fax application for their new computer system. Both were competent users of fax machines, understood the concepts behind sending faxes from a computer, and were skilled users of the Windows 95 operating system. However, as new users of the Windows 95-based fax product, they were confused about the sequence of events required to set up the fax system and send a fax. They finally got the fax set up and ready for use but only after a confusing sequence of trial-and-error attempts. At the end of the usability session, one of the users commented that he "had no idea how [he] did that."

A few weeks later, however, after they had installed the fax product once again and used it to send and receive faxes, these users had developed a comprehensive mental model of the way to do tasks in the new product. They commented that they could easily set up the system again because they now understood that they had to create a folder to receive a fax before they could complete the set-up process. They understood the new process even though they continued to view the required sequence as somewhat peculiar. In fact, the required sequence continued to violate their previous mental model of the task. They asked, "Why must I have a folder set up to receive faxes, when I only want to send a fax?" However, they now knew they had to do it. In the process of gaining competence at using the product, they had acquired a conceptual understanding that would help them diagnose and correct problems using the software in the future.

In observing competent computer repair technicians, we noted that they were frequently able to diagnose problems on products entirely new to them because they were able to apply a sophisticated mental model of how similar computers worked. They were able to distinguish between significant and insignificant differences among products.

Competent performers are more likely to use job aids provided with an interface to increase their understanding of how the product works. They are often anxious to learn additional tasks and have sufficient understanding of the tool to understand detailed task-oriented instructions. Competent performers with considerable subject-matter knowledge and experience using similar interfaces are also more likely use tutorials and computer-based training to quickly gain familiarity with common tasks and the conceptual model designed into the product. Since competent performers are also involved in diagnosis and error correction, they are also more likely to use documentation to gain insights into how things are supposed to work and what might have gone wrong. They are likely to prefer, however, straightforward problem-solution tables to more conceptual discussions of the design and the theories behind the design.

The ability to create a plan of action to perform a task and follow it to a successful conclusion, plus the ability to recognize, diagnose, and solve problems while attempting to perform a task are the hallmarks of a competent performer. When you conduct your field studies, try to discover what percentage of your users have achieved competence by observing their ability to perform complex tasks and to solve problems. In distinguishing between competent performers and advanced beginners, look for the diversity of tasks performed. Advanced beginners are likely to know how to perform fewer tasks overall than are competent performers.

Expert performers

As competent performers continue to gain experience performing tasks and troubleshooting problems, they increase the richness of their understanding of how the product interface supports their ability to reach their goals. Competent performers become experts when they are highly motivated, use the product frequently and as an integral part of their jobs or personal activities and hobbies, have considerable subject matter knowledge, and are skilled at solving their own problems and the problems of others. Figure 3-17 highlights the characteristics typically found with expert performers.

- Focus on developing a comprehensive and consistent mental model of the product functionality and the interface
- Ability to understand complex problems and find solutions
- Interest in learning about concepts and theories behind a product's design and use
- Interest in interacting with other expert users

Figure 3-17 Characteristics of expert performers.

In most instances you will find few experts in your user community. Most people simply lack the time or motivation to become expert in more than one area and with more than a small number of products.

We can often identify expert performers by the number of competent performers who refer us to them. The experts are the few individuals in an organization who are clearly recognized as more skilled in that particular area than anyone else. They solve the most complex problems and often do the most difficult and infrequently performed tasks. They are the people who work on the support lines, teach the workshops, and serve as consultants for the rest of the user community.

Expert performers have the kind of comprehensive understanding of the whole that allows them to create their own more efficient ways to perform tasks. They are continually experimenting to increase their understanding. They often own five or six books on the subject and read the journals and magazines that discuss their areas of interest and the products and tools they use or need to know about. There may be little in task-oriented documentation to interest expert users, but they are often skilled and frequent users of documentation. They use the information to gain the small insights that will enrich their understanding and to learn to perform new tasks, especially with new versions of the product.

Expert performers are often engaged in a dialogue with product engineers and interface designers, pushing the envelope of the functions the product will perform and asking for alternative approaches to be included in the interface. Because they are already using the products to the fullest extent, they are always asking for more. The danger, of course, is that you may allow yourself, as a designer, to spend too much time catering to the needs of people at this stage of use. Certainly your most expert customers will assist you in moving your product and its interface into new, uncharted areas. However, if they represent only a small percentage of your users, as is likely, they may sap your energies and move your attention from the needs of less proficient users. In fact, one of the dangers of enlisting expert users to serve on user requirements panels or to take part in focus groups to define new product features is that they will preempt your design time. For many designers and expert users, talking together is fun. Of all the user groups, experts may be the most like the designers. The fallacy of relying on the experts, even if you enjoy being with them most, is that they are not representative of most of your users. Figure 3-18 reminds you to pay attention to all four stages of use.

JoAnn worked on one interface design where the engineers spent most of their design time working on the exceptional and obscure tasks that some users wanted to perform. As a result, the primary functions served by the product and of interest to most users were neglected. The interface was difficult to understand and use, proving inaccessible to novices, advanced beginners, and even competent performers.

Applying the stages of use to your field studies

As you plan your field studies, consider how you will identify the stages of use within your user community. Plan your site visits (see chapters 7 and 8) so that

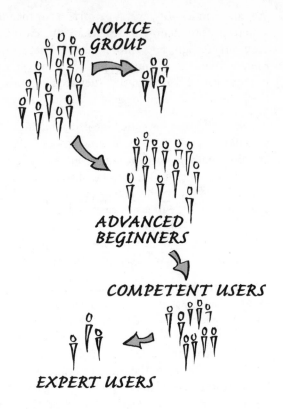

Figure 3-18 You will find users at all four stages of use, but many users will always remain advanced beginners and few users will ever become experts.

you will see how novices, advanced beginners, competent performers, and experts are distributed among your users. If you have no users yet, consider finding out about the characteristics of potential users. Are they likely to be infrequent or frequent users? What subject-matter knowledge will they bring with them? What knowledge and experience in the technology will they bring with them? Do they have experience using similar products and interfaces? How much training and documentation will they require to move through the stages?

Try to avoid having your site visits dominated by any one type of user. Some of your customers may want to steer you to their inhouse experts because competent performers and experts are likely to be more motivated and articulate in defining the problems with a product and its interface. Also, they want to show off their best performers. However, you should insist on seeing less competent but more typical users if advanced beginners are the most typical people among your users.

As you construct the profiles of your users, identify them in terms of stages of use. Consider what percentage of your user community is likely to fall within each stage. Consider how your users are likely to move through the stages in their interaction with your product. Consider the possible relationships between stages of use and other user characteristics such as subject-matter knowledge, technology knowledge, and personal characteristics like learning style, all of which were discussed in chapter 2.

As you can see, developing a picture of stages of use provides a link between the characteristics of your users, especially their prior knowledge and experience, and your task analysis. If you observe only novices, you are unlikely to gain much insight into the performance of more than a few tasks. If you study only experts, you will have difficulty designing for those who are unfamiliar either with similar tools or with the subject matter.

One word of caution. Do not assume that your own personal characteristics are common to your users. You may prefer to read all the documentation before you begin to use a new software application, but that does not mean that all your users will choose the same course. You may prefer hacking your way through a new software application interface, but your users may be more timid about first-time use and prefer to have some training or built-in job aid as a way to start.

References cited in the chapter

Benyon, David, The role of task analysis in systems design, *Interacting with Computers*, 4 (1), April 1992: 102-123.

Diaper, Dan and Addison, Mark, Task analysis and systems analysis for software development, *Interacting with Computers*, 4 (1), April 1992: 124-139.

Dray, Susan and Mrazek, Deborah, A day in the life of a family: An international ethnographic study, in *Field Methods Casebook for Software Design*, edited by Dennis Wixon and Judith Ramey, NY: John Wiley & Sons, 1996a, 145-156.

Dray, Susan and Mrazek, Deborah, A day in the life: Studying context across cultures, in *International User Interfaces*, edited by Elisa M. del Galdo and Jakob Nielsen, NY: John Wiley & Sons, 1996b, 242-256.

Dreyfus, Hubert L. and Dreyfus, Stuart E., *Minds over Machines*, NY: Macmillan, 1986.

Ehn, Pelle, *Work-Oriented Design of Computer Artifacts*, Hillsdale, NJ: Lawrence Erlbaum Associates, 1989.

Ehn, Pelle, Scandinavian design: On participation and skill, in *Participatory Design: Principles and Practices*, edited by Douglas Schuler and Aki Namioka, Hillsdale, NJ: Lawrence Erlbaum Associates, 1993, 41–77.

Juhl, Diane, Using field-oriented design techniques to develop consumer software products, in *Field Methods Casebook for Software Design*, edited by Dennis Wixon and Judith Ramey, NY: John Wiley & Sons, 1996, 215-228.

Norman, Donald A., *The Design of Everyday Things*, NY: Doubleday, 1988 (originally published as *The Psychology of Everyday Things*, NY: Basic Books).

Simon, Herbert A., *Administrative Behavior,* NY: The Free Press, 3rd edition, 1976.

Other books and articles for further reading

Cooper, Alan, *About Face: The Essentials of User Interface Design,* Foster City, CA: IDG Book Worldwide, 1995.

Kirwan, Barry and Ainsworth, Les K., *A Guide to Task Analysis*, London: Taylor & Francis, 1992.

Rubinstein, Richard and Hersh, Harry, *The Human Factor: Designing Computer Systems for People*, Bedford, MA: Digital Equipment Corporation, 1984.

Shneiderman, Ben, *Designing the User Interface: Strategies for Human-Computer Interaction*, 3rd ed., Reading, MA: Addison-Wesley, 1998.

Wixon, Dennis and Ramey, Judith, Eds., *Field Methods Casebook for Software Design*, NY: John Wiley & Sons, 1996.

Zemke, Ron and Kramlinger, Tom, *Figuring Things Out: A Trainer's Guide to Needs and Task Analysis*, Reading, MA: Addison-Wesley, 1982.

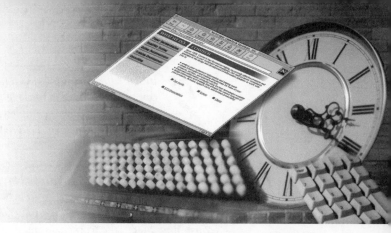

4

Thinking about the users' environment

When conducting field studies to learn about your users and the tasks they want to perform, you must also consider the physical, social, and cultural environments in which the users work. When you observe and interview users in their work environments, you can hardly avoid having that environment color your observations. But if aspects of the users' environment are to influence your thinking about the design of the product and its interface, documentation, and training, you will find it useful to have considered which aspects of the environment are likely to be most important. You must also try to become aware of your own cultural biases. That awareness will help you see the users' world in their own terms, rather than your own.

Why is environment important?

People do not perform their work in isolation. They are influenced by the activity around them, the physical characteristics of the workplace, the type of equipment they are using, and the work relationships they have with other people. If the products you design do not fit into the environment, they may be difficult or frustrating to use. They may also result in complete rejection by the users who will return to their previous ways of working or find ways to subvert the systems imposed upon them.

In one company, workers on the loading dock were given a new computerized system for logging incoming materials. In the existing system, the manager completed a form in the office. The new system required that the workers use the computer outside. The environment on the loading dock was fast-paced, noisy, dirty, and frequently windy. The loading dock was not an environment conducive to learning how to use a new computer system and entering complex data using a keyboard.

In part because they were given little training in using the new system, but primarily because they found the interface too complicated, awkward, and time-consuming to use, the workers found a way to bypass the new computers. They found that they could use the system defaults to log materials without identifying the types and quantities each time. It was months before the company was able to track the shortages they were experiencing in inventory to the loading-dock problems.

In another case, insurance salespeople were given a very large manual that described the insurance policies and other services the company provided for its customers. The manual contained detailed information that would help the salespeople answer customer questions about policies and services. However, the salespeople generally visited customers' homes to discuss insurance needs. They never carried the manuals with them. They argued that their customers expected them to be knowledgeable and not need to look up information, especially in a huge, awkward, difficult-to-access manual. The manual made them look bad in front of their customers. (See figure 4-1.)

Figure 4-1 A large manual will not work in some environments.

What aspects of the environment are important?

As you observe your users' working environments, note aspects of the environment that may influence how people will use your product and interact with your interface, documentation, or training.

Physical environment

The physical aspects of the environment are likely to be immediately significant. Light levels will affect the users' ability to see screens or controls. How many of us have tried to read dark letters on black backgrounds on our televisions or VCRs? Or tried to see small fonts on a screen placed at a distance? The placement of controls may make them invisible or difficult to reach (figure 4-2). A computer interface that

Figure 4-2 Many users have their VCRs in cabinets below the TV. Reaching down to find the controls is awkward.

requires a mouse may not be usable in a public place where mice have short lives. Touch screens that work just fine in an office environment may last only minutes or hours in an oily or dusty environment. Paper manuals may not be accessible to users working at customer sites or may be inadmissible to the manufacturing "clean room." Information on CD-ROMs or Web pages may be inaccessible to users without CD-ROM drives on their computers or access to the Internet.

Issues to consider about the physical environment:

- ■ How much space do the users have to work in? Can they spread out materials? Is there space for manuals? Can they reach all pieces of equipment needed? Can you really add another piece of equipment?

- Do the users have their own equipment or do they borrow equipment from one another? If they borrow equipment, do they move it to their workspace or go to another workspace? Is all the information they need available in the area where they perform the tasks?

- Is the users' environment noisy? Does the noise make it difficult to hear, to read, to concentrate?

- Do the users have adequate light to see the computer screen and the documentation?

- Do dirt, dust, pollution, or other environmental hazards affect the users' workplace and make working difficult?

- Do the temperature, humidity, and other weather-related factors affect the users' ability to use your product effectively?

- Is power easily available to the users so that they can operate all the equipment they need? Is the power steady or are power interruptions common?

- Are there dangers in the environment that will affect how the users work?

 The instructions telling what do in an emergency were posted in large signs on the walls of the workplace. The users were directed to telephone for assistance if they had a problem. However, no telephones were available in the area where the problems occurred and the users could not leave the location to go for help.

Recognize that the users' physical environment may substantially affect the success of your design. Look for as many clues as you can observe or discuss with users that will help you avoid design mistakes.

Social environment

The social environment, either within the users' immediate group or in a larger group of coworkers and customers, may make a particular design difficult to use. Workers under pressure to perform functions quickly will be frustrated by interfaces that don't support them adequately. Customers waiting on the phone or in long queues may be equally frustrated.

 Denver International Airport requires that all drivers that have either dropped people off, picked them up, or parked in the short-term or long-term parking lots must exit through the same toll booths. The computer system used to determine the amount of money to be paid for parking requires the worker to enter several keystroke sequences

(more for credit card payments) and perform several separate actions. As a result, each transaction takes two to several minutes to complete. The result is long lines of cars with many irate drivers because of the failure of the interface designers to optimize the speed of the human-computer interaction.

Issues to consider about the social environment:

- Do the users work in situations where they must perform their tasks quickly and accurately? Are they pressured to go fast? Are they pressured not to make mistakes?

- Are resources available that help users answer questions and solve problems? Is the documentation easily available? Do they have access to phones to call for help? Are there other people nearby who can assist if a problem occurs? Are there system administrators on site or do users have to call the manufacturer for help?

- Do the people who share information work in the same location? Are they separated into different departments in the same building? Are they in different buildings, in different cities, in different parts of the world? How does geographic separation affect their work?

- How do your users work together and share information? Do they communicate by talking informally or holding meetings? Do they communicate by telephone, fax, e-mail, video conference? Do they share information informally or by formal means?

- What is the social hierarchy in the organization? How do end users work with supervisors? How do users interact with system administrators or technicians? How well do coworkers interact?

- How do the physical and social environments interact? Where do coworkers sit? Does each user have an individual office? Or do they all sit in an open space? Do they work in cubicles? How does the seating arrangement affect working together? Do they interact with each other a lot as they work?

- Are many users at home? Do they work alone? What are the implications for your design of telecommuting or independent consultants working at home?

- What is the relationship between your users and their customers? Do they interact with customers in person, by telephone, by mail, or by other means? How sensitive to "bad impressions" is this environment? How quickly must users respond to customer needs? Are they timed, tracked, or otherwise evaluated on their performance with customers?

These and other questions will help you to find out about the social environment and to make decisions about how the social interactions of your users should affect your design.

One company tried to develop a better training program for workers who staff remote call centers. Because people work in very small groups of three or four individuals, the company's training organization decided that computer-based training (CBT) would be more economical to deliver than instructor-led training. Even though the CBT was well designed and initially well received by the users, it shortly became obvious that the users were not using it.

When JoAnn investigated, she learned that the call-center workers had been selected largely for their pleasant telephone manner and gregarious natures. As soon as JoAnn's team entered the workplace, it was obvious that the workers enjoyed interacting with customers on the telephone and with each other between calls. As extroverts, these users gained energy from being with other team members. The CBT system, however, required that individuals go to another room and sit quietly and alone in front of a computer terminal. Since none of the members of the team wanted to work alone, they took few opportunities to use the CBT system as a learning tool. The CBT experiment failed because it neglected the call-center environment and the social interactions of the team members. (See figure 4-3.)

Figure 4-3 Users who work in a people-rich environment will often feel isolated and neglected if they are forced to learn alone at a computer.

Cultural environment

The users' cultural environment is not only about their ethnicity or nationality but also an entire range of experiences related to their corporate, regional, professional, and socioeconomic backgrounds. You may learn, for example, that you cannot use obtrusive sounds to signal computer errors in a culture where users may lose face if they think someone else knows they have done something wrong. You may want to design a system that provides autonomous decision making if you learn that the users' culture values independent actions. You may learn that visual images that you thought communicated well are incomprehensible or offensive to people from a different culture.

 Pictures often have stronger cultural connotations than words. A group from the Program for Appropriate Technology in Health (PATH) tested material they had prepared to teach women in Sudan how to treat children with diarrhea. They used a picture of a woman wearing a tobe *(a long piece of cloth women in Sudan typically wear over their dresses when they go outside the home). Because of that and other features of the picture, people thought the woman was in an office. It took four rounds of drawing and testing to find one that worked (Forslund 1996).*

In another case, users were unable to understand the picture of a pregnant woman carrying a heavy load with an X over the picture. This Western symbol for "do not" meant nothing to women in Kenya (Forslund 1996).

In these examples, the national culture affected how a message was received. Interpretations of messages can also be affected by professional or gender-related cultures. For example, many ordinary computer users, as well as some usability specialists, have observed that messages appearing on the screen are often insulting to the users. The tone of the messages appears to reflect a computer-hacker culture dominated by young men. The systems are used by people of different sensibilities, ages, genders, religions, and so on who may be offended by the message tone. The culture of the users is not the same as the culture of the developers, and the contrast makes using the computer less pleasant for the users than it might be.

Remember also that your users may be a diverse group. The cultures you see depend on where you do the site visits. Even if you cannot visit all the cultures your product will reach, try to find out about those cultures from experts.

Issues to consider about the cultural environment:

■ Will the users' national cultures influence how they work, how they perform tasks, what they value, or what their work environment is like?

What specifically should developers be aware of for the users of your product?

■ Do your users work in different cities, states, regions, and so on in the same country? If so, can you observe differences in their cultural environments that may affect your design?

■ Do your users belong to a professional culture that has particular values, styles of working and interacting, or task emphasis that must be taken into account?

■ Do you users belong to socioeconomic groups that will affect their experience with your design? Are there metaphors that they will find obscure or inappropriate?

■ Do your users have culturally determined references for the structure of information in manuals or online help?

■ What cultural biases might you be bringing to the observations? If you are aware of them you can be more open-minded to see how others work.

What should you look for in the physical environment?

It is impossible to anticipate all the characteristics of the users' physical environment that might have an impact on your design. However, characteristics you may want to take into account when you visit your users include

■ working environment (home, office, laboratory)

■ working space

■ noise

■ dirt

■ lighting

■ temperature

■ speed

■ power sources

■ proximity to information sources

■ danger

This list is not meant to be exhaustive but to encourage you to think about the users' environments as factors in your design problem. In the following sections, we discuss some of these factors in more detail.

Do your users work at home?

Many interfaces appear to have been designed under the assumption that the users work alone in pristine office environments with easy access to manuals and power outlets, with good lighting and adequate workspace, and free from excessive noise and interruptions. Only recently have designers begun to be aware of the special circumstances in which their users do their tasks.

David Mitropoulus-Rundus and Jerry Muszak (1997a, 1997b) and Susan Dray and Deborah Mrazek (1996a, 1996b) have described their visits to users for Kodak and Hewlett-Packard to discover what it is like to install and use equipment and software when constantly being interrupted by children and pets, when work space is limited and power sources awkwardly placed, or when lighting is not designed to make seeing controls easy. JoAnn's staff has visited users who work out of their homes. The staff discovered manuals used to block the sun coming in the window in the late afternoon and manuals stored out of easy reach in a bookcase in a hallway to the outside so that the users could claim the hallway on their income taxes.

As more users work at home with computers, either for family use, independent businesses, or for telecommuting, designers will need to understand more about the home environment and its effect on interface and information design. You may learn, for example, that your product needs to come with a longer power cord for home use or that the users need an interface with an automatic save feature because they are frequently interrupted by children's emergencies. You may learn that you have to partition tasks differently when the users and their spouses work on different parts of a task.

You need to consider what percentage of your users are likely to work at home. If that percentage is high, you may need to provide alternative designs that accommodate home use. For example, you may be able to depend upon users in an office having T1 lines to connect them to the Internet. If they work at home, they may have access only via much slower modems. The difference may require two separate strategies for allowing users to get to the information they need.

Do your users work in an office with adequate space to perform tasks?

Even seemingly "standard" office environments may not be as standard as you assume. If your users are going to use your interface in an ordinary office environment, will they have adequate working space? Is there room for a mouse or detached keyboard to be used with the computer system? Is there room for paper manuals or should manuals be online? Is there adequate space to establish an optimal viewing angle for a monitor? Can the controls be seen easily? Will the user be able to reach the controls of the equipment in a restricted workspace?

JoAnn's staff encountered users who worked with their equipment in laboratories but used their computers in their office cubicles. That made it difficult for them to access information stored on CD-ROM or on a Web site while they were using the laboratory equipment. In a factory environment, the staff discovered that the computers were on small stands with no room for manuals. The users were not permitted to clutter the work environment with sticky notes. (See figure 4-4.)

Figure 4-4 Users may have no space to use manuals.

You are also likely to discover that office space is configured differently in different cultures. JoAnn discovered that bookcases in Japan are narrower than American bookcases, making it especially difficult to store large manuals. Work and storage space in general is more limited in the typical Japanese office than American designers might assume. Desks are narrower and are placed closer together. Cubicle walls dividing individual space are also rare.

A company planned to introduce a new system that required new computers on everyone's desks. The company was willing to provide the new computers. However, when the designers visited the users' site, they learned that the users also worked on other programs that ran only on the older machines. There were no plans to change these programs, which meant that the users would have to have two computers in their workspace. The limited workspace made this accommodation impossible. No one had thought through the potential problems the new computers might introduce until they did the site visits.

Do users work in a noisy environment?

Is the users' environment noisy enough to make learning and performing tasks difficult? If people are using your system at home, will they be distracted by barking dogs and screaming kids? Are the sound cues (bells, beeps, and cheeps) included in your interface design likely to annoy coworkers? Will users be able to hear audio warnings? Will they be able to listen to audio instructions with people talking, machines running, and telephones ringing?

Noise that may be tolerable to people with normal hearing may present special difficulties to people with impaired hearing. Users of hearing aids often report that they find it difficult to distinguish particular sounds when there is lots of background noise. If people are talking and machines are running, your users may find it difficult to hear the warning sounds coming from their computers. (See figure 4-5.)

Figure 4-5 Some environments are very noisy.

Do users work in a dirty, dusty, or windy environment?

Is the users' workplace dirty enough to require a special type of keyboard or other controls? Will a touch screen be usable if the screen smears from oil? Do users work in a clean room that requires dust-free paper for manuals or no paper at all? If users work outside or in places other than offices, you must consider how that will affect your design.

Workers at a mine site had to devise covers for computer keyboards because the fine dust in the environment quickly made them unusable. Maintenance technicians who work high on utility poles found that the large foldout sheets containing the mechanical or electrical diagrams they needed quickly became flying objects in the slightest wind.

Do your users have adequate lighting to see the screens or controls?

Is the lighting adequate to see the computer screen, the manuals, the controls on the equipment? If the users have to dim the lights to see an image, can they see the controls at the same time? If the users have special lighting in place, will it affect the colors that will be visible on the screen? Will colors for warnings or cautions be adequately visible on the screen? (See figure 4-6.)

Figure 4-6 Not all users work in the typical lighting of designers' offices.

Ginny found that users of VCRs had difficulty seeing black words on black buttons in the normal subdued light of a living room. The designers most likely designed the buttons in the bright light of a laboratory or design studio.

Do temperature problems affect your users' ability to work?

Will the equipment you are designing be used under a variety of environmental conditions, including extremes of temperature or elevation? One customer had difficulty using a disk drive at a mine site located at an elevation over 12,000 feet because there was not enough air pressure to float the disk above the read mechanism. Will very cold temperatures make it difficult for users to manipulate controls? Will users be wearing gloves because of cold temperatures? Will high temperature and humidity fog screens or make hands slip?

Professor Judy Ramey of the University of Washington teaches workshops on usability testing. A participant in one of her workshops reported on problems the designers encountered when they visited the users of their inventory software for distributors of wholesale frozen goods. Warehouse people were given handheld devices to enter product codes as they worked through their pick lists in the warehouse. After the new system went into use, the managers quickly discovered that the information being entered into the database was extremely inaccurate. The designers went on site to see how the devices were being used. They found that the warehouse workers had to handle 100 pound sacks of frozen food, wearing work gloves to protect their hands. With the work gloves on, these workers could not accurately press just one key at a time on the handheld device.

How quickly will your users expect the system to react?

You may find that your users are measured on their ability to react quickly to their customers, especially if their customers are standing in line or are on the phone. For example, the design of a computer system used by librarians made it so difficult and time-consuming for the users to shift between book checkout screens and other parts of the interface that long lines of angry patrons resulted. Customer service representatives talking on the phone with customers want their computers to quickly find the customer records they need. Travel agents want computers that search very quickly for the best airline flights at the best prices so that they don't have to keep their customers waiting.

Earlier in the chapter, you saw a story about the computer system for checking people out of the parking lot at Denver International Airport. Because it is so slow, requires so many operator steps, and has made so many airport customers unhappy, the city is considering eliminating the checkout lanes and replacing the entire system with something that will reduce the long lines and the travelers' frustration.

Tourists trying to use the automatic ticket machines at the Sydney, Australia, monorail found the design of the interface so obscure that the transit authority was forced to put human assistants at each machine to help tourists use the machine and keep long lines from forming, as shown in figure 4-7.

We have all experienced the frustration of being in the grocery-store checkout line when a new clerk is struggling to learn a difficult computer system. In each of these cases, the designers failed to account for the impact of slow and difficult-to-use interfaces on the entire set of user interactions.

Figure 4-7 If a system is too difficult to use, human support may be needed—an expensive solution.

Do your users have adequate and accessible sources of power?

Are adequate sources of power available to the users? Will they have to take special measures to ensure adequate power? Are cables long enough to be useful in typical or unusual work areas? Anyone who has used a laptop computer with an LCD panel knows that short interconnecting cables reduce the ease of use for the presenter.

Power sources are substantially different internationally, as you most likely know. When planning products, think about whether power sources are as accessible in offices, hotels, or homes as they are in the United States? Even in U.S. hotel rooms, users may find that outlets are inaccessible or filled with plugs for other devices.

Are users able to get the information they need?

Will users be able to access the information they need to do their jobs? If information is paper based, where will it be stored? Will everyone who needs information be able to find it when they need it? If information is delivered electronically, do all of the potential users have electronic access? Do they have CD-ROM drives to view manuals or access to the Internet? If your product requires users to upgrade their systems or buy new equipment, is that a realistic expectation given users' economic and cultural situations? If users will need to call customer support for assistance, are telephones accessible to the areas where the work takes place? Are support personnel available when customers are likely to perform tasks, such as late at night or on weekends?

At one manufacturing plant, technicians often found themselves making repairs at in-plant locations more than a mile from their office space, making paper-based manuals inaccessible. In another case, technicians rolled computer and test equipment on carts into the worksite. They had no place to store or access manuals, which led to the introduction of online information, including graphics to aid in setting up and configuring the test equipment.

Are users in any danger?

If the interface you design is difficult to use, will your users be in danger? Will they endanger others? What happens when users make mistakes? Will mistakes produce catastrophic results or cause loss of data?

Banks have found that ATM machines have become focal points for robberies. To safeguard customers, they have had to place the machines inside code-locked and bullet-proof rooms. (See figure 4-8.)

Figure 4-8 Some environments are potentially dangerous.

Summarizing issues about physical environments

As you investigate your customers' physical environment, pay attention to factors that may affect your product, information, training, or support design. Ask about extreme environmental conditions that you may not have an opportunity to observe directly. Be alert for reports to customer service that indicate special conditions. Discuss issues with field engineering groups or application engineers who visit customer sites regularly. During your site visits, be alert for environmental conditions that will change your design specifications. In one case, technical communicators decided to increase the font size in the maintenance manuals after they learned that the maintenance engineers had to place the manuals on the floor beside the equipment and had difficulty reading the company's standard 10-point Times Roman. Look for opportunities to improve upon a design so that users will be able to use it under different physical conditions.

What should you look for in the social and cultural environment?

Every workplace is a social and cultural environment. In chapter 2, we discussed looking at users' personal characteristics in terms of social or cultural factors that might affect your design. The ways that users behave together and behave in relation to their work are also likely to affect design.

Paying attention to social environments

The social environments of your users may also affect the way you design the product, its interface, and its documentation and training. Workgroups frequently divide responsibilities for a process among themselves, with some individuals specializing in the part of a process where they have more expertise. For example, in many organizations, one or two individuals assume responsibility for fixing office machines when they break down. Those who have not acquired maintenance and repair expertise simply alert the specialists, who then take care of the problems. This division of labor may affect the design of "maintenance" interfaces and maintenance documentation. You may encounter less technically skilled people doing basic data manipulation, while more complex tasks are performed only by people with more experience and expertise. You may also encounter situations in which individuals work in isolated places, such as telecommuters working at home. They find themselves having to take responsibility for aspects of a task that they might never have had to perform as part of a workgroup. You may find that users typically have to share equipment so that if one user takes a long time, others have to wait, or if one user has a problem, many users spend time trying to solve it. These interactions cost companies money for "down time." (See figure 4-9.)

Be careful in assuming that the characteristics of one work environment are typical. You may find that user sites vary, particularly in terms of how work is subdivided.

Does your users' work situation include integrating a series of tasks? If so, will the design of your system and its interface permit easy task integration? In one instance, users had to work with five or six completely different interfaces from different computer applications to accomplish a single integrated task. The cognitive burden increased learning time and increased the number of errors.

Figure 4-9 Everyone may have to share the same equipment.

Sometimes the lack of an integrated workflow with incompatible interfaces requires that the same tasks be performed many times. In an episode of the television series *This Old House,* employees of a stair maker had to continually reenter the same data as the work moved from one incompatible computer system to another.

Paying attention to cultural environments

Not only do the social situations involving groups of workers or workers and their customers affect product design, differences among cultures are likely to also. For example, you probably know that you must anticipate space needs of other languages in your designs. Words that easily fit on a computer screen in English are unlikely to fit once they are translated into German or Swedish. You also know that icons that are meaningful and acceptable in the United States may be incomprehensible or insulting elsewhere. But there is more to culture than translation and icons. Other cultural issues may be more difficult to detect even with direct observation in the workplace.

For example, work done in the U.S. by technicians may be performed in other countries by degreed professional engineers or scientists. These users may need a very different level of technical information in support of product use than the average technician needs. In many countries, we find far less familiarity with computers than we see in the United States. For example, researchers report that users in the United Kingdom are far less comfortable using online help systems than are U.S. computer users (Ellison 1997). JoAnn found that at one customer location in the early 1990s, users were typing text on electric typewriters rather than using computers because of a social and national requirement for full employment.

Regional differences within the same society may also require modifications in design assumptions. In a U.S. government agency, workforce availability in various parts of the country requires accommodations for language differences, education level, and work style among members of teams, some of whom divide work among the group differently from other teams. In one case, developers found that wage differences for certain jobs in some parts of the country affected the skill levels of the workers. In lower wage areas, the clerical workers were much less computer-literate than in the higher wage areas.

Corporate cultures may affect how products and information are used. In an insurance company, male managers frequently withheld documentation from employees as a way of maintaining control over the largely female workforce. Other organizations bar some workers from Internet access because of fears of abuse through opportunities to access games or pornography or simply to use work time for personal activities. The company culture, in such cases, frowns on frivolous activities.

Union requirements at some companies require that interfaces, documentation, and training be approved by union representatives before they can be rolled out. There is concern that tasks may be designed that are too difficult for the average worker to perform, a situation that might lead to loss of jobs.

A Canadian insurance company learned that workers at company offices in British Columbia had established a different workflow and interacted with the home office in Ontario differently than workers at company offices closer to headquarters. The time zone differences made interactions with headquarters difficult.

Ginny once conducted an entire project by fax (before the days of e-mail) because the time difference did not allow telephoning. Some companies have a culture of faxing because of time difference.

As you do site visits, be aware that companies and organizations have cultures. If your product is just for your company, it should probably reflect your company's cultural norms. If your product is going to be used in many different companies, be wary of building in your own company's culture and vocabulary.

Disciplines, too, have their own cultures and vocabularies. If you are writing for experienced telephone workers, using telephony vocabulary may be necessary. However, be careful to find out if the users really know those words since the vocabulary may be limited to specialists. The people doing the work your product supports may not be those specialists.

As you go out and do site visits, you may see ways of working and hear vocabulary that surprise you. Be careful that your own cultural biases are not influencing your perceptions.

What are the trade-offs?

In your study of the environments in which your users do their work, you will encounter many situations that may affect your product, interface, documentation, and training. The final decisions about which situations to take into account and which to ignore will have to be made in consultation with others in your organization. Each trade-off must be evaluated in terms of its impact on customers' ability to use products effectively. You may choose to ignore some users' environments that require expensive alternative designs likely to affect only a small number of potential customers. In other cases, you may have to incorporate design alternatives because of legal requirements to accommodate potential environmental hazards or because the customers affected are likely to represent an important market segment for your product.

Just as with your analysis of user characteristics and the work users will perform with your product, environmental analysis serves as data to inform your decision making. Without data, you are likely to make mistakes that will profoundly affect the success of your product and the ability of customers to learn and use your product effectively.

References cited in the chapter

Dray, Susan and Mrazek, Deborah, A day in the life of a family: An international ethnographic study, in *Field Methods Casebook for Software Design*, edited by Dennis Wixon and Judith Ramey, NY: John Wiley & Sons, 1996a, 145–156.

Dray, Susan and Mrazek, Deborah, A day in the life: Studying contest across cultures, in *International User Interfaces*, edited by Elisa M. del Galdo and Jakob Nielsen, NY: John Wiley & Sons, 1996b, 242–256.

Ellison, Matthew, Help in the UK, *Proceedings of the WinHelp 97 Conference*, Seattle, WA, 1997.

Forslund, Charlene J., Analyzing pictorial messages across cultures, in *International Dimensions of Technical Communication*, edited by Deborah C. Andrews, Arlington, VA: Society for Technical Communication, 1996, 45–58.

Mitropoulos-Rundus, David and Muszak, Jerry, Criteria for determining if consumer "in-home" usability testing is feasible for your product, *Common Ground*, 7 (1), January 1997a: 10–12.

Mitropoulos-Rundus, David and Muszak, Jerry, How to design and conduct a consumer in-home usability test, *Common Ground*, 7 (2), April 1997b: 1, 8–14, 19.

Other books and articles for further reading

Andrews, Deborah C., *International Dimensions of Technical Communication*, Arlington, VA: Society for Technical Communication, 1996.

Del Galdo, Elisa M. and Nielsen, Jakob, Eds., *International User Interfaces*, NY: John Wiley & Sons, 1996.

Hoft, Nancy, *International Technical Information*, NY: John Wiley & Sons, 1995.

Jones, Scott, Kennelly, Cynthia, Mueller, Claudia, Sweezy, Marcia, Thomas, Bill, Velez, Lydia, *Developing International User Information*, Bedford, MA: Digital Equipment Corporation, 1992.

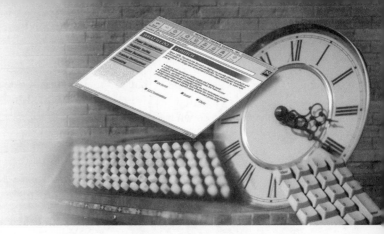

5

Making the business case for site visits

You've decided that you need to meet your users, watch them at work, and hold conversations with them to understand how they think about the tasks they do. Now you must convince others in your organization who may present objections based upon their previous experience with customers and their strongly held ideas about how users should be defined. Many marketing professionals, for example, have traditionally used focus groups, surveys, or questionnaires to understand customers. They may feel that they already have sufficient information about potential users that makes further study unnecessary. Product developers may have interacted with customers at trade shows where they often get ideas about functional requirements for new or updated products. They may believe that such informal meetings are sufficient. Supervisors may want to inform you about their workers and may believe their analysis of user characteristics is sufficient. How do you counter these arguments and show that carefully planned interactions with users in their real work environments will lead to important new information?

Challenging or verifying your assumptions

First, recognize that a primary reason for traveling to user sites is to challenge or verify your assumptions. In study after study, designers have learned just how easy it is to create unusable designs based upon assumptions that prove to be either completely untrue or significantly misleading to the design process.

People in your organization have made many assumptions about users that affect their design decisions, whether they recognize them or not. Even you have made assumptions that you may not recognize you are making. Many designers, meeting users for the first time, are shocked to find that the users are very different from what they thought.

In the following cases, product developers, information developers, and instructional designers learned that their initial assumptions were mistaken. Review the stories presented here and think about the tremendous value of what these people learned when they met with actual users.

Some of the cases come from published articles; in those cases, we have provided the reference. Others come from our experience or experiences others have told us about. The sources and their companies do not want to be mentioned. In some cases, we have changed some of the particulars to disguise the source.

Automated directory assistance

You might think that what directory assistance operators do could easily be automated. When Michael Muller and his colleagues (1995) at US West analyzed actual interactions between the operators and customers, however, they realized that what the operators did was complex. Directory assistance operators are, in fact, knowledge workers, doing as much cognitive work that would be difficult to automate as physical work. They use their understanding of the structure of directories, the organization of state, city, and regional governments, and frequent and typical requests in order to answer the wide range of questions customers ask. Studies by Muller and his colleagues, combining qualitative and quantitative data challenged assumptions that many developers might have held.

Right-handed machine for a left-handed environment

The engineers had ergonomically designed the controls of a new diagnostic machine for optimal right-hand use. They discovered a few weeks before the initial release of the new product that technicians always used the machine controls with their left hands while they held the probe in their right hands. The completed control panels had to be ripped out, redesigned, and reconstructed before the equipment could be shipped to the customers.

Noisy, cramped conditions

The information developers who visited the workplaces of their technician customers found them doing repairs in extremely noisy, cramped conditions. The technicians had absolutely no opportunity to refer to a complicated manual. The manual would not even fit into the limited space between the open door and the back of the machine. The information was redesigned to include easy-to-access quick reference cards.

Manuals on the factory floor

The information developers for an automotive manufacturer believed that their manuals were going to be used at the work site. When they visited the factory floor, they discovered that the manuals were back in the technicians' offices rather than where they were needed. They redesigned the information to be usable from the computers the technicians could access at each work site.

Linking software

The developers of software that allowed users to link files between their desktop and laptop computers were surprised to discover that the blank area at the upper right-hand corner of the screen did not convey the concept of a "shared space." Users, following the step-by-step instructions in the manual, did manage to drag and drop files into the "shared space" but were unable to explain why they had done so or what the action would accomplish. The conceptual model on the screen failed to correspond to the users' mental model of the task, requiring a complete rethinking of the interface.

Medical equipment

A company was designing a completely new type of medical diagnostic equipment for use in Southeast Asian hospitals. The lead designer was a 6-foot 2-inch American male, who designed the machine so that it had to be adjusted by reaching overhead and moving the machine along a track in the ceiling. Only after the machine was installed did they discover that the nurses who typically performed the tests were rarely more than 5 feet tall. They had to use stools or chairs (with the danger of falling and injuring themselves) to move the machines high over their heads.

Customer service system

Designers of a customer service system thought the people answering customer calls performed the same task over and over again. When they actually listened in on the customer calls, they learned that every customer service call required a different approach to the task and that some of the calls required actions that were performed very infrequently.

Automated telephone answering system

The developers of an automated answering system assumed that the users would be able to negotiate the choices provided by the automated attendant so that, by the time they reached human clerks, the clerks would have the needed information about the users displayed on their computer screens. As it turned out, the users' questions and concerns were so poorly articulated that they selected choices almost at random. Consequently, the clerks often had the wrong information displayed. The designers had to rethink the way they presented information to the clerks to account for the users' confusion.

Medical records system

Programmers designing a medical records system completely changed their initial conceptualization of the software interface after they visited medical records departments, watched people performing tasks, and interviewed the medical records staff about the nature of the work. They discovered that the workflow among departments and individuals proceeded in a different manner than they had imagined.

Classified documents control system

When the developers of a classified documents control system for a nuclear weapons plant observed users performing the task manually, they discovered that their assumption that all the control tasks were different was completely wrong. The workers they interviewed all insisted that the tasks they performed on their document types were unique; in reality the tasks were all done in the same way with very minor differences. It was clear in this instance that observing the users at work provided far different information than had been collected at meetings with the workers in conference rooms.

Unless you challenge your assumptions by observing and talking with users and others in the real work environment, you are likely to design according to your own or your team's unexamined assumptions. The danger is that you won't realize how profoundly your assumptions have controlled your design until your organization or your customers begin having problems with sales and support. It is better to get the design right in the first place than to have to recover from a disaster.

Designing from reality, not assumptions

The case studies point out that many designers, upon first meeting users, are shocked to find that the users are very different from what they have assumed. As Rubenstein and Hersch (1984, p. 29) say in their description of the development of the ATM machine: "In the absence of detailed information, we all work from assumptions about who the user is, what he or she does, and what type of system would meet his or her needs. Following these assumptions, we tend to design for ourselves, not for other people."

As you begin the design process and throughout the development life cycle, you must make many assumptions about what your users will or will not be able to do, what they will or will not be able to understand. The assumptions most often come from your own interactions with products and from the interactions of people you work with, especially your coworkers. You unwittingly assume basic skills, elementary understanding, specific mental models, and even advanced experience and knowledge.

When you make the wrong assumptions in your day-to-day interactions with family and colleagues, you receive instant feedback that tells you if you have assumed incorrectly. For example, when you assume that the person you are talking with understands the words you are using, you learn quickly if you are wrong. A quizzical look or a direct request for definitions and clarification helps you correct your assumptions. When you are designing products for users and you do not interact directly with them, you make many of the same assumptions. The problem comes when you fail to get feedback to learn if your assumptions are correct.

Through site visits, interviews, telephone calls, usability assessments, and other techniques of increasing your contact with users, you will find ways to assess the validity of your design assumptions.

Countering objections to doing user and task analysis

You may meet resistance to the idea that you should go out to users and watch and listen to and converse with them as they work. If no one in your development organization, including documentation and instructional design, has ever visited users in their work environments before, you are likely to encounter objections when you first raise the possibility. Here are some of the arguments we've heard and our answers to them.

We're changing the process; why go out to see the current process?

You may hear the argument that no one is performing tasks today in the way they will be performed in the future—with your new product. Even so, you can still study the environment in which potential users work, how work flows in their workplaces or their homes, and what types of tasks they perform there today. If the tasks you are designing will require too much of a stretch from the current environment, how do you expect your users to learn to perform them? Be aware that you may be designing a system that few will be able to learn to use or that will be incompatible with their environments.

But you may hear: "We're going to totally change the work environment." If the product is for use inside the company, you can respond with questions about the workforce that show how important it is that you know the users. If the company does not intend to hire new people, but will expect the current workers to do different types of work than they do now, ask: How will we handle the human resource problem, the acceptance or lack of acceptance of change? How will we deal with the problem of skills transfer? We have to know what users are like and what they do now to facilitate that transfer.

If the company intends to hire new people to perform the new tasks, will those people not come with their own prior experiences and knowledge? Will these experiences affect how they will learn and what they will find easy or difficult to understand? We have to know what these new users will be like.

Even if your organization or your customers plan major process changes, you need to observe the users at work today. Only by observing the current process can you learn what is necessary to the way they do business and what is redundant and can be streamlined. Processes often have ramifications for other groups or even for external customers that have to be considered when process changes are planned. Without site visits and user and task analysis, especially for users outside your organization, these ramifications may not become known until after the product is released. Unhappy customers and costly fixes may be the result of not going out to see and understand the current process.

Company A decided to change the process for doing a major part of its business and thought they could sell it to their customers because it would eliminate a lot of the paperwork between the customers and Company A. They thought they knew the old process really well and that they didn't need to go out to watch users before they changed the process. Shortly after they put out the new version of the product and extolled the new process with its paperless system, they got angry calls from users who wanted to know how they could print out one of the old reports. Company A said: "But you don't need to send us that report anymore." The users said: "But we still need it for other reasons. We have to send it to this department and that department within our own company. They're not on your system and they can't work with your new process." Company A had to hastily figure out how to let customers generate the same old paper report.

Even if the users are inside the organization, task analysis is needed to ensure a successful transition to new processes. Unless the organization plans to fire all the current users and hire an entirely new workforce, the users doing the new process will be the same as those who did the old process—or at least some of the same people if the new process requires fewer people. As we discussed in chapter 2, users are not blank slates. They bring all the baggage of their previous experiences with them. You cannot put new processes into place and expect them to be followed immediately. Transitions for users have to be carefully planned, and knowing a lot about the users and how they work today will help you create smooth transitions.

Developers of an automated system that nurses and other care workers would use to record patient vital signs and when they administered medications failed to consider the power of prior instruction and experience. The nurses and others had been taught always to write down exactly when and how they had given medications or administered other types of care. Writing something down was the guarantee that the actions had actually taken place. The caregivers viewed the written document, the physical piece of paper, as a confirmation of their correct action. Without it, they might be blamed for making a mistake.

The new system did not allow them to "write down" what they had done. Rather, they recorded the action by clicking buttons on a screen. The new process made them so uncomfortable that they continued to create their paper records and often "forgot" to use the new computer system. Bypassing the new system meant the designers were unable to rely on a complete patient database to use in other parts of the system design. Screen redesigns, additional training, and lengthy discussions about liability and hospital policy were required before the transition to the new system could proceed.

This is totally new; there's nothing to go out and see

You may encounter the objection from marketing, designers, and developers that because you are designing a completely new product for a new market, you have no users to study. You don't know who the users will be. Therefore, you have nothing to go and watch because nothing happening today is comparable to what users will be doing tomorrow.

In the first place, in our experience, it is exceedingly rare to be designing a product so new that no manual analog or other automated product exists that can be studied. At the very least, consider if someone in the organization, such as marketing, has been studying the potential market for the product. In that study, have they begun to define potential users? If not, how will the product be sold, and to whom? In most cases, you will find people whose lifestyle and workstyle make them good potential buyers and users.

If you were inventing the first fax machine, would you watch how people sent messages by hand? Do they think about addressing the envelope before they write the message or afterward? What is the sequence of the tasks in the existing environment? Should you take that sequence into account when you design a new way to perform the task?

If something is entirely new to the user population and you cannot think of an analogous system to study, consider rapidly developing a prototype of the conceptual model you have for the system and taking it to the users. You may discover that the users build their own analogies to things they already do. Listen to their conversations about the prototype design; focus on how they compare the new system with something they already know. You will be experiencing the process your users will take to make sense of what they see and experience. The analogies your users find will provide you with something to study that already exists in your users' environment.

It certainly may be true that you will have limits to what you can learn the first time around in your design process. But you will have many opportunities during the design process to check your assumptions. You will have opportunities to review how well your assumptions fit reality during prototype usability evaluations, as well as during the traditional alpha and beta site testing. It may be that the second version of your design will be much more usable than the first version. However, the relative truth of that conclusion does not mean that you should neglect to learn about your potential users now.

Users all do it differently; how will you know whom to watch?

On the one hand, you are likely to see individual differences in how people do a task, even if the organization has standards on how to do tasks and even if users have received training in those tasks. People do differ, and they develop their own workarounds and shortcuts. Organizational cultures also differ. Even within the same organization, tasks may be done differently at headquarters and in branches, in different geographic regions within the same country, and certainly in different countries. For retail products sold to consumers, you may have an even wider ranger of users than inside a company. That's why one observation is not enough for a task analysis.

In chapter 7 on planning site visits, we discuss how many users to observe and how to select appropriate users based on preliminary analyses of the different types of users. In chapter 11 on analyzing data from site visits, we discuss how to reconcile individual differences that you see and how you might want to consider those differences in design.

You are likely to find, however, much less variation than you assumed. Users may think that they each have individual ways of doing tasks, but when you actually analyze what they are doing, you may find that the procedures are, in fact, very similar. The differences may be minor and easily accommodated in a single design.

The developers of a small retail business inventory system spent time studying how their potential users organized information about their inventory. They found that some of them kept file cards with each item in the inventory identified by source, quantity, color, and so on. Others created word-processing tables in which they typed lists of their inventory items. Others created spreadsheet files with each item in a different spreadsheet cell. Using spreadsheets permitted them to sort items in different ways and to add various quantities of items they had in stock. They could also use the spreadsheet to record how many items were sold and how many remained on the shelves or in the storeroom. The differences, although significant to the users, tended to appear more similar than different with respect to the new system being defined.

By studying all of these diverse behaviors, the designers were able to construct a new computer-based inventory system that users were immediately able to understand. The objects in the system had the same features as the objects in their real world and the actions they could perform on the objects, such as sorting them into different groups, had obvious analogs to the functions they already knew how to perform.

We're just changing one part; you don't need to look beyond that

The people who come to talk to you about doing a task analysis may have a very narrow view. Often a group is given responsibility for designing or fixing up only one part of a system or even just one new function. The issue to consider is whether even that part will be successful if you constrain the task analysis and subsequent design to just that part.

For example, if a team approaches you to do a task analysis because they are building data entry screens for a database, you should push them to also think about the users of the database. If getting information out is too difficult, who will use the database? If no one uses the database, the effort that went into designing good data entry screens will have been wasted.

To take the opposite example, if the assignment is only to consider users who generate reports, you should push to also consider the users who will put the information into the system and their goals and tasks. If putting information into the system is too difficult, there won't be any good information to put into the reports. No matter how easy it is to generate the reports, if there isn't good information, the effort that went into designing the report generator will have been wasted.

Although you may not always get the resources to do the broader workflow analysis that you realize is necessary, pushing for it makes the point that, in the real world, specific users and tasks don't occur in isolation. Tasks are the parts of a process. Success for a product usually occurs only when all the users in the process can easily and quickly accomplish their goals.

What can we learn from only a few users?

Most user studies that we recommend here include small numbers of users who are representative of the user community as a whole and can be expected to provide a great deal of information about the intended design. Such small-scale studies are typical of usability testing as well. From studies of sample size in usability testing, we have learned that we can understand a very high percentage of user needs from a relatively small sample—six or eight individuals for each user group (novices, experts, technicians, clerks, and so on) (Nielsen 1993; Virzi 1992).

Marketing research typically uses much larger sample sizes, in the range of 120 to 150 customers for a representative study. The intent is to use the larger sample to achieve statistically significant results. Such results are needed to make decisions about the direction a marketing campaign must take in light of user preferences. Large-scale, statistically significant studies are usually not necessary when the problem is to understand user behavior in reference to the overall structure and detailed design of a user interface. The patterns that will be important for the interface design emerge very quickly with small numbers of users. The remaining users simply repeat the patterns already observed with a few minor variations. What you need for interface design is the richness of the data you get from extended time observing and talking with a small sample of users in the context of their work.

A small-scale study can be accomplished quickly and within most development budgets. If the small study reveals differences that require critical decisions about the product's direction, you can always do larger studies to investigate and validate the differences.

Why not just use the information that we already have?

How will you handle the objections of managers and colleagues who tell you that they already have ways of studying users that are less expensive than field studies? They may have completed a series of focus groups, and they will be more than willing to give you the answers to any questions you may have about the users. Business analysts, marketing researchers, systems analysts, and others in your organization may all know a lot about the users. You will certainly profit from their contributions. On the other hand, they may be focusing on different issues and may not be able to give you the kind of information you need to design a product, its documentation, or its training materials. They may not have gotten down to the level of detail that you need for interface design and decisions on documentation or training.

The product lead on a development team was a user who had been brought in from the field. He was convinced he could represent all users and that there was no need to do site visits. Unfortunately, he came from a country where the typical process had many elements that were strongly influenced by the local culture. Later site visits showed that the ways in which users accomplished major tasks differed considerably in other countries. Until the site vists were made, there had been no plans to accommodate individual, regional, or other culturally influenced differences.

Are other researchers in your organization asking your questions about the users or are they addressing someone else's questions? User studies conducted by market researchers often focus on marketing's need for an analysis of potential buyers rather than users. Marketing may be more interested in the preferences and habits of the gatekeepers—managers and decision makers—than of the actual end users. Even when the same individuals buy and use the product, if you are looking at them as buyers, you are focusing on different issues and questions than if you are looking at them as users.

Understanding users' buying patterns may be just as critical to the success of a product as use patterns, but if the product is not usable and does not meet users' expectations of how it should function, no amount of marketing will result in long-term product success. (See figure 5-1.)

Figure 5-1 Not every happy buyer becomes a happy user.

You should make every effort to find out who is gathering information and discuss with them the techniques they are using and what they have learned. Recognize, however, that the typical market research techniques will not lead to the same types of information as site visits.

Other objections

Some of the objections you may hear are covered later in the book. In chapter 7, you learn how to recruit users, which will help you counter objections such as, we don't want to impose upon the users—they're too busy, marketing owns the customers, the salespeople will object.

In chapter 10, you learn how to talk with users and establish rapport, which will help you counter objections such as, you'll embarrass the company, you'll let company secrets out of the bag, you'll make promises we can't keep.

A way to counter these and all the other objections we have mentioned is to use the example studies at the beginning of this chapter as cases in support of the need to visit user sites. Another way to counter the objections is to create a business proposal that includes an analysis of the return on investment promised by gaining a better, more detailed understanding of user needs.

Preparing a business proposal

A major objection you are likely to hear when you propose user site visits is that visiting users and performing task analysis is too expensive and will take too long. To get the time and funding that you need to conduct user site visits, prepare and present a business proposal for your decision makers. Your business proposal might be as simple as a memo or as lengthy as a detailed plan. In either case, you should focus your proposal on explaining how the benefits of understanding your users will outweigh the costs, and you should respond to any objections you are hearing.

Analyzing the return on investment

User site visits, like almost any other new attempt to meet and study users, will likely represent a new immediate cost to you and your development organization in terms of resources and time. However, you need to take a longer view of costs and benefits, looking beyond the immediate expenditures. You may need to argue on the basis of return on investment (ROI). The expense today will result in greater savings or greater revenue later.

Without a detailed understanding of user characteristics, tasks, and environments, your organization is likely to experience much greater costs in the future. Increases in customer-support costs, more costly documentation and training, and last-minute changes to poorly designed interfaces may all result if you do not have the information you need to design effectively from the beginning. The organization that had to tear apart manufactured machines to correct a critical, show-stopping usability problem decided to test usability early in the design process the next time around. The director of materials management at the utilities warehouse came to regret that they had not studied their users' physical characteristics before they purchased computers with keyboards too small to be used by people with large hands. The president and investors of a start-up company were not happy when they had to scrap a new product and write off one-and-a-half years of development after they learned that users could not make sense of the graphical user interface that had been designed.

An investment in user and task analysis early in the design and development process will reap considerable benefits in cost savings later in the process. One interface designer told us that he was saving months of development time that otherwise would have been spent going in the wrong direction because he understood early in the process exactly how his users thought about the tasks he was designing into the new interface.

An effective cost-benefit analysis that supports early user involvement might point to the case of Digital Equipment Corporation (Wixon and Jones 1996), a story we mentioned in chapter 1. A new product with little involvement by human factors professionals experienced disappointingly low initial sales. The second version was developed with extensive involvement by usability professionals using a variety of usability techniques. As a result, sales exceeded predictions by 30 to 60%. Customers, as it turned out, considered usability to be the second most important factor in their purchase decision.

In a second case, a cross-functional team at Digital Equipment Corporation worked closely with potential users to understand users, their tasks, and their environments and to decide if a product developed for one platform could be extended to another platform. Through their field studies, the team revised many of their original assumptions and concluded that the existing metaphor would not work in the second environment.

The team decided not to build what they had originally planned because it was not what users needed or wanted and would not have fit in their environment. A solution that did match their way of working was much less costly and more successful in meeting users' needs (Wixon et al., 1996).

To prepare your ROI calculation, consider the costs that might be avoided if you deliver a more usable interface and the revenues that might be realized if users are more enthusiastic about how the new design will help them work more effectively and easily. For more information on calculating ROI, see Redish and Ramey (1995) and Bias and Mayhew (1994).

An Australian insurance company, working with the Communication Research Institute of Australia (CRIA), set out to improve the quality of the company's forms. Part of the extensive process that CRIA used was an analysis of errors on the old forms and the cost of those errors to the insurance company. They took a sample of the forms, categorized errors, counted the number of errors in each category, and estimated the time needed to fix each category of error (in part by observing and timing staff as they worked on fixing the errors). By knowing the level and salary rate of the type of person who was involved in fixing each category of error, they were able to estimate the cost to the company of getting those errors fixed. (The true cost to the company was probably higher; customers' time and loss of business from customers' unhappiness weren't included in the estimate.)

They changed the forms through a process that involved detailed interactions with users and other relevant groups in the client company, learning about the client's social and political cultures and working within those cultures, and developing iterative designs with iterative diagnostic usability evaluations. Through this process, they were able to develop forms that greatly reduced the error rate. They repeated the error analysis six months after the new forms went into use. Errors in the samples of 200 forms went from 100% of forms having errors to 15%. Total number of errors in the sample of 200 forms went from 1,560 to 44. As a result, the company saved more than $500,000 (Fisher and Sless 1990).

Meeting or exceeding the competition

Look at the competition in your industry as you prepare your business proposal. Are your competitors already conducting usability studies? Have they been conducting user and task visits to users' workplaces? Is user and task analysis a regular part of their design and development process?

One company decided that contextual inquiry and usability studies would give them a competitive edge in an industry that had not yet discovered that it needed to pay attention to users. In fact, their field is so competitive that they hired JoAnn's company to conduct the studies as an outside firm and they disguised all references to their company on the prototype products. Taking a position of industry leadership in conducting user and task analysis, especially when your product's market is moving toward a more conservative buyer, may give you as much as a two-year lead over the competition. It often takes time to convince a reluctant management to invest in user and task analysis. If you can get out in front by doing it first, it may take your competition significant time to catch up.

Finally, if you learn that the competition is already ahead of you, be prepared to argue your case in terms of meeting and possibly exceeding their efforts. If they are conducting usability tests late in the development life cycle, you might introduce early user and task analysis to reduce development costs and avoid the problems and high costs of making late changes to provide or enhance usability. If the competition is doing inquiries at customer sites, find ways to involve users as directly as possible in the development process throughout the life cycle. Your efforts will eventually pay off.

Calculating the time required to conduct a user and task analysis

In calculating the hours and costs of a user and task analysis, you need to account for several key activities, including deciding who to visit, preparing for the visits, conducting the visits, and analyzing and reporting the results to others on the development team. The cost of implementing the design is already included in the development time for the project.

In Table 5-1, we estimate the hours and costs for a typical small-scale project involving visits to six user locations in the United States with two team members on each visit. The estimated hours represent the time of three or four different people, including a human factors expert, a senior member (possibly the project manager) of the product development team, and two or more other people from the human factors group or the development team. The estimated hours usually take place over three to six weeks, depending primarily on the logistics of setting up the user visits, which includes identifying, contacting, and scheduling each user selected for the analysis. The estimated hours do not include the time to travel to the sites, which will vary according to their distance from the team's location and the team's ability to set up several visits on consecutive days.

The total costs are figured on an average of $70 per hour, a typical inhouse fully burdened cost for a development professional. The costs do not include the costs of travel, nor do they include the costs of gifts or payments to user participants. Ordinarily, company employees are not paid but may be offered a gift of nominal cost, such as a T-shirt or a mug. External customers may require a budget for gifts, software or hardware, or even payments for time spent on the site visits.

Table 5-2 shows estimated hours and costs for a larger international study. In this study, six United States and six European site visits are planned with two observers at each site.

Task	Hours per task	Labor cost per task
Brainstorming an initial user/task matrix and outlining the proposed site visits	80	$5,600
Planning the site visits	34	2,380
Recruiting participants	42	2,940
Conducting six days of site visits/two observers	120	8,400
Analysis and report	80	5,600
Total hours and labor costs	356	$24,920

Table 5-1 Estimated hours and costs for a small-scale U.S.-based user and task analysis.

Task	Hours per task	Labor cost per task
Brainstorming an initial user/task matrix and outlining the proposed site visits	80	$5,600
U.S. site visits		
Planning and recruiting	120	8,400
Pilot study	20	1,400
Visits to six U.S. sites/two observers	60	4,200
Initial trip reports	56	3,920
International site visits		
Planning and recruiting	76	5,320
Two weeks (80 hours) in Europe/including travel/six locations/location planning and setups	242	16,940
Trip reports	80	5,600
Final analysis and report	120	8,400
Total hours and labor costs	854	$59,780

Table 5-2 Estimate of hours and costs for a larger international user and task analysis.

The estimates in table 5-2 do not include the cost of travel or the cost of gifts or payments to participants. Neither do they include the cost of interpreters if interviews are to be conducted in languages that team members do not speak fluently. The total costs are based on $70 per hour, as in table 5-1.

Like the U.S. site vists, the duration of the international site visits will depend upon the logistics of planning and preparing for the visits, setting up the visits, and recruiting the participants. Typically, a user and task analysis of this size can be accomplished in about six weeks, especially if several team members are involved.

Helping management understand that plans may change

Important as it is to prepare your business case and estimate costs for user and task analysis, it is also important to remember that plans may change based on what you learn when you first go out. You may need to revise your plan and reestimate costs. Both you and your managers should understand that the point of the study is to challenge or verify assumptions. As you learn more about reality compared to assumptions, you may find you need to meet other users, look at different aspects of the work, see more environments, or make other changes to the plan.

References cited in the chapter

Bias, Randolph G. and Mayhew, Deborah J., Eds., *Cost-Justifying Usability*, San Diego, CA: Academic Press, 1994.

Fisher, Phil and Sless, David, Information design methods and productivity in the insurance industry, *Information Design Journal*, 6(2), 1990: 103–129.

Muller, Michael J., Carr, Rebecca, Ashworth, Catherine, Diekmann, Barbara, Wharton, Cathleen, Eickstaedt, Cherie, and Clonts, Joan, Telephone operators as knowledge workers: Consultants who meet customer needs, *Proceedings of CHI'95*, Denver, CO, ACM, 1995: 130–137.

Nielsen, Jakob, *Usability Engineering*, San Diego, CA: Academic Press, 1993.

Redish, Janice C. and Ramey, Judith A., Special section: Measuring the value added by professional technical communicators, *Technical Communication*, 42(1), February 1995, 23–83.

Rubinstein, Richard and Hersh, Harry, *The Human Factor: Designing Computer Systems for People*, Bedford, MA: Digital Equipment Corporation, 1984.

Virzi, Robert, Refining the test phase of usability evaluation: How many subjects is enough, *Human Factors*, 34(4), August 1992, 457–468.

Wixon, Dennis and Jones, Sandy, Usability for fun and profit: A case study of the design of DEC rally version 2, in *Human-Computer Interface Design: Success Stories, Emerging Methods, and Real-World Context*, edited by Marianne Rudisill, Clayton Lewis, Peter B. Polson, Timothy D. McKay, San Francisco, CA: Morgan Kaufmann Publishers, 1996, 3–35.

PART 2

Getting ready for site visits

In part 2 we focus on the decisions you need to make and the activities you need to perform to set up and prepare for your site visits.

In chapter 6 we present an overview of the many techniques available to answer the questions and get the information you need to design effective interfaces and documentation. The way you gather the information may vary considerably, depending on your information needs and the users' situations. You may use direct observation to learn about the interaction of user characteristics and work environments. You may perform formal or informal task analyses to understand the processes you need to support and how your users think about these processes. You may ask users to show you examples of their work.

You may also find yourself interacting in your information gathering with other people in your organization who are also interested in knowing the users. You may find yourself working with those doing market research or collecting data about customers. You may find yourself interacting with people in human resources who are responsible for evaluating new hires and orienting them to your organization. You may find that your company has already sponsored studies that will assist you in better understanding the people who have to use your products and interfaces. You may be part of development teams involved in systems analysis for the design of products.

Chapters 7 and 8 lead you through the process of creating a site visit plan and an observer's notebook. Included at the end of chapter 8 is a sample site visit plan that you can use as a starting point for your own work. A template of the site visit plan can be found in appendix A. Included in planning your site visits are suggestions for defining your specific goals and objectives, deciding on the number and characteristics of participants to visit, deciding which customer locations to visit, determining a schedule for the site visits, recruiting actual customers to participate, and scheduling the visits.

Planning activities continue into chapter 8 which focuses on selecting and preparing your site visit team, preparing guidelines for the team to use during the study, deciding on activities that you want to observe or that you will role play with the users, collecting the materials you will need, and planning for data collection including videotaping and audiotaping, if appropriate. Chapter 8 closes with a brief discussion of determining how you will analyze and report your findings to the rest of your organization. More detailed information on analyzing results appears in chapters 11 and 12.

By following the guidelines in chapters 7 and 8, you will be fully prepared to venture out on your first visit. Remember, however, that if you are new at this, you may want to enlist the help of a usability or human factors specialist to guide you through the preparation and serve as a coach and mentor during your initial visits. With such coaching, you are more likely to conduct a series of visits that will provide you with the information you had hoped to gain and that will be favorably received by others in your organization.

6

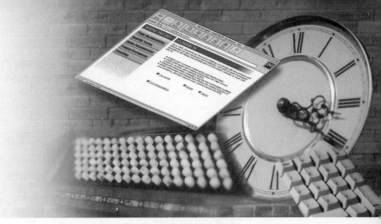

Selecting techniques

Now that we have convinced you (we hope) of the importance of understanding your users, their work, and their environments, let's discuss techniques that you can use to develop that understanding. The techniques you need—and the specific ways of applying those techniques—depend on several factors, including where you are in the product life cycle, the level of detail you need at this moment, how much time and other resources you have, and how much you can get involved with the users and their work. In this chapter we introduce several techniques for gathering predesign data from users—and variations on them. We discuss

- observing, listening to, and talking with users (contextual inquiries)

- interviewing users and others

- working with users away from their work sites

- using more traditional market research techniques, like focus groups

- using more traditional systems development techniques, like requirements-gathering sessions

In the chapters that follow, we expand on the main techniques we discuss here— site visits in which you observe, listen to, and talk with users as they work in their own environment. Chapters 7 and 8 help you plan and set up the site visits. Chapter 9 gives you tips for conducting successful site visits and details on how to collect useful data while observing users. Chapter 10 helps you listen to and talk with users; it's about asking useful questions.

However, we know that working with users at their sites, observing, listening, and talking with users as they work isn't always possible. It may not even be the best technique to get the information that you need for your design project. Therefore, in this chapter, we discuss several other techniques that you may want to use in addition to or instead of the main technique that we focus on.

Observing, listening to, and talking with users

You can learn most by actually being with users: watching them work; observing how the physical, social, and cultural environments affect the work; listening to users explain what they are doing as they worxk, interjecting questions to elicit even more from users about themselves, the work, and the environment (see figure 6-1).

Figure 6-1 The best way to understand users is to go to their workplaces and observe, listen to, and talk with them as they work.

Conducting site visits as "contextual inquiries"

Both of us have been doing site visits for more than 20 years, using many of the features of what has come to be called "contextual inquiry" long before the technique was given that name. Nonetheless, our current view of site visits owes a lot to the work of Michael Good, Karen Holtzblatt, John Whiteside, Dennis Wixon, and others who developed contextual inquiry at Digital Equipment Corporation and who continue to write and teach about it. [For more on contextual inquiry, you might read Beyer and Holtzblatt (1997); Holtzblatt and Beyer (1996); and Whiteside et al. (1987). For specific applications of contextual inquiry, you might read Beabes and Flanders (1995) and Raven and Flanders (1996).]

Contextual inquiry is a philosophy as much as a technique. Here are some of the main points of contextual inquiry, which we urge you to adopt for any type of site visit:

- Plan. Understand the issues and objectives for the visits.

- Select users to represent the diversity in the user group.

- Treat the user as a partner.

- Watch, listen to, and talk with users, usually one at a time, about their work as they work in their own environment. (That's the "contextual" part of "contextual inquiry.")

- Make the conversation concrete. Talk about what the user is doing or just did.

- Take your cues from the user. Share your emerging understanding with the user to make sure you are interpreting what you see and hear correctly.

Different issues and objectives, different situations, may require variations on the general theme of observing, listening to, and talking with users. On the next several pages, we discuss some of the variations. Select the technique or combination of techniques for observing and talking with users that best meets your situation.

Getting users to think aloud while doing the task

The best understanding of how users do their work usually comes from talking with the user about the work while it is being done. Even immediately after doing a task, users may not be able to recall why they did something or what they were thinking while they were doing the task. If you are with the users during the task, you can be part of a dialogue in which the user is telling you what he or she is doing and you are asking questions. As part of that dialogue, you may want to encourage the users to "think aloud"—that is, to tell you at each step what they are doing, why they are doing it, what they think about it, in fact, everything they are thinking (figure 6-2). This is the same technique that we use during usability testing and the purpose is the same—to get at users' inferences, intuitions, and mental models as well as their reasons for the specific steps they take and decisions they make while doing the task.

Talking right after the task (when you can't talk during the task)

Despite the advantages of doing so, you can't always talk with the user during the task. Here are five of many situations in which you would probably choose to be an unobtrusive observer ("like a fly on the wall"), watching and listening, but not talking, while the task is being done:

- The task involves helping another person who either calls on the phone or comes into the user's work space. This might happen with customer service representatives, telephone operators, travel agents, hotel reservation clerks, or network administrators dealing with a crisis.

Figure 6-2 When users think aloud, you hear their insights and inferences.

■ The task involves safety and must be done without interruption. Working with air traffic controllers on the job would require unobtrusive observations and discussions after the fact (figure 6-3).

Figure 6-3 With some jobs like air traffic controller, you can't talk with the user while the user is working.

- The task requires that the users maintain a high degree of concentration while they are working. Users trying to solve complex mathematical problems may find that any interruption disrupts their thought patterns.

- You are timing the task.

- The user is on a deadline. Seeing how the work is done under the pressure of a deadline might be one of your objectives, but talking during the task might keep the user from meeting the deadline.

In these cases, you can take notes (as well as videotape or audiotape) and then talk to the user immediately after the task. Immediate recall is better than later recall, although not as good as concurrent discussion for really capturing what was in the user's mind.

Role playing and staged scenarios during site visits

When you find yourself in a situation where you must be an unobtrusive observer (where there is a customer or another person involved) or you are unlikely to observe a particular task that occurs infrequently, you can create a situation in which you *can* observe and talk during the task. Role playing data is not as credible as data taken under actual conditions, but it may be the only substitute available. You or someone else on the site visit team or a colleague of the user can play the role of the customer in a relevant scenario or you can stage a scenario that is typical of what your users may encounter under particular, but infrequent circumstances.

Usability specialists at American Airlines SABRE Travel Information Network were helping to design new software to make booking cruises easier for travel agents. They went to travel agencies that specialize in cruises. But even in these agencies, travel agents aren't booking cruises all day. On a particular morning, a travel agent might make many travel reservations, but not have a single request for a cruise. So the SABRE team took along scenarios of typical requests for cruises, and if there wasn't a real situation to observe, one of them became the client who wanted to go on a cruise. In addition to making sure they got to see the travel agent do the tasks they were studying, role playing as a technique allowed them to stop the action and talk about the task while the travel agent was working on it.

Role playing and staged scenarios do take some of the reality out of the situation. You need to ensure that you have relevant scenarios, including the types of questions typical customers would ask and the information that typical customers would bring to the tasks. In many cases, such as our story about travel agents or where the application you are observing is about customer service (customers ordering items, querying bills, asking for help on how to do something), you might well be a customer. Coming up with scenarios would not be difficult. If you are at a site with several people who fit your user profiles, you can have one user act as the customer while another user does the work you came to observe. These users have probably had lots of experience with many customers and many scenarios. Just listening to the scenarios they choose to act out can be very insightful. If you don't know enough about typical situations to come up with scenarios for role playing on your own, having one user role play for another in the first few site visits might be a good way to gather several relevant scenarios for other site visits.

JoAnn used role playing to ensure that the observation team would see users of laboratory instruments take several types of measurements. The team was concerned that the infrequent situations they wanted to see were unlikely to occur during a site visit. Consequently they created several situations that they asked the users to work through, similar to the scenarios we might create for usability tests. The staged situations were performed at the work site and followed observations in which the users worked through their own problems with their own equipment. The staged scenarios enabled the team to understand how the users would approach particular types of problems.

Role playing and staged scenarios have the added advantage that you can use the same scenario on several site visits and thus observe, listen to, and talk with different users as they do the same task. You can combine role playing with other types of observations during a site visit.

Cueing recall with videotapes

Sometimes even when you can observe unobtrusively, you can't get the user's time immediately after the task either. Sometimes you can't be present to do the observation. How can you capture what the user does and have a contextually based discussion about the work?

A technique that has been used successfully in several field studies is cued recall with videotapes.

Judy Ramey and client (the firm funding the project) wanted to understand how radiologists work to see if there was an opportunity to design software for this market and how to design it so these doctors would use it. The radiologists did not want to be interrupted while they were interpreting images and dictating their analyses, but they were willing to have a video camera set up to record both pictures and sound. After they had recorded each radiologist for a period of time, Ramey's field study team went through the videotapes, noting places where they wanted to understand better what they were seeing. They met with each radiologist individually in a conference room and together looked at selected parts of the tapes. The tapes served as a cue for the discussion that would have taken place during the observation—if they could have done a real-time contextual inquiry (Ramey et al. 1996)

Barbara Means and colleagues needed to understand how air traffic controllers do their job. In particular, they were interested in understanding how controllers handle cognitive tasks—how the controllers mentally structure the parts of the task, how they set up and choose among alternative decisions during the task. However, Means and her colleagues could not interrupt the controllers' work, so they videotaped the controllers and used the videotape to cue discussions later (Means 1993).

Interviewing users and others

Interviewing is a part of the observation techniques that we've just described. Sometimes, however, observations aren't appropriate or possible and you need to gather information about users, their work, and their environment just by talking with them. You also might want to gather information by interviewing other people whose knowledge, attitudes, and insights may be valuable to you in planning and designing your product: those gatekeepers that we've been mentioning all along (supervisors, managers) and people who are peripherally involved with the process you are looking at. Therefore, in this section, we discuss some interviewing techniques that may be especially appropriate as you gather predesign information.

Doing a process analysis

You can ask users to walk you through the task or the process you are interested in. For example, you might want to know what a typical day is like for the user. You can ask users to imagine walking in the door and then have the users tell you all the tasks they are likely to do. As you gather a list of tasks, you can ask questions, probing for more information about when, how frequently, and how the user does each task.

You might instead be interested in a particular work process that might extend over several days. In that case, you would ask users to tell you how the process starts and then to walk you through it. You can handdraw a process map as shown in figure 6-4. You would ask questions and probe for an understanding of these aspects of each part of the process:

- when the first task in the process happens

- what triggers it

- who does it

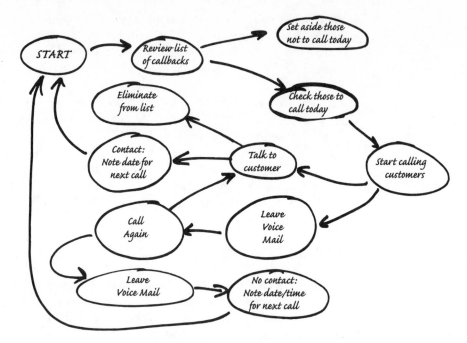

Figure 6-4 A process analysis ends up in a large map of the entire workflow.

- what information the person has when that task starts

- what the major steps are in the task

- what information comes out of it

- who is the next person in the chain of the process

- when does the next task happen

You then repeat all the questions in this list about the next task. And you continue in this way going through each task until you come to the end of the process. At the end, you want to make notes on

- what lets users know the process is completed

- whether the process connects to other processes

- whether the process is ever reopened, and if so, under what circumstances and what happens then

For each part of the process, you might also probe to find out if there are other possible triggers and how often each occurs, if there are alternate pathways and when they would be chosen, and if the output goes to more than one person or group and what those other people use it for. With a work process interview, you can get a good overall picture of a group's process in just a few hours of discussion. If at all possible, you should also try to observe the users doing the process, even if it means returning to the site at different times over several days.

Depending on the situation, you may want to interview one user at a time or a group of users. If you are trying to get a thorough picture of a process, you probably want to have representatives of all the groups involved in the process. Each one can talk in turn about his or her part of the process. The others can also contribute their understanding of the part of the process that others do. Process analysis sessions like these are often very informative not only for the interviewer but for users who learn a lot about how the whole process works and what others in the process do. Misunderstandings—or different understandings—among people who do different parts of the process can lead to discussions that illuminate issues, problems, typical and rare cases of the process, and other information that leads to the deep and rich understanding you need.

One caveat: Be sure that you talk to the people who actually do the process. If you let supervisors or managers tell you what their staff does, you may get an unrealistic picture of the real work.

Conducting ethnographic interviews

Larry Wood (1996) suggests starting with interviews with "key informants" before doing observations. He finds it useful to conduct semistructured interviews to understand the general context of the work, the users' vocabulary for the work, and the users' issues about the work before observing the users doing the work (see figure 6-5). He suggests that you interview the user, go away and absorb the information, use it to plan your next interview or to plan your observations, and then return to the same user. Because the methodology draws on work in anthropology and ethnography as well as cognitive psychology, Wood calls his approach "ethnographic interviews." He characterizes this approach as "top down" because he starts by getting a general framework from the interviews and then uses that knowledge to structure and understand his observations.

Wood contrasts his top-down approach to contextual inquiry, which he characterizes as "bottom up" because it emphasizes first observing and gathering large samples of work and then using those to inductively develop workflows and descriptions of the work.

Wood suggests that the initial interviews make you a more knowledgeable observer and help you ask better questions while observing. If you are working in a domain that is new to you, you should certainly get some familiarity with the users' world before you do observations. Interviews with one or two users would be a good way to begin.

Figure 6-5 Beginning with an interview can help you understand the user's overall work and the user's vocabulary.

Woods says he develops most of his understanding from one user and then confirms or challenges that understanding with other users with whom he spends less time than he does with the first user. In most cases we suggest that you observe and interview more than one user. Working primarily with one user may be appropriate in some situations, especially where there are relatively few users, the users are all in one location, and there is relatively little diversity among the users. The example that Wood gives in his article met those conditions. If you have a large and diverse pool of current and potential users of the product you are developing, however, concentrating on one user as you gather data may not be wise. You run the very serious risk that the user with whom you are developing your understanding is not typical.

Collecting artifacts and holding artifact walk-throughs

You can and should collect artifacts from observations as well as interviews. As you see users working or hear about a process, ask for examples of the various artifacts that are mentioned.

Artifacts are usually paper, although they might be screen shots (see figure 6-6). Typical artifacts are

- "cheat sheets" and other hand-done manuals that people have created for themselves

- forms that trigger data entry or the start of processes

- forms and reports that get printed at various times during a process

- examples of output from tasks, even if the output typically gets passed on electronically

- hand-written notes or logs that users keep as reminders or to track progress in a process

Figure 6-6 Try to collect examples of artifacts: cheat sheets, input forms, output documents, what people write for themselves, what they print.

You should try to get not only blank versions of these artifacts, but filled-out examples as well. If people are leery of sharing private data with you, ask them to fill out a "fake" example that indicates the way the real example would be filled out.

One caveat: Don't go overboard in what you ask for. Don't expect people to copy whole manuals for you. Consider how much work it is for the users to get you copies of the artifacts. Consider how much you can carry or want to ship back. Think about what you are going to do with the artifacts. Watch people's body language and facial expressions to know when you are asking for more than is reasonable or for something they really don't want to share.

Artifacts can be extremely useful in understanding how processes get done now as well as what needs to be continued and what can be streamlined in developing new processes, new software, new documentation. The "cheat sheets" and private manuals that users create for themselves tell you both about tasks they need to know how to do and about what is difficult for them to remember. You can use these items to focus on simplifying those tasks, on finding innovative ways to help users through those tasks, or on how to explain tasks in the manuals and online help for the new product.

Forms and reports that feed into and come out of the process probably have connections to other groups and other processes. If you plan to eliminate or change these documents, you need to understand how the change will affect those other people and those other processes. This is actually a very important point: Products have failed because designers did not take into account users' needs that went beyond the immediate part of the product they were designing. Understanding how the artifacts are used in the larger organization or even among organizations may be critical to designing a successful product.

You can also use artifacts to stimulate a useful discussion of the process. You can ask users to bring copies of their documents to a process or artifact analysis session. You can use the artifacts collected in one set of observations or interviews to stimulate a discussion of the process with another set of users. For example, you can use the artifacts from the process in one regional office to find out if the process and its accompanying artifacts differ from region to region.

Collecting stories, the critical-incident technique

Another way to collect task-based data from interviews is to gather stories of real situations. John Flanagan, founder of the American Institutes for Research, developed a data gathering technique that allows an interviewer to get many stories of real situations and real behaviors from users in a very short time (Flanagan 1954). It is called the "critical-incident technique" because you first ask each interviewee to recall a specific critical incident. Then you probe for more information about that incident with questions that you have planned in advance to learn more about each incident. When you have gotten all the information you need about that incident, ask the interviewee to recall another specific incident and go through your probing questions about that second incident. With this technique, you can often gather detailed information about several incidents in an interview that lasts less than an hour.

This is a story from the early days of the Document Design Center (DDC), which Ginny started in 1979. One of DDC's first goals was to understand the types of documents that caused problems for most people, why those documents were problems, and whether the documents and problems differed for different groups of people. Ginny and her colleagues did a critical-incident study through interviews with people in "helping agencies" such as Legal Services for the Elderly. They included agencies that helped different groups of users from the elderly to low-income people to immigrants to anyone who sought advice. In each interview, they asked the interviewee to "think of the last time someone came to you with a problem and the situation involved a document." When the interviewee had an incident in mind, they probed for more details about the user's characteristics (not names, but relevant demographics), about the document, about the specific problems the person had with the document, and about the outcome. They gathered more than 100 incidents in a very short time. Then they took apart each incident, writing relevant sentences on separate index cards. Sorting the cards into piles of related sentences allowed them to identify several different categories of problems. Just a few examples of the categories were: specific words that users didn't understand, instances in which a document required information users didn't have, situations in which users were overwhelmed by the sheer size and poor layout of the document, the very fact that forms are the type of document that users must deal with, and that forms have seldom been designed by people who understand either human factors or document design.

Asking about specific incidents allows you to concentrate on behaviors and tasks even when you are only talking about and not observing the work. With good probing questions, you can get down to quite specific levels, such as words to use or not use in your design.

The stories that you gather this way are just like the stories you get while observing users doing the actual work. They are stories of real situations in which real users are doing or trying to do real work in real environments. They can be the bases of scenarios that you can use for scenario-based design. (See chapter 11 for more on developing scenarios from the data that you gather. See chapter 12 for more on using scenarios in design.) However, they are stories that you are being told. It would be best to also see for yourself the users trying to do the work, not only hearing about it.

Asking your users to tell stories about actual events is, nonetheless, better than asking them to generalize about their experience or to give you opinions about what they think they need in a new product. Stories keep your users situated in their real experience rather than speculating about what might occur.

Bill Hackos was doing a series of observations and interviews with users of a call-logging system. One of the users complained vociferously about the number of keystrokes required to perform a task. He wanted the new software to eliminate keystrokes. The designers might have considered his comment significant information about the design until they observed him logging a call. When he typed his paragraph of free-form text into the system, he made nearly 40 typing mistakes that necessitated lots of backspacing and retyping to correct. The total number of keystrokes was huge but seemed not to perturb the user. It was clear that keystrokes were only important when he was doing a part of the task that appeared to deserve fewer keystrokes than it required. The observation, and its distinct difference from the generalization, led the design team to reevaluate the level of importance of each task that the system supported.

Working with users away from their work sites

Although you lose the insights of seeing the user in his or her own environment, there may be good reasons for wanting the observations to take place away from the user's site. Resource issues may make it easier for the users to come to you than for you to travel to them. For example, you may be able to get users to work with you when they come to a user group meeting or a vendor's conference. Security reasons or other rules may make it impossible for you to be on site in users' workplaces. You may want others to observe in real time rather than from videotape excerpts later. You may have equipment already set up in a laboratory or conference room and not have portable equipment to take to the users' sites.

Bringing the users' work to your site with "usability roundtables"

You can use a usability laboratory, conference room, or other space to bring the users' work into close view for observation and analysis. Rather than settle for a focus group or other group interview and rather than set scenarios for users as you would in a usability test, in many cases, you can do the same things you would do in a real site visit. You can ask users to bring examples of their own work with them so that the tasks they do are real tasks for them (see figure 6-7). You can have them do real work of their choosing and observe, listen to, and talk with them just as you would in their own environment.

Figure 6-7 You can have users bring examples of their work to a discussion of process.

For example, Butler and Tahir (1996) discuss a technique they call "usability roundtables." Instead of going out to users' work sites, they invite users to come to them (individually or with a coworker) and bring examples of their work that "show[s] their use of the feature or work pattern" that the development team is interested in. They use the work samples as the context.

Working with customer partners

Customer partnering combines several techniques, including user site visits, task-oriented focus groups (see more on traditional focus groups later in this chapter), and participatory design, to involve a small group of users in data gathering, providing feedback for design ideas, and responding to design prototypes. JoAnn originally introduced customer partnering as a method to allow developers to interact with users for longer periods of time, in contrast with the typically limited interactions of site visits. Customer partners, chosen as typical representatives of the user community (rather than as experts), participate in a series of group meetings in which they are asked to role play tasks, examine and comment upon artifacts, analyze tasks and workflow, evaluate competing design ideas, and view, interact with, and comment on early design prototypes. In addition, members of the design team visit the partners' workplaces, using the techniques of observation and interview described earlier in this chapter.

Typically the customer partners participate in five or six working sessions with the design team, with intervals of two to three weeks between sessions. The time between sessions allows the design team to work out new ideas to present to the partners and allows the partners to keep diaries of use and do small-scale data gathering in their own workgroups. The partners are given specific "homework" assignments, including gathering demographic data on other users, observing users performing a particular task, gathering artifacts, looking at competing product designs, and keeping logs of task performance and workgroup interactions. The "homework" is highly structured (questionnaires, forms to complete, lists of activities) to reduce the time burden on the partners and to ensure that the data collected is reasonably uniform. JoAnn has found that the partners are amazingly cooperative and conscientious about completing the homework assignments.

In developing a customer partnering, you need to invite participants who meet the individual characteristics that you discussed in the brainstorming sessions outlined in chapter 2. The participants should be actual users, not official user representatives or others who supervise or manage users. You most likely will choose a particular segment of your user population and invite a group to participate that is reasonably homogeneous, rather than drawing from different user communities and thus having a single representative of each community. We have found the partnering group to work better when the partners have much in common (similar to the homogeneous groups that might take part in a focus group or a usability test). Be certain that you make it clear to partners that participation in the partnering group requires a time commitment. They must be willing to attend all sessions and complete the homework assignments for the duration of the partnering. In most cases, we recommend that a formal contract be signed with responsibilities and compensation (if required) clearly outlined. (For more on customer partnering, see Hackos et al. 1997).

Doing usability evaluations of an existing product or process

You can also do usability evaluations (usability testing in a laboratory or conference room) as a predesign technique. You may want to gather baseline information on users' performance with the existing version of a product or with similar products. For example, you may want to know how much time users take to do a particular task today in the best of circumstances, that is, without the interruptions that may occur in their real environments. You may want to count the steps and errors they make. You may want to see how several users do the same task. That will help you set usability goals for the tasks in your new design. (See chapter 12 for more on setting measurable usability goals as an important step in design.) You may simply want to identify problems with the current product and opportunities for new features and functions.

For this kind of detailed quantitative or qualitative analysis, you may find it easier to do usability evaluations away from the users' work sites. In usability evaluations, you usually give all the users the same tasks to do. When you use usability evaluations along with site visits, the tasks and scenarios you choose for the evaluations often come out of the site visits.

JoAnn's team did a series of international site visits for Federal Express to gather information on how users at local sites interacted with policies and procedures manuals developed at corporate headquarters. Through the site visits, they learned that users found the manuals difficult and time consuming to use. They frequently could not find the information they sought, requiring lengthy long-distance phone calls to find the answers. Or they simply made their own decisions on how to perform tasks when they could not find the information.

The team decided, however, that the observation evidence did not provide enough detail about the problems to lead to design solutions. As a result, they devised a usability test in which they asked representative users to find the answers to typical questions using the set of procedures that would be available to them. The usability tests led to details about the access problem and the lack of understandable information. It also led to a cost-benefit analysis that showed the cost to the company of the time spent looking for information in the old manuals. The average search time of nine minutes yielded an estimated cost in lost time of $38 million in North America alone (about half the users), and 52% of the time the users found and acted upon incorrect information. This cost-benefit analysis led to funding for redesigning and rewriting the policies and procedures manuals (Hackos 1995).

Especially with existing products, you can generate design ideas by observing how users are likely to perform given realistic scenarios. In some situations it may be easier to simulate proposed changes to the working environment in the context of a usability evaluation. If you test with actual users rather than with user surrogates, you are likely to be able to learn more about user characteristics with a usability evaluation, as well as gain further insight into how users perform the tasks.

As you develop design ideas, usability evaluations will become a more critical technique for having users try out those ideas. In the predesign phase, however, we see usability evaluations (bringing users into a more controlled environment and watching and listening as they do tasks you set for them) as an addition to but not a substitute for site visits. Site visits show you the tasks that appear in the context of real work and show you characteristics of the workplace that affect performance. You cannot as easily learn about those tasks and workplace characteristics in the laboratory. [For more on usability testing, see Dumas and Redish (1993) and Rubin (1994).]

Using more traditional market research techniques

In this section and the next, we discuss techniques that you or others on the design team may already be familiar with. We are not covering them in this book beyond the discussion in this chapter. But we do want to bring up some of the more traditional market research and systems design data gathering techniques so that we can discuss their strengths and weaknesses and compare them to the more user-centered techniques that we are focusing on in this book.

If you come from a background in marketing or are working with people from a marketing department, you (or they) may be more familiar with techniques like focus groups, user surveys, and meeting with users at trade shows. Here we describe these three techniques and discuss what can (and what cannot) be learned by using them. You may want to use some of these in addition to the data gathering techniques we have discussed in the earlier sections of this chapter. We emphasize, however, that these are not the main techniques you should use. They are not substitutes for actually observing, listening to, and talking with users in their own work environments.

Meeting with users in focus groups

In their most common manifestation, focus groups are group meetings held with existing or potential customers and moderated by a facilitator who is skilled in eliciting attitudes, opinions, preferences, and reactions to new product ideas, customer requirements for new or updated products, problems and shortcomings of existing products, and more. A typical focus group includes 8 to 12 people plus the facilitator. The facilitator follows, at least loosely, a script or plan that has been decided in advance with the market researchers, laying out the issues to be covered or the questions to be addressed. The facilitator makes sure that no single person dominates the discussion, that the discussion stays close to the issues to be covered (that's the "focus" part of a "focus group"), and that all the issues in the plan are covered.

Focus groups usually meet away from any work site and last about two hours. During a focus group session, the facilitator may ask questions about how users do things, what they have done in the past, and what they think they would do in certain situations. The facilitator may present ideas or demonstrate products and ask for immediate reactions. Focus groups are, therefore, a good way to get opinions, attitudes, preferences, and reactions from people.

Limitations of focus groups for understanding users, tasks, and environments

For the type of analyses you need to design successful products, focus groups have several limitations. They don't show behavior. They aren't held in the users' environment. They often include gatekeepers, not users. They may be dominated by a few individuals.

In most cases, focus groups do not examine users' behaviors with a product and are not held in the users' environments. Therefore, they are usually not a good way to understand how people work or how they behave on the job. What people report about their work in a focus group and what happens on the job may differ, perhaps significantly. Much of the work that people do is so automatic that they forget to mention it when just talking about it. But the steps that don't get mentioned in a focus group may be critical to include in a new design or to document in a manual for new users.

Focus groups often bypass users. In many cases, we find that market researchers are talking to gatekeepers—the supervisors, managers, and other decision makers who will buy the product—and not to the people who will actually use the product. Pleasing these gatekeepers is important, but the information they give you may not help you design the interface or write the documentation that will really meet the needs of the people who do the work.

Another limitation of focus groups is that some individuals will be more outspoken than others and are likely to influence the direction and conclusions of the group. With user site visits, you observe users one at a time. With focus groups, you observe a group of people in an interactive discussion. In the hands of a skilled facilitator, the group interaction encourages a wide variety of ideas and opinions, with one participant influencing another to expand upon an idea or add a new concept. On the other hand, group dynamics may also affect the users negatively and limit the variety of responses. An outspoken individual may dominate the conversation and lead the group to a consensus of opinion that individuals would not have reached on their own.

Suggestions for overcoming some of the limitations of focus groups

In a typical focus group, participants only talk about what they do. To help participants be more aware of their behaviors as the basis for a focus group discussion, you can build some task work into the focus group session. We call these "task-based focus groups."

In a project to revise appliance manuals, Ginny held focus groups with consumers who owned a particular appliance from the client's company. At the beginning of each focus group, she handed each participant a set of scenarios and the manual for one of the client's products. She asked them to find the information they needed in the manual and to write down what they looked up in the table of contents or index, what page(s) they looked at, the answer they found, and how confident they were (on a five-point scale) that they had found the information they needed. The discussion that followed was far richer than focus groups Ginny had done without having users do these tasks. Users not only referred to the tasks they had just tried to do, but the just-completed tasks triggered memories of other experiences they had had with these and similar manuals.

If you do hold focus groups as part of your predesign data gathering, be sure that at least some of the focus groups are with users, not gatekeepers. You may also want to keep focus groups with users separate from those with gatekeepers. Users may not talk as freely when their bosses are there.

Good professional facilitation goes a long way to overcome the problem of one person dominating a focus group discussion. In addition some companies now have facilities for computer-assisted group discussions. Each participant is at a computer and all contributions to the discussion come typed through the computer. Because all contributions are anonymous, more timid people sometimes participate more fully in computer-assisted discussions. These newer, automated systems that allow all participants to "vote" on the issue at hand help to avoid the influence of dominant individuals and ensure that more introverted individuals have the opportunity for full participation without having to speak out in a group.

Focus groups can indeed be an effective addition to your user site visits, enabling you to test ideas formed when you visited users in their workplace. Focus groups provide you with a larger and potentially more diverse audience for new ideas than you might be able to visit in a reasonable amount of time or within a limited budget. Focus groups can provide significant insight into the perceptions that potential users will have of a new product or the requirements that users would like to add to the existing product specification. They do not, however, provide you with direct observations of users at work, of how users interact with the product in the workplace, learn about the product on their own, or solve their own problems in their actual use environment. And those are the most important types of data you need to develop successful designs.

Doing user surveys

Direct-mail questionnaires, telephone surveys, and surveys conducted by fax or through the Web are broadcast techniques designed to gather information from a large group of users. For example, once you know the critical characteristics of your users, you can use a survey to find out how the entire population of your users fits into the categories you have developed. You can use surveys to get more information on typical environments. For example, if you are considering building a product for a particular platform or Web browser, you can find out how many people in your existing or potential market have that platform or Web browser.

You can use surveys to investigate further an issue that you noticed on a site visit. For example, you may have noticed that many of your users were not provided with the user documentation when their product was installed. A survey might permit you to discover how high (or low) a percentage of your entire user population does not receive the documentation with the product. Surveys can help you decide if the circumstances you have observed at site visits are representative of a wider user population. Surveys can also help you focus on the types of information you may want to obtain as you conduct site visits or focus groups.

But surveys have several serious limitations for the type of data you most need for product design. Perhaps the greatest difficulty in using broadcast survey techniques is your own expertise in survey design and data analysis, especially if you do not have the opportunity to consult with experienced designers. Without a good design, it is easy to get bad information from a survey and analysis. Awkwardly phrased questions may lead to misinterpretations among respondents. Limited experience among people making telephone calls to users may result in incomplete or inaccurate information. A few misunderstood questions might make the difference between a successful and an unsuccessful product design. Surveys that ask for an immediate response outside of the workplace context may lead to misrepresentations of user opinions or characteristics.

Another potential serious problem is response bias. If you have a large user population and get a very small return on your surveys, you have to consider whether the people who responded represent only a specialized subset of your users.

Furthermore, surveys generally consist of closed questions—ones for which you already know all the possible answers. You ask respondents to select from the list of possible answers. Although you can ask open-ended questions on a survey, analyzing the answers is extremely time consuming and may not yield the information you are looking for. To develop closed questions for a survey, you have to know the critical questions and all the possible answers. That information can come from the open-ended observation and interviewing techniques that we focus on in this book.

Nonetheless, a well-designed survey allows you to get many more responses to a specific question than you are likely to get through site visits. Because we cover developing questionnaires to use on site visits in chapter 8 and how to ask questions in interviews in chapter 10, you may find useful advice later that can help you develop surveys.

Meeting users at trade shows

Trade shows and user group meetings can give you opportunities to meet many users who can tell you about themselves and their potential use of your product. Trade shows and user group meetings may allow you to take one less expensive trip in lieu of many, perhaps more expensive trips to user sites. It may be easier to get users' time at trade shows or user group meetings than at their work sites. Meeting with users at trade shows and user group meetings might be a way to get users excited about participating in other predesign usability activities.

JoAnn's company once held a panel on user documentation at a product user group meeting. The panel was attended by several hundred people who were interested in what the company was doing to improve their documentation. The participants were anxious to make their opinions known to the manufacturer. In addition to valuable input about their experiences with documentation, several participants volunteered to participate in site visits, focus groups, and usability tests.

Usability specialists at another company used the occasion of their industry trade show to do usability testing. They set up a portable usability lab at the trade show and signed up participants when they visited the company's booth. The users then came one at a time to a separate room where the portable lab was set up. The usability specialists gained useful information from a larger and more diverse group of users than they might have been able to visit in their workplaces or get to come to their site.

For the most part, however, user groups and trade shows find the users out of context. Often they are attending the events to gather information themselves, not to provide information to you. They are out to have a good time and don't want to be diverted by a time-consuming usability test or detailed interview. They are often reluctant to answer specific questions you might have because they view the activity as unnecessarily time consuming.

Perhaps the most troublesome aspect of relying only upon information gathered at trade shows and user groups is the demographic mix of the users who attend. Many companies send their most experienced people to these activities, both to offer them a perquisite and to make the most of the opportunity. Experienced users often serve as technical evaluators of new products in the field or may have the budgets to participate in user groups that are instrumental in influencing the functionality of new versions of the products. Unfortunately these experts are often unaware of or insensitive to usability issues.

To the extent that trade show and user group participants are not typical users and are being interviewed outside the work environment, their information may be less useful than what you might uncover in a site visit. However, talking with users at trade shows and user group meetings may add to the database of information about users that you are collecting.

Using more traditional systems development techniques

When you work with systems analysts and developers, you may find that they are used to other techniques for gathering predesign data about users and tasks, especially bringing users to requirements-gathering sessions, including a user representative on the team, and modeling work just by thinking about it or using analytic techniques while sitting at their own desks. While these are useful techniques, they miss many of the critical aspects that you get from working with users during site visits.

Bringing users to requirements-gathering sessions

Gathering user requirements is a necessary step in developing products. But the traditional method of gathering user requirements through systems analysis and through extended requirements-gathering, working sessions away from the users' work, does not necessarily lead to understanding users, the way that they work, their mental models, what they are likely to find intuitive and usable, or what will work in their environments.

What might you be missing if you do all the requirements gathering through requirements-gathering sessions? Here are several critical points to think about. Notice that these points are valid for focus groups as well as for requirements-gathering sessions.

■ Although you may develop some useful information about users through requirements-gathering sessions, in most cases these sessions focus on functionality rather than usability. Defining the functional requirements for a product leads to defining database elements, writing algorithms, and defining transactions. Usability requirements differ from functional requirements.

■ What people say they do and what they actually do may be different. Some tasks or steps are so automatic that users don't even mention them.

■ When users talk about situations, they usually think of a typical case. When you go out and watch, you may find that you see many atypical cases—situations that no one mentioned in a requirements-gathering session.

■ What people say they need and the best way to solve their problems may be different. In system-focused requirements-gathering sessions, participants tell you what they think they need to get a job done. When you go out and watch users do the tasks, you may discover that there are other, more innovative ways to help them meet their goals. You may find that the people you were talking with are reacting to a symptom of a problem and are not seeing the real problem or the best solution to it.

■ You may not be talking to the people who actually do the jobs. Even if you think you are inviting users to the requirements-gathering sessions, you may find that supervisors, managers, or people who used to do the job come to represent users. It does not take very long for people to forget what it is like to go through the work process all day every day. When you go out and watch, you may find that reality is different from what you heard in these sessions.

■ Even if users do come to the sessions, you may be losing information because of the group dynamics. This is one of the most serious problems with using meetings of this type to try to understand how users work. When you have a lot of people together in a group meeting, the dynamics of the group can strongly influence what happens. Important insights or problems may never be mentioned because some people are unwilling to talk in the group setting. The group may reach a consensus because one dominant personality sweeps reluctant participants to a decision. Participants may not speak up because they don't want to be different. They may think, "If everyone else agrees, I must be wrong to have a different opinion." Participants may not speak up because they don't want to take responsibility for advocating a specific point of view. They may think, "There are lots of people here. If none of them are taking responsibility, why should I put myself forward." Not everyone in the group operates at the same pace. Participants may be reluctant to reopen a discussion even though they disagree with how it ended. The developers may feel much more at ease in the requirements-gathering session than the users do. Users may be the most reluctant to speak up. When you go on site visits to observe, listen to, and talk with users, you work with one user at a time. The social dynamics that affect groups are lessened.

■ You don't get to see the work environment when all the requirements are gathered through meetings. Discussing the workplace instead of seeing it may lead to generalizations about product use that are inaccurate.

> *A team was designing a new system for use by clerks who registered patients in a hospital. The requirements sessions were dominated by physicians and hospital administrators who knew little about the relevant characteristics and specific work environment of the clerical-level users. The interface design that emerged led to numerous errors and decreased productivity.*

Contextual inquiries with users at users' sites are a better way to understand the usability requirements for a product. You get to see and talk with the actual users. You get to see the tasks they do and how they do them. You get to see the workarounds that they have developed. You get to see their self-developed quick reference sheets. You get to see how the physical setting influences the workflow. You get to see how social and cultural influences affect the way that the work is accomplished. Even if you plan major changes to the work process, you will come away with a better understanding of the people who will do that new process, the environment in which it will be done (or the changes that need to be made to that environment), the goals the users have, and their problems. You may come up with more innovative solutions to their problems and, therefore, a better design than you would gathering all the information through function-oriented requirements meetings.

Including a user on the design team

Including users on the design team is often a great idea that should definitely become part of a sophisticated user-centered design process. In the case of the development of a printing production system described by Pelle Ehn, users from the graphic workers' union contributed significantly to ensuring that the new system would function well in the workplace. The users who knew their traditionally performed jobs played a critical role in planning to automate their environment. They did this not through elaborate data flows but through a "design-by-doing" approach (Ehn 1993, 58).

Having a user or users on the design team is a great idea, but it is not enough. Do that in addition to, not instead of, doing site visits with more users.

Q *JoAnn worked on a project in which the representative user was a pediatrician. As a result, the first version of the physicians' interface had a decided pediatrician focus that surprised users from other medical specialties. Moreover, this user was not typical of most users of the system because he was interested in the details of the interface design and had taught himself Visual Basic. His knowledge of interface issues was helpful to the team but his design expertise also led the team to overestimate the computer sophistication and interest of the majority of users.*

One user cannot represent the entire user population. Furthermore, there is a tendency for the users who volunteer for design teams to be more expert than the typical user. And even if the users on the design team begin working with the team as typical users, the experience of working with the designers quickly taints them. They begin to think and act like designers and stop thinking and acting like users. As a result, it is often necessary to bring in "fresh" users during the design process.

Summary

In this chapter we've covered many techniques that you can use to understand the people who will be working with the product you are designing, the goals they have, the tasks they now do and the way they do those tasks, how those tasks fit into larger processes, and the environments in which the people work. In the rest of this book we concentrate on the techniques that we recommended in the first half of the chapter, particularly contextual inquiry and variations on ways to observe, listen to, and talk with users as they work in their own workplaces. This is the best way to get the information that you need to design usable and useful products.

References cited in the chapter

Beabes, Minette A. and Flanders, Alicia, Experiences with using contextual inquiry to design information, *Technical Communication*, 42 (3), August 1995: 409–420.

Beyer, Hugh and Holtzblatt, Karen, *Contextual Design: Defining Customer-Centered Systems*, San Francisco, CA: Morgan Kaufmann Publishers, 1997.

Butler, Mary Beth and Tahir, Marie, Bringing the users' work to us: Usability roundtables of Lotus Development, in *Field Methods Casebook for Software Design*, edited by Dennis Wixon & Judith Ramey, NY : John Wiley & Sons, 1996, 249–267.

Dumas, Joseph S. and Redish, Janice C., *A Practical Guide to Usability Testing*, Greenwich, CT: Ablex, 1993.

Ehn, Pelle, Scandinavian design: On participation and skill, in *Participatory Design: Principles and Practices*, edited by Douglas Schuler and Aki Namioka, Hillsdale, NJ: Lawrence Erlbaum Associates, 1993, 41–77.

Flanagan, John C., The critical incident technique, *Psychological Bulletin*, 51 (4), 1954: 327–358.

Hackos, JoAnn T., Finding out what users need and giving it to them: A case-study at Federal Express, *Technical Communication*, 42 (2), 1995: 322–327.

Hackos, JoAnn T., Elser, Arthur, and Hammar, Molly, Customer partnering: Data gathering for complex on-line documentation, *IEEE Transactions on Professional Communication*, 40 (2), June 1997: 102–110.

Holtzblatt, Karen and Beyer, Hugh, Contextual design, principles and practice, in *Field Methods Casebook for Software Design*, edited by Dennis Wixon and Judith Ramey, New York: John Wiley & Sons, 1996, 301–333.

Means, Barbara, Cognitive task analysis as a basis for instructional design, in *Cognitive Science Foundations of Instruction*, edited by Mitchell Rabinowitz, Hillsdale, NJ: Lawrence Erlbaum Associates, 1993, 97–118.

Ramey, Judith, Rowberg, Alan H., and Robinson, Carol, Adaption of an Ethnographic Method for investigation of the task domain in diagnostic radiology, in *Field Methods Casebook for Software Design*, edited by Dennis Wixon and Judith Ramey, NY: John Wiley & Sons, 1996, 1–15.

Raven, Mary Elizabeth and Flanders, Alicia, Using contextual inquiry to learn about your audiences, **The Journal of Computer Documentation*, 20 (1), February 1996: 1–13.

Rubin, Jeffrey, *Handbook of Usability Testing*, NY: John Wiley & Sons, 1994.

Whiteside, John, Bennett, John, and Holtzblatt, Karen, Usability engineering: Our experience and evaluation, in *Handbook of Human Computer Interaction*, edited by Martin Helander, NY: Elsevier Science Publishing, 1988, 791–817.

Wood, Larry E., The ethnographic interview in user-centered work/task analysis, in *Field Methods Casebook for Software Design*, edited by Dennis Wixon and Judith Ramey, NY: John Wiley & Sons, 1996, 35–56.

Other books and articles for further reading

Wixon, Dennis and Ramey, Judith, Eds., *Field Methods Casebook for Software Design*, NY: John Wiley & Sons, 1996.

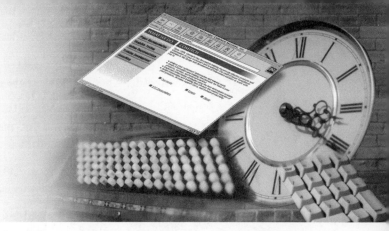

7

Setting up site visits

Planning is as critical to site visits as it is to any project. Don't skimp on the planning and just go out on a fishing expedition. If you don't have any sense of what you are trying to learn, you are likely to miss seeing and hearing information that is critical to the decisions you need to make.

Moreover, you may find that the process of planning is valuable in itself. Sitting down to do a site visit plan may make the project team think about issues that may not have come up before, such as how little the team really knows about users and their work, what markets the company wants to focus on, or what the team is really trying to accomplish.

At the same time, you should be prepared to remain open minded. If you have not visited users before, or if you are starting a new project with a new perspective on your users, your initial site visits may lead to a whole new set of plans. You may need to throw out your initial plans because you have learned that what is important about your users is different from what you originally expected.

If you have done usability testing, you will see that the plan for a site visit covers the same topics as a usability test plan, plus a few more related to the fact that you are going out to users rather than having users come to you. In planning for site visits, you have to think about and make decisions on

- ■ **Issues and objectives.** What do you (your group, your company, your agency) want to learn through these site visits?

- ■ **Participants**. Who should you observe and interview? How many participants should you include? What types of users should participate?

- ■ **Locations**. Where should you go to observe and interview?

- **Schedule**. When should you go? How long should you plan to stay for each visit?

- **Recruiting**. How will you find the people you need to visit? How will you convince them to let you come?

- **Data collection techniques**. Which techniques will you use to gather the data? How unobtrusive or participatory will you be? How much will you structure the visit?

- **Site visit team(s)**. Who should go? How many people should you send at one time? What roles should the different team members have? How should you train them?

- **Materials**. What materials will you need in order to recruit participants and prepare for the site visit? What materials will the team need during the site visit? What will you plan to bring back?

- **Media**. Will you use videotape? Audiotape? Will you use a laptop? Paper and pencil? Prepared forms? What else will you need to bring?

- **Data analysis and reporting**. What will you do with the data? Who can expect feedback from you and when?

In the rest of this chapter, we discuss the first six parts of a site visit plan through the topic of data collection techniques. In the next chapter, "Preparing for the site visit," we pick up on the last four parts and give you detailed advice for them, especially on preparing materials and selecting and training the team. At the end of chapter 8, you will find the entire site visit plan. In appendix A, you'll find a template to use for your own plans. Feel free to use it or modify it for your own situation.

Issues and objectives

The first decisions you need to make concern the purposes for your site visits. What are the issues that are driving you to go out on site visits? What objectives does your project group or the company or agency have for your site visits? What questions are you trying to answer? What information do you want to bring back? As you think about issues and objectives, consider the following points.

Realize that you have limited time

You'll typically have only a few hours with each user on a site visit. Although we've both done site visits that last a whole day or even longer, in most cases, you simply cannot ask users to take much more than half a day to spend with you. Even if you are watching them do their own work, you are still an interruption in their regular working arrangement.

You also probably have to limit each site visit to just a few hours for time and cost reasons. You will want to see several users, and spending more than half a day with each would make the site visit project take longer and cost more.

The time limits mean that you cannot learn everything. You have to make choices and, therefore, you have to think about issues and objectives before you go. Even if you could stay longer, you would probably not be able to absorb more. There's a limit to how much information any of us can take in at one time. You'll almost certainly find that you need to leave the user's site, think about what you've seen and heard, share insights with other team members, and plan for the next site visit. You may even find that you need to rethink your entire approach because your users are much different than you expected.

You could, of course, go back to the same user, and in some situations that will be appropriate, as in the case reported by Wood (1996). However, as we discuss in the section on participants, our experience is that observing several users is more valuable than going back to the same user over and over again. One is rarely enough unless all your users are very similar. One may be dangerously limiting. You may initially choose to visit each user twice to confirm your observations, and then cut back to one visit per person as you feel more secure in your planning.

You can also have several users who are working with you over time, which is typical of participatory design teams (Ehn 1989; Muller 1993) and is part of the technique of customer partnering that we discussed in chapter 6.

Involve all the "stakeholders" in deciding on issues and objectives

If you want what you learn to be used, it's a good idea to involve all the stakeholders in your decisions about what to focus on in the site visits. Stakeholders are all the people who need to pay attention to what you learn, as shown in figure 7-1. Depending on the product and situation, "stakeholders" may include business analysts, developers, documentation specialists, interface designers, marketing and sales representatives, system analysts, trainers, and the managers who will make decisions on direction, budget, and schedule. Getting "buy-in" beforehand smoothes the way for acceptance when you bring the data back.

To get at issues and objectives for one set of site visits, you should also consider what you already know as well as the questions that came up during earlier work on this and other products. Information might come from

- earlier discussions of the feasibility of the product

- attempts to put together a preliminary model of the users. (See chapter 2 for more on how to do this with brainstorming.)

Figure 7-1 Involve all the people who will use your data or whose support you need in deciding on issues and objectives for the site visits.

- technical support's knowledge of typical users' problems

- your own or others' earlier observations of users

- usability testing observations

- issues raised in focus groups and customer surveys

- issues that people in different areas within the company have raised (marketing, sales, development, documentation, human factors, training, usability)

If all the stakeholders agree on a set of issues and objectives that are feasible for a set of site visits, you can go ahead. However, you may also need to make trade-offs because you may not be able to gather all the information that each of these groups wants. In this case, you need to work with the stakeholders whose issues you will not be addressing. How can the data they want be gathered? Is there some other source for getting that data without doing site visits? Would another set of site visits at another time be a better way to get that data? Should you extend your plans for this set of site visits? What implications would extending the site visits have for the design process and project schedule?

Don't neglect the issues that a group of stakeholders raises. If you do, those people may lose interest in the project and may not continue to support your usability activities.

Write down the objectives and issues

Your list of objectives and issues may be declarative sentences that are objectives, questions that reflect the issues for which you want answers, verb phrases, or a combination of these.

Ginny's team at the Document Design Center did site visits as the first step in a project to revise a company's benefits handbook. The impetus to do the entire project was the need to update the information in the handbook. Because they had to redo the handbook anyway, the company took the opportunity to prepare a handbook that would work better for users. They also had an economic incentive. The benefits department was fielding many phone calls. A handbook in which users could find what they needed and understand what they found might reduce the calls. In planning site visits, the team realized they needed information on the following issues:

- *Did users even know they had a copy of the current handbook?*
- *Where did users keep their copy of the handbook? How available was it?*
- *Had the users ever consulted it?*
- *Did it look used? Did it have bookmarks or paper clips or notes in it? If it did, where were the bookmarks? What did the notes say?*
- *When would the users consult the handbook? (That is, what situations had actually arisen in the users' lives for which they should have gone to the handbook?) Did they?*
- *If they didn't use the handbook, how did they get the information? Why did they go to another source?*
- *If asked to use the handbook for the situation they mentioned (or for another relevant scenario), could they find what they needed? How did they search? Did they go to the table of contents? To the index? What words did they use in searching?*
- *How did they interpret what they found?*
- *How long did they search before giving up?*
- *How confident were they that they understood what they found?*
- *Did they want to consult another source even after they used the handbook? Why?*

Ginny worked with a group that was planning to replace a traditional command-based system with a GUI version. They wanted to make changes to the users' process at the same time. The client and Ginny agreed that site visits would be important to

- *understand the users' current process*
- *see how much variation there is in the way that different users do the process and what triggers that variation (Individual preferences? Number of*

transactions different users do? The way that information comes to the user? Other reasons?)

- *gather the users' vocabulary for the steps in the process and for the objects they deal with during the process*

- *find out what technology the users have and what they would need to replace to use the planned new system*

- *learn more about the users' level of experience with the subject matter and with Windows-based software*

- *get information on what matters most to users (Flexibility in ways to do tasks? Speed of system response? Straightforward paths through the software? Handholding help such as wizards or cue cards? Something else?)*

In figure 7-2, we introduce the SuperSales case study that is represented in the sample site visit plan at the end of chapter 8. The case represents the study planned by an in-house team developing new software that will assist store personnel in planning, implementing, and managing special sales. The list of issues and objectives was generated by the development team and other stakeholders from marketing, documentation, training, and customer service. The issues and objectives represent questions that the team hopes will be answered during the planned observations and interviews.

Note that the sample plan is for a fairly elaborate field study that seeks to answer questions of both feasibility and design. Your site visit study may not be this elaborate, but you should still do a plan with objectives or issue. The example is continued in chapter 8 where you will find forms and tables that fit this plan and a sample observer's notebook for the field study.

A caveat: Yes, planning is critical. You should put down your issues and objectives. You should plan the activities you will do during the site visits to focus on those issues and to meet your objectives. But when you actually go out on the site visits, you must also be alert and interested enough to notice what you did not expect to see. The most interesting and useful information from a site visit may well be something you had never thought to include in your objectives or issues. You must be flexible enough to change what you planned to do when something special happens (see figure 7-3).

Participants

Once you have some idea of what you want to learn, you have to decide which users you should visit. You'll want to decide on the number of users, the types of users, and how much variation there needs to be among the users you see. In figure 7-4, you learn how the participants will be selected for the SuperSales case study. Note that the study will include 27 total participants representing different

ISSUES:

These are the questions we want to be able to answer after this study.

- How do people in supermarkets plan and implement sales on food items?
- Who decides what to put on sale?
- Who decides how to advertise the sale?
- Who actually implements the sale? Who ensures that everything is ready?
- How do people decide what to put on sale? In what ways do they use computers or computer-generated information in those decisions?
- What materials do people create or arrange to have created to advertise in the store? outside the store? How do they now use computers in those tasks?
- What procedures do they use to ensure that everything is ready for the sale?
- How much variation is there in roles and tasks in different supermarkets?
- What varies?
- What are the main variables in that variation? (size of store? personal choice of people involved? roles set by company procedures?)

OBJECTIVES:

- Understand roles (who does what) in preparing for and implementing a sale
- Understand the overall sales process from first decisions to closing down sale
- Understand specific tasks in each part of the process
- See problems users have today in doing any part of the process
- Decide whether integrating modules to do all three functions is necessary and understand why or why not
- Understand what users value most
- Learn users' vocabulary for items and tasks

Figure 7-2 Issues and objectives for the SuperSales case study.

size stores and different levels of experience in several job categories. The team decided to look at three different size stores, given the assumption that the tasks might be done differently in smaller stores than in super stores because of a different division of labor. The team also wanted to look at the three primary tasks: planning, advertising, and implementation. In addition, the team considered it important to look at three different groups of participants: those with little experience (less than 1 year), those with much experience (more than 3 years), and those in between (1 to 3 years). It is always possible, however, that the

Figure 7-3 On site visits, stay alert for the unexpected.

first few visits will lead to rethinking these assumptions and revising the participant plan.

To develop a list of potential participants for your site visits, consider the issues addressed in the following discussion.

Start small

As with usability testing, you can learn a great deal from a relatively small number of participants. If you need to convince management of the value of the technique, don't ask for huge resources for a new way of doing things. Your proposal is likely to be rejected. Instead, get permission to do a small study. Even visiting two or three users may be enough when you first start out. Bring back useful data—and insightful videotapes—from a small number of users. You'll then be more likely to get the resources to do more.

If your site visits are in support of a specific project, the rest of the design and development team is probably very anxious to move ahead—and is probably under the pressure of deadlines to do so. Short small studies fit better into the typical development cycle than a long site visit project with many users and with a proportionately longer time for analysis and reporting. If you want the data to be used, you need to fit it into the ongoing product process, while perhaps at the

PARTICIPANTS

- 27 people will participate; 3 people in each of 9 stores
- All will actually work in our supermarkets and have a role in food sales.
- They will be store managers, assistant store managers, or department heads who actually do one or more of the three tasks: decide what to put on sale, decide on advertising for the sale, and implement the sale.
- The two characteristics that we believe may make a difference in what we learn are size of store and years of experience of the employee.
- Size of store may make a difference because roles and tasks may be divided among people differently in stores of different sizes. Interest in an integrated computer-based system may differ in stores of different sizes.
- Years of experience in the grocery business and in doing these tasks may make a difference in participants' general knowledge of sales and number of sales they have arranged.
- We therefore plan to observe and interview in three sizes of stores and at three levels of experience. We will visit three stores in each size category.
- That gives us the following matrix. We will observe and interview at least one person in each of the 27 categories of this matrix.

The matrix shows how 27 participants will be chosen by store size and years of experience.

Task	Store Size		
	Medium (40,000 to 50,000 sq. ft.)	Large (50,000 to 90,000 sq. ft.)	Super (170,000 to 240,000 sq. ft.)
Sale decisions (numbers = yrs of experience)	<1 1-3 3+	<1 1-3 3+	<1 1-3 3+
Advertising (numbers = yrs of experience)	<1 1-3 3+	<1 1-3 3+	<1 1-3 3+
Implementing (numbers = yrs of experience)	<1 1-3 3+	<1 1-3 3+	<1 1-3 3+

Figure 7-4 Participants for the SuperSales case study.

same time raising people's awareness of the need to change the process to accommodate more user-centered activities.

If you keep each study small—5 to 10 well-chosen participants—you may be able to do more studies. Just as iterative usability testing (design, have users try out the design, find problems, redesign to fix the problems, test again with other users) is the best way to move forward during the design and development phase, iterating site visits may give you the best information during the predesign phase. After the team has used the information from the first round of site visits, you may discover new questions, refine old issues, or see the need to visit another group of users.

Note that longer studies are sometimes feasible and appropriate as in our SuperSales example. If the project has a very long lead time, you may be able to do extensive studies up front. If the company is enlightened enough to have included usability throughout the product's life cycle, you may have several weeks of predesign field studies built into the schedule. The best situation for extensive field studies is when companies agree to do projects that are not attached to any specific product or development project but are information for the company's long-range strategic goal setting.

With Leslie Cahill of the SABRE Travel Information Network, Ginny conducted site visits with 41 travel agents in 29 travel agencies in 15 states over a four-month period. The impetus for the study was twofold: to get information that would be used immediately in designing a new product and to get information that would help the company plan future enhancements to its flagship software system. After the first few weeks of site visits, Ginny and Leslie reported back to the team designing the new product so they could incorporate the intermediate findings into their ongoing design work. After the entire field study project, Ginny and Leslie reported on the findings in several meetings to a variety of development teams and to upper-level management (see Redish and James 1996).

Look for patterns to know when to stop

Again, as with usability testing, the best answer to how many participants you need is that if you keep finding important differences, you want to keep visiting more users. When you have seen the same process, the same user profile, the same problems several times in different user groups and different locations, you will decide that you have the data you need. So look for patterns. The caveat to this advice, however, is that you need to select even your first few users to represent at least some of the major categories of diversity among users.

Decide on the user types to visit

One of the objectives of your site visits is almost certainly to learn more about your users. However, you must know at least something about the users or potential users of the product you are designing to decide who to visit. Using the information in Chapters 2 and 3 to help you understand how to characterize and categorize your users, you should create tentative user profiles.

To characterize your users in order to choose participants for site visits, you will almost certainly start with a definition that relates to their jobs, as shown in figure 7-5. If you are building an application for small businesses, the users will be the people who work in small businesses. For example, if you are replacing a legacy system with a graphical user interface, the users are the people who now work with the legacy system. If you are developing a new CD with information about financial aid, the users are potential students and their parents. Once you've begun with those job-related statements about users, however, you need to ask other questions to help you think about user types for your site visits.

Figure 7-5 Select users to represent differences that you have reason to believe will be meaningful for your design.

For the legacy system. Do people use it in different ways? For different tasks? With different frequencies? Are there novices? Advanced beginners? Competent users? Experts? You might decide that if you can only do six site visits, you want to work with two advanced beginners because that is the most common stage of use, two competent users, one novice, and one expert.

For the small business system. What is the title or role of the person who does the tasks your product will handle? You might decide that you want to visit a few one-person consulting firms where the business owner does everything and visit some businesses with five or more employees where the person doing these tasks has a more specialized role.

For the CD about financial aid. How much computer experience do these students and their parents have? You might decide to visit some families where both students and parents have been using computers for a long time and some where they are just now getting a computer. What educational background do the students and parents in your target market have? Even if all the students in your target market have finished or are close to finishing high school, you might still be concerned about the range of literacy levels among the potential users of your CD and therefore plan to visit students from schools in different areas. Are some of the programs on your CD aimed at the older, returning student, who has been out of school for a while? You might decide to visit with people in different age ranges. Where will these students be looking at the CD? If you are thinking of putting it in libraries and schools, you might plan to visit in those environments and include as users the librarians or school aides who are likely to be helping students and their parents.

Sometimes you may have to do some preliminary research to find out who the users of your product actually are, especially if the company is shifting its marketing and sales strategy.

JoAnn's team at Comtech kicked off a study of the users of satellite television systems by conducting a brainstorming session with people from marketing, sales, support, training, and engineering. It quickly became clear that the brainstorming team had a lot of knowledge of the wrong customers. All the company's previous focus had been on dealer sales. Their new strategy was to sell directly to end users. Unfortunately they knew almost nothing about the end users and their dealers were not about to tell them since the company's new direction threatened their livelihood. The team decided to use other techniques to identify users, in particular working with the companies that sold satellite TV guides to end users. These companies, as it turned out, had extensive demographic data on the end users because they needed this information to sell space to their advertisers. The demographic data provided the basis for segmenting the end-user community and planning the site visits.

Strive for breadth of representation

Even with 5 to 10 participants, you can get some breadth among the participants in your field study. Don't spend all your time with one user. The chances are great that that user is not typical.

If your product will be used both inside and outside the company, don't do all the site visits with employees. There are already far too many examples of products that were developed based on internal processes that then failed when the company tried to sell the product outside. The differences between internal processes and the ways others do the work outside the company is extremely likely to be too great for an internally focused product to succeed. The vocabulary that works inside the company may totally confuse the outside users.

If people in different roles will use different parts of the product or do different parts of the process that the product supports, plan site visits with at least a few people in each of the relevant positions. As we suggested in both chapters 3 and 6, you may be most interested at first in a workflow analysis, looking at the larger process to see how the piece you are designing fits in.

If you are looking at workflows that involve people in different roles, you may need to include more participants from each site in your site visits. Don't see just one clerk and one system administrator.

In this book we emphasize the importance of working with users during site visits, not with their supervisors. But if supervisors will have tasks to do in the process or with the product, then they may well be a user type that you want to include in your site visits. In the SuperSales case study, the users are the managers and department heads.

Work with marketing to decide on participants

If your company has a marketing department, you may be able to link up with marketing specialists who are familiar with the product you are replacing or with your project to design a new product. They may be able to help you develop preliminary user profiles, decide on the user types to focus on, and select appropriate locations. They may even be willing to make initial contacts for you.

You may also, of course, have to convince marketing and sales that you have legitimate needs for talking to their customers. They may have quite realistic fears that you will not know how to handle yourself and the customers properly. We find that by being open and inclusive you will get much farther than by being defensive about the implied criticism. Recognize marketing's and sales' expertise and make use of it. However, also show that development needs are different, requiring more detail and a much closer look at the users rather than the buyers. Invite marketing and sales to participate in the brainstorming, planning, and implementing of the field study if possible. In this way, you will both become aware of the differences in information needs as well as the similarities.

Many marketing departments gather lots of information about customers through focus groups and customer surveys and by mining data available through various databases the company keeps. For example, in many companies, the marketing department can tell you the volume of business they do with different customers, the type of interactions they have with different customers, how often a customer buys from the company or contacts the company, etc. They may be able to give you lists of all the customers in a given geographic area with data on size, number of users, types of work, and other data.

A few caveats are in order for you to think about when working with marketing specialists:

Press them to take a long-range view

When products are first being developed, they are often aimed at specific market segments. We urge you to press your marketing colleagues or clients to consider planning for the future. Will this product always be restricted to that market segment? What is likely to happen in a year, or two years, or five years? If the same or a similar product is going to be marketed to other users later, considering them now is crucial. Otherwise design decisions made for the first market segment will constrain what can be done later to meet the needs of users in other market segments. In the long run, the company will get the greatest benefit by thinking long term and having you do site visits with a range of users in a range of markets.

Marketing's information is usually about "customers" not users

Marketing can usually tell you about a customer or client "shop." If they've been talking to people in focus groups or by doing surveys, they've most likely been talking to gatekeepers, the decision makers who buy, and not to the users, the people who do the work. Your site visits are to understand users and how they do the work. You need to be sure the marketing specialists you are working with understand the distinction. When marketing specialists understand the distinction, they can often be helpful about helping you get to the users you want to see.

Your intuition about the characteristics that matter may not be correct

As we discussed in chapters 2 and 5, we all have assumptions about users, their work, and their environments. The purpose of going out to the users is to challenge and clarify those assumptions. We also all have assumptions about which characteristics of users, work, and environments are going to be the major features distinguishing one user type from another. These assumptions, like the ones we discussed in chapter 5, may turn out to be false.

JoAnn worked on a project in the banking industry, where people in sales and marketing were sure that users would be different in small banks and in large banks. So JoAnn and her colleagues used size of the organization as a factor in deciding on participants for site visits. They included some users in banks with few employees and some users in banks with many employees. What they found, however, was that the size of the organization was less relevant to how users worked. What was more relevant was the internal structure of the departments in different banks.

Ginny worked with a group that also thought that size of the organization might match differences in what users were like. And in this case, size did correlate with differences, but not in the direction that Ginny and her clients assumed they would find. They had assumed that users in large organizations would be more technically sophisticated than users in small organizations. They found just the opposite. Users from organizations with few employees were more knowledgeable about Windows; had newer, more sophisticated computer equipment available to them; and were more likely to be competent performers, interested and able to consider new ideas than users from large organizations. In thinking about the finding, Ginny and her clients realized that indeed what they saw made sense. In the smaller organizations, the users had more roles to play and often had more responsibility. In the larger organizations, users were more likely to be in a clerical position and to be people who are happiest without decision-making responsibility. Smaller organizations that only have to outfit one user can perhaps afford to update their technology more often than large organizations that have to replace many computers at once. Change may be easier for small organizations to accept.

Use your preliminary models of users and their communities to decide on participants

In chapter 2 we talked about different ways of viewing users and urged you to think about your users along several dimensions. We suggested that you think of individual users in terms of characteristics such as

- jobs they hold and tasks they do
- subject matter knowledge and experience
- tool knowledge and experience
- frequency and level of use of the product
- language, literacy, and culture
- learning styles
- motivation

We also suggested that you think of users as part of user communities, so the environment in which users work would be part of your thinking about which users to include in your site visits. Use the procedures we discussed in chapter 2 to come up with preliminary models of users and user communities. When you are ready to select participants for site visits, work from those preliminary models.

P *For the site visit project that Ginny did with Leslie Cahill of the SABRE Travel Information Network, the company had user profiles from past work that suggested that travel agents who primarily book corporate travel work very differently from travel agents who primarily book leisure travel. The team decided to try to do half the site visits with corporate travel agents and half with leisure travel agents. The team also suspected that users with different levels of subject matter expertise (years as a travel agent) and tool expertise (time with and frequency of use of a graphical user interface) would be having different experiences with the current software and would have different expectations of new software. They strove to do site visits with users at different stages of use with the current software and different stages of use with the graphical user interface that would be used for new versions of the software.*

Insist on advanced beginners and novices if that is what you want

You may need to convince account executives, managers, supervisors, union reps, or whoever else you need to go through to get permission for site visits that you really, really do want to see the less skilled users. The gatekeepers you have to work with to set up site visits understandably want themselves and their clients, their workers, their union members to look their very best. Therefore their natural inclination is to suggest that you work with the person at the site who knows the most—that is, the expert.

But you don't want to see the expert, or at least not only the expert. You want to see typical users, who are often the people we called advanced beginners in the section on stages of use in chapter 3. And you may in fact want to see the least experienced people—absolute novices—to know what life is like for those who are first learning the subject matter or the tool.

You may be the first person that these gatekeepers have dealt with who is doing this type of information gathering, predesign site visits. Educating them about the purposes of the site visits, what will be done with the data, and why it is critical to see the nonexpert may well be part of the task you need to accomplish. Don't leave it to chance. From many, many experiences, we both assure you that if you leave it up to the gatekeeper, you will be working with the atypical expert (see figure 7-6).

Use site visits to get user profiles from more people

Part of the materials for site visits should be a user profile form—a questionnaire that you fill in when recruiting users or that you have users fill in about themselves either before you come or when you start the visit. (See figure 7-10 for an example of a screening questionnaire and figure 8-4 for a demographic data form, both of

Figure 7-6 Help people understand why it is so important for you to work with typical users and not just experts.

which get you the type of information you need to develop better profiles of your users.)

You may want to use that same form to get information about many more users than you have time to actually observe and listen to. When you go to a location with several users, even though you only work with one of them, you can ask all of them to fill in your user profile form. That way, you have at least some demographic data about all the users in that location.

You can also send the form as a type of user survey to people in other locations, even ones that you cannot visit. You can use the filled-in forms to expand your understanding of the users' backgrounds. You can also use them to build a database of potential participants for future site visits and for other usability activities.

Locations

Now that you know the types of users you want to include as participants, you have to decide where you will find them. Your thoughts about user communities may also lead to decisions on different locations to include in your field study. Time and budget are likely to keep you from going to all the types of sites that you would like to see, but do consider the different locations, environments, and market niches that users work in. If you can't get to all of them in the first round of site visits, you may be able to later. And it may be crucial to keep the people you did not visit in mind—and to make sure that developers keep them in mind also.

In the SuperSales case study, the locations are in three different metropolitan areas, representing a range of locations for the nationwide chain. Within each geographic area, three sizes of stores—medium, large, and super—will be included, as explained in figure 7-7.

LOCATIONS

We have selected three locations in our nationwide chain: Denver, Colorado; Fort Worth, Texas; and the Washington DC metropolitan area. All three are areas with grocery stores of all sizes and both urban and suburban locations. They represent distinct areas of the country with different user profiles. The Human Resources Department has already spoken with the regional managers in those areas, and they have agreed to cooperate in the study.

Within each location, we will visit one store of each size. If possible, we will want to have a variety of experience levels among the study participants in each store.

Figure 7-7 Locations for the SuperSales case study.

Not all user and task analyses are done at users' sites. In chapter 6 we discussed several valuable techniques for working with users to understand who they are, what they do, and how they work without being present at their work. For our detailed "how-to" chapters, however, we are concentrating on doing user and task analysis by observing, listening to, and talking with users as they do their own tasks in their own environments. For our discussion here, conducting a site visit means being on site with the user. How then do you decide which sites to visit?

Strive for at least some geographic spread even in one country

If all the present and future users are in one geographic area, that's where you'll be doing your site visits. However, most companies have users in different parts of their own country and in different countries. Even within one country, you many well find differences from region to region in the physical setup of environments, in corporate cultures, in expectations of workloads and productivity, and in the background of users. Seeing a range of these locations will give you the broader user and task analysis you need to design an interface or write a document that will serve all these users.

A telecommunications company has its headquarters in one state and regional offices in several other states. When they were developing a new customer service application, they realized that the way work is done at headquarters might not be the way it is done in the regional offices. At first they planned to learn about the users and their current process by

observing and talking with users at headquarters and at one regional office. When the usability specialist talked with others in the company who were knowledgeable about customer service, however, she realized that it would be important to visit at least two of the regional offices. She discovered that environmental influences— climate and expectations in the local community about the relationship between work hours and nonwork activities—differed in the different regions. But more relevant to the application that she was helping a group to develop was the discovery during her site visits that people with different skills did the same job at different locations. In one location, customer service work was considered a low-level clerical job while in another it was considered a mid-level job for people with much more experience who were expected to be making decisions.

One way to get more geographic spread is to share data—to leverage what you and others are learning on different projects. Time and budget may limit you to one geographic region for one round of site visits. However, as the techniques of user and task analysis become more widespread in your company, you (as the usability specialist working with different teams) or others (going out as their own teams) may go to different areas. Even if the specific projects concentrate on different users and different tasks, the observers on one team may well be gathering information about the overall physical environment, culture, user population, work practices, and tasks that will help other teams. Develop ways to share that information.

Ginny was working with a company in which several development teams were simultaneously working on the same product. There were several releases in the works at the same time as well as different product modules for different users, all of whom would be doing their own jobs while drawing on the same database. Each development team could only afford the time and cost of a few site visits. By being aware of the needs of all the development teams, Ginny and the people who went on the site visits were able to gather some information for everyone while concentrating in each round on the specific users and issues of one of the development teams. Representatives from all the teams came to all the debriefing sessions.

Think globally, even if you can't go abroad right away

When we talk about understanding all the users and how they work, if you are part of a global company, your first thought is probably that you need to do an international user and task analysis. And you are correct. However, if the idea of getting out to users' sites is new for your company, you are probably not going to get the resources to do a global study right away. Start with what you can do. But keep reminding people that what you learn in one country may not apply around the world—in fact, it almost certainly does not apply to all countries. Once you show the value of a user and task analysis and feel more comfortable with your own skills, you can expand your work to other countries.

JoAnn's team at Comtech conducted both U.S. and European site visits to study the documentation and training needs of the users of the client company's software. They found that the equipment operators in France and Italy had considerably more hours of classroom training than operators of the same equipment in the United Kingdom and the United States because France and Italy have laws requiring companies to invest in worker training. They concluded that the mix of documentation and training would have to be different for U.K. and U.S. users than for continental European users.

In another study for a telecommunications company, JoAnn and her colleagues learned that people doing routine maintenance on equipment in the United States tended to be trained technicians. In the Middle East and Africa, the same tasks were being done by degreed engineers. Their information needs were considerably different from the technicians in the United States. In fact, the engineers preferred the maintenance manuals to be in the original English rather than translated into their local languages.

Also remember that international markets differ. Western Europe, Eastern Europe, different parts of the Middle East, Africa, and Asia include many different cultures, languages, and physical environments. You cannot do an international study in just one place and expect what you learn to represent the entire non-U.S. market.

Consider present—and also future—markets or user groups

Many products are initially developed because a particular group asks for them or needs them. In the beginning, that group is the only market being considered, and you may be encouraged to visit only users in that group. You should probably start there, but you should also ask about future plans. Even if no one has future plans for the product, ask what would happen if the product were given or sold to other user groups in the future. Decisions made for the initial group will constrain what can be done later, so thinking broadly and into the future will let you produce a product that works for wider audiences.

Ginny worked with a group that usually starts its product development by talking with its major customers. The major customers are large companies with many users, so it is natural that the development managers listen to them. However, site visits to a broader range of customer shops showed many, many differences between these few large customers and most others. In the large shops, users work with the client's software all day long. Most users are extremely proficient with the parts of the software they use regularly. These users value speed over ease of use. The customers have in-house technical specialists who build add-ons and workarounds to accommodate specific uses of the software for their business.

In the smaller shops (of which there are many more, although each has only a few users), most users are still advanced beginners. They do many tasks, instead of specializing. They value ease of use more than speed because they use more features but use them less frequently. The pace of work is much slower and the atmosphere encourages more personal contact than in the larger shops, which do most of their business by telephone. Many users in the smaller shops still use paper whenever they can rather than the software. What is needed to satisfy these two groups differs.

The market differentiators that you might consider include

- size of the user companies

- technical sophistication of the user companies

- job and task differences (for example, for a medical product: doctors, nurses, paramedics; for inventory software: people who work in offices, people who work on the factory floor, people who work on the loading dock)

Schedule

As you think about participants and locations, you will also need to think about schedules. For scheduling, consider

- how long you want to spend with each participant (including "meeting and greeting" time with site managers both before and after the time you spend with participants)

- how long it will take to travel to each location (including middle of the day travel if you are going to two sites in one day)

- how much time you can leave after every one or two site visits to go over your own notes, prepare trip reports, share observations within the team, and plan any changes for the next site visits

The schedule for the SuperSales site visits is based upon the shifts at the store and negotiations with the store managers (see figure 7-8). Note that the team makes sure that it has sufficient time to discuss what they have observed and make changes to the plan if necessary.

Plan around users' schedules and the cyclical nature of the work

The people you want to visit may prefer that you come only on certain days of the week or month. David Mitropoulos-Rundus and Jerry Muszak (1997b) suggest that home visits are best done between 5:00 P.M. and 8:30 P.M. because that's when

SCHEDULE

We will spend approximately four to five hours in each store, beginning either in the morning (first shift) or mid-afternoon (second shift) at the store manager's convenience. We will visit only one store on each day and use the rest of that day to review our notes, prepare trip reports, and begin to analyze the data.

Recruiting and further planning will be done in July. The data will be collected in August and early September. Analysis of the data will be ongoing during August and September. Findings will be presented no later than October 1.

The detailed schedule is shown in the matrix:

Location	Date	Time
Denver super store	August 10	7 A.M. to noon
Denver large store	August 11	9 A.M. to 2 P.M.
Denver medium store	August 12	7 A.M. to noon
Washington medium store	August 20	2 P.M. to 7 P.M.
Washington large store	August 22	7 A.M. to noon
Washington super store	August 25	7 A.M. to noon
Fort Worth large store	September 3	9 A.M. to 2 P.M.
Fort Worth super store	September 4	7 A.M. to noon
Fort Worth medium store	September 6	2 P.M. to 7 P.M.

Figure 7-8 Sample schedule for the SuperSales site visits.

families are home and during mid-week so that you don't disturb valuable family time on Friday nights or on the weekends.

In many businesses, you will see very different situations on different days of the week or days of the month. For example, in some businesses—or some areas of the business—Monday is a very busy day because work accumulates over the weekend and has to be dealt with on Mondays. In other businesses, Monday is a slow day because work does not accumulate, and the users you are working with have to wait until other divisions generate work for them.

Many types of work are cyclical throughout a month. If you want to watch payroll clerks generating paychecks, there may be only two days in the month when that happens.

The irony is that users may least want you to come at just the time when you most want to be there. They feel they can give you more time when their work is slow. You may feel that you most need to understand the tasks they do and how they do them when they are under the greatest pressure.

Consider your issues and objectives when deciding how to handle scheduling conflicts like these. If seeing users at their busiest time is not crucial to your objectives and if you most want to talk with users and perhaps role play specific scenarios, ask for a time when they are not so busy. If seeing them at their busiest is crucial, plan to be unobtrusive (observing quietly and out of their way with little time spent talking), and assure the users and their managers that you will not interfere with their meeting their deadlines.

You may need to compromise. If seeing the users in their own sites is critical and you cannot get permission to come on busy days, then take what you can get. Go when they will let you come, observe and listen, and ask about the other times. If you cannot convince managers and users that you will not be in their way, you may be able to get them to let you set up video and audio recording equipment to capture what happens during those very busy times.

Consider cultural differences in your schedule

Be certain that you are aware of cultural differences that could have an impact on your schedule. Here are several examples:

- In some parts of the world, certain holiday months preclude site visits. If you plan site visits to businesses in France in August, you're likely to be the only one there.

- Some cultures place great value on punctuality. Dray and Mraczek (1996a) report that their site visit team went out of their way to be sure they were on time for visits with German families.

- Other cultures don't place the same value on punctuality. One team doing site visits in Italy was delayed several hours because of transportation problems. It wasn't a problem to the users. In South American cultures, you may find that the users you are going to visit have a different sense from yours of when *they* need to be there.

- Some cultures place great value on time spent building rapport before getting down to work. One company found that account representatives in Europe could not meet the same quotas for customer visits as their counterparts in the United States. The European customers expected each visit from the representative to last much longer than the U.S. customers expected.

Try to leave time so the team is fresh and alert for each visit

Like usability testing, observing and listening to users at their sites is exhausting work. Team members need to be constantly attentive to new environments, new people, new processes. Each user and each site brings new perspectives. That's why we suggest that you schedule no more than two visits in one day. To minimize travel, you may want to visit with more than one user at each site.

In the study that Ginny and Leslie Cahill did, one of the most interesting observations was how much the individual travel agents controlled the way that they chose to do their tasks, deciding when to use the computer and when to use the phone, deciding whether to fax from the computer or from a fax machine, deciding how much attention to give to a customer. Observing and talking with two agents in the same travel agency often revealed as many if not more differences in a given day than did changing sites in the middle of the day.

If you do get to do site visits abroad, don't plan to start observing users the moment you arrive. You'll have jet lag. Try to start with a day for the team to adjust to the time difference and to the new overall surroundings before having to take in the specifics of the users' work or home environment.

Consider whether half a day is the right amount of time

Although we are suggesting two to three hours for a typical site visit, that may not be the best schedule for your situation. You may want to spend an entire day at a user's site because you want to engage the user and other people at the site in different activities.

Ginny did a study to help her client understand how users of their software now do their work and how those users' tasks fit into the larger picture of the user companies' processes. In the morning, Ginny and her observation teammate met in a conference room at the site with all the groups involved in all parts of the process, not just the user of Ginny's client's software. With Ginny's facilitation (asking questions, probing for more information), the group did a workflow analysis, laying out the entire work process, with the person responsible for each part of the process taking the lead as his or her turn came up. The user whose work was of primary concern also talked through that part of the process. Ginny's observation teammate took extensive notes and the entire group developed an elaborate process flow on large sheets of paper which became the main artifact from the session. In the afternoon, Ginny and her observation teammate did a contextual inquiry while the user actually carried out his part of the process with the software. The two techniques complemented each other to give both a broad picture of the overall work process and a detailed picture of one part of the process.

Recruiting

Once you decide on the geographic areas, types of environments, and types of users you want to observe and talk with, you have to arrange the visits. Figure 7-9 shows the recruiting plan for the SuperSales case study. Note that the team plans to work closely with the regional managers, who are directly responsible for the stores in their region and whose approval is necessary for the study to succeed. You will often find that you must seek out and obtain the appropriate clearances from people who may be concerned about the purpose of your study and the amount of time it may take from the work schedule of their employees.

RECRUITING

The Usability Department will do the recruiting based on information from Human Resources. Our first contact will be with the regional manager in each of the regions. These people have already been contacted by Human Resources and are expecting to be called. We will ask the regional manager to suggest stores for us to visit and to make the initial contact with the store manager for us.

Materials needed: Screening Questionnaire; Calendar for Site Visits; Letter of Introduction to be sent as soon as a site is put on the calendar

---

Figure 7-9 Recruiting information for the SuperSales case study.

Work through appropriate channels

Depending on your situation, you may need to work through account managers, site supervisors, or union representatives to get permission to talk with users, even to arrange the site visits. Find out what the protocol is in your company and in the users' companies. For your first excursion into site visits, leave plenty of time to go through the appropriate channels. Here are some tips for working through appropriate channels:

- If you are in a commercial company with account managers, appreciate that they have legitimate reasons to worry about who is visiting with their customers and what will happen. They don't want to lose a customer.

- Recognize that salespeople are almost always on commission. Their job is to sell. If you need to work with the sales force to reach users, you must convince the salespeople and their managers that what you are doing is going to help them sell more.

- Realize that predesign site visits may be a totally new concept to these people. They need to understand what you are going to do when you are there, what you are going to do with the data, and why the technique is so critical. They need to be reassured that you know how to talk with customers.

■ Get on the agenda of the monthly meetings of these people or their managers to explain the process and its value. Put an article in their internal newsletter. Get permission to put information onto the company's Web site in a place where these people are likely to browse.

■ When you hear the objection that "We don't want to impose on the users, they're too busy," talk about how in other companies, people thought that but when they asked users if usability specialists could come watch them work, they found that users were thrilled to have someone come to find out how they do their jobs.

■ But also realize that users are busy and that you cannot impose on the same users over and over again.

■ Invite the account manager or sales representative to come with you on a site visit. They may want to see what happens to understand what you are doing and to convince themselves that you are not embarrassing the company. However, make sure that you work out beforehand just what the account manager or sales representative's role in the site visit will be. This is *not* a sales visit.

■ Get permission from the managers of accounts or sales to develop a database of users that you can use for future site visits so that you do not need to go through a two-step recruiting process each time (getting to the account manager and then getting to the users). That will lessen the burden on account managers of helping you do recruiting.

■ If the person who helps you get to the user is at the site (site supervisor, user's manager, union representative), stop in to say hello and thank the person when you first get to the site.

■ After the site visit, thank anyone who facilitated the visit as well as the users.

■ Never share information about a specific user with that user's manager or anyone else who could use the information in a negative way. Just as in a usability test, you are assuring as much anonymity to your site visit participants as you can, even though they are your partners in understanding their work and their environments.

■ But do share information with the account manager or other people who can solve a problem that you hear about.

 On a site visit for a client, Ginny heard a story about a negative experience that the user had had with a particular individual on the client's support line. Another person in the customer's shop, overhearing the conversation, chimed in with the perception that the

person in question was often rude and unhelpful. Ginny relayed the story to her contact in the client company who then followed up with the manager of the support line and with the client representative handling that account. It was very important to Ginny's client that customer complaints be taken seriously and handled well.

Once you get to the users, you may find that they are eager to participate in field studies. After all, you want them to help you understand enough to develop a product that will work well for them. They like the fact that the company is interested in what they think and do. They love the idea that the people who are developing the products they will have to work with care enough to come to see them at work. In chapter 9 we offer tips on how to make the site visit successful when you get there.

Get lists of potential users or sites

The marketing or sales department may be the best place to get lists of users in the geographic areas you want to visit. The sales representatives for a particular region and product line are frequently key sources for customer names and will often volunteer to make the first contact for you and tell the customer about you and why you want to visit.

The customer support department may have the names and telephone numbers of users who call for information. Field engineering personnel may know the customers to whom they provide assistance. The company's training organization probably has lists of people who have attended training courses. They may also be able to tell you something about the users' experience levels.

If you have done usability testing or other usability activities on the product or other products that the same users work with, you may want to work with some of the same people again in site visits. Or you may want to ask them to suggest colleagues or others they know through professional networks as potential people for your site visits. Dealer representatives may be willing to provide names of their customers although, if they are in competition with your company or client, they may be reluctant to share this information.

Expect to make several calls to find each place to visit

All of the groups we listed in the last few paragraphs may be good sources of names, addresses, and phone numbers. Every potential lead should be checked so that you get the broadest list of potential participants that you can. Not everyone will be willing to or able to participate. You will probably need three to four times as many contacts as you need participants in the study.

Ask the people who supply the names to make the first contact

We strongly recommend asking the people who provided the leads to make the initial contacts for you or lend their names to an introductory letter. We have found that customers are more likely to return phone calls from your team if they know you will be calling. They are also more likely to provide you with information if they don't suspect that you're a spy for the competition. We have found customers to be quite protective of their sales representative or of their relationship with a favored vendor.

If people are willing to introduce you and the project to their customers, provide them with a script that explains the purpose of the study and provides the names and phone numbers of the people who will be calling to schedule a visit. Without a script, we have found that customers often get a very distorted view of what you are up to.

For other types of users, consider working through a recruiting agency

If you are trying to recruit from a broader population and not within a structure that has account managers or equivalents, you can send out a general broadcast to all the users in an area by e-mail or letter. However, expect a very small return from a general request.

If you are looking for home users, the general public, or specific types of individuals (accountants, lawyers, nurses), you can work through temporary agencies, firms that recruit for focus groups, or professional societies, which often have chapters in different geographic areas. If you work with a temporary agency, give them explicit instructions on the types of users and environments you need.

Use a screening questionnaire

A screening questionnaire is a script for you or someone else to use to ask people where they, and possibly their organizations, fit in the dimensions you have decided are critical to your site visits. The purpose of the screening questionnaire is to allow the recruiter to decide whether to include that user in the site visit plan and, if so, which of the user types you want to visit that particular user represents.

Part of the screening questionnaire can be a schedule form that the recruiter uses for working out a date and time for the site visit with the user. If you work with a recruiting agency, give them a screening questionnaire to use.

Getting participants for site visits is very much like getting them for usability tests. In chapter 2 you learned how to brainstorm about your potential users and examine your assumptions. Earlier in this chapter, you learned how to gather user information and make decisions about the best users to visit. You will need to recruit participants for your study even after you have identified suitable people and sites.

In your recruiting efforts, it will be important to ensure that the people you want to observe and interview will be available during your visit. If you want to interview new users, you will have to arrange a time to visit when new hires have just come on board. If you want to interview managers, you will have to be certain that they are available. You may want to observe and interview individuals with particular types of experience, training, or knowledge. You will need some way of determining if the right people are available at a particular site.

A screening questionnaire is always useful to guide your thinking when you interview potential users by phone. However, a screening questionnaire is essential when you use professional recruiters or people in your organization to do the recruiting. They need specific questions to ask and paths to pursue to help them decide which users are appropriate for the site visits.

The screening questionnaire consists of a series of questions that enable you to tell if the person you are talking with has the characteristics you are looking for in your user community. For example, you may want to meet with network system administrators who have experience with both UNIX and PC operating systems, are familiar with three generations of your network server, and are skilled in a number of tasks, including installation, configuration, troubleshooting, and repair. You might use a screening questionnaire to ensure that the people you have selected have these basic characteristics. If one of your goals is to analyze the initial configuration task, it will be less than useful to meet with a system administrator who has no initial configuration responsibilities and who has only worked with a system that someone else has configured.

In designing your questionnaire, think about the questions that will produce the results you want. Include questions that specify the nature of experience and knowledge among your users. Ask basic questions first to eliminate those who do not have the characteristics you are looking for. Then ask more detailed questions to narrow your selection.

Remember, however, that part of your intent in the user studies is to discover the characteristics of your users. Be open in your administration of the questionnaire to characteristics or levels of knowledge and experience that you have not anticipated. You may, for example, want to interview people with considerable prior experience. However, during your discussions with potential participants in the study, you may find that most people have considerably less experience than you anticipated. Be prepared to shift the focus of your investigation to take the realities you perceive into account.

Figures 7-10 and 7-11 provide examples of a typical screening questionnaire and a screening grid. The questionnaire is designed to find out about store size, type of tasks performed, and years of experience. The grid is based on the user/task matrix discussed in chapter 2, outlining the user segments to be included in the site visits.

SCREENING QUESTIONNAIRE

Hello, my name is //give your name// and I am calling about a project for //name the company.// Your name was given to us by //name your contact// as a person who would be interested in helping us better understand how supermarkets plan and implement sales on special items. I understand that //name// has already mentioned the project to you.

[If the user remembers the project, go on. If the user does not remember the project, use the following description.]

Our company is developing a new software system that will help people in supermarkets plan and implement sales on food items. We want to learn how you decide to put a certain item on sale, how you put the sale in place with advertising both inside and outside the store, and what procedures you go through to ensure that everything is ready for the sale. The best way we know of to understand how this process works is to visit your store for 4 to 5 hours. During the visit we want to watch the process you use without interfering in your work. Then we want to ask you some questions about how the process works. If possible, we'd like to observe and talk to 3 or 4 people in the store who are involved in the process of setting up a sale.

[If the user is still confused, suggest that you will have a member of the project team call them to explain the project further. If the user seems satisfied, go on to the next item.]

If you have a few minutes, I need to ask you a few questions about your experience and the type of store you work in.

1. I understand that you are the store manager. Is that correct? _____
   If not, what is your job title? _____
   [If you do not have the store manager, assistant store manager, or department head, ask if one of them is available, transfer the call, or get the number and a time to call back, if possible. End the call.]
   [If you are talking to the store manager, assistant store manager, or a department head, continue with the questions below.]

2. Is your store medium (40,000 to 50,000 sq. ft.)? _____ Large size (between 50,000 and 90,000 sq. ft.)? _____ Super (more than 170,000 sq. ft.)? _____
   [Check your grid. Do you already have three stores that fit the size criterion? If so, explain that we most need people from different size stores. Ask if it would be possible to call back if someone cancels? End the call.]

Figure 7-10 Example screening questionnaire for the SuperSales visits.

3. Are you responsible for deciding to put an item on sale? _____
   If no, ask who in the store decides on a sale item. _____

4. Are you responsible for setting up the advertising for a sale? _____
   If no, ask who is. _____

5. Are you responsible for implementing the sale in the store? _____
   If no, ask who is. _____
   [If the user answers no to questions 3, 4, and 5, explain that we want to observe the actual people who do the tasks. Explain that we would like to set up the visits with the people who do the tasks. Can he or she help to facilitate those visits? If no, ask if you can speak to anyone who is able to facilitate the visits? Or if the answer is still no and it's clear this person does not want to take part, thank them politely for their time and end the call.]
   [If the individual you are speaking with answers yes to question 3, 4, or 5, ask the following questions as appropriate.]

6. Is there more than one person in the store who handles sales? _____
   If yes, ask if each department handles its own sales. _____

7. How many years' experience do you have deciding on sales? Less than one? _____ One to three? _____ More than three? _____
   [Check your grid again. Do you have at least one person with this level of experience for the size store? If no, continue the questions. If yes, fill in the person's name in the grid and continue the questions.]

8. How many years' experience do you have handling sale advertising? Less than one? _____ One to three? _____ More than three? _____
   [Check your grid again. Do you have at least one person with this level of experience for the size store? If no, continue the questions. If yes, fill in the person's name in the grid and continue the questions.]

9. How many years' experience do you have implementing a sale? Less than one? _____ One to three? _____ More than three? _____
   [Check your grid again. Do you have at least one person with this level of experience for the size store? If no, continue the questions. If yes, fill in the person's name in the grid and continue the questions.]
   [If the person does not fit on the grid because all the space for this experience level are filled in, explain what is needed and ask if anyone else in the store has more or less experience. If no, explain the problem, thank the person, ask if you can call back in case of a cancellation, and end the call.]

Figure 7-10 Example screening questionnaire for the SuperSales visits. (Continued)

10. Do you currently use a computer in your work? _____
   If no, do you use a computer at home or did you use one on a previous job? _____
   If yes, what do you use the computer to do? _____
   _____

11. Do you consider yourself a beginning, medium level, or expert computer user?
   If medium or expert, what type of computer software do you ordinarily use?
   _____

Once you have completed the questions, consult your schedule list and establish a date and time for the site visit. Explain that you will send a letter confirming the visit, explaining the purpose of the study, and explaining the agenda for the visit.

If the person has further questions, tell him or her that _____ will answer their questions. Check to see if _____ is immediately available. If not, explain that _____ will call back with more information. Establish a time for _____'s return call.

Figure 7-10 Example screening questionnaire for the SuperSales visits. (Continued)

SCREENING GRID (USER/TASK MATRIX)

We need at least one person in each of the 27 categories. If possible, we want to have a variety of experience levels at the same locations to minimize travel.

Task	Store size		
	Medium (40,000 to 50,000 sq. ft.)	Large (50,000 to 90,000 sq. ft.)	Super (170,000 to 240,000 sq. ft.)
Sale decisions	<1	<1	<1
	1-3	1-3	1-3
	3+	3+	3+
Advertising	<1	<1	<1
	1-3	1-3	1-3
	3+	3+	3+
Implementing	<1	<1	<1
	1-3	1-3	1-3
	3+	3+	3+

Figure 7-11 A screening grid (user/task matrix) for the SuperSales visits.

Offer an incentive if you need to

In most cases you'll want to bring a small thank-you present to give to the people you work with at the end of the site visit (see figure 7-12). You don't need to tell people about thank-you presents when you are recruiting them.

Figure 7-12 You might need to offer an incentive to compensate users for their time.

However, you may need to offer a more substantial incentive to get people to allow you into their homes or offices. If you do that, you'll want to tell them about the incentive when you are recruiting them and setting up visits.

Whether an incentive is appropriate, what form it should take, and how large it should be depend on the situation. We can't give you definitive rules.

 On one project, Ginny worked with an organization whose customers were eager to have people visit. The users at those customer shops are all on salary, not on commission. They are in a somewhat captive market niche where they have to use Ginny's client's software to accomplish some of their tasks. So a new version of the software is of great interest to them. In the past, customers have willingly come to meetings at Ginny's client's headquarters at their own expense. So they did not expect compensation when usability teams from the organization came to observe and listen to them at their own sites.

On a different project, however, Ginny worked with an organization that is in an industry where many users of Ginny's client's software are or used to be on commission. Users who work on commission lose money if a site visit keeps them from doing as much work as they

otherwise would. Even though Ginny and the usability team from the client found during the site visits that today many of the users are on salary, not commission, the mentality in the industry is such that offering money was a necessary incentive.

When they were conducting studies of how trained technicians used medical diagnostic equipment, JoAnn's team at Comtech found they had to pay the technicians' regular hourly rate. The best way to find technicians to visit was temporary placement agencies, since most technicians in this field worked as independents through the agencies. Paying the users their regular fee was essential to getting their full participation.

If the users are employees of the company that is developing the software and doing the site visits, only a thank-you present is usually needed. If the users are on commission or otherwise losing an opportunity to make money during the time you are with them, you should probably plan to pay them for their time.

If you are going to pay people, your accounting department may prefer that you use petty cash rather than asking for checks. If you don't want to carry a lot of cash, consider gift certificates as described in the list at the end of this section. If you are using cash or a gift certificate, put it in an envelope or a "thank-you" card. Don't just hand cash to users. Even though you are compensating them for their time, they usually see it more as a gift than as payment.

If you are going to offer money to a user who is an employee in another company and who is using company time for the site visit, check out that arrangement with the user's supervisor or manager before you recruit and before you tell the user what to expect. You may find that in small businesses, at least, the business owner thinks the company should be compensated and not the individual user who is participating in the site visit.

If the users are going out of their way to work with you, as families are to let you into their homes, you probably need to offer an incentive. Dray and Mraczek (1996a) found that bringing dinner to their home visits worked very well both in the United States and in Europe (France and Germany). Dinner was a gift so the family didn't need to cook; eating with the family provided time at the beginning of the visit to develop rapport. Dray and Mraczek also report that they gave each family an honorarium, although they don't say how much it was.

If you are going to do site visits in other cultures, check with people who know the users' culture to be sure the incentive you plan will be well received and not taken as an insult. Sometimes their perceptions are wrong: the European market research firms that did the recruiting for Dray and Mraczek's study were initially skeptical of the researchers' idea of bringing food as part of the incentive, but the dinners were well received and appreciated. Nonetheless, it is always a good idea to check the cultural appropriateness of your plans for the site visits, including your planned incentives.

Other incentives you can offer, besides money, include

- company products such as software or hardware, which would cost the user much more to buy than it costs you to provide from inside the company

- technical help at the end of the visit

- gift certificates through a credit card company, which you charge but which are equal to cash for the user

- dining certificates, which are good at many restaurants in the user's area

Data collection techniques

Part of your site visit plan should be to consider how you are going to collect the data. Select techniques that will get you the data you need to answer your questions, provide information on your issues, and meet your objectives. (See chapter 6 for an extensive discussion of different techniques you can use.)

A variety of data collection techniques are planned for the SuperSales case study (see figure 7-13). The team will send out a demographic questionnaire to gather basic information about the participants in the study. A sample of this questionnaire appears in chapter 8. They also want to include observations about the environments in the various stores they visit since they suspect that environmental issues will be critical to introducing computers into the process. They want to bring all the participants together for a workflow analysis so that they clearly understand how tasks are spread among staff members and how information is shared.

Following the workflow analysis, in which all the participants are together with the site visit team, the team members will meet individually with each of the participants to observe their individual activities. Under the best circumstances, the participants will actually have a sale to arrange while the team members are present. However, the team members are prepared to ask them to run through their individual processes in a role-playing exercise.

The team plans to audiotape the sessions and take some pictures but not use videotape. They decided that videotaping would be too intrusive in the store environment, especially since there will be customers present.

DATA COLLECTION TECHNIQUES

We will use these techniques:

- demographic questionnaires for each participant to enhance our user profiles
- environmental protocol (list of points to observe) for each location
- process analysis in groups to understand the workflow from the decision to have a sale through implementation
- observation and concurrent discussion (contextual inquiry) with each person as he or she does part of the workflow (decision making, planning advertising, implementing the sale)
- audiotaping of all discussions for later analysis
- pictures with a still camera for user and environmental profiles
- notetaking on observers' forms

Figure 7-13 Data collection techniques planned for the SuperSales site visits.

Combine techniques in one visit, if appropriate

One site visit may include several different techniques. You may do contextual inquiries, watching, listening, and talking with users as they work, and also do interviews with other people, such as managers, at the site. If you are trying to understand users' current work processes, you probably want to come away with both a process map and a more detailed understanding of parts of the process. You would therefore combine workflow analysis and contextual inquiries. If users have examples of work from situations that had come up in the past, you may want to combine contextual inquiries of the work happening today with artifact-driven interviews about work that had produced those other examples.

If you are trying to understand how users work with documentation and their future documentation needs, you probably want to both observe and interview them. You want to pay particular attention to uses of documentation as well as times when they could have but didn't go to documentation. You want to make note of all user-constructed documentation from sticky notes around the computer to what they print out that they could have read online to the individual user manuals they create for themselves. If they are willing to share their individual documentation with you, collect copies of as many of these artifacts as you can. When you cannot get copies, you might be able to capture pictures of them with a video or still camera. Pictures of users' computers festooned with sticky note reminders may be the best way to convince those who do not go on the site visits of the need for better documentation or a more intuitive interface.

Lay out a schedule of what you will do during the visit

Although lots of things may interrupt your plans and make you change what you do during a site visit, you should have a tentative plan for how you and the users will spend the time during your site visit. Knowing what to do at different times helps structure the experience for the site visit team. However, don't overstructure the experience. Remaining flexible is a key to successful site visits.

In figure 7-14, you see a tentative schedule for the visits to the supermarkets. The team has several activities planned and definite ideas about what will happen during the visit.

The following is a tentative schedule for each visit. We expect to be flexible and to find that in many, if not all, site visits, we may have to deviate from this plan, but we hope to accomplish all the activities on it during our time at the location. Breaks will occur as needed at people's convenience. Logical breaks would come in between activities.

SCHEDULE FOR EACH VISIT

Time	Activity
5 minutes	Greet store manager, go over plans for visit
10 minutes	Greet all participants together, go over plans for visit; set up equipment
one hour	Do process analysis of overall workflow
one hour	Observe and interview person who decides on sales
one hour	Observe and interview person who does advertising
one hour	Observe and interview person who implements sales
10 minutes	Thank all; distribute gift certificates

NOTES ON SCHEDULE

• At the beginning of individual session with each participant, the person who is doing interviewing (not note taking) will go over the demographic questionnaire with the participant.

• The notetaker on the team will be responsible for filling out the environmental protocol during the visit.

• Depending on our starting time, the schedule might include a break for lunch. The lunch time may be used for additional discussion with the participants and perhaps with others in similar roles at the store.

• If we find that all participants are in the same general area and we will be able to thank them all together at the end of the visit, we will distribute gift certificates then. If we find that we will not see the participants again after the time with them, we will distribute the gift certificates at the end of each individual session.

Figure 7-14 Plan what you expect to do throughout the site visit.

Summary

In this chapter we've helped you build the first several parts of a site visit plan, covering the decisions you need to make about issues and objectives, participants, locations, schedules, recruiting, and data collection techniques.

In the next chapter we continue building the site visit plan with ideas for you on team building and training, materials, media, and data analysis and reporting.

References cited in the chapter

Dray, Susan and Mrazek, Deborah, A day in the life of a family: An international ethnographic study, in *Field Methods Casebook for Software Design*, edited by Dennis Wixon and Judith Ramey, NY: John Wiley & Sons, 1996a, 145–156.

Ehn, Pelle, Scandinavian design: On participation and skill, in *Participatory Design: Principles and Practices*, edited by Douglas Schuler and Aki Namioka, Hillsdale, NJ: Lawrence Erlbaum Associates, 1993, 41–77.

Mitropoulos-Rundus, David and Muszak, Jerry, How to design and conduct a consumer in-home usability test, *Common Ground*, 7 (2), April 1997b: 1, 8–14, 19.

Muller, Michael J., and Kuhn, Sarah, Eds., Special issue on participatory design, *Communications of the ACM*, 36 (4), June 1993.

Redish, Janice C. and James, Janice, Going to the users: How to set up, conduct, and use a user and task analysis for (re)designing a major computer system, *Proceedings of the Fifth Annual Conference UPA '96*, Dallas, TX, Usability Professionals' Association, 1996.

Wood, Larry E., The ethnographic interview in user-centered work/task analysis, in *Field Methods Casebook for Software Design*, edited by Dennis Wixon and Judith Ramey, NY: John Wiley & Sons, 1996, 35–56.

Other books and articles for further reading

Dumas, Joseph S. and Redish, Janice C., *A Practical Guide to Usability Testing*, Greenwich, CT: Ablex, 1993.

Mitropoulos-Rundus, David and Muszak, Jerry, Criteria for determining if consumer "in-home" usability testing is feasible for your product, *Common Ground*, 7 (1), January 1997a: 10–12.

Rubin, Jeffrey, *Handbook of Usability Testing*, NY: John Wiley & Sons, 1994.

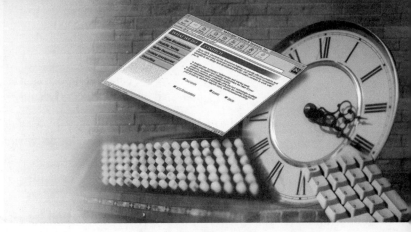

8

Preparing for the site visits

To ensure the success of your visits to users, you and your team members must be well prepared. It is not enough simply to schedule a visit and arrive. You must make careful plans to ensure that the right people are available and that you have selected the best techniques to answer your questions. You must also ensure that you will be able to gather the type of information you need once your arrive. Careful preparation ensures that you make best use of your users and their valuable time.

By coming prepared with an agenda that includes what you want to observe, what questions you need answers to, and what activities will assist the analysis, you will ensure that you use the time most productively. As you prepare for the visits, you are likely to make hypotheses about user behaviors and characteristics that you will want to test, in addition to noticing behaviors and characteristics that you did not anticipate. By defining your hypotheses up front and observing or staging events that will help you prove or disprove them, you will be able to tell the differences between expected behaviors and those that are truly unusual.

In chapter 7 we introduced the site visit plan and covered the first six elements of the plan (issues and objectives, participants, locations, schedule, recruiting, and data collection techniques). In this chapter, we cover the last four elements:

- organizing and training the team

- preparing the materials

- selecting the media to use to gather data

■ analyzing the data and reporting it to all the team members and others interested in the results of the study

At the end of the chapter is the complete site visit plan, which brings together all the pieces you have seen during this discussion.

Issues to consider as you prepare

As you prepare for the site visits, consider what you need to have ready to make the visits a success:

■ **Site visit team(s).** Who should go? How many people should attend? What roles should the team members assume? Note taker, taping person, watching the red light? What is the role of the user? Do you need or want more than one team? How will you train the team?

■ **Materials.** What materials will you need to recruit participants and prepare for the site visits? What materials will the team need during the site visits? Prepared forms? Rating sheets? Note taking sheets? What will you plan to bring back? Your equipment? Sample artifacts?

■ **Media.** How do you plan to take notes and record observations? Will you use videotape? Audiotape? Will you take notes on a laptop computer? Paper and pencil? Prepared forms and notebooks? What else might you need to bring? Post-it notes? Paper? Flip-charts?

■ **Data analysis and reporting.** What will you do with the data? Will you write trip reports, plan debrief sessions? Who will expect feedback from you and when? How will you archive materials and other records?

These issues are discussed in detail in the next sections. Techniques for observing, including notetaking, are discussed in chapter 9.

Organizing the team

As you progress from creating your site visit plan to preparing for the visits, you will decide which members of your planning team or others are going to conduct the site visits. You definitely want the leader to have experience in conducting site visits. You want other team members who are learning to conduct visits and who are able to serve as note takers. You may also want to include developers, managers, marketers, or others who need to experience the users' environment firsthand. For political reasons, you may want to include some people who are skeptical about the usefulness of the visits. If you are a consultant, you may be training a client team or may want to ensure that client representatives attend at least some of the site visits so that they have greater ownership of the results.

As you select people to participate in the site visits consider people who are empathetic, not intimidating. Team members should have good people skills, especially if they assume the role of administrator. You need good listeners on your team, and people who are able to establish rapport quickly with the users.

Figure 8-1 describes the team make up for the SuperSales case study. Note that the team is led by the usability specialist who is experienced in doing field studies and is responsible for training the other observers.

The Senior Usability Specialist will go on all the site visits. Two people from Information Systems (IS) and one from Human Resources (HR) will also participate in the study. Each site-visit team will include two people, the Senior Usability Specialist and one IS or HR person. The entire team of four people will work together to develop the Observer's Notebook and other materials for the site visits. The Senior Usability Specialist will hold a training session for the other team members, and the training session will be open to other interested IS and HR staff who might want to participate in future site visits or usability evaluations. The time and location of the training will be announced over e-mail, and registration for the training will be handled through HR.

Figure 8-1 The team make up for the SuperSales case study.

The team leader

The individual who leads the team should have experience doing field studies, or at least experience doing usability testing. To do a field study, you need training to know what to look for, how to ask questions, how to interact with users, and more. The team leader may be a usability specialist or may be a developer or information designer who has been trained by a usability specialist in the techniques of site visits. If you do not have any expertise in-house, you may want to consider hiring a usability specialist who will lead the visits and train you and your staff to do later studies on your own.

Two-person teams

The ideal for a site visit is a two-person team, one to lead the interaction with the user and the other to record what has happened. The lead role is similar to the role of the usability test administrator. The second role is similar to the role of the data collector in usability testing. User site visits can be conducted with only one person if absolutely necessary, but one is less desirable. When you are working alone, you cannot possibly observe everything that is going on, particularly if you are trying to take notes, observe, and ask questions.

Even if you are in the lead on the site visit, you'll find it extremely helpful to have someone with you to take notes, make independent observations, and discuss what you each observed.

Larger teams

Teams larger than two may present logistics problems. Too many people at a customer site might interfere with the customer's business and create traffic jams. A larger group may also have difficulty adequately observing what is going on in the user's environment. If you must support the involvement of a larger team of people, consider alternating the team roles and having more than one team working simultaneously, either at the same site or at different sites.

Multiple teams

Multiple teams will, of course, enable you to visit more user sites in less time. You lose the consistency of observation that occurs with a single team, but consistency is not always the most important parameter to take into account. The politics of participation in site visits should also be part of your planning strategy. You want to have the right people out there to see what users are really doing. A user site visit sometimes has the affect of changing the views of otherwise unsympathetic designers.

At the same time, you don't want to have too many observers or you won't have enough comparable data. Since you are looking for repeated patterns of user behavior, a few observers are more likely to notice patterns than if every visit is conducted by a different team. If you are training team members, we recommend pairing an experienced observer with a less experienced observer during the first two or three visits. Only then should the less experienced observers be paired to conduct visits together.

Roles of the team members

It is critical that developers and technical writers who serve on the site visit team understand that they are there to listen and learn, not to show off how much they know or to show users what to do. In chapter 10 we discuss how to keep your body language neutral but interested and how to ask questions that get useful information without biasing the user. You will find that the usefulness of a site visit can be called into question if team members do not conduct themselves properly.

Cultural issues for teams

We would like to believe that the teams handling the user site visits will be viewed impersonally by the users, but that may not always be the case. You will have to decide if you will ignore the cultural biases in your users' community or take them into account as you plan your team. In some user communities, because of ethnic, religious, or even professional or technical biases, women will have a difficult time as members of the site-visit team. You may not want to send women to interview men in countries that do not permit women to work in the same workplaces as men.

Even in Western countries, biases exist in the workplace that may make observations and interviews difficult. Age, gender, even dress and hair styles may, unfortunately, have to be considered. Your intention, you must keep in mind, is to be reasonably unobtrusive in the users' environment. Decide how to configure your team to make this possible.

On the other hand, you may also discover that your identification with your company or your status as a "researcher" may balance possible cultural biases. In Japan, where there are few professional women in the workplace, women with research credentials are treated with respect and politeness. Even being a foreigner can be an advantage. JoAnn has found that in Australia, users went out of their way to explain what is different or unique about how they work, especially in comparison to how "the Americans" do it.

Team dress

How you dress at your users' site is surprisingly important.

In one study, the team members wore what they thought was standard business dress. The users, however, were dressed very casually. They felt uncomfortable with the team members because their dress made them look like the feared auditors who visited unexpectedly several times a year.

Be certain that you choose a style of dress that will help you fit in with your users' environment, although you may not want to go much past "business casual" at most offices. If you are out in the field, however, be sure to dress for safety and comfort. That may mean slacks or even jeans for women, running or hiking shoes or even waterproof boots for everyone. You may even have to don special equipment at your users' site, including safety glasses, hardhats, steel-toed shoes, clean room clothing, and so on.

In some cultural environments, you may want to consult local customs about dress. Some cultures expect people to be dressed fairly formally, especially women. You may find that women need to avoid slacks and short sleeves or wear a head covering to be unobtrusive.

Interpreters

Visits to sites where people speak different languages than you speak will usually require an interpreter. Remember that an interpreter is not the same as a translator. An interpreter is able to speak for the users and for you, translating nearly simultaneously. A translator works on written text, a very different skill. When you look for an interpreter, use your contacts in the country to find professional services. Avoid using staff members of your in-country office. They aren't trained to be fast or neutral. If possible, find an interpreter who has some familiarity with the subject matter, especially if the users are very technical. You might even want to help the interpreter prepare by developing a glossary of terms you are likely to use.

If you are using an interpreter for the site visit, remember to account for the interpretation in your schedule. The conversations proceed much more slowly when they are conducted in two languages rather than one. You will most likely need extra time on site.

Avoiding defensiveness

If you are meeting with users who use existing versions of the product and its documentation, you may not want the original designers or writers to conduct the site visits unless you can trust them not to become defensive. If you have to include the actual designer, writer, or instructional designer, we recommend that you not tell the user. Users may hesitate to be frank if they are concerned about insulting the person who is interviewing them.

Everyone on the team should be very careful about becoming defensive about previous designs. It is difficult to remain neutral when someone is criticizing your work. However, a defensive posture will close down user conversation immediately. The user feels, and rightly so, that you are making excuses for an aspect of the design that presents them with significant problems. It is never a good idea to bring up company policies or politics that may indeed have kept you from implementing an effective design. You will find more about defensiveness in chapter 9.

Training the team

Conducting effective user site visits requires that the leader train and mentor team members. Team members need to be trained in the subject matter to be analyzed, observing and interviewing skills, note taking and other data collection techniques, and using the equipment.

Subject-matter knowledge

If team members do not know much about the subject of the inquiry, you may want to have them spend time talking with subject-matter experts in your organization, reviewing data gathered by marketing research or in previous studies, reading documentation and using software and hardware, and attending training classes to become familiar with the processes they will be observing and hearing about. The more you become familiar with the interests, personalities, and professional vocabularies of your users, the more credibility you will have and the easier it will be for you to establish rapport. If you are very ignorant about the users' field (and show it), users may feel that they are wasting their time trying to explain something to you. On the other hand, you also don't want to be so expert that you cannot see beyond your personal understanding of how the work "should" be performed. A certain amount of naiveté about the subject matter may in fact help you see what is really there. What we are trying to say is—there's a fine line between knowing too much before you go out and knowing too little.

JoAnn's team spent about 40 hours learning to use lab equipment to prepare for their site visits. They read the documentation for the existing equipment and competitors' equipment, read applications, talked to the client company's in-house experts, and practiced using the equipment themselves. One of the team members even spent a weekend with a friend, who used similar equipment, getting more instruction and practice. This training helped them understand what the users were talking about, understand the vocabulary used in the field, know how to run the equipment themselves in case of problems, and know how to clarify the problems they asked the users to run through. At the same, the team members were not experts. That meant they could ask "dumb" questions to get the users to explain what was really happening.

You may also decide, in some cases, that you cannot possibly develop the expertise you need to understand the users' tasks without the assistance of a subject-matter expert. When you recruit an expert to advise your team or join you on the site visits, be certain to make the expert's role clear. He or she should be there to assist you in understanding what the users are telling you, not to teach the users how to do their tasks properly.

Observing and interviewing

New team members may need training and practice in observing and interviewing before the site visits. As a starting point, you may want everyone to attend a workshop on conducting site visits or even one on conducting usability tests. A consultant hired to conduct the workshop might also serve as a coach to the team.

Team members might conduct mock site visits with other team members or in-house staff under the watchful eye of the coach or the experienced team leader. You could videotape each team member and then have everyone critique the videotapes. Team members might participate in usability testing, taking notes or learning to serve as test administrators. Team members will, of course, continue to learn throughout the actual visits by observing the team leader and coach and then being observed in turn.

Learning to use the equipment

Team members also need to be certain that they know how to operate all the data-gathering equipment they will take on the site visits. They need to check out video and still cameras and tape recorders and practice using them. If the equipment is complicated, they may need to have a short class conducted by an equipment expert. We have seen unfamiliar equipment completely ruin a visit. Avoid the problems through adequate training and practice.

Materials for the site visits

Developing the site visit plan and the materials, including the observers' notebook, discussed later in this chapter, is one of the best methods we know to prepare the team members for specific site visits. We use notebook development as a primary training tool for the site visits. The exercise of creating the site visit plan and the notebook allows team members to reach a consensus about what is to be learned.

Preparing the materials

Preparing materials carefully and in advance of your visits will provide you with greater consistency across site visits, help to prepare your team for the visits, direct their focus on the issues you want to study, and save you time later in analyzing your results. Without a well-crafted plan in place, you will find yourself going on fishing expeditions, hoping to catch something useful along the way.

You will need to create three types of material in preparation for your customer study:

- material to use during recruiting and as preparation for the site visits

- material for the team to use during the site visits (the observer's notebook)

- material to be used to facilitate information gathering

What materials will you need during recruiting and advance preparation?

Part of your site visit plan should include a list of all the materials that you have to remember to gather and take with you. In fact, you should make a checklist of those materials and have copies in the travel folder that you actually use each time you go out. These materials should include

- letters of introduction explaining the purpose of your visit

- formal agreements to be signed by appropriate management

- demographic questionnaires to be completed by participants before you arrive

- videotaping and audiotaping release forms

- confidentiality agreements

All of these documents and others will help you set the right tone for your visits and ensure that the right people and information will be there when you arrive.

Letter of introduction

As you continue your discussions with people at potential user sites, you will often be asked for a formal written description of your study. Individual participants must inform their managers of the study; managers must often obtain permission from senior management or company headquarters. They will need a statement to transmit to others involved in the decision making.

Your statement should be brief, stating

- the purpose of the study

- the outcomes expected

- the kinds of people you want to meet

- the kinds of tasks you want to observe

- how long you will be on site

- how much time you expect to spend with each individual

- what feedback you will provide to the customers about the results of the study

- what equipment you will be using on site

- what assistance, if any, you will require from the customer

Suggest that your participant use the letter to communicate to management or to staff, as appropriate. Also volunteer to call managers or staff to answer any questions they may have. You are trying to convince people that it will be in their best interest to assist in the study. Be upbeat about the study but be scrupulously honest about the impact of your visit. You do not want to raise expectations that you cannot meet. Be sure that your letter also makes it clear that you are not trying to sell anyone anything.

Figure 8-2 is an example of the letter of introduction used for the supermarket study.

LETTER OF INTRODUCTION

Dear //person's name//:

Thank you for agreeing to participate in our supermarket study. The purpose of the study is to help us understand how you and your staff handle food item sales. We are just beginning the process of designing new computer software that will help store personnel to decide which items to put on sale, arranging in-store and external advertising for the sale, and implementing all the logistics required to ensure that the sale is handled smoothly. The outcomes of the study will help us ensure that the software meets your needs and the needs of your staff.

We hope to spend one shift, either morning or afternoon, at your store. During that time, we hope to observe you and your staff as you perform three tasks:

- deciding which items to include in a sale

- setting up the advertising for a sale

- implementing the logistics for a sale

If possible, we hope to observe and talk with those who perform these tasks at your store location. We hope that our observations will not interfere with anyone getting their tasks done. However, we want to spend the first hour with the entire team so that we can learn about the whole workflow of setting up a sale. Then we will spend no more than one hour with each participant.

It is especially important that we meet with _____, who you have indicated is a new assistant manager and has never handled a sale before. _____ will help us understand how the new computer system needs to support new users as well as more experienced managers like yourself.

As we mentioned, we will be taking notes on our observations and taking still pictures of the work areas. We also will want to audiotape each person performing their tasks individually. We will bring release forms for each person who will be photographed and audiotaped to sign.

We hope that you will be interested in helping us test the new software as it is designed. Your assistance will be invaluable to ensuring the system's success in your store.

As we mentioned, we will bring gift certificates for each participant we work with.

Thank you again for your generous cooperation. Please feel free to call me at //phone number// or _____ at //phone number// if you have any other questions. We'll be calling you on _____ to schedule the visit.

Sincerely,

//Your name// Head of the study team

Figure 8-2 Sample of a letter of introduction for the SuperSales case study.

Formal statements of agreement

In some situations you will need to provide a formal statement of agreement for the signature of the responsible manager in the users' organization. You may be able to use your letter of introduction as an agreement by adding a signature page at the end. Or you may need to prepare a separate statement, as shown in figure 8-3. Once again, keep the statement simple, straightforward, and nonthreatening. Always give the user an opportunity to cancel the visit if necessary. Include provisions to reschedule the time of the visit. Remember that your customers are taking time out of a busy schedule to accommodate your request. Be certain to make clear that you will accommodate their needs as much as you can and yet maintain the integrity of the study.

STATEMENT OF AGREEMENT

I agree that our store will participate in the sales process study. We understand that the information will be used to judge feasibility and to design and develop software to assist the sales process. Our participation will enable the development group to obtain a thorough understanding of what we do today and how we do it.

Name

Signature

Date

Figure 8-3 Sample letter of agreement for the SuperSales case study.

Demographic questionnaire

A demographic questionnaire allows you to confirm the characteristics you identified when you initially screened the users. It also allows you to gather additional information that will help you associate particular tasks and behaviors with categories of users. For example, you might want to know more about the types of equipment your users have had experience using. A questionnaire with check-off boxes listing possibilities, with space to add more, will help you identify if your customers have the same, more, or less experience than you expected.

In one case study, JoAnn was interested in learning if users had previous experience analyzing print production problems. In the questionnaire, users were asked about the types of problems they had dealt with in the past. This experience was then compared with the strategies that they used to solve a troubleshooting problem with the new product.

You may want the users you intend to visit to complete the demographic questionnaire before the visit. If the questionnaire is completed earlier, you don't have to spend precious observation time asking users to complete it. You also have an opportunity to review the data, compare it with your earlier assumptions, and make adjustments to your field study plan.

We recommend sending the questionnaire by e-mail or fax so that you are certain it has been received. Send the questionnaire a few days before the visit, check to ensure that it has been received, and verify that it has been completed on schedule. Occasionally we ask users to have the questionnaire ready when we arrive. Then we spend a few minutes at the beginning of the observation and interview reviewing the information. Often the questionnaire information may lead us to ask questions of the individual that were not in our original plan. Just in case, take additional copies of the questionnaire with you to replace lost, misplaced, or forgotten forms.

You may, of course, decide to use the questionnaires as an activity during your visit. If so, carry them with you and hand them out at the time in your schedule when you think they will be most useful. We often hand them out at the beginning of the visit so that we will have the information to consider later.

Also consider having several people at a single site complete the demographic questionnaire even if you are interviewing only one. The additional demographic information may be useful for comparisons and contain ideas for future studies.

The questions for the demographic questionnaire shown in figure 8-4 come from the original issues and objectives you determined for your site visit. They reflect what you want to learn about your users, such as their previous experience with computers, their experience with the subject matter, and their job history. The answers to the questions should assist you in profiling your users according to issues that are related to your interface design.

Photograph, videotape, and audiotape release forms

Remember that you must have written permission to photograph or tape both from customers and employees. Be sure that users know that you plan to photograph or videotape before you go and confirm that they will give you permission. You must have permission and a signed release form to photograph or videotape anyone or even to audiotape a conversation.

When recruiting users and again when you get on site, explain that the videotape allows you to go back and review what happened because, of course, you won't capture everything in your notes. The videotape is also to show other people who are developing the new release, the new application, or the documentation how users do their work. You must assure users that you will not use their full names, that you usually show just snippets of tapes, that you usually show several

DEMOGRAPHIC QUESTIONNAIRE

Thank you for participating in our project to understand how you plan, advertise, and implement a food item sale at your store. To help us better understand your activities and experience, please take a few minutes to complete this questionnaire. Please fax the questionnaire back to us at least one day before our scheduled visit on _____. The fax number is //fax number//.

Name _____ Store name _____

Position held in store _____ Years in this position _____

Previous positions held in this store or other stores Years in this position _____

_____

_____

_____

1. Do you make decisions about which items will go on sale?

Yes ☐   No ☐

If, yes, how often?

Daily ☐   Several times a week ☐   Once a week ☐   Other ☐

How long have you been doing this task? _____

2. Do you plan and set up the advertising for the sale?

Yes ☐   No ☐

If, yes, how often?

Daily ☐   Several times a week ☐   Once a week ☐   Other ☐

How long have you been doing this task? _____

3. Do you set up the internal logistics for the sale?

Yes ☐   No ☐

If, yes, how often?

Daily ☐   Several times a week ☐   Once a week ☐   Other ☐

How long have you been doing this task? _____

4. Do you use a computer at your job?

Yes ☐   No ☐

If yes, how often do you use the computer?

Daily ☐   Several times a week ☐   Once a week ☐   Other ☐

Figure 8-4 Sample demographic questionnaire for the SuperSales case study.

5. If no, do you use a computer at home?

Yes ☐   No ☐

If yes, how often do you use the computer?

Daily ☐   Several times a week ☐   Once a week ☐   Other ☐

6. As a computer user, do you consider yourself

Very experienced ☐   Experienced ☐   Moderate user ☐   Beginner ☐

7. Do you use word processing software?

Yes ☐   No ☐

8. Do you use spreadsheet software?

Yes ☐   No ☐

9. Do you use a database?

Yes ☐   No ☐

10. What is your favorite business-related software? _____

11. What do you like about it?_____

Figure 8-4 Sample demographic questionnaire for the SuperSales case study. (Continued)

different users doing the same thing. You must also assure them that you will never have a public showing of the tapes; they will only be used internally by the development team. In our experience, very few users refuse to be videotaped. Once the tape is set up and rolling and users are doing their work, they quickly forget about the videotape.

In most cases you will have little problem obtaining signatures on photograph, video, and audiotape release forms (see figure 8-5). But in some cases, especially at customer locations, individuals and managers may have concerns about allowing photographs or taping. You should always mention your intent to tape in your letter of introduction and reiterate your intent in discussions you have with people at the site. If you sense any hesitation, it may be best to send the release forms in advance so they can be reviewed and discussed. You do not want to take the chance of arriving with taping equipment only to learn that your users are unwilling to be taped or have been refused permission by their managers.

One of the responsibilities of the lead observer in the team should be to ensure that the release forms are signed and collected. You also do not want to find yourself with several hours of tape that you cannot use because you've forgotten to obtain the required releases.

PHOTOGRAPH RELEASE FORM

If permitted, //company name// will photograph your work area. Photographs will aid us in analyzing your work environment and making recommendations for improving //name the product//.

//company name// will use site visit photographs for internal purposes only. //company name// will not disclose the names of participants or their companies in relation to their comments, experiences, criticisms, or suggestions.

Please read the following statements and ask site visit facilitators any questions you may have. Indicate that you understand and agree to the conditions stated in this form by signing and dating below.

❏ I give //company name// permission to photograph myself and my workspace during the site visit. I understand that the photographs will be used in //company name// analysis and recommendations and that my name and my company's name will not be associated with my comments or discussions of company affairs.

❏ At the completion of the site visit all photographs will remain in //company name// possession. //company name// may use the photographs for future analysis with no obligation to me. The photographs will not be used for commercial advertising.

❏ I have been given the opportunity to ask questions and have had my questions answered to my satisfaction.

Participant's Signature

//company name// Representative

//company name// Representative

date

Figure 8-5 Sample of a photo release form.

Confidentiality or nondisclosure agreement

In some cases you may need to ask your users to keep the information you discuss with them confidential. Confidentiality is needed when you are developing a completely new product or service and want to ensure that competitors don't learn what you're doing. If information is very confidential, you may want to consider hiring an outside firm to conduct the user studies without reference to your company's name. User companies may also ask you to sign confidentiality agreements as well. They need to protect the confidential information you are likely to learn during the site visit from disclosure. Figure 8-6 shows a typical confidentiality agreement.

CONFIDENTIALITY AGREEMENT

//company name// is obligated to keep information about its clients and products confidential. All site visit participants must sign this confidentiality agreement.

Please read the following statements and ask the site visit facilitators any questions you may have. Indicate that you understand and agree to the conditions stated in this form by signing and dating below.

❏ I understand that I will see unannounced //company name// products and product ideas during this site visit. I will not discuss unannounced product ideas with anyone outside //company name//, or with any employee of my company not authorized to know that particular information.

❏ I will not disclose to anyone outside //company name//, or to any employee of this company not authorized to know that particular information, any confidential information relating to other site visit participants, their companies, their views, or their activities.

❏ I will not attempt to obtain information confidential to //company name// that I have not been authorized to obtain.

❏ I have been given the opportunity to ask questions and have had my questions answered to my satisfaction.

Participant's Signature

//company name// Representative

//company name// Representative

date

Figure 8-6 Sample of a confidentiality agreement.

What materials will you need for the team to use during the site visits?

To prepare your team for the site visits requires a variety of guidelines, documents, and forms, collected into an observers' notebook. The notebook contains

- a restatement of the goals and objectives of the study (from the site visit plan)
- guidelines for observing, asking questions, staging events, role playing, and others
- forms to be completed by or with the customers, including question-and-answer forms, opinion surveys, and mechanisms for ranking choices

In addition to preparing the team for the site visits, the observers' notebook is used for collecting data about user tasks and is critical to the success of the field study. It must be carefully designed and developed with the participation of all the team members. Creating the documents that make up the observers' notebook is a critical part of the training for your team. By creating the documents, you reach consensus about the nature of the study and how team members will conduct themselves at the user sites. The process of putting the observers' notebook together is as important as the notebook documents themselves.

Observers' notebook

Use the opportunity in building your observers' notebook for observers to establish the focus of your site visits and to educate your team. To create the guidelines, go back to your site visit plan and review the list of questions you would like to have answers to. Consider how you will answer these questions through observations and interviews. In your site visit plan, you have already indicated the techniques that you feel are most appropriate for gathering the information you need.

You will want to observe users performing a task they ordinarily work on. For example, in a study of the check-in/check-out process in a library, the team may want to observe the process through the day, including peak hours and slow times. During parts of the observation, the team may have a series of questions prepared that they want to ask the librarians or assistants who are working at the check-in desk. During slow periods or in another location, they may want to ask critical-incident questions about especially memorable situations that have occurred at other times but which they have not had an opportunity to observe.

In the sample notebook in figure 8-7, the observers want to learn how the users go through the process of deciding on advertising and implementing a sale. The guidelines are designed to remind the team to observe the entire process workflow and note the sequence of activities before they interview individual users. They are also to observe and inquire about the decisions that led the users to adopt a particular course of action.

SuperSales Systems

Site Visit Study

Observers' Notebook

Date:_____

Customer visited: _____

Facilitator:_____

Observer:_____

Figure 8-7 Sample observers' notebook for the SuperSales study.

GOALS AND OBJECTIVES

Before each site visit, review the goals and objective of the project.

PURPOSE

The purpose of the site visits is to learn about the potential users, their workflow, and their tasks in preparation for designing the new SuperSales system, including the user interface and the underlying system design.

GOALS

- to identify the Supermarket personnel who are involved in the process of identifying items for sale, advertising the sale, and implementing the sale

- to understand the workflow from the initial decision to hold a sale through the completion of the sale and the analysis of sale results

- to identify the objects currently associated with the sale process, including forms, cheat sheets, calculators, advertising copy and layout, signage, and so on

- to understand the procedures used by each staff member involved in the sale process

- to understand the mental model that the users bring to the complete process

- to understand how individuals involved in the sale process interact with one another

OBJECTIVES

The primary objective of this project is to understand how the supermarket sale process is currently done. To meet this objective, we will consider the following questions:

- Which personnel are involved in the process from start to end? How different are the personnel in each store visited?

- Where and how is the sale process initiated? What are the trigger events? How do these events differ under different circumstances?

- How is the decision made to place an item on sale? What parameters are involved in the decision-making process? What information does the decision maker use? Are any artifacts used in the decision-making process? Does one person make the decision, or does a group decide together or provide input to the decision? What alternatives are looked at?

Figure 8-7 Sample observers' notebook for the SuperSales study. (Continued)

- Once a sale item is selected, what happens next? Is advertising started? Inhouse changes started? What is the overall workflow and what variations exist in the workflow?

- How is the advertising process started? Who is responsible for in-store advertising? Who is responsible for external advertising? How are decisions made about doing one or the other? How much of the advertising design and writing is done in-store, at headquarters, by outside agencies? How is the cost of advertising figured into the process and the decision making?

- What is the internal process for implementing the sale? How is signage changed? Who makes the decisions? What decisions are made? Who is responsible for making the signs, putting them in place? How are the signs created?

- How are the price changes implemented in the signage and in the existing computer system? Who is responsible? Who signs off? Who actually makes the changes? How are the changes verified?

- How are the cashiers informed about the sale items? Are they alerted? If so, how? Do they need to know? What about the department personnel? Are they informed and in what way?

- What problems have occurred in the past with sale items? Critical incidents? Errors? Unhappy customers?

Figure 8-7 Sample observers' notebook for the SuperSales study. (Continued)

STORE MANAGER #1 //THIS SECTION WILL BE DUPLICATED IN THE WORKBOOK TO ACCOMMODATE ALL PERSONNEL TO BE INTERVIEWED DURING THE VISIT.//

Name _____

Store name _____

Job Title _____

Full time or part time _____

Store location and size _____

INTRODUCTION (PARTICIPANT'S BACKGROUND)

What are the participant's responsibilities within the store?

How long has the participant had this job?

How long has the participant been working in the store?

What other jobs has the participant had in this store?

What other jobs has the participant had in similar stores?

For how many years?

Does the participant have computer experience? What kind?

PC? Windows? Mouse? CD-ROM? Business software? Word processing? Spreadsheet?

How many years of computer experience

Does the participant use a computer at the store? What kind?

What tasks does the participant do with a computer in the store?

Figure 8-7 Sample observers' notebook for the SuperSales study. (Continued)

OBSERVING THE SALE PROCESS

The goal of this activity is to review the entire sale process with as many of the players as possible. Discuss with the store manager before the visit how you will schedule the joint session. You may have to meet early in the morning or late in the evening to get all the people involved to take part. The company is committed to the new system development, so the store managers have been given the OK to pay overtime as needed for this activity.

When you begin the session, ask the participants first to quickly identify the large parts of the tasks and who performs them in the store. Have the participants sketch these on the poster paper. Ask what tasks are done sequentially and what tasks can be done simultaneously. Ask if participants ever collaborate when they perform the tasks.

Then, ask each participant in the process, starting at the beginning, to sketch and explain what he or she does. Record the process on the poster paper. If possible, put the poster paper up on the walls so that everyone can see the process emerging.

Go through each participant until you have the entire process at a high level. Encourage discussion and additions as you go along.

Issues to discuss during the workflow analysis:

Who does each part of the task? Does this ever change? For what reasons?

How do parts of the whole workflow interrelate? Do people use information from previous steps in their part of the process?

INDIVIDUAL OBSERVATIONS

Schedule individual meetings with each participant. Ask to watch the participant perform his or her part of the overall process. If possible, watch an actual process rather than a demonstration.

- What is the goal of the task? How does the user state the goal? Is the goal for this task part of a higher-level company goal, like encouraging customers to come to the store more often or more regularly?

Figure 8-7 Sample observers' notebook for the SuperSales study. (Continued)

If direct observation is not possible, ask the user to describe the process he or she goes through to handle a part of the sale-item process. List problems encountered, troubleshooting approaches, etc. during the following three phases:

- Getting started: how does the process start? What is the trigger event? What problems can occur in getting started with the task?

- Main flow: what are the steps performed? What about exceptions? When do most problems occur? Describe a typical problem situation? (Keep going until you run out of problems.) Are any other people involved in assisting the user? Can you speak to them?

- Completing the task: how does the person decide the task is done? Where does it go next? Where do problems occur? Describe a typical problem situation. (Keep going until you run out of problems.)

- What has to happen for the task to be completed? Are there things that take place that aren't related to the goal?

- What conditions have to exist for the task to be successful? What information does the participant need to start with? Any documents? Other artifacts?

- Are there any artifacts that are used as part of the task? Ask if you can have examples. Be certain the user describes exactly how the artifact is used.

- Can the user identify the critical parts of the task? If these are missing, the task can't be started or completed.

- What are the business rules that control how the user does the task? What can they never do? What do they have to do?

Figure 8-7 Sample observers' notebook for the SuperSales study. (Continued)

Role playing or staged scenarios

The observers' notebook also provides your team with a set of activities to conduct at the user site which you decided on in the site visit plan. You need to obtain information about specific tasks. What actions are you going to ask people to perform? Will you suggest a particular set of activities or simply wait to see what happens?

In many cases you will not be able to observe all the activities you need to see if you simply wait for them to happen. You will save time in the investigation by suggesting some activities to the users. For example, if you want to know what happens when the librarians have a long line of people waiting to check books in and out, you may have to suggest that scenario. If you want to know what happens when the users open the box of new equipment, you may want to provide the box and observe them opening it.

What sequence are you going to use in your approach to the users? What will you ask them to show you? How will you ask them to proceed? Each of the activities should be outlined in your notebook for the field study.

Once the observers' notebook is prepared, we recommend that you review it with other people who are not part of the immediate team. Representatives from marketing, the rest of the development group, instructional designers, and technical communicators should be given an opportunity to review the plans. They are likely to assist your team in refining the material by adding and clarifying issues, and eliminating some issues from the list.

What materials will you need to facilitate information gathering?

As you prepare for your site visits, consider the media and equipment you are planning to take with you. The list might include

- video equipment: portable lab, camera and tripod, scan converter
- audio equipment, if separate from video equipment: microphones, cassette recorder
- regular still camera or digital camera (instead of or in addition to video)
- videotapes
- cassette tapes for audiotaping
- film for the still camera or disks for the digital camera
- cables
- power strip
- extension cord (that accommodates the types of plugs you have)

- converters and correct plugs (if going abroad)
- extra batteries for every piece of equipment that has batteries
- laptop with cords and extra battery
- diskettes for backing up files
- portable printer (if you want to print files while on the road)
- notebook, pens
- poster paper, colored markers, sticky notes (if you are going to create process flow diagrams with users in a conference room or with the team in a hotel room after the site visit)

The table in figure 8-8 illustrates the material list for the SuperSales study. Note that the team must indicate who is responsible for preparing the information, when it needs to be prepared, and who will review the materials before they are added to the observers' notebook.

Material	Person responsible	Date ready	Reviewer
Screening questionnaire	Name	Date	Name
Letter of introduction			
Schedule for teams			
Demographic questionnaire			
Environmental protocol			
Release forms			
Observers notebook with:			
goals and objectives			
schedule for each visit			
list of activities with guidelines			
observation and interview protocols for each role			
copies of forms			
Artifact log			
Site visit report template			

Figure 8-8 The list of materials for the SuperSales case study.

If you take no other visual recording equipment, consider a still camera, possibly an instant camera, to take pictures of the users and their environment. These informal portraits will serve as good reminders of users and their needs during the design process.

Make sure you have everything reserved well in advance. If you can't carry the equipment yourself, figure out how it will be shipped, who will receive it, and who will track it to see if it has arrived. Remember to keep your packing boxes to reuse when you return the equipment to the office.

Be certain to collect emergency call numbers you can use if equipment doesn't work. You may also want to find possible locations for repair at remote sites, as well as investigate the possibility of obtaining backup equipment.

Will you videotape? Audiotape?

Lugging equipment around, especially when traveling by air, is not fun. But pictures of the users' real environments and of real users at work are likely to be the most convincing data you bring back. If you have anyone to convince of users' needs, getting the video equipment to users' sites will be well worth the effort. Also, if you want to do a detailed task analysis at the level of developing flowcharts, you are likely to need the videotape later. You probably cannot capture enough detail in your notes to do a complete, detailed flowchart.

One organization used videotaping to record the user's actions because no observer was able to be present in the cockpit with a military jet pilot. They later reviewed the videotape with the pilot, a form of cued recall discussed in chapter 6. You will find videotaping especially useful when an action is difficult to observe. In other cases, researchers have used videotape to record a complex action so that they could slow the action and review the tape nearly frame by frame.

With today's portable labs that fit into a wheeled, carry-on suitcase, you can take even very sophisticated equipment fairly easily. See appendix B for a list of companies that assemble and sell portable lab equipment and figure 8-9 for a photo of a portable lab.

A portable lab is most important if you will need a scan converter to get a steady, clear picture of a computer screen. A scan converter lets you videotape a computer screen without the image rolling because of the difference in frames per second between the computer and the videocamera. Without a scan converter, you may be unable to see what you have spent so much time recording. If you don't need a scan converter, taking a camcorder (the one you have at home will do) and a tripod may well be enough.

Figure 8-9 This photo shows a portable lab. (Photo courtesy of Norm Wilcox Associates, Inc., Jefferson, Maryland.) See appendix B for information on vendors of portable labs.

Some situations do not lend themselves to being videotaped. In others, you must be sensitive to what you may or may not capture on the tape. If the users you are working with have customers who come to their sites, you may not want to include those customers in the videotape. You may want to stop taping when a customer comes in. If you do continue to tape, you must get a release form from the customer as well. For home visits, you should establish with each family what is off-limits to your video camera. [See David Mitropoulos-Rundus and Jerry Muczak (1997b) for more information about videotaping on home visits.]

When taking any type of recording equipment through an airport, be sure you have cables and plugs with you. You may need to turn on the equipment to get through security. If you plan to take recording equipment to another country, make sure it will work where you are going. Voltages differ. Outlets differ. In some countries, the type of plug you need may vary with each outlet in the room. The distance you have to go to get to an outlet may differ.

In some cultures you may not be permitted to take photographs or videotapes at all. Be certain to ask in advance to find out if there are cultural taboos at work.

Figure 8-10 shows the media plan for the SuperSales case study. Note the team has decided not to use videotape for the study because of the disturbance it is likely to cause in the environment.

Teams will use these media:

- large poster paper, markers, sticky notes for documenting process flow
- audiotape for all discussions (group discussion during process flow and contextual inquiries of individuals)
- still camera pictures of people and environment
- notetaking with laptop or paper, depending on team's and users' comfort

We will not use videotape for this study because of the environmental conditions. During the group discussion of a process analysis, videotaping would be difficult because we would need someone to move the videotape to capture the speaker. The artifact of the process diagram will serve as the record of that discussion.

We anticipate that in some stores, the individual conversations will take place in closed offices, but that in others, they will be in more open areas where videotaping would be considered an intrusion.

Figure 8-10 The media plan for the SuperSales case study.

Audiotaping

You may find audiotapes useful for recording information when it is impossible to videotape or if you are concerned that something might happen to the videotape and you will lose critical information. For example, the detailed conversations that occur in a call center between the service person and the customer may be audiotaped for later analysis. You might supplement the tape with your notes on the actions that the support person takes in finding information to assist in answering questions and solving problems.

Transcribing tapes

If you do make audiotapes or videotapes, you are likely to use the tapes only for spot checking what you observed. However, sometimes you want a detailed analysis of part or all of the tapes. In these cases, have the tapes transcribed by a transcribing service. You will rarely have time to review a tape in real time, but you may want to make notes on a transcription.

Tape recording your notes

If you find it difficult in the user's environment to take detailed notes, you may want to use a tape recorder to record your observations immediately after the visit. We often find that going out to the car and recording observations either with a tape recorder or by hand will facilitate remembering what has just happened.

It is vitally important to get a lot of information down immediately and thoroughly. You can't go back and recapture something that you have inadequate notes about. Most people later regret having too few notes, not having too many notes.

Using a laptop computer

One of the most useful tools may be your laptop computer. If you are a good touch typist, you can often type notes while watching users, something most of us cannot do with handwriting (not if we want to read it later). Using a laptop can help you take many more notes than you might take with handwritten notes. And the notes will be readable later. Don't worry about spelling—you can check that later when you turn the notes into a trip report.

On the other hand, you may find that typing is distracting to your users. Typing makes more noise and puts a screen between you and the user. Laptops also require power cords and outlets, which may be in short supply or inconvenient at your users' location. They often require that you have a surface to put them on, despite the name.

The best way to use a laptop computer or to take voluminous notes is to have one member of the team as a dedicated note taker. Then the person with the laptop sits in a less obtrusive location. In fact, we do not advise using a laptop if you are the only observer. The laptop makes note taking appear too formal and obtrusive.

Note taking

Note taking on paper is the simplest method to use and requires no equipment. A combination of paper and other techniques may be appropriate under certain circumstances, especially when you want to record the details of a task. As you plan your site visits, consider the nature of the tasks you want to observe and decide which method of note taking will work best under the circumstances.

The most critical issue will be the quality and completeness of the notes you take. Your goal should be to capture both the general feel of the user's environment and details about the performance of tasks. You may find that two different levels of inquiry require different levels of note taking:

- High-level analysis of users, tasks, and environments in which you are seeking to take away general impressions rather than specific performance details may lead to less formal note taking. Just be certain that you write legibly enough to interpret the writing later. You can use a free form of recording with a notepad, or you can take your notes directly in the spaces provided in your observers' notebook.

- Low-level analysis of user tasks, in particular, may require you to complete prepared forms that list actions, decisions, and circumstances surrounding the detailed performance of a task. In this case, you may still want to emphasize handwritten notes rather than trying to complete elaborate computer-based forms. You can fill out the computer forms later.

Deciding what you will do with the data

Just as your issues and objectives shape the focus of your site visit, your plans for analyzing and using the data shape what you collect, the detail required in the data you collect, and how you collect it. In the last section we reviewed the mechanics of data gathering and note taking while you are at the users' site. In this section we discuss briefly how best to preserve the data you have collected immediately upon completing the site visits and upon returning home. In chapter 11 we cover what to do with the data in more detail.

Debriefing team members

If two of you have attended a site visit, you will find it advantageous to debrief each other as soon as you leave the session with the users. Go over key points from your notes, discuss your observations, and make additional notes. Do not, under any circumstances, wait until you have completed several visits. You will find it difficult to remember what happened at each visit.

The SuperSales development team has carefully planned how they will handle the data they collect, as shown in figure 8-11. They plan to produce user profiles, environment profiles, process flow diagrams, task lists, detailed task flows, and procedural flow charts of the tasks they observe. Although they may decide on other data collection and analysis methods as the study proceeds, their initial plan helps them organize their note taking from the first.

Plan for a team meeting at the end of each day or two of visits. If other team members are nearby, invite them to attend. Discuss your observations, ask and answer questions, and discuss the conclusions you are beginning to draw. If the full development team is not participating in the site visits, you may want to schedule meetings with them by phone or in person to discuss preliminary results, especially if development is proceeding while the site visits are taking place.

Trip reports

Once you are away from the customer site, during the evening on a trip or immediately upon returning to the office, prepare a detailed trip report of each customer visit (see figure 8-12). Immediacy is important so that you still have a fresh memory of the events and can capture details. Enhance your report with still pictures, audio inserts, and video clips if you have the facilities to do so. Such an annotated report could be viewed online by others in the organization. The addition of other media will enhance the quality of the experience of reading the report. Sun Microsystems has had good experiences with presenting online, multimedia versions of usability reports. The same can and should be done with site visits.

Just as you might prepare data flow diagrams when you analyze the flow of information through a system, you may find it useful to sketch informal flow

DATA ANALYSIS AND REPORTING

To meet the objectives, we anticipate presenting our findings in these forms:

- user profiles, including information on job experience including overall time in the grocery business and time in the specific job, computer experience and attitudes towards using computers for this type of work, users' views of competencies needed to do this type of work

- environment profiles, including information on where users do their work; where computers do or might reside; physical characteristics of the environment such as space, noise, lighting, access to computers, privacy to work; cultural and social characteristics, such as value placed on computer literacy, on speed in completing a task, on working by oneself versus working collaboratively

- process flow diagram of the entire work process from conceiving the idea of a sale through decision-making process, advertising planning and implementing, sale planning and implementing, including any record keeping, archiving, using information from past sale experience, and other tangential tasks that users do or think would be important to do, plus notes on differences in the process flow across sites

- task lists from each participant of tasks that person does in that part of the process

- detailed task flow and procedural flowcharts of tasks as each participant does his or her part of the overall workflow

- report organized by the list of questions in this plan with insights and recommendations: we might use affinity diagramming from our note logs and site visit reports to arrive at our insights

We also anticipate having artifacts to share from the site visits.

We will involve the extended SuperSales design team in analyzing and understanding the data. We will summarize the findings into a presentation to the IS and HR management team by October 1. If the decision is to go ahead with the project to create the integrated SuperSales product, we will use the various flow diagrams and the other data to begin to plan the overall design and flow of the new SuperSales product interface. We plan to invite selected users from the local region to review our flow diagrams and to work with us in developing and doing usability testing of task lists, task flows, and interface designs for SuperSales.

Figure 8-11 The data collection plan for the SuperSales case study.

SuperSales Trip Report #4

Site visited: store #25, Denver, Colorado
Location type: suburban
Store size: medium, 50,000 square feet
Date visited: August 12, 19…
Site visit team: Tom R. (Usability); Jenny P. (Information Systems)

Photo of outside of store with sale signage	Photo of inside of store with end of aisle sale and signage for it.

.Store personnel who participated in visit:

1. Paul R., Store Manager

   • makes decisions on sales in conjunction with regional office and with department heads in store

   • 18 years in grocery business

   • 5 years as manager

   • 7 years experience in sales decisions (had been department head and then assistant manager in another store in the same chain)

   • 7 years experience with computers, but limited to occasional word processing of memos and letters

2. Annette L., Assistant Manager for Customer Relations

   • in charge of all advertising in store

   • liaison to advertising group in regional office

   • also responsible for other aspects of customer relations

   • 2 years experience in grocery business

   • 2 years experience in advertising

   • had come from customer relations work in another field

   • 5 years experience with computers, word processing, drawing programs, rates self as fairly adept with computers

Figure 8-12 Sample trip report.

3. John Z., Department Head, Groceries
   - responsible for recommending in-store sales of groceries
   - responsible for setting up and taking down grocery sales, both in-store manager's specials and regionally-decided sales
   - requests and receives inventory reports to make recommendations
   - responsible for giving advertising information to Annette L. for in-store sales
   - responsible for conveying information about changed prices to computer inventory group
   - 8 years in grocery business
   - 6 months in current position
   - 18 months experience with computers but says is very limited; knows how to request certain reports about inventory and prices, but not much else

Photo of these three people posed with "Special: This Store Only" sign for sale starting next week.

[More detailed narrative profiles might go here or at the end of the report.]

Profile of the environment:
   - Store #25 is at one end of a strip mall in a middle-class neighborhood.
   - It is a very clean and airy store with wide aisles.
   - Promotional items are prominently displayed at the ends of each aisle.
   - Large signs advertising the sales are hung in the front window so they are visible from the parking lot.
   - [More details about store, sales, and signage, about office space where people work, about where computers are and how accessible they are might go here.]

How a sale gets decided, advertised, and implemented in store 25:

[A workflow picture might go here. See figures 6-4 and 11-8 for examples.]

Insights from site visit notes:

1. People try to coordinate what they are doing about sales, but there is no computer support for it.
   - Department heads meet with the store manager to decide on in-store (manager's specials) sales.
   - They have to balance what they want to do in that particular store with regional office directives about region-wide sales.
   - Most information gets passed on paper in the form of memos and filled-out forms.

Figure 8-12 Sample trip report. (Continued)

2. Computer-generated reports of inventory and price histories are used as input to sales decisions, but there is no decision-making, "what if," tool with that software.

3. When a decision is made, department heads communicate decisions, new prices, and dates prices will be in effect, to Information Systems to be put into pricing data base.

   • Decisions are often not final and changes are made.

   • Changes don't always get communicated clearly.

   • Mistakes get made in putting in new prices and often there is no check on it until a problem shows up.

   • John Z., Department Head for Groceries, says problems are rare, but they are embarrassing when they occur because a customer gets to the check-out line and the wrong price comes up on the register.

   • The customer gets angry at the check-out person, but it's not that person's fault.

4. Annette L, Assistant Store Manager for Customer Relations, has to coordinate with all the department heads.

   • Because the decisions are not on computer, she meets regularly with each department head.

   • She says department heads don't realize the lead time needed for signage.

   • They can't print the signs in store because the signs are too big. She has to coordinate through the regional office and that takes time.

   • She has a computer linkage to the advertising people in the regional office, but she can't check prices and dates on her computer because she and the advertising group are on a different kind of computer than the pricing data base is on.

   • Decisions, prices, and dates change a lot before they are finalized. When changes are needed after she has ordered the signs, that's more time and money.

Figure 8-12 Sample trip report. (Continued)

diagrams that show the way work flows through the people part of the organization. Charts that show the movement of paper and the interrelationship of team members will give an important perspective on the users' immediate work community and help you preserve information and perspectives that you've gained.

Quantitative data

Tabulate the quantitative data that you have collected. Create tables, graphics, spreadsheets, and diagrams showing the information that you have obtained about users, tasks, opinions, practices, and more. For example, you may have asked users to rank certain tasks they perform by frequency and difficulty. Create graphic representations of the results of your inquiry. You will learn more about analyzing this data in chapters 11 and 12.

User artifacts

You will often have an opportunity to collect artifacts at a customer site that will help you understand how users approach their work activities. We have found that forms, job aids, procedures, and other items provide you with additional insights into how your users perform tasks. If you believe that artifacts may exist and be helpful, include collecting them as part of your observers' notebook. Be certain that you have a plan in place to analyze and store the information you have collected.

During the SuperSales site visits, the team expects to collect numerous artifacts to help them understand the sales process, as shown in figure 8-13.

We will also try to collect artifacts at each site. Artifacts of interest would be whatever participants use to document the process for themselves today and whatever outcomes participants create during the process. So, for example, we would be interested in copies of paper notes, forms, logs, and other materials used by participants who do the process today on paper. We would be interested in memos or electronic mail that participants use in the decision making process, advertisements created by participants with responsibility for advertising, and checklists or other documents used by participants responsible for implementing the sale. We will be open to whatever artifacts we find being used in the participant's current process.

Figure 8-13 The artifacts collection plan for the SuperSales case study.

Staying organized (building in record keeping)

Once you have planned how to collect and organize your data, be certain that you also establish a plan for archiving the information you have collected. How will your reports be archived? Where will you store tape recordings and other handwritten data? What will you do with photographs and artifacts that you collected at the users' site. By planning in advance, you will ensure that the information will be available if it is needed for comparative studies in the future.

Site Visit Plan

In this section we have reassembled the site visit plan for the SuperSales project from the pieces we presented during the detailed discussion. A template for a plan like this appears in appendix A.

Site visit plan for *SuperSales*
A few notes on the site visit plan that follows:

This is the plan for a fairly elaborate field study that seeks to answer questions of both feasibility and design. You may not be doing nearly as elaborate a field study as this. You may be planning three quick visits to users' sites in one week with analysis the next week and immediate feedback into a design session. That's fine. You should still do a plan. You should still include these topics in your plan. It will guide you as you are getting ready to go out, when you are out there, and when you get back. It will let other people know what you are doing. By writing the plan and circulating it to all stakeholders, you will be making sure everyone understands what you are doing.

You may also be in a much more exploratory mode than this plan seems to cover. Your first objective may be to visit a few users and see what is going on and then come back and think about what you have learned so you can decide how to focus later visits. That's fine, too. You should still do a plan for those first few visits and then revise the plan for later visits.

Site visit plan for *SuperSales*

The SuperSales development team will visit nine of our supermarkets in three geographic areas to gather information to be used in designing SuperSales, an integrated system for supermarkets to plan and implement sales on food.

Issues and objectives

Issues:
These are the questions we want to be able to answer after this study.

- How do people in supermarkets plan and implement sales on food items?

- Who decides what to put on sale?

- Who decides how to advertise the sale?

- Who actually implements the sale? Who ensures that everything is ready?

- How do people decide what to put on sale? In what ways do they use computers or computer-generated information in those decisions?

- What materials do people create or arrange to have created to advertise in the store? outside the store? How do they now use computers in those tasks?

- What procedures do they use to ensure that everything is ready for the sale?

- How much variation is there on roles and tasks in different supermarkets?

- What varies?

- What are the main variables in that variation? (size of store? personal choice of people involved? roles set by company procedures?)

Objectives:

- Understand roles (who does what) in preparing for and implementing a sale.

- Understand the overall sales process from first decisions to closing down sale.

- Understand specific tasks in each part of the process.

- See problems users have today in doing any part of the process.

- Decide whether integrating modules to do all three functions is necessary and understand why or why not.

- Understand what users value most.

- Learn users' vocabulary for items and tasks.

Participants

■ 27 people will participate; 3 people in each of 9 stores.

■ All will actually work in our supermarkets and have a role in food sales.

■ They will be store managers, assistant store managers, or department heads who actually do one or more of the three tasks: decide what to put on sale, decide on advertising for the sale, and implement the sale.

■ The two characteristics that we believe may make a difference in what we learn are size of store and years of experience of the employee.

■ Size of store may make a difference because roles and tasks may be divided among people differently in stores of different sizes. Interest in an integrated computer-based system may differ in stores of different sizes.

■ Years of experience in the grocery business and in doing these tasks may make a difference in participants' general knowledge of sales and number of sales they have arranged.

■ We therefore plan to observe and interview in three sizes of stores and at three levels of experience. We will visit three stores in each size category.

■ That gives us the following matrix. We will observe and interview at least one person in each of the 27 categories of this matrix.

| | Store Size | | |
Task	Medium (40,000 to 50,000 sq. ft.)	Large (50,000 to 90,000 sq. ft.)	Super (170,000 to 240,000 sq. ft.)
Sale decisions (numbers = yrs of experience)	<1 1–3 3+	<1 1–3 3+	<1 1–3 3+
Advertising (numbers = yrs of experience)	<1 1–3 3+	<1 1–3 3+	<1 1–3 3+
Implementing (numbers = yrs of experience)	<1 1–3 3+	<1 1–3 3+	<1 1–3 3+

Locations

We have selected three locations in our nationwide chain: Denver, Colorado; Fort Worth, Texas; and the Washington DC metropolitan area. All three are areas with grocery stores at all sizes and both urban and suburban locations. They represent distinct areas of the country with different user profiles. The Human Resources Department has already spoken with the regional managers in those areas, and they have agreed to cooperate in the study.

Within each location, we will visit one store of each size. If possible, we will want to have a variety of experience levels among the study participants in each store.

Schedule

We will spend approximately four to five hours in each store, beginning either in the morning (first shift) or mid-afternoon (second shift) at the store manager's convenience. We will visit only one store on each day and use the rest of that day to review our notes, prepare trip reports, and begin to analyze the data.

Recruiting and further planning will be done in July. The data will be collected in August and early September. Analysis of the data will be ongoing during August and September. Findings will be presented no later than October 1.

The calendar for the site visit is as follows:

Location	Date	Time
Denver super store	August 10	7 A.M. to noon
Denver mid store	August 11	9 A.M. to 2 P.M.
Denver small store	August 12	7 A.M. to noon
Washington small store	August 20	2 P.M. to 7 P.M.
Washington mid store	August 22	7 A.M. to noon
Washington super store	August 25	7 A.M. to noon
Fort Worth mid store	September 3	9 A.M. to 2 P.M.
Fort Worth super store	September 4	7 A.M. to noon
Fort Worth small store	September 6	2 P.M. to 7 P.M.

Recruiting

The Usability Department will do the recruiting based on information from Human Resources. Our first contact will be with the regional manager in each of the regions. These people have already been contacted by Human Resources and are expecting to be called. We will ask the regional manager to suggest stores for us to visit and to make the initial contact with the store manager for us.

Materials needed: *Screening Questionnaire; Calendar for Site Visits; Letter of Introduction to be sent as soon as a site is put on the calendar*

Screening questionnaire
Hello, my name is //give your name// and I am calling about a project for //name the company.// Your name was given to us by //name your contact// as a person who would be interested in helping us better understand how supermarkets plan and implement sales on special items. I understand that //name// has already mentioned the project to you.

[If the user remembers the project, go on. If the user does not remember the project, use the following description.]

Our company is developing a new software system that will help people in supermarkets plan and implement sales on food items. We want to learn how you decide to put a certain item on sale, how you put the sale in place with advertising both inside and outside the store, and what procedures you go through to ensure that everything is ready for the sale. The best way we know of to understand how this process works is to visit your store for 2 to 3 hours. During the visit we want to watch the process you use without interfering in your work. Then we want to ask you some questions about how the process works. If possible, we'd like to observe and talk to 3 or 4 people in the store who are involved in the process of setting up a sale.

[If the user is still confused, suggest that you will have a member of the project team call him or her to explain the project further. If the user seems satisfied, go on to the next item.]

If you have a few minutes, I need to ask you a few questions about your experience and the type of store you work in.

1. I understand that you are the store manager. Is that correct? _____
   If not, what is your job title? _____
   [If you do not have the store manager, assistant store manager, or department head, ask if one of them is available, transfer the call, or get the number and a time to call back, if possible. End the call.]
   [If you are talking to the store manager, assistant store manager, or a department head, continue with the questions below.]

2. Is your store medium (40,000 to 50,000 sq. ft.)? _____ Large size (between 50,000 and 90,000 sq. ft.)? _____ Super (more than 170,000 sq. ft.)?
   _____
   [Check your grid. Do you already have four stores that fit the size criterion? If so, explain that we most need people from different size stores. Ask if it would be possible to call back if someone cancels? End the call.]

3. Are you responsible for deciding to put an item on sale? _____
   If no, ask who in the store decides on a sale item. _____

4. Are you responsible for setting up the advertising for a sale? _____
   If no, ask who is. _____

5. Are you responsible for implementing the sale in the store? _____
   If no, ask who is. _____
   [If the user answers no to questions 3, 4, and 5, explain that we want to observe the actual people who do the tasks. Explain that we would like to set up the visits with the people who do the tasks. Can he or she help to facilitate those visits? If no, ask if you can speak to anyone who is able to facilitate the visits? Or if the answer is still no and it's clear this person does not want to take part, thank them politely for their time and end the call.]
   [If the individual you are speaking with answers yes to question 3, 4, or 5, ask the following questions as appropriate.]

6. Is there more than one person in the store who handles sales? _____
   If yes, ask if each department handles its own sales. _____

7. How many years' experience do you have deciding on sales? Less than one? _____ One to three? _____ More than three? _____
   [Check your grid again. Do you have at least one person with this level of experience for the size store? If no, continue the questions. If yes, fill in the person's name in the grid and continue the questions.]

8. How many years' experience do you have handling sale advertising? Less than one? _____ One to three? _____ More than three? _____
   [Check your grid again. Do you have at least one person with this level of experience for the size store? If no, continue the questions. If yes, fill in the person's name in the grid and continue the questions.]

9. How many years' experience do you have implementing a sale? Less than one? _____ One to three? _____ More than three? _____
   [Check your grid again. Do you have at least one person with this level of experience for the size store? If no, continue the questions. If yes, fill in the person's name in the grid and continue the questions.]
   [If the person does not fit on the grid because all the space for this experience level are filled in, explain what is needed and ask if anyone else in the store has more or less experience. If no, explain the problem, thank the person, ask if you can call back in case of a cancellation, and end the call.]

10. Do you currently use a computer in your work? _____
    If no, do you use a computer at home or did you use one on a previous job? _____

If yes, what do you use the computer to do? _____

_____

11. Do you consider yourself a beginning, medium level, or expert computer user? If medium or expert, what type of computer software do you ordinarily use?

_____

Once you have completed the questions, consult your schedule list and establish a date and time for the site visit. Explain that you will send a letter confirming the visit, explaining the purpose of the study, and explaining the agenda for the visit.

If the person has further questions, tell him or her that _____ will answer their questions. Check to see if _____ is immediately available. If not, explain that _____ will call back with more information. Establish a time for _____'s return call.

Letter of Introduction

Letter of Introduction
Dear //person's name//:

Thank you for agreeing to participate in our supermarket study. The purpose of the study is to help us understand how you and your staff handle food item sales. We are just beginning the process of designing new computer software that will help store personnel to decide which items to put on sale, arranging in-store and external advertising for the sale, and implementing all the logistics required to ensure that the sale is handled smoothly. The outcomes of the study will help us ensure that the software meets your needs and the needs of your staff.

We hope to spend a half day, either morning or afternoon, at your store. During that time, we hope to observe you and your staff as you perform three tasks:

■ deciding which items to include in a sale

■ setting up the advertising for a sale

■ implementing the logistics for a sale

If possible, we hope to observe and talk with those who perform these tasks at your store location. We hope that our observations will not interfere with anyone getting their tasks done. However, we want to spend the first hour with the entire team so that we can learn about the whole workflow of setting up a sale. Then we will spend no more than one hour with each participant.

It is especially important that we meet with _____, who you have indicated is a new assistant manager and has never handled a sale before. _____ will help us understand how the new computer system needs to support new users as well as more experienced managers like yourself.

As we mentioned, we will be taking notes on our observations and taking still pictures of the work areas. We also will want to audiotape each person performing their tasks individually. We will bring release forms for each person who will be photographed and audiotaped to sign.

We also hope that you will be interested in helping us test the new software as it is designed. Your assistance will be invaluable to ensuring the system's success in your store.

As we mentioned, we will bring gift certificates for each participant we work with.

Thank you again for your generous cooperation. Please feel free to call me at //phone number// or _____ at //phone number// if you have any other questions. We'll be calling you on _____ to schedule the visit.

Sincerely,

//Your name//

Head of the study team

Data collection techniques

We will use these techniques:

- demographic questionnaires for each participant to enhance our user profiles

- environmental protocol (list of points to observe) for each location

- process analysis in groups to understand the workflow from the decision to have a sale through implementation

- observation and concurrent discussion (contextual inquiry) with each person as he or she does part of the workflow (decision making, planning advertising, implementing the sale)

- audiotaping of all discussions for later analysis

- pictures with a still camera for user and environmental profiles

- notetaking on observers' forms

The following is a tentative schedule for each visit. We expect to be flexible and to find that in many, if not all, site visits, we may have to deviate from this plan, but we hope to accomplish all the activities on it during our time at the location. Breaks will occur as needed at people's convenience. Logical breaks would come in between activities.

Schedule for each visit:

Time	Activity
5 minutes	Greet store manager, go over plans for visit.
10 minutes	Greet all participants together, go over plans for visit; set up equipment.
one hour	Do process analysis of overall workflow.
one hour	Observe and interview person who decides on sales.
one hour	Observe and interview person who does advertising.
one hour	Observe and interview person who implements sales.
10 minutes	Thank all; distribute gift certificates.

Notes on schedule:

■ At the beginning of individual session with each participant, the person who is doing interviewing (not note taking) will go over the demographic questionnaire with the participant.

■ The note taker on the team will be responsible for filling out the environmental protocol during the visit.

■ Depending on our starting time, the schedule might include a break for lunch. The lunch time may be used for additional discussion with the participants and perhaps with others in similar roles at the store.

■ If we find that all participants are in the same general area and we will be able to thank them all together at the end of the visit, we will distribute gift certificates then. If we find that we will not see the participants again after the time with them, we will distribute the gift certificates at the end of each individual session.

Teams

The Senior Usability Specialist will go on all the site visits. Two people from IS and one from HR will also participate in the study. Each site-visit team will include two people, the Senior Usability Specialist and one IS or HR person. The entire team of four people will work together to develop the Observer's Notebook and other materials for the site visits. The Senior Usability Specialist will hold a training session for the other team members, and the training session will be open to other interested IS and HR staff who might want to participate in future site visits or usability evaluations. The time and location of the training will be announced over e-mail, and registration for the training will be handled through HR.

Materials

The following chart indicates the materials that we will have for the study, who will be responsible for each, when we will develop each, and who will review each.

Material	Person responsible	Date ready	Reviewer
Screening questionnaire	Name	Date	Name
Letter of introduction			
Schedule for teams			
Demographic questionnaire			
Environmental protocol			
Release forms			
Observers notebook with:			
goals and objectives			
schedule for each visit			
list of activities with guidelines			
observation and interview protocols for each role			
copies of forms			
Artifact log			
Site visit report template			

Media

Teams will use these media:

- large poster paper, markers, sticky notes for documenting process flow
- audiotape for all discussions (group discussion during process flow and contextual inquiries of individuals)
- still camera pictures of people and environment
- notetaking with laptop or paper, depending on team's and users' comfort

We will not use videotape for this study because of the environmental conditions. During the group discussion of a process analysis, videotaping would be difficult because we would need someone to move the videotape to capture the speaker. The artifact of the process diagram will serve as the record of that discussion.

We anticipate that in some stores, the individual contextual inquiries will take place in closed offices, but that in others, they will be in more open areas where videotaping would be considered an intrusion.

We will also try to collect artifacts at each site. Artifacts of interest would be whatever participants use to document the process for themselves today and whatever outcomes participants create during the process. So, for example, we would be interested in copies of paper notes, forms, logs, and other materials used by participants who do the process today on paper. We would be interested in memos or electronic mail that participants use in the decision making process, advertisements created by participants with responsibility for advertising, and checklists or other documents used by participants responsible for implementing the sale. We will be open to whatever artifacts we find being used in the participant's current process.

Data analysis and reporting

To meet the objectives, we anticipate presenting our findings in these forms:

- user profiles, including information on job experience including overall time in the grocery business and time in the specific job, computer experience and attitudes towards using computers for this type of work, users' views of competencies needed to do this type of work

- environmental profiles, including information on where users do their work; where computers do or might reside; physical characteristics of the environment such as space, noise, lighting, access to computers, privacy to work; cultural and social characteristics, such as value placed on computer literacy, on speed in completing a task, on working by oneself versus working collaboratively

- process flow diagram of the entire work process from conceiving the idea of a sale through decision making process, advertising planning and implementing, sale planning and implementing, including any record keeping, archiving, using information from past sale experience, and other tangential tasks that users do or think would be important to do, plus notes on differences in the process flow across sites

- task lists from each participant of tasks that person does in that part of the process

- detailed task flow and procedural flowcharts of tasks as each participant does his or her part of the overall workflow

- report organized by the list of questions in this plan with insights and recommendations: we might use affinity diagramming from our note logs and site visit reports to arrive at our insights

We also anticipate having artifacts to share from the site visits.

We will involve the extended SuperSales design team in analyzing and understanding the data. We will summarize the findings into a presentation to the IS and HR management team by October 1. If the decision is to go ahead with the project to create the integrated SuperSales product, we will use the various flow diagrams and the other data to begin to plan the overall design and flow of the new SuperSales product interface. We plan to invite selected users from the local region to review our flow diagrams and to work with us in developing and doing usability testing of task lists, task flows, and interface designs for SuperSales.

Checklist of supplies to be taken on each site visit.

Check	Supply to be taken
——	still camera
——	film for camera
——	batteries for camera
——	audio recorder
——	cassettes for recorder
——	batteries for recorder
——	laptop with cords and extra battery
——	diskettes for backing up files
——	portable printer with cords and cable
——	notebooks
——	pencils, pens
——	folder for each site visit
——	copy of letter of introduction that went to that site
——	demographic questionnaires that those participants have already filled out
——	blank demographic questionnaire for any participant lacking a filled-out one
——	blank demographic questionnaire for other users at sites
——	release form for each participant at site (and extras)
——	supplies for process flow: poster paper, colored markers, color sticky notes
——	observers' notebook with environmental protocol and observation and interview protocols for each participant
——	artifact log (file on laptop)
——	folder to put artifacts in
——	gift certificates for each participant

Reference cited in the chapter

Mitropoulos-Rundus, David and Muszak, Jerry, How to design and conduct a consumer in-home usability test, *Common Ground*, 7 (2), April 1997b: 1, 8-14, 19.

PART 3

Conducting the site visit

In part 2, you decided why you were doing site visits and who you would visit. You created your site visit plan, developed the guidelines and action plan for your team members, and assembled all the tools and materials you intend to use to interact with the users.

In part 3, we give you tips for successful site visits and help you hone the skills you need to make your observations and interviews effective. In chapter 9 we focus on logistics for site visits and then on observation skills. In chapter 10 we concentrate on interviewing skills.

In many cases, of course, you'll be observing and interviewing users at the same time. There's so much to say about observing and interviewing, however, that we've divided the material into two chapters.

If you follow the sound observation practices in chapter 9, you will return from your visits with a rich picture of your users, their tasks, and their environments. You will be able to identify the users' goals, the tasks they do to achieve those goals, where they think each task starts and ends, what triggers a task and what keeps it going, what problems users have doing their tasks, and how they solve their problems.

You will also be conscious of the differences between observations and inferences. The most useful information for design comes from taking careful notes on what actually happens, what you can observe or see. However, you'll also find yourself making inferences about the meaning of what you see and taking notes on users' inferences about what is happening. Inferences are important, too, but you need to clarify your inferences with users. It is important to know when you are taking down facts and when you are interpreting those facts.

In chapter 10 we move from observations to interviewing skills. As we've said, in many site visits you'll combine observations with interviews, talking with users as they work or right after they've finished a task. Just watching users is almost never enough. You have to listen to and talk with users to understand the mental work they do as well as their processes, hypotheses, inferences, and other experiences.

There may also be times when you do interviews without observations. Some of the activities that you need to understand may not take place while you are on site. Others may take place over a longer period of time than you can be present. You may also have questions that go beyond the specific tasks you can watch.

Interviewing skills are critical both for talking with users during observations and for talking with users and others apart from observations. Chapter 10 should help you realize that the key to getting useful information is to listen more than you talk and to really hear what users are saying, capturing their words, not translating them into what you want to hear. Chapter 10 should help you find the right type of questions to get the information you need, keep a conversation going without dominating it, be attentive to nonverbal signals, and be attuned to cultural differences in conversation styles and expectations.

9

Conducting the site visit—honing your observation skills

In chapter 8, we discussed preparing for your site visits. In this chapter and the next, we help you conduct the site visit.

We begin with some pointers on logistics. The first section and figure 9-1 give you an overview of how a site visit is likely to go and some tips for successful site visits. In the rest of the chapter, we concentrate on improving your skills as an observer.

What you do during the site visit depends, of course, on the decisions you've made about what you want to learn, where you are going, and which techniques are most appropriate for your project. (See chapter 6 for more on different techniques and when they are most appropriate. See chapter 7 for more on making decisions as you plan.) Here we concentrate on the techniques of observing users and talking with them either during the observation or immediately afterward.

If you can, you want to both observe and talk with users at the same time. Because we have much to say about both observing and talking, however, we've separated our discussion into two chapters. First, in this chapter, we consider what to focus on as you observe users, with a few suggestions for questions you might want to ask. Then, in chapter 10, we discuss in detail how to talk with users and how to ask useful questions.

Here are the topics we cover in this chapter:

- handling the site visit

- learning more about the user

- taking notes on the user's environment

- understanding the user's goals

- understanding the user's tasks

- asking the user to talk to you and to think out loud

- noting where the user starts the task

- noting what triggers the task

- taking down the level of detail you need for your issues

- capturing interactions with other resources: people, paper, programs

- separating observations and inferences as you watch users

- noting where the user ends the task (what happens next)

- noting whether the user achieved the goals

- thanking the user, distributing presents, and taking your leave

At the end of the chapter, we provide a paper form that you can adapt to capture notes. Of course, you can also adapt the ideas from this form for your laptop.

Handling the site visit

Here's an overview of what generally happens in a site visit:

- Your team arrives and is greeted by someone from the site. You may have to sign in if there is security. You get to the general area of the group you will be working with.

- You introduce yourselves and meet the user you will be working with and that person's colleagues and managers.

- You set up to observe. If they have set up for you in a different location than the one you want to work in, politely but firmly explain what you need to do and where you need to be. In our experience, no matter how clearly you or others may have explained what a site visit is all about or what a contextual inquiry means, you may find when you arrive at the site that they have planned for a conversation in a conference room or expect you to provide a demonstration of something. When you explain again, right there, they're usually happy to accommodate you.

■ If you are there to see an actual user do his or her work in the actual work environment, you really want to do that even if it means squeezing into a small cubicle. If you know that typical users have very small working spaces, don't take three people. You won't fit. If the only place to put a tripod is going to be in the narrow space where people have to walk between cubicles, consider a desktop tripod. You may need to think creatively about how to work in the space available.

■ If you have a team, one person might be setting up the recording equipment while the other does these next few steps. Sit down with the user in the work space. Confirm your expectations of what is going to happen. Confirm the schedule. If expectations differ, negotiate, then stick with what you negotiate.

■ You might engage in a little social chit-chat to build rapport, but how much time to spend in chit-chat depends a lot on culture. Try to find out from account representatives and others who have visited these users what is appropriate—and pay attention to body language signals from the user.

■ Before you tape record or take photographs, confirm that you have permission. Have the user sign the release form.

■ If you are collecting demographic data, you might ask those questions next.

■ Another person on the team might be taking notes and photographs of the environment at this time. (If the user is hesitant about your taking photographs, wait until the end and ask again.)

■ Now you're ready to have the user do his or her work while you observe and take notes. Depending on the user's work and the technique you are using, you may interrupt with questions as the user is working or you may hold your questions and ask them when the user finishes a task.

■ If a customer happens to come in or call while you are working with a user, you'll probably want to melt into the background and be on your best behavior. The user may need to explain your presence to the customer. That's fine. We often find that the customer is happy to participate in the site visit and let you continue to observe, and sometimes to ask questions. If the customer does not want you to hear the conversation, however, you'll have to leave the space and perhaps observe another part of the operation with another user for a while. If you do stay to observe, the customer may want you to turn off the videotape. If you do continue to tape, you'll need to ask the customer to sign a release form.

- You now let the work flow naturally while you observe, take notes, ask questions, and collect examples when you can. Take breaks when the user does, although of course you can ask the user if you need a break. (We've found that users may be used to working far longer than we are without breaks.)

- Watch the time so that you don't overstay your welcome and so that you can move on to other aspects of the site visit if you have planned to meet with others or to do other activities with the user.

- At the end of the visit, you might ask permission to videotape or photograph the user and the environment for your user and environment profiles.

- Last, you pack up your recording equipment, thank everyone, give out gifts, and leave.

Figure 9-1 gives you more tips on what to do before, during, and after each site visit. One caveat to everything we've said so far and to the tips in figure 9-1: Your situation may require changes from what we suggest here. And always, be flexible; take advantage of opportunities to see what you did not expect. Treat the users with respect and solicitude, even if it means changing your plans.

In the rest of the chapter, we expand on the part when you are sitting with the user, learning more about the user, the environment, the user's goals, how the user does tasks, etc.

Learning more about the user

If you haven't used a screening questionnaire or had users fill out a profile before you get to the site, you might start with one when you sit down with the user. It lets users tell you important information about themselves. When you analyze the data that you bring back, you'll almost certainly want to know where each user is on the dimensions that we discussed in chapter 2 and the section on stages of use in chapter 3. Adapt the questionnaire from chapter 7 for your own needs.

Even if you have a filled-out demographic questionnaire from the user before you get to the site, you probably want to go over it with the user. Doing so gives you the opportunity to verify and expand on the information. The user may have misunderstood a question. You may have learned in another site visit that a question is ambiguous and now need to know how this user interpreted it. You may want to ask more questions about a topic, such as not only how many years of computer experience a user has, but what applications the user works with and how frequently the user works with each one.

TIPS FOR SUCCESSFUL SITE VISITS

BEFORE YOU GO

1. Don't arrive unannounced.

    • Arrange the logistics with managers and users.

    • Let them know (in general) what you and the user will be doing (especially whether the user will be doing his/her own work).

2. Work through channels.

    • managers

    • unions where necessary

3. Think about the best day and time for your visits. What you see may vary by the day or time.

    • Monday may be spent dealing with a weekend's worth of crises.

    • Mid-week days may be "slow."

    • Consider coming after the user starts the day.

    • Leave time for lunch.

4. Confirm the visit

    • with a fax as soon as it is arranged

    • with a call the day before

5. Ask for directions if you need them.

    • You don't want to be late because you can't find the place.

    • Users feel good that they get to help even before you come.

6. Practice setting up the equipment in your space before you go to users' sites.

WHEN YOU ARRIVE

1. Greet the manager as well as the user.
   Greet the user's colleagues, especially if they share space.

2. Ask permission again before setting up your AV equipment.
   Ask for space that you need, but don't interfere with others' work.

3. Verify expectations about the length of your visit and what you plan to do.

Figure 9-1 Tips for a successful site visit.

WHILE YOU ARE THERE

1. Make it a cooperative venture.

   • Work to build rapport.

   • Remember you are interested in what users do—whatever and however they do it.

   • Don't let the user make you the "expert" who can explain how to do it.

   • Reassure users if necessary and remind them that they are not being tested.

2. Be flexible about schedules, breaks, other tasks users have to do. (This may all be part of the data that you want to capture.)

3. Watch your own verbal language and body language so that you stay friendly, but neutral.

4. Take lots of notes. Write down everything. Overdo the note taking. We know many people who have regretted not taking enough notes. We don't know many people who thought they took too many notes.

WHEN YOU ARE LEAVING

1. Thank the manager as well as the user.

2. Give the user a gift (even if you are paying for the visit).

3. Pack up quickly and quietly.

AFTERWARD

1. Send a thank you to both the user and manager.

Figure 9-1 Tips for a successful site visit. (Continued)

As you work with the user throughout the site visit, you may observe or hear about other user characteristics that designers and developers should know about. Be sure to take notes on those characteristics. You can put them in your notes with a **U** so they are easy to find when you sort your notes later. (Be careful of what you write down and how you say it. Take notes as if you are going to share all those notes with the user.)

What are important notes about users? Here are some from various situations:

■ In the dim light of a typical TV room, the middle-aged user took off his bifocals and squinted at the tiny, black-on-black buttons of the remote control.

- The user says she is "a people person." She likes the job because she gets to talk with people on the phone and help them. She doesn't think she'd like to look everything up on a computer when she can call quickly with her speed dial and get a person to answer her questions.

- The user speaks and reads English quite well even though she's only been in this country for six months. She says she understands the menu names on the screen, but the abbreviations and shortened words that come up as column headings and in messages are very hard for her to figure out. She's been embarrassed to find out from coworkers so she often completely misinterprets the messages.

Taking notes on the user's environment

Early in the site visit, take a few minutes to make specific notes about the environment. If two people are doing the site visit, one might take notes on the environment while the other is filling out or verifying or adding to the demographic questionnaire with the user. Bringing back pictures of the user's environment can be very useful both for letting designers and developers know "what it's really like out there" and for keeping users and their situations at the forefront throughout the design and development process.

What are important notes about environments? Here are some examples:

- The user's computer is festooned with sticky notes. Some are telephone numbers. Others are the user's own "quick reference cards," reminders of how to do a task. (Try to capture the essence of the sticky notes that seem relevant to your project. Note which tasks they are. You might ask the user why those tasks? How often does the user refer to the notes?)

- The users all work in one large open space. They can all see and hear what the others are doing. This arrangement means that users don't want their computers beeping at them all the time. The open arrangement also means there is very little shelf space for manuals or even for posting reminder sheets. The lack of easily accessible manuals and the open arrangement both contribute to users going to colleagues rather than books for help with problems. If management wants to reduce the time users spend solving each other's problems, you need to build solutions into the users' computers that are quicker and easier than getting the information from colleagues.

- The environment is a factory floor. You've had to put on a special smock and eye-protector goggles to be out there. The user, wearing thin gloves, carries one of the devices that has just been assembled over to special equipment attached to the PC and hooks it up to run the testing programs. A single sheet of instructions for the tests sits next to the PC, but there's no room to open a large manual and the user could not carry both a manual and the device that is about to be tested.

As with your notes about users, you may observe or hear about other relevant features of the physical, social, or cultural environment as the site visit continues. Capture them in your notes, perhaps marked with an **E** so that you can find them easily when analyzing your notes later.

Understanding the users' goals

Once the preliminaries are over and you have some sense of who the user is and what the user's environment is like, you are ready to pay attention to what the user is doing. The first thing you have to understand is "What is the user trying to do? What's the user's goal?"

People use software, hardware, other machines, and documents to accomplish goals. Both at work and at home, these goals are often quite specific. The people you are observing may be trying to arrange a trip, sign up for a retirement program, resolve a discrepancy over a medical claim, bake cookies, set the VCR to tape a sports event, write a report, pay bills, or any one of a myriad of other goals.

Focusing on the users' goals and the ways they think about the tasks they do to meet those goals will give you the information you need to design usable products. Too many designs focus on features and functionality without considering why and how users work. A product can have database elements that are all correct, algorithms that work as intended, calculations that are totally reliable, and yet be so frustrating to users that the users give up on them.

Consider the cellular telephone. The user's goal is to communicate with other people in all types of locations, without the hassle of having to find a phone. When the cellular telephone rings, the user's goal is to answer the phone to find out who is calling and what that person wants.

All cellular phones have the functionality of receiving calls as well as sending them. But for the new user, cellular telephones are immensely frustrating because the interface does not make it at all obvious how to meet the goal of receiving a call. Users just want to "answer the phone." The functionality requires them to press the SEND key.

When new users learn that the correct response is to press the SEND key, they respond with complete incredulity at the illogic of the design, as shown in figure 9-2. "Press SEND?" they reply. "How can that possibly be true?"

They don't understand the underlying logic of the engineer who tells them that a cellular phone is not a telephone at all but a radio, hence the SEND key is

Figure 9-2 New users are often frustrated trying to use cellular phones to answer calls.

used for both incoming and outgoing calls. "Well it doesn't look like a radio. It looks like a phone," users say. "It is even called a phone. How can it be something else? Why doesn't it behave as I expect it to behave?"

That the underlying architecture is closer to a radio than a telephone is irrelevant to users. Users care about what they are trying to do. Their mental model is that the device is a telephone so they expect it to work like a telephone. If designers had watched and listened to users meeting the same goal (receiving a call) with their earlier devices (plugged-in telephones), the designers might have created cellular telephones that let users answer just by picking up the phone and talking into it or by having both SEND and RECEIVE buttons or at the very least by labeling the one button SEND/RECEIVE.

Even if you are planning drastic changes to the users' work processes, understanding the users' goals is critical. The users' goals are not likely to change. Users still want to get the report the boss needs, feed their hungry families, talk to their friends on the phone. In fact, understanding users' goals is the best way to make reengineered processes work. If your group is reengineering work processes, your goal is to help the users achieve their goals more effectively and efficiently than before. A well-designed product can drastically change the mechanics of how the user performs tasks and make users even happier than they were before, but only if it respects the goals and values that the users bring to it.

If you don't get the information you need about users' goals and don't apply it effectively during the design and development process, you are likely to end up with products that meet the requirements but that users find frustrating, awkward, time-consuming, confusing, and ultimately defeating.

So how do you find out about users' goals? You can ask users directly what they are trying to do, but you should also listen for some interesting implications in the users' statements and situations of what they are trying to do.

The goal may be for the benefit of others

One aspect of goals that you should look and listen for is "Who else benefits? Who else's tolerance for time and error must we consider in creating a useful product?"

In many cases, the person you are observing is doing the work so that someone else will benefit. Are you observing an individual making his or her own travel plans or are you observing a travel agent making plans for a client? Are you observing an individual filling out benefits forms for a new retirement program or a human resources staff person filling out the forms with an employee? Are you observing the person who was ill trying to resolve a problem with a medical claim, or a relative who is doing this on someone else's behalf, or the medical claims agent on the phone with a distraught and frustrated customer?

Even in home situations, the user's goal often includes satisfying someone else. The cookie baker may have hungry watchers waiting for the job to be done. The person setting the VCR may be doing it so someone else will be able to watch the tape later.

Even if these other users will never put their hands on the interface or document that you are creating, you have to consider them as you develop requirements and create products. Airplane mechanics might be willing to hunt around in the documentation to find out how to fix a particular part if they are doing it in the hangar. But when they are called to fix a part at the gate, the goal is "to find the problem and fix it safely and quickly so that these 125 passengers can get on their way." That pressure is going to affect the choices they make in meeting the goal. Part of the goal in many situations is to satisfy someone else—a customer, a supervisor, a family member. Include that information in your statement of the user's goal. Use that information later when you are setting measurable usability goals. (See chapter 12 for more on usability goals.)

Goals are often, but not always, specifically action oriented

Users' goals at work are almost always directed at getting something done. It is perhaps surprising how often that's also true at home and in our personal lives outside of either home or work. However, sometimes the user's goal is much broader and less clearly defined. You could be observing a user in the library who has a very specific goal of "finding a copy of John Grisham's new novel." You could be observing a user in the library who wants "to see if there's anything I'd like to take out to read in the next few weeks." Those are quite different goals that would probably generate quite different search strategies.

Users on the Web are much like the users in the library. They may be looking for a particular piece of information. They may be "surfing," content to wander around looking for something interesting. If your product is likely to have users with both "doing" goals and "browsing" goals, try to observe users in both those situations. Also try to estimate the relative frequency of the different types of goals.

Even specific action-oriented goals may encompass many tasks

Don't confuse the doing/browsing difference with goals that cover many tasks but which are in fact still action oriented. When you observe and talk to users, you may hear goals that range from solving a very immediate, very specific problem to goals that reflect the larger situations of which the immediate problem is but a small part.

That is, you may hear: "My goal right now is to get the boxes in my chart all lined up neatly." You may hear: "I'm trying to create an organization chart to go in the annual report." You may hear: "I'm in charge of creating the design for the annual report. I need to get good page templates set up." The levels of users' goals that you are most interested in observing and talking to users about depend in part on what *you* are trying to accomplish. That's why we said in chapter 7 that defining the issues for your site visits is critical.

You may be tempted to concentrate on very low-level goals because they are easiest to observe and analyze. However, observing users dealing with the larger process may be more fruitful in the long run. In fact, understanding how different goal statements relate to each other in a hierarchy is also very important.

Goals come at different levels and are hierarchical

As you listen to users articulate their goals, you will often find yourself probing to get the broader and bigger picture of what they are really trying to accomplish, as shown in figure 9-3. Users may say that what they "are trying to do is to …"

- change channels using the remote control
- turn on the new computerized oven
- read notes on the last contact with this customer
- get the computer fax modem to work
- use the ultrasound machine correctly
- use the clinical patient information system

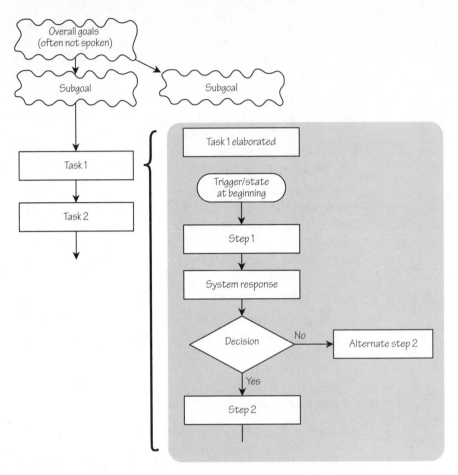

Figure 9-3 Goals and tasks are hierarchical and come at different levels, but the boundary between what is a "goal," a "task," and a "step" is fluid. All are stated as verb phrases.

What they are really articulating are tasks they believe they need to do. By probing for "why" they are doing what they are doing, for "what they are really trying to achieve," you can sometimes get the users to articulate the goal behind the task. Sometimes the user's real goals only emerge from the discussion as the user is doing the work. Sometimes the real goal is never explicitly stated. You need to be thinking about underlying goals, however, because they may lead you to insights about how to improve products—perhaps even eliminate tasks. These insights may allow you to help users to achieve these often unstated goals faster and more easily.

■ The user probably wants to find out how to change the channels with the remote control to watch a particular program. The user probably wants to watch the program to be informed or entertained.

- The user probably wants to turn on the new computerized oven to cook something, perhaps to bake the holiday turkey. The user probably wants to bake the turkey to feed the hungry guests and make everyone stuffed and happy.

- The user probably wants to read notes about the last contact with the customer to respond more effectively to the customer's questions and possibly secure a sale.

- The user probably wants to install and use the computer fax modem to communicate with someone more quickly than before.

- The ultrasound technician probably wants to examine the patient as quickly and accurately as possible, perhaps in this case to assist the radiologist in discovering if a lump is benign or cancerous.

- The doctor probably wants to use the clinical patient information system to find out something, perhaps to see the test results with the real goal of making a better diagnosis and curing the patient.

Goals may not necessarily imply a specific task sequence

As we discussed in chapter 3, sometimes it is critical to understand the goal apart from the tasks you—or the users—assume they will do to accomplish the goal. Users trying to tape a program on a VCR may tell you that what they want to do is "program the VCR." Although they state that as their goal, it is really a task, not the goal. What they really want is to have a tape of a program so that they or someone else can watch it. Programming the VCR is a task they may have to do in their current system to accomplish the goal of watching the program at some later time.

Why is understanding the *real* goal apart from the tasks so important? If you are looking for ways to improve products, to make users' lives simpler, focusing on the high-level goal rather than on the current tasks will allow you to see possibilities for offering users other ways of accomplishing their goals. VCR Plus was a solution to help users meet their real goal of getting a particular program on tape without the task of programming the VCR.

By probing for the goal behind using the remote control, you may realize that if you found a way to help users change channels more effectively and more quickly than by using a remote control, the television watcher might be even happier. By trying to understand the goal behind turning on the oven, you may realize that what the user told you is only the first of many tasks that the user may need to do to accomplish the real goal. By probing for the goal behind reading the customer contact notes, you may realize that users don't want to spend time and effort to get to those notes. The customer may be on the phone with the user and the real goal is to make the sale. Your new design will have to make retrieving those notes very fast and very easy or the notes may go unread.

The real goal and problem domain may be large and messy

When you listen for users' goals, you may find that the problem the user is trying to solve is not easy to state in terms of simple tasks that can be done with one software program or with one piece of hardware. The user may even have difficulty figuring out how to attack the problem, that is, what software or hardware to use. You should see such situations as opportunities for new market niches and new solutions.

Barbara Mirel (1998) has been studying these complex situations that occur frequently in the real world. For example, a manager has to figure out where the apparent overrun comes from in the budget report she just received from the accounting office and decide what to do about it. To do so, she has to apply her knowledge of likely sources, perhaps go into several different databases, set up queries, get the answers to her questions, consider the implications of the answers, use a different program to do some "what if" modeling, figure out what changes to make to the project plans, etc. If the different databases have been set up by different people or use different underlying software, she may have to know how to set up queries several different ways and remember which way is needed in which software.

By listening to this user state her goals (get this mess straightened out; get the project back on track; look good with her bosses for not having more overruns; keeping her job) and by watching her try to meet her goals (using different products; being frustrated over inconsistencies; making mistakes because she has so much to learn and remember), you may see the need to have more integrated software applications or at least more consistent families of products.

Don't confine yourself to one part of the process if attending to the whole process is necessary to really make users productive.

Summarizing how to get information on users' goals

- Create opportunities for users to explain what they are trying to accomplish in their work.

- Probe to discover why they want to achieve a particular goal. The first "goals" they state are likely to be tasks or secondary goals, only part of the higher-level goals you really want to uncover.

- Try to create a hierarchy of goals. Sketch the hierarchy or use sticky notes to represent the goals in a hierarchical relationship so that you understand how lower-level tasks or secondary goals relate to higher-level primary goals. You may not be able to do this all at once at the beginning of the site visit. It may emerge through the visit.

- Review your understanding with each user.

- Make changes as needed to clarify the user's goals.

Understanding the users' tasks

Once you have started to understand the user's goals, you are ready to watch the user work on the goals using existing tools in the current environment. For example, if your intent is to design an automated system for sending and receiving faxes through a computer modem, you might ask the user to send a fax the way he or she now does it. You might then be watching the user with an office or home fax machine. You might learn, for example, that the user follows these steps:

1. Decides to send someone a message by fax.

2. Creates the message or document.

3. Looks in a file and finds the fax number of the recipient.

4. Fills out a cover page in pen that has previously been printed out and that already has information about the sender but which needs the name, address, phone number, and fax number of the recipient.

5. Puts the document into the fax machine (right side down).

6. Starts to dial and says: "Oops. I never remember the fax number."

7. Takes the document back out of the machine. Grabs a pencil and scrap of paper and jots down the fax number.

8. Puts the document back into the fax machine.

9. Dials the fax number and waits for the fax machine tone.

10. Starts the fax process.

As you observe the user performing the steps, take note of the order in which the user does them. Try to find out which steps the technology requires and which are optional. Discover if the particular order that you observe is one that the user always follows or if variations are possible or desirable. Find out to what extent the steps and the sequence are determined by the current tools and work environment: Does the user do the steps in this order because that is the logical order or because the system requires the steps in that order? Consider which steps are essential to meeting the goal and if any are not necessary, why the user does them. If the user suggests that variations happen, ask if the user has relevant work to do that would give you the opportunity to see the other ways of working or to see how the user handles other scenarios.

You might learn, for example, that all the users you observe create the document first and then look up the recipient's fax number and that they think that is the logical order of the steps when they have a separate document to fax. You might also find out that some of them use that same order when they are only sending a short message while others send short messages right on the cover sheet and so address the message before writing it. You might then plan to be flexible about when users have to put in addresses in your computer fax design.

As you observe the users doing the tasks, take notes on how the physical, social, and cultural environments affect the task. As an example of the impact of physical environment, you might learn that at one site, the fax machine is in the office manager's work area, and users have to interrupt the manager's work to use the fax machine. You might hear that in that office users are reluctant to fax because of the way the fax machine fits into the physical environment and would welcome software that allowed them to fax from their own space.

As an example of the impact of the social environment, you might discover that in some offices, support staff send out most of the faxes while in other offices everyone is responsible for his or her own. You might learn that many users fax only occasionally and do not want to have to relearn how to use the more intricate features of the fax machine each time they have to send a fax. You might learn that users feel they are always harried and are always dealing with a recipient who needs the fax "immediately if not sooner." You might conclude that users of fax machines value having a process that is easy to remember and follow without mistakes and so realize that your design for fax software must be better than a fax machine at making the steps obvious to users.

As an example of the impact of the cultural environment, you might learn that in some offices a handwritten cover sheet is considered not professional enough, and the users have to create and print a fax cover sheet every time they send a fax message. For those users, you would probably recommend that an essential design feature for your new software be templates for easy-to-create cover sheets where users can include a company logo and place the fields they need where they want them to be. You would probably also say that it is essential that the design make it easy to fill out the sheet for each fax.

Asking the user to talk to you and to think aloud

Observing users doing tasks is likely to give you information about the task that you would not get if the users just told you what they did without actually doing it. When users just talk about a task without doing it, they often forget to mention some of the steps because they do those steps so automatically that they don't think about them. In fact, they may not even realize each step they are taking while they are doing the task. Thus, watching users do the task, you may see behaviors they fail to notice themselves. Observations are critical.

To design a usable product, you must almost always understand more about the tasks than you can learn through observations alone. In almost all tasks, including some seemingly simple physical actions, users are evaluating what they see in the interface, making decisions, making choices for reasons you wish you knew, and doing other mental tasks. You cannot see the mental tasks. You can only hear about them if users tell you what they are thinking as they work. So hearing what is going on in the user's head is critical.

You get inside the user's head by asking the user to "think aloud" while working. The recording of the user's thinking aloud is called a "protocol," so these are often called "verbal protocols" or "think-aloud protocols." By listening and recording the verbal protocol, you will be able to clarify behaviors that are difficult to interpret through observation alone and to detect cognitive activities that may not be visible at all.

If you are sitting with the users, you can engage them in a more natural dialogue than if you must ask them to think aloud with no one present. Just tell the users to say everything that's going through their heads, to tell you at each step what they are doing and why. You can prompt the users when they are quiet by asking, "What are you thinking now?" "What are you looking for or trying to do?" You can also ask clarifying questions. (For more about how to ask useful questions, see chapter 10.) If you have a reluctant talker, you might find that it works to suggest that they imagine that you (the observer) are on the telephone rather than sitting right there. "Imagine that you're on the phone with a friend explaining what you are doing step by step as you're doing it."

Of course, there are situations in which you cannot observe the users doing the task. There are even more situations in which users cannot give you a think-aloud protocol while they are working because the work involves them talking with someone else, often on the telephone. In those cases, you gather what you can by listening to the natural conversation and try to fill in the gaps when the call is over.

As you observe and listen to the user doing the task, you might want to make specific notes on the aspects of the task that we cover in the next several sections.

Noting where the user starts the task

Whenever you do a task analysis, write down the situation at the start of the task. Later when you are planning documentation or designing an interface, you will want to know how each task connects to the larger process. For example, if the user's task is to send a fax to a regular correspondent, your expectation of what the user will do next will differ if the fax machine is still in the box, if it is out of the box but no return information or speed dial numbers have been set up, or if it is all set up and has been used before to correspond with the recipient.

If the users have difficulty while you are watching, the problem may not be in the task the users told you they were doing or in the task you came to watch. It may be in getting from where the system is to the place where you expected the users to start the task.

> *Q* *Ginny was watching a user as he was trying to program a VCR that he had not used before. The VCR and the TV were both set up. However, the system was not linked to a cable box. Therefore, it was not automatically set to channel 3. After looking for buttons to press, the user reluctantly went to the manual. He looked in the table of contents and found a page about "recording a program." He went directly to that page, skipping over all the previous pages of the manual as users typically do. On the page he looked at, he learned that he would have to fill out a menu on the TV. He tried to follow the instructions on that page to make the menu appear, but they did not work. After much trial and error and many hypotheses that did not work, the user realized that he had to put the TV on channel 3. That information was not on the page he went to in the manual. That page apparently assumed his starting point was after following instructions on earlier pages. It had no quick reminders that made the instructions there match his starting point.*

Capture the starting point in a set of declarative sentences that indicate the state of the hardware, software, documentation, etc. at the time the user starts the task during your observation. An example might be

> Task: Reserving a room in the hotel

> Starting point: Computer is on. Application is at Main Menu where "Reservations" is one of the choices.

You might ask the user if that is the way everything typically is at the start of the task. You might learn: "No, usually I have to get out of whatever function someone else has left it in and find my way back here before I can start." You might learn: "Well, sometimes I'm the first one in and I have to turn everything on. Then I have to remember where on the network to go to log into this program."

Noting what triggers the task

In your notes about the starting point of the task, make a particular point of indicating what makes the user start the task. These triggers can be internal to the user (satisfy own hunger or curiosity) or external to the user. If it is external, you should also always try to figure out if someone else is benefiting from the user doing the task.

An external trigger might be a phone call, a request in person, a piece of paper, or something appearing on the user's screen.

For example, a hotel reservation is usually triggered by a phone call from the traveler or from a travel agent. But it could also be triggered in person by a traveler who is checking out from one visit and making a reservation for the next visit.

In any of these cases, you probably want to note not only what form the trigger takes, but also where it comes from, what information the user is getting as input, who controls the flow of that information, and whether the user just gets it or has to ask for it or go looking for it. You might also be interested in why that is the trigger.

At one site, Ginny watched users keying in data from printed sheets. The printed sheets meant that the data was already in a computer somewhere in the company. When Ginny asked where the print-outs came from and why the users couldn't just get the data electronically, the user Ginny was working with sighed and said, yes, she knew it had already been keyed in by people in another part of the company, but the two systems weren't compatible. They had tried to download the information from one system to the other, but it came over with so many mistakes and had to be reviewed so carefully that it was quicker and easier just to retype it all. Understanding that situation could lead to new possibilities for simplifying the larger work process by working on intersystem compatibility.

You may be planning on changing the way the task is triggered. For example, you might be planning to have what used to come to the user on paper now come on the computer. Or the old paper form was never in logical order and has items that no one needs any more so you're going to change it. Or users want the screen to look just like their paper form but you know that doesn't take advantage of the options you now have for good document design. Even if you are planning to change the trigger, however, you still need to understand why users start their tasks.

As you learn about the trigger, you might also want answers to questions like these:

- How often does this trigger happen?
- Is this the only way the task gets triggered?
- What variations are there?
- How often do these variations happen?
- Does the trigger provide complete information?
- What happens if some information is missing?
- Does the trigger provide unnecessary information?
- What information is unnecessary?

Taking down the level of detail you need for your issues

It's hard to take notes and watch, listen, and talk with a user all at the same time. That's why it helps to have two people on a site visit. One concentrates on taking notes while the other concentrates on interacting with the user. That's why it helps to capture the visit on audiotape or videotape.

You'll almost certainly find that you cannot take down everything. We do recommend that you *overdo* the note taking. You won't regret having too many notes. You can also help yourself by taking the type of notes that best matches your issues and what you plan to do with the notes.

Are you trying to do a workflow or process analysis? Then focus on capturing the major stages of the process with notes on who does each stage, what triggers it, what come out of it, how does that get to the next stage, who does the next stage, etc.

Are you trying to do a detailed task analysis? Then focus on capturing the specifics of each step the user takes from the starting point to the end point of that task. This can be a bulleted or numbered list. User does X. Y happens. User does Z, etc., as shown in figure 9-4.

TASK LOG

U stands for User; O stands for Observer

–U points to screen, runs finger around screen, over all the fields, staying about an inch from the screen itself.

–U "just checking to see if I've filled in everything I need before I go on. Okay, it's all here."

–O "I see you went over that screen with your finger hovering near the screen."

–U "I did? Yeah, I guess I do that. On some screens, the fields are all over the place and it's easy to miss one, if you're not careful."

–U uses mouse to click on Next button.

–Tax information screen comes up.

–U "This screen always confuses me. It got so I printed out the Help that tells me which code means what."

–U opens desk drawer, pulls out notebook.

–O private note: notebook looks dog-eared, has sticky notes for tabs. (Reminder: After task is done, talk more about notebook. Ask to see it.)

–U opens notebook using sticky note that says "tax fields."

Figure 9-4 A fragment from site visit notes where the goal is to understand in detail how a user does the task now.

Are you primarily looking for problems users have doing the task now and how they try to solve those problems? Then focus on capturing places where the unexpected happens, where users take wrong turns, repeat steps, express frustration, or give other indications that the process isn't smooth for them. Think aloud protocols are especially important if you are focusing on problems because you hear the users' interpretations of what the problems are and their hypotheses about how to solve the problems.

Are you primarily looking at when and how users go to documentation? Then be especially alert to all the times when the user might go to the documentation. Capture where and how the user gets information, even if it is from a colleague or the help desk. Try to get exactly what question the user asks and try to capture it in the user's words. Try to write down all the words the user looks up in a print index or online search. Capture users' reactions to what they find to give you insights for developing new documentation.

Of course, you may be focusing on more than one of these aspects of users and their tasks, but even if you are focusing on only one, don't let useful information about other aspects slip away. For example, you may be concentrating on when and how users go to online help and what their experiences are with the help. In the course of observing and listening to users in the site visits, you are going to learn a lot about the interface. Don't ignore what you learn. When something important comes up, take notes. And take that information back to the interface designers along with the information you are taking back to the documentation specialists.

Capturing interactions with other resources: people, paper, programs

To achieve the goal, the user may use other resources besides the product that you are interested in. Sometimes these resources are a necessary part of the task. In work that involves direct interactions with customers or clients, for example, those interactions are an ongoing part of the task. You need to note not only the initial trigger for what the user you are observing is doing, but all the intermediate triggers and the ways in which they direct or redirect the way the user does the task.

There is likely to be more variability in what happens in tasks that involve interactions with other people than in tasks like data entry or payroll in which the user has no one to change the task once the user has started it. Therefore, if the task you are observing includes ongoing interactions with other people, you probably want to do more observations (more site visits) than you need to do for repetitive tasks that don't change once the user has started them.

Sometimes the other resources are required only at certain points in the task. The main issue you probably want to observe is what users do when the other resources are not immediately available. Sometimes users turn to other resources because the product they are working with fails them at a given point in the work.

> *Ginny once observed a user get out of the program he was using, open another program, import the data into that program, print a report, get out, and go back to the original program to continue working. When Ginny asked him why he did that when the first program had a similar reporting function, the user said that the first program (the one Ginny had come to observe) didn't allow him to include all the information that he wanted on the report and that the format of the report wasn't as easy to use. For various reasons he had to use the program that Ginny had come to observe as the basis of his work, but this user had developed his own workaround for part of the task—an important observation for Ginny to bring back to her client.*

Separating observations and inferences as you watch users

As you watch and listen, you are seeing actual behaviors, and you are hearing the users' words and the users' hypotheses about what is happening. You are also almost certainly making your own judgments about the user and your own inferences about what's going on in the user's head.

For example, you see the user open the manual, stare at the table of contents, turn to a page, say "no, that's not it," scratch his head, frown, turn back to the table of contents, try a different page, frown again, and put down the manual. Those are all behaviors. That's what you should write in your notes. If you write in your notes: "User is confused by the way the manual is organized," that's an inference. It may be a correct inference, but it's still your judgment of the user's state of mind and of the problem.

Behaviors are what users do and say. Inferences are your interpretations of what those behaviors mean. When you take notes, try to capture the user's actual behaviors. Note your inferences separately. On the paper note form that we offer at the end of this chapter, the left two-thirds of the page is for behaviors. The right third of the page is for your inferences and for questions you want to ask the user if you cannot interrupt the task.

Why is it important to capture behaviors and to separate the users' behaviors from your inferences? First, your inferences may be wrong. For example, frowns don't always indicate confusion, as shown in figure 9-5.

Second, behaviors are more useful than inferences in understanding users' needs and in developing interfaces and documentation, as shown in figure 9-6.

Figure 9-5 Users may not always be thinking what you think they are thinking.

OBSERVATIONS ABOUT THE USER'S BEHAVIOR:

- The user sent a reply, looked at the screen, said "It looks just like it did before," and sent a second identical reply, even though the first had gone correctly.

OBSERVATION ABOUT THE SYSTEM:

- The system did not send a feedback message to tell the user that the reply had been sent successfully.

INFERENCE ABOUT THE USER: (LESS HELPFUL THAN OBSERVATIONS)

- The user doesn't understand how the system works.

Figure 9-6 Capturing what users—and systems—actually do gives better insights into how to develop products than inferences, especially inferences that blame the user.

How do you know when you are noting behaviors and when you are making inferences? A behavior is something you actually see. Inferences include words indicating something you cannot see. See figure 9-7 for examples of behaviors and inferences.

EXAMPLES OF BEHAVIORS:

- User clicked on print icon.
- User walks over to shelf on other side of office and takes down the *Employee Benefits Handbook*.
- User selects first item and drags mouse down three more rows, saying, "I'm trying to select these four items because they're the ones I want to work on."
- User pressed F3 three times even though nothing happened.

EXAMPLES OF INFERENCES:

- The manual is *confusing* the user.
- The user doesn't *understand* selection controls.
- The user *forgot* to save the file.
- Went to Edit menu *by mistake*.
- User *is lost* in the help system.
- User *thinks* she needs to type data in. (*Doesn't see* that it's already on the screen.)

Figure 9-7 Inferences include words for actions that you cannot see (based on Prail 1990).

Do write down your inferences. They are also important and may well be very useful insights. Just realize that they are inferences. Verify them in conversation with the user. One of the principles of contextual inquiry is "clarify your assumptions with the user." In chapter 10, we discuss how to ask questions to clarify assumptions in ways that do not put words into the user's mouth or make the user feel stupid or guilty.

You may observe behaviors and not know how to explain them, not be able to formulate a reasonable hypothesis for them. That's why you need to talk with the users as well as watch them.

When Judith Ramey and her colleagues gathered videotapes of radiologists working, they observed that radiologists who were looking at X-rays changed their body and head positions a lot. The radiologists were doing manual "zoom and roam." They were focusing close in on a spot and then zooming out and back in, scanning a whole board of perhaps 80 images for a split second and then focusing down on a single image. Ramey and her colleagues weren't sure what those motions meant and what was critical to being able to duplicate what the radiologists were doing in a computer system. Only by talking with the radiologists with the videotapes as cues did they learn that the radiologists could "see" differences better as they went through these motions but only as long as the motions were continuous. Having to look away to type a computer command destroyed the continuity of the in and out viewing. Zooming on the computer wasn't continuous, each zoom produced a different image. The researchers then realized that the technology available at the time they did the study would not permit them to provide the seamless and continuous zoom and roam that the radiologists needed. They decided that a computer-based record archive would be useful (and even that certain kinds of imaging workstations might also be useful), but that a diagnostic workstation upon which radiologists would perform primary diagnosis probably would not be accepted by the radiologists (Judith Ramey, personal correspondence, 1997).

Noting where the user ends the task (what happens next)

Just as you captured the situation at the start of the task, you also want to know how and when the user thinks the task is done and what the situation is at the end of the task. In a site visit you should let the user tell you when the task is completed. Even if the user does more than is necessary or does less than is necessary, you need to know what the user thinks the end point of the task is.

Users sometimes do more than is necessary.

Observing users working with a new e-mail program, Ginny saw several users reply to a message, correctly completing the task they were trying to do. Then, they looked at the screen, which was back in exactly the same setup as before they sent the reply. They wondered if they had actually done the reply and then did the same task again. A few users sent three identical replies before concluding that even though they weren't getting any feedback they were going to assume the replies had gone off correctly.

Users sometimes do less than is necessary.

The user whom Ginny watched trying to program the VCR finally got the programming menu on the screen. He had several problems filling out the screens that followed the menu, but eventually he did get all the data in correctly. He then declared that he was done. In fact, although he had finished putting in the programming data, he had not finished setting up the VCR to record the program. He had not put a tape into the VCR and nothing on the screen reminded him to do so.

As you observe and listen to users concluding a task, try to get a sense of the user's confidence level. Try to capture what brings closure to the task for the users. What types of feedback are the users looking for? Do the users take some action to get feedback or to verify success? Do the users express a wish for some indicator of closure that they aren't now getting? Do the users assume the task is completed even when it isn't?

You'll also want to record times when users abandon the task, simplify or change the task because they are having problems, or even change the goal.

Noting whether the user successfully met the goal

Users may complete the immediate task and still not meet the goal. The user Ginny observed trying to program the VCR is going to be disappointed when he comes back to watch the program later and finds that it was never recorded.

The goal may require more tasks than the immediate one you are observing. You may need to observe another user or the same user doing another task before you can draw conclusions about the goal.

Going on to the next observation or the next part of the site visit

In a single site visit, you may watch the same user do many tasks. You may watch the same user do the same task several times. You may watch different users as you follow a work process through its different stages. Which you do, of course, depends on the situation and your issues.

Observing what is ostensibly the same task several times may be very informative. You may be surprised at how much variability there is in even seemingly simple tasks.

A human factors specialist told Ginny about going out to observe people who take orders over the phone. The expectation she had been given was that these people do the same task over and over. She was told she'd be bored observing and listening to their tasks for an hour. She wasn't at all. In the first hour she was there, observing and listening to one individual order taker, every call that person worked on had some variation on the task.

You may also see other effects of the environment or other triggers as you observe and listen to what otherwise seems to be the same task. For example, the user may have gotten all the way through the task the first time you watched, but the second time the user may be interrupted, have to suspend the work, do something else, and then get back to the task. Or the user may get to a point and discover that this time there is information missing, so even without an external interruption, the user has to stop the task. Even if you don't observe the rest of that task, you'll note for the designers that the user needs a way to be able to pick up on the task at that place when the information comes later.

Thanking the user, distributing presents, and taking your leave

Don't overstay your welcome. Abide by the agreement of how long you will be at the user's site. If you are getting terrific information and could get more by staying longer, of course you can ask to do so. However, as in any social situation, you need to be attuned to all the signals from people's words and their body language to decide if users and their managers genuinely want you to stay longer or are just being polite in response to your request.

Pack up your materials unobtrusively. If there are two of you, one can be packing up while the other starts the process of thanking people.

Whether the users have volunteered or are being paid, you probably also want to give out token gifts just to say "thank you." After all, the users have invited you into their space, have let you look over their shoulders as they are working, have shared their thoughts with you. They are helping you. In selecting token gifts, think about the users and their environments. In some cases, a mug, mouse pad, wrist rest, or other desktop item with your company's logo is something users would like—especially if their managers have been to lots of meetings and brought those back for themselves but the users haven't received those gifts before.

If the users already have lots of items with the company's logo, you'll have to come up with other ideas. Pen sets, candy in dishes that remain as desktop items, or gift certificates to local stores or restaurants work well as "thank you" gifts. Be sure the gifts are acceptable. People at home and in most companies can accept gifts, but some government workers cannot accept vendor gifts of any kind.

As you leave, be sure to thank the supervisors, managers, or others who facilitated the visit as well as the users whom you worked with.

Send a thank you letter after the visit to each user whom you worked with and also to anyone who helped arrange the visit or did something special during the visit. If you can make the letters personal by recalling a specific event or discussion, do so. However, be very careful not to make any promises in the thank you letter about what will or will not happen based on what you learned.

Note taking form

You may want to use or adapt the form shown in figure 9-8 for taking notes as users do tasks. Notice that the form is divided into two columns. The large left column is for taking notes on users' behaviors; the smaller right column is for you to jot down questions you might want to ask the users, especially if you cannot ask the users while they are working, or inferences about the users' behaviors. Be sensitive as you take your notes that they won't hurt or embarrass the users if you share them.

OBSERVING A USER WHO IS TRYING TO DO A TASK

Project:
Observation #:
Observer:
Date:_____/_____/_____
Page:_____ of _____

Inferences/Questions:
_____

User's goal: _____   _____
_____   _____

User's task: _____   _____
_____   _____

Notes about the user: _____ _____
_____   _____
_____   _____
_____   _____

Notes about the environment: _____   _____
_____   _____
_____   _____
_____   _____

Situation at starting point: _____   _____
_____   _____
_____   _____
_____   _____

Time task was started: _____ : _____ A.M. P.M.

Figure 9-8 Note taking form.

Page: _____ of _____

Observations   Inferences/Questions:

_____   _____
_____   _____
_____   _____
_____   _____
_____   _____
_____   _____
_____   _____
_____   _____
_____   _____
_____   _____
_____   _____

Time task was stopped: _____ : _____ A.M. P.M.

Situation at end of task: _____
_____   _____
_____   _____
_____   _____

End point that will show goal has been met: _____
_____   _____
_____   _____
_____   _____

Figure 9-8 Note taking form. (Continued)

References cited in the chapter

Mirel, Barbara, Minimalism for complex tasks, in *Minimalism Since the Nurnberg Funnel,* edited by John M. Carroll, Cambridge, MA: MIT Press in cooperation with the Society for Technical Communication, 1998.

Prail, Amanda, Suggestions on collecting observational data, *Common Ground,* 1 (2), 1991: 3–4.

Other books and articles for further reading

Dumas, Joseph S. and Redish, Janice C., *A Practical Guide to Usability Testing,* Greenwich, CT: Ablex, 1993.

Holtzblatt, Karen and Jones, Sandra, Contextual inquiry: A participatory technique for system design, in *Participatory Design: Principles and Practices*, edited by Douglas Schuler and Aki Namioka, Hillsdale, NJ: Lawrence Erlbaum Associates, 1993, 177–210.

Schriver, Karen A., *Dynamics in Document Design*, NY: John Wiley & Sons, 1997.

Schriver, Karen A., Plain language through protocol-aided revision, in *Plain Language: Principles and Practice*, edited by Erwin R. Steinberg, Detroit: Wayne State University Press, 1991, 148–172.

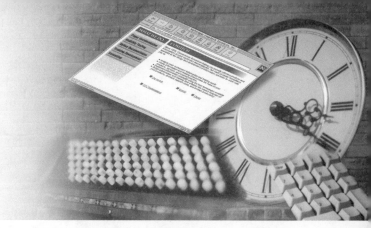

10

Conducting the site visit—honing your interviewing skills

In chapter 9, we focused on getting information by watching users. In this chapter, we focus on getting information by asking questions and listening to users. In many cases, of course, you'll do both. Indeed, for site visits, we recommend that, whenever possible, you conduct concurrent contextual interviews, that is, you combine observing, listening, and asking the user questions in the context of the user's work as shown in figure 10-1.

Concurrent, contextual interviews are, however, only one of several ways of talking with users. Depending on the nature of the tasks you need to learn about, the ability and willingness of the users to talk with you as they work, how much time you have with the users, and other factors, you may choose a different way of interviewing users. To review the various techniques that we introduced in chapter 6, you may decide to

- probe for information while the user is performing the task (concurrent, contextual interviews)

- record what the user does and talk about it immediately after the user completes the task (immediate recall interview)

- record what the user does and talk about it sometime later, perhaps while you and the user watch parts of the videotape (cued recall interview)

Figure 10-1 Talking with the user while the user is performing a task.

- interview users individually or in groups to understand an entire process or work flow (process interview)

- interview one user first (as a key informant) and then later interview others and conduct observations with discussions during the observations (ethnographic interviews)

- collect artifacts from the user and construct an interview around the artifacts, particularly about differences in the way the user dealt with seemingly similar artifacts (cued recall interview or discourse-based interview; artifact walkthrough)

- interview users about specific situations when you cannot observe them (critical incident interview)

- interview users individually or in groups about attitudes, desires, preferences, experience, etc. (group interview or focus group)

- interview users away from their work sites with examples of their work as stimuli for the discussion (usability roundtables)

- work with a group of users over time with interviews as one of the techniques (customer partnering)

No matter which of these techniques or combination of techniques you use, there are some fundamental skills you should practice to be a successful interviewer. That's what we cover in this chapter. In this chapter, we discuss

- listening—the most important part of interviewing
- setting expectations about roles and knowledge
- planning the questions or issues for site visit interviews
- knowing what you are trying to learn
- realizing the power of different types of questions
- asking neutral questions
- probing to get additional information
- respecting silence
- watching body language and other signals from users
- capturing exactly what the user says
- staying close to your site visit plan
- giving users opportunities to answer the questions you didn't ask
- handling questions from users

Overarching all of these topics is a philosophy of interviewing that will set the tone for all your interactions with users. As you plan and conduct interviews with users, keep these three points in mind:

- Treat the user as a partner, not as a research subject.
- Assume the user knows a lot about his or her work.
- Listen far more than you talk.

Listening—the most important part of interviewing

The most important point to remember about site visits for a user and task analysis is that you are there to listen and learn from the user. This is not a training session; you are not there to teach or talk. This is not a demonstration session; you are not there to show off the product. This is not an ego trip for you or anyone else on the team; none of you is there to show off how much you know.

Listen → Learn

The best way to learn is to open your eyes and ears and truly see and hear what the user is telling you. Whether the user is a novice or an expert on the tasks you are observing, you are there to see how the user does the tasks. In this situation, the user is always "right," because whatever the user does, however the user works on the tasks is that user's process. That's what you are there to see.

When you think about interviewing, concentrate on listening, not on talking. If you are there to learn, you must listen. Any time you spend talking is time that you cannot be listening.

Setting expectations about roles and knowledge

At the beginning of a site visit session, you may want to set expectations with the user about your respective roles and knowledge. That's when you explain who you are, why you're there, and what you hope to get from the session. That's when you convey your interest in the user and the user's work, that the user is your partner in helping you to understand the realities of the user's work situation and work processes. That's when the user also gets to express what he or she expects the session to be like and what he or she wants to have as a result of the site visit.

In many cases, users, especially nonexperts, will try to put you, the observer, in the position of expert, especially if you come from the company that put out the product or from the development team if it is an internal product. You must guard against that. Even if you think you have agreed on roles and knowledge, during the session, the user may turn to you and ask, "Am I doing it right?" or "Did I do the right thing there?" Resist the temptation to answer from the product or development team's point of view. Respond with, "Whatever you do today is 'right.' We're here to see how *you* do the task. You're the task expert. We're trying to understand how the people who do the work do these tasks. We want to know what makes sense to you."

While there is some advantage to having the primary interviewer in site visits *not* be an expert in the system, it is also important that the interviewer not be totally naive either. An expert in the system may find it more difficult to note what users are doing without reinterpreting the users' words and actions into the terms of the current system. An expert in the system may find it more difficult to ask the seemingly naive question that gets the users to talk more about their actual work processes.

But the primary interviewer should have done at least some homework on the system before doing site visits. You don't want to sound stupid about the product or process you are observing. We have both found that knowing something about the system helps both in making sense of what we see and hear and in giving the users we are working with confidence that we will be able to understand and use what they are showing and telling us.

Planning the questions or issues for site visit interviews

The interviews we are talking about in this book are different from surveys in that you are not likely to be asking exactly the same questions in exactly the same words of all the people you talk to. If we consider a survey to be a completely structured interview, the types of interviews we are talking about here range from unstructured to semistructured.

For a concurrent, contextual interview, most of the questions you ask will be spontaneous, driven by something you see the user do or a comment the user makes. For an immediate recall interview, most of the questions will also be driven by something you saw or heard as the user was doing the task. However, even for these interviews, you should know what issues you are trying to learn about before you do the site visits. (See chapter 7 for more on setting out the issues as part of your site visit plan.)

Other interviews that are not responses to an immediate situation during the site visit merit even more attention to the specific questions that you want to ask. For a cued-recall interview, you review the artifacts or videotapes and plan which cues you want to give users and what questions you want to ask from those cues.

For semistructured, individual interviews apart from observations, you should write out a questionnaire (also sometimes called a "protocol" or "script"). It's usually for you to use, not to hand to the user. In the end, you may not ask every user all the questions. You may ask them in a different order. You may ask different follow-up questions of different users. But having the questions in writing reminds you of what you want to cover and helps keep you focused on the specific questions for which you need answers. Similarly, for focus groups, you prepare a list of the issues you want to cover and then make sure the open discussion covers the issues on the list.

In a typical site visit, you may well combine interviewing techniques. For example, your site visit plan might include both talking with the user while observing the user doing tasks and also getting answers to specific questions that your team or client wants to know about. In that case, you would do a spontaneous, unstructured interview that differs from user to user while doing the observations, and you would also do a semistructured interview apart from the tasks, in the user's space or in a conference room, repeating the questions that you ask of all the other users. Alternatively, you might observe one or two users individually and then meet with a group that includes those users and others to ask the more structured questions. Or as Larry Wood (1996) suggests, you might conduct interviews first, take back what you learn about the users' work from the interviews, and use that information to plan for observations.

The point is that whichever of these techniques you use, spend at least some time before you go planning what you will ask and how you will ask it.

Knowing what you are trying to learn

Questions are your way of getting the user to talk more—and to talk about issues that concern you. As you plan the questions to ask, it may help to think about the types of information you want to get in different situations. In chapter 6, we gave you a list of the questions you would ask in doing a process analysis. Here are a few other situations you might be interested in and suggestions for what you might want to learn.

While you are watching users work

In the context of watching users work, you probably want to ask questions that help you to

- clarify what the user actually did (It may have happened so fast, you weren't sure what you saw. Something may have obscured your vision. You may have looked away for a moment.)

- understand why the user took a particular action

- understand why the user didn't do something else

- find out if the user always does it this way

- find out what triggers different choices if the user does have variations

- verify your interpretation of what is happening

If you are primarily interested in documentation

If documentation is one of the topics you want to focus on, you may be interested in learning

- whether the user has a copy of the manual for the product

- where the documentation for the product is kept

- when and how the user typically goes to different types of documentation (print manuals, online help, tutorials, etc.)

- reasons or experiences behind the user's attitudes toward and typical use of different types of documentation

- whether the user has created personal documentation (his or her own "cheat sheets" or other types of notes) and if so, what it covers and how it is written

As the user works, you may want to be sure to capture

- specific words or phrases the person uses when searching for information

- what the user expects to find as a result of each search
- whether each search was successful from the user's point of view and if not, why not

For an excellent article with questions and examples for semistructured ethnographic interviews, see Wood (1996). In the next few sections, we give you an overview of types of questions for any kind of interview with examples and suggestions about using them.

Realizing the power of different types of questions

Figure 10-2 offers a taxonomy of question types. As you plan an interview, consider which types will be best for your situation. In a typical interview you will probably combine several of the types. All have their place in interviews, except leading and blaming questions which we discuss later in the chapter.

Closed versus open questions

In large-scale surveys, the questions are almost always all closed. That's for ease of doing data entry and analysis. In face-to-face interviews, which is what we are talking about in this book, you can favor open-ended questions. You will generally find that open questions get you much richer data than closed questions. They are basically invitations to the user to talk about a specific issue. A closed question can be useful, however, especially as the ice-breaker to get into a topic.

Closed question:	"Do you have a PC at home?"
Participant answers:	"Yes"
Open question:	"What do you use it to do?"

General versus specific questions

Both general and specific questions have a place in face-to-face interviews. In many cases, a general question is a good way to open up a topic. You can then use specific questions to probe for more details or to keep the user going on the topic.

General open question:	"What are you trying to do in this task?"
Participant answers:	"Well, this customer called yesterday and wants to go visit her sister in Phoenix. She's open about when to go so I need to try out a whole bunch of itineraries to find her a really low fare."
Specific open question:	"Okay. What's the first thing you're going to do now?"

Type	Definition	Examples
Closed	Structured, limits responses	Do you use a PC? How long have you worked here?
Open	Broad, no fixed response Invites discussion	Who? What? When? Where? Why? Tell me about…
General	Focuses on big picture	What do you do when a client asks for…
Specific	Focuses on details	After you type in the zip code, what do you do next?
Factual	Can be verified	What did you do just then?
Hypothetical	Speculative	Do you think you would…? What would you do if…?
Judgmental	Asks for opinion	What do you think about…?
Comparative	Asks for judgment about two or more alternatives	Would you rather use the first product you worked with or the second? How does this compare to…?
Neutral	Even-handed Includes no value words	What do you think of…? How does this software work for you?
Leading (Don't do it!)	Includes value words, suggests the right answer	Don't you think that…? Is it easy to…?
Blaming (Don't do it!)	Asks so directly that user appears at fault	Why didn't you do…? (Note: Tone of voice matters here.)
Request for suggestions	Lets interviewee offer an opinion	How would you like this to work? If you could tell the developers just one thing about this product, what would it be?
Request for questions	Lets interviewee shape questions; lets you capture what you didn't think of	Is there anything you'd like to add? Is there something else that I should have asked?

Figure 10-2 Types of questions for interviews.

Factual versus hypothetical questions

Users generally find it easier to answer factual questions than ones that ask them about hypothetical situations or that ask them to create their own new products or processes. In our experience, you can get useful responses from users about future possibilities if you keep the questions very specific, especially if you bring screen prints or other pictures of the types of changes or new products or processes you are considering.

However, asking users to "think outside the box," to "blue sky" about how to change products or processes often yields very few exciting insights. Users, especially users who have been doing the same tasks with the same system for a long time, have absorbed that system to the point where it is second nature to them. It is just "the way we do things." They cannot imagine a different way of doing things even when it is obvious from your observations that the current process is cumbersome, inefficient, and even frustrating.

Factual question:	"How often do you get a customer who wants to rent a car without also making an airline reservation?"
Hypothetical and specific question:	"If we had a screen like this with these fields [show new screen], would you have the information to fill out each of these fields? Where would that information come from?"
Hypothetical and general question ("blue sky"; "think out of the box"):	"If you could design the ideal system for your needs, what would it look like?" "How would you change the process?"

Judgmental and comparative questions

When you think of doing user and task analysis, you probably think first of gathering objective information: demographic facts about the users and observed facts about how the users do the tasks. But you also want to get subjective information from the users. You want to know their attitudes, opinions, motivations, expectations. Asking users what they think about their work, their tasks, their processes, and the products they are using may be an important part of your interviews. When you ask subjective questions, however, you need to be especially careful to ask them in a neutral manner so that you get the user's real opinion and not what the user thinks you want to hear. That's why we devote an entire section to how to ask neutral questions.

Asking neutral questions

One of the most difficult but critical guidelines for a successful interview is to keep the questions neutral. You don't want to put words in the user's mouth. You don't want to lead the user by suggesting the value you want the user to select. You don't want to blame the user or make the user feel stupid. Asking questions so that you don't lead or blame the user is not easy. It takes practice. But it is very important to learn how to do if you want to truly learn what users think.

Neutral versus leading questions

Sometimes, of course, users are very unhappy with products or situations and grab the opportunity of your site visit to complain or to be very negative about companies, products, documents, or even individuals. Most users, most of the time, however, want to please. When you ask questions, they try to give you the answer that they think you want. If you put value words in your questions, they will pick up on those value words and give you answers that are slanted in the direction of those values.

Here are some examples of leading questions and ways to probe for the same information in a more neutral manner:

Leading question:	"That was difficult, wasn't it?"
Neutral question:	"How did that task go for you?"
Leading question:	"You didn't really have problems with those menus, did you?"
Neutral question:	"What do you think about the way the menus are organized?"
Leading question:	"Would the new screens work for you?"
Leading question:	"How did you like the new screens?"
Neutral question:	"What do you think about the new screens?"

Even the question that includes matching value words is a leading question. Users are likely to pick up on whichever word you give first.

Leading question:	"How easy or difficult was that?"
Neutral question:	"How was doing that task?"

Even after you've done several site visits and consider yourself an expert, you need to watch for leading questions. You may have to walk a fine line between being sympathetic to the user and keeping the questions neutral.

Ginny had just watched a user struggle through a complex task. The user had taken information from a customer and promised to call back with the answer to the customer's query. She persevered because she wanted to make the customer happy. She had to remember commands she didn't use regularly. She had to interpret cryptic messages from the computer. She tried in vain to get help from the online information system. At the end, when she finally succeeded at the task and was ready to call the customer back with the answer, Ginny found herself saying out loud what she was thinking:

"Wow. That was difficult, wasn't it?" Ginny's first thought had been to be empathetic toward the user. The user certainly needed some positive stroking and support. The software really hadn't made her task easy. But it was not Ginny's place to judge the software for the user, so it was a leading question.

How do you avoid asking leading questions? Use open-ended questions or requests such as

Neutral question:	"How did that go?"
Neutral question:	"How was doing that task for you?"
Neutral request:	"Tell me how you feel after doing that task."

Russ Branaghan (1995) suggests that the ability to ask questions neutrally and to really hear what the user is saying and not reinterpret it to be what you want to hear is one reason to be sure that you include a usability professional on the site visit team. Asking neutral questions also means not setting up the user so that it is obvious how you want the user to answer. Branaghan tells the story in our next example to show how easy it is to fool yourself about what users think. If the company in Branaghan's story puts out the product with the problem unfixed, users are likely to have difficulty and be unhappy despite what this developer got the user to say. Dialogues like this are not the purpose of site visits.

Recently [Russ Branaghan tells us], I observed a software developer interviewing a user. A small portion of that dialogue is shown below. Developer: "Unfortunately, there is really nothing we can do to fix Feature X. It would take us several more months, and the managers will not stand for that. Besides, the users will only make this mistake a few times and then they'll catch on. This isn't too unusable, is it?"

User: "No, I suppose it's not too bad. I guess it's OK."

The developer then informed us that the users didn't seem to mind the problem with Feature X. (Branaghan 1995, 12)

Neutral versus blaming questions

Blaming questions suggest that the user should have acted in a different way. Blaming questions often start: "Why did you…?" or "Why didn't you…?" Here are two examples of blaming questions and ways to probe for the same information in a more neutral manner:

Blaming question:	"Why didn't you read the manual first?"
Neutral question:	"I noticed that you first tried to do the task without the manual. You picked up the manual later. Is that how you typically use manuals?"

| Blaming question: | "Why did you do that again? The first reply went just fine but you did the whole task a second time. Now the person who sent the message has two replies." |
| Neutral question: | "The first time you tried to send a reply, you typed your response and chose Send. I noticed you seemed to be thinking about it and then you retyped the same response. What was happening there?" |

Research shows that users tend to blame themselves

If you've done much field research or watched and listened to users in a usability test, you know that when something goes wrong, users tend to blame themselves rather than the product, manufacturer, or manual. They say things like: "Oh, I'm so stupid." "That was dumb of me." In fact, Karen Schriver (1997) found in two different studies that users blame themselves more than half the time. This finding came from both a survey and observations.

In Schriver's survey, users were asked "If you experienced a problem of any sort while you were trying to use your product, where did you assign the blame?" Of the five choices (manual, machine, manufacturer, self, don't remember), 63% of the respondents chose "to myself." Men and women gave remarkably similar answers (males, 62%; females, 65%). The result also held true across age from people under 20 to people over 60, with the one exception being that people in their 50s were less likely to blame themselves.

Schriver and her group also noted who users blamed during usability test sessions. They asked users the blame question before the test and again after the test. They also analyzed statements the users made while they (the users) were working with the products. We think that the statements users made while they were working are particularly revealing. The 35 users made a total of 331 relevant statements during the usability tests. That's an average of more than nine blaming statements per user while they were working. And in just over half (51%), users blamed themselves for the problems they were having (Schriver 1997, 219).

Work on making sure you don't encourage users to blame themselves

When you ask questions in ways that users might interpret as telling them they should have done something different, you only fuel the users' tendency to blame themselves. How can you avoid blaming the user as you ask questions? As the examples we gave earlier show you, one successful tactic is to feed back the user's behavior as you saw it and then ask a more general question about the situation or that type of behavior or the user's past experiences. You can also not ask a question but just open the way for users to start talking.

Another successful tactic is to be sure to use an even tone of voice when you talk about the user's behavior. The same words can come over as neutral or as blaming depending on your intonation and the way you emphasize the words in what you

Neutral question:	"It was really interesting to see how you did that reservation. In this case, you printed out the itinerary, went and got it from the printer, and then faxed it over to the caller. Have you ever tried other ways to do it?"
	(User responds "yes" and goes on, on her own, to explain when and why.)
Neutral statement leading to an opening for user to talk:	"If I understand correctly, you create most of your assembly drawings by modifying older ones. Can you tell me more about that process and under what circumstances it happens?"

say. Consider the sentence, "You didn't start by looking at the manual." Said in an even, neutral tone, it can be a statement of fact. Said with a frown or with rising intonation as in a question, it can come across to users to mean: "Why didn't you…?" or "I think you should have started with the manual." As you talk with users, pay attention to your tone of voice.

Keeping the conversation going

To get as much information as possible about the users and the way they do their tasks, you may need to probe for more information than you get as an answer to the first question that you ask. How can you get users to keep talking? Figure 10-3 describes some of the reasons why you might want to probe and the types of responses you might give for each.

When you want to	Try this
Keep the conversation going	"Uh-huh." "Yes, that's interesting." "I see."
Encourage continuation and show that you are following what is being said	Paraphrase or repeat back.
Get more details	"Tell me more about…" "And what did you do then?"
Clarify something you're not sure you understood	"If I understand, you're saying that…"

Figure 10-3 Types of probes you can use in interviews.

Linguists who study conversation have seen that when two people are talking, they give each other signals to indicate whose turn it is to talk. When one person stops talking, that's a signal to the other to begin. But in conversation with users during a site visit, you often want the user to talk longer. You don't want to take your conversational turn. When you respond with general comments or just friendly noises like, "That's interesting. Tell me more," you are signaling to the other person that you are listening, that you are interested in what that person is saying, and that you do not want to take your conversational turn.

Using active listening

Another way of signaling that you are listening but that you want the user to continue to be the person giving information is to use a technique called "active listening." In active listening, you repeat back part of what the other person said and you do it in a tone that indicates you are very interested and want the person to continue talking.

User:	"Then I went looking for the manual for the stove, but I couldn't find it, so I decided to see if I could do it on my own." [User stops and is quiet.]
Interviewer	"So you decided to see if you could do it on your own."
User:	"Yeah, so I went back to the stove and…"

By repeating back part of what the user said, the interviewer has taken a turn in the conversation without changing the conversation or adding to it. What the interviewer has done here is to send a signal that is equivalent to saying: "I heard you. I'm listening. I know you stopped so it was my turn to speak, but I'm not adding any information here, so I'm giving the conversational turn back to you." Of course, the interviewer doesn't want to be that explicit out loud, but that's what is accomplished by the active listening repetition of part of what the user said. When the interviewer stops talking, the user picks up the signal that it's his or her turn to talk again, and the user goes on with the story.

Getting more details

Paraphrasing part of what the user said is a good technique when you don't know what is going to come next. When you want more details, you can often be more direct. Sometimes it's appropriate to just say, "Tell me more." Sometimes it's appropriate to ask a direct question that focuses the user's attention on what you want to know more about, as in questions like these: "And what happens next?" "What did you do then?" "Who gets the information at that point?" "Do you print any other forms?" "Does anyone else ask for that kind of information?" "Is that a typical situation for you?"

Clarifying and checking your understanding

In site visits, you are trying to understand the user's world. That often requires that you make sure that you are correctly interpreting what you are seeing or what the user is telling you. In many cases, the purpose of probing is to clarify your own understanding. In chapter 9, we talked about the importance of separating observations and inferences—separating the user's behaviors that you actually see from what you think the user's behaviors mean. Just as important is separating what you actually hear from what you think you hear. If you are not sure, probe for clarification. You can do that by saying something like, "I want to be sure that I understand what you're saying. I hear you say that (paraphrase the user's point). Is that right?"

You may find that it is especially important to clarify the meaning of words. One critical guideline for interfaces and documentation is that they use the users' words. As you listen to users, you are gathering their vocabulary. However, you should also probe to be sure you understand what they mean by the words they use. You may assume that because you hear a word you know, you and the user have the same meaning for that word—and that may not be true.

Respecting silence

In typical conversations, silence is a signal from one person to the other to take over the conversation. As we've been saying, in a site visit interview, you may not want to take your turn right away. You may want the user to keep talking. Silence can be a powerful probe.

Give the user time to think. If the user stops talking but seems to still be thinking, wait for the user to say more. Some of the most interesting information comes from respecting silence and waiting for the user to continue.

Silence is a tricky probe. If you let silence go on too long, the user may become uncomfortable. You may want the user to be a little bit uncomfortable, to think more deeply about a topic than he or she may have done before. But you certainly do not want the user to be overly uncomfortable. We can't give you a specific number of seconds to wait. It varies with the people, their culture, and the topics involved. With practice, you'll find you can recognize from the user's body language when the user is likely to have more to say, and you'll get a sense of how long to wait.

Watching body language and other signals from users

People signal interest, boredom, frustration, happiness, and other feelings with more than words. Facial expressions, gestures, and posture are also ways of signaling feelings. In face-to-face observations and interviews, body language can be very important. Watch your body language as shown in Figure 10-4. Use it to show interest, but don't use it to send signals that the user is doing something wrong or that you are bored with what is going on. Watch the user's body language. Be aware of signals that the user is frustrated with the interview, thinks it has gone on too long, feels pushed beyond what he or she wants to do, etc., as well as signals that the user is doing fine even when you are getting frustrated.

Figure 10-4 Be sensitive to the signals you send with your body and facial expressions.

Practice will help you find the right balance

Here again, practice will help you find the right balance. We aren't suggesting that you sit there like a rigid log with a blank, stoic expression. You are part of the conversation. You want to be animated and interested, and a friendly expression is part of that. You want to see what the user is doing and that may well mean leaning in toward the user. You want to be empathetic but not to the disparagement of the product or process you are watching.

Be sensitive to cultural differences, especially in international situations

If you are going to be interviewing users from another culture, learn about the meaning of different physical signals (what we are calling body language—facial expressions, gestures, and posture) in that culture as well as other cultural differences before you do the site visits. Norms for these physical signals and other aspects of conversations differ from culture to culture. For example, two Australians talking to each other in everyday conversation will typically stand closer to each other than will two Americans. Masao Ito and Kumiyo Nakakoji (1996) suggest that Japanese users typically display more patience for learning a system than users in other cultures. They say that Japanese users are unlikely to explicitly show strong opinions against their company and are even more likely than others to blame themselves when things go wrong.

Many users, especially sophisticated computer users and technical professionals, may have spent some time in your culture. Those users may be more aware of cultural differences and may be more comfortable in cross-cultural situations than you are. You may find that because they know that you are a foreigner, they do not expect you to adapt entirely to their way of doing things.

However, some people in the culture you are visiting may not have had these cross-cultural experiences. They may not be aware of the differences between their culture and yours, and what they do is normal for them. Therefore, you must understand at least the basics of the norms in the culture you are visiting, both so that you do not misunderstand the signals users send to you through their body language and so that you do not inadvertently miscommunicate with or insult the people you are visiting.

Consider getting local help in understanding how to behave in that culture. For example, Susan Dray and Deborah Mraczek (1996b, 252), who did site visits to users' homes in Germany and France, report that "we relied on our local translator to coach us about when and how to shake hands, whether to offer to help clear the table [after the dinner that they had brought to the family], and how to show respect and interest regarding specific local holiday customs and decorations."

Be sensitive to cultural differences even within your own country

As we discussed in chapter 4, social interactions and culture affect all environments. You do not have to go abroad to find cultural differences. For example, Ito and Nakakoji (1996) talk about different expectations about what is politely called "communication overlap"—whether it is acceptable for people to interrupt each other in conversations. They say, "In many of the Western languages, [speakers] alternate; in the Asian languages, they alternate and pause for a while; and in the Latin languages, the two conversations overlap."

You'll find differences in the acceptability of overlapping conversations even within English-speaking groups. Deborah Tannen (1986) found that in some groups, defined by ethnicity and geography, conversations in social situations proceed by interruptions, not waiting for the speaker to finish, while in other groups, interrupting is considered socially unacceptable. If you are going out on site visits, be aware of your own conversational style, especially if you come from a culture that accepts interrupting, and be alert to the expectations of the users you are interviewing.

Be sensitive to individual differences, too

It is difficult not to project your own expectations and frustrations on the situation you are observing and on the user you are interviewing. In chapter 2, in the discussion of understanding users, we talked about personality differences. These can affect those body language signals that you and the person you are observing or talking with send to each other and how you both interpret each other's signals.

For example, you may be a very methodical person who quickly turns to the online help when you don't know how to proceed. The person you are interviewing may be a "hacker," a person who never goes to help and who works best by trial and error, playing around in the system. Thus you may be frustrated with the system long before the other person is. Or you may yourself be a "hacker" and be impatient with users who proceed slowly and carefully and who spend a lot of time in the documentation.

Ginny was on a site visit with two other people watching a user try out the prototype of a new version of a software product. This particular user bypassed all the "just in time" tips that the product offered, never used the performance aids that had been built into the product, and moved so quickly past messages and menus that she didn't seem to get any help from them. She plunged right in to trying to work with the screens, took many wrong turns, went back to places over and over, got lost several times, but kept going. Ginny found it very difficult to observe with a friendly but unconcerned expression and to ask neutrally what the user was doing without jumping in to suggest that the user take advantage of the tips and performance aids. In fact, after a while, Ginny did suggest using the built in aides, but the user tried it once briefly and then went back to the trial-and-error approach. After the session, the observers disagreed on how frustrated the user had been. Although the user had expressed mild frustration in a few places, she had not given up and had never been upset. After discussing what had happened, the three observers realized that they had been reacting from their own personal ways of working with software. Ginny and one of the observers would not have worked the way this user did. The other observer said that she was just like this user and that the user's way of rapidly trying and rejecting pathways was also her way of learning.

Capturing exactly what the user says

Just as we urged you in chapter 9 to try to capture the user's actual behaviors in your observation notes, we urge you to try to capture the user's actual words in your interview notes. Getting down exactly what users say—in the words they use—is critical for two reasons. First, quoting users in their own words brings them alive for the team members who were not there. Often a quote from a user will have a greater impact on the people who have not been to users' sites than all your more technical reports. Second, successful products incorporate the users' vocabulary. One of your goals for a user and task analysis is very likely to be to learn what words users use for the objects and actions the product will include.

Unless you are a very fast typist, you probably won't be able to take down every word the user says, but for the words you do take down, don't translate. If you put down your words instead of the user's words, you are interpreting what the user is saying. (You can, of course, also take notes on your interpretations and on your own thoughts. Just make sure you indicate clearly when your notes refer to what the user said and when they refer to what you thought about what the user said.)

When you watch and listen to users, you may feel more comfortable about an inference you are making if the user not only did something but talked about it, too. If the user says, "I'm confused here," you have the user's report of his or her state of mind, not your inference about it. That's why getting users to talk while working is so critical.

You may need to make a special effort to keep what the users say in their own words. Many inexperienced analysts find themselves translating what users say. A client whom Ginny was mentoring into becoming a usability specialist realized this on her own after being the note taker in an observation. She said, "I found myself translating what the user said into our internal jargon. I was thinking I need to get this in words the developers will understand. But in fact what I need to do is keep it in the user's words because we're trying to tell the developers that the users don't know either our internal jargon or the operating system's software terms."

If you are videotaping or audiotaping the site visit, you will have the user's words on tape. However, just as most teams rely more on their notes from usability testing than on the hours and hours of videotape, most teams don't have the time to transcribe and study all the tapes from site visits. You are likely to find yourself relying on your notes.

If you use the tapes at all, you are likely to go looking for specific moments from the site visits that you remember or ones you marked in your notes as being particularly insightful. If you find that you cannot get everything the user said on a topic and it is important enough for you to go back to or if you want to include it in a report or a highlight tape, mark the place in your notes with a special symbol and also write down the tape time if you can. That will make the place easier to find on the tape.

Staying close to your site visit plan

If you have a list of issues or topics that you want to be sure to cover in a site visit, you have to subtly stay in control of the situation. Here are some hints for how to do this:

- When you start to work with the user, verify or establish how long you both expect the session to last.

- You might start with some social chit-chat to build rapport, but don't let it take up too much time. Take the lead on moving to the business at hand in a polite but firm way. (You may find that the user has been waiting for you to do this. As the external person, you will likely be seen as the lead in how the site visit will go. You're the one who has come into the environment with a plan that makes this day different from other days for the user.)

- There is a cross-cultural corollary to the last point: Expectations of the amount of time spent in rapport building differ from culture to culture. Be aware of expectations in the culture in which you are interviewing.

- Pace the site visit. Have some idea of where you should be in your agenda or interview when the time is half up. Adjust your plans if your timing is off. You might decide to skip some questions, to probe less deeply into other questions, or to ask for more time.

- Don't just assume you can finish the interview no matter how much time it takes. Renegotiate the amount of time part way through if it looks as if you will need more time. Understand that no matter how far you have come, how important you think the site visit is, or how much you want the information, if the user cannot spare more time or doesn't want to continue, you must respect that choice.

- Know which are the most important issues or questions for the team you represent so that you can make wise choices if you cannot cover everything.

Being flexible

Despite all the bulleted items in the list we just gave you, sometimes *not* following the plan will get you the most important information. Take advantage of the unexpected if it is likely to yield relevant information even if (perhaps especially if) it shows you an aspect of the situation that no one on the design team has even thought about.

JoAnn was visiting a customer site and happened to arrive early for an interview with the field office manager. While waiting in the general workroom where employees were sorting items for delivery, she was able to observe by pure chance a significant event in which the team of employees consulted the manual to answer a question about a procedure. The shift leader referred the team to the manual and worked with them to find the appropriate procedure in question. They discussed the recommended action, the alternatives available, and decided how to proceed. This serendipitous experience gave JoAnn insight into the group's behavior in finding critical information. Of course, she took notes on what she observed even though it had not been in her plan.

Giving users opportunities to answer the questions you didn't ask

One of the reasons for doing site visits is to understand aspects of the users' world that you had not imagined. As part of every interview, therefore, you should ask the users if there is anything else they think you should know. You can ask this in several ways:

- "Is there anything else about the process that we haven't covered?"

- "Are there any questions that you had expected me to ask that I didn't?"

- "Is there anything else you'd like the design team to think about when they're working on the new product?"

- "If you could tell the developers just one thing, what would it be?"

- "Have we covered all the types of situations you deal with? Are there any other situations I should have asked about?"

Handling questions from users

The people you visit for your user and task analyses are going to be curious, too. They may well have questions for you. You need to let them ask the questions, but you also need to be very careful about your responses.

Here are some suggestions for handling questions from users:

- No question is a dumb question. Treat every question with respect.

- You probably do not want to answer questions about how the product works while the user is working. That would become a training session, not a task analysis in which you learn how the user does the tasks. If the user asks how to do something, you might say something like, "We're here to see how you do the tasks. However you do them is what we want to see." In some cases, if you do indeed know some tricks for the product that the user doesn't know, it might be appropriate to offer to answer some of those questions at the end of the session.

When Denise Carlevato was doing user and task analysis site visits for Visio Corporation, the incentive for the users to let the field research team come and observe was the promise that at the end of a two-hour observation, the user could ask the technical person on the site visit team for a half-hour of technical assistance. The technical person would explain or help the user learn whatever aspect of the software the user wanted to know more about (Judith Ramey and Denise Carlevato, personal communication, 1997).

- Never promise that something the user asks for will happen. Just say that you're not the person who will make the decisions about what gets done.

- Always promise that you will take the users' concerns, requests, praise, or other comments back to the appropriate people. And do it. Users want to know that they are being heard. One of the major reasons to do predesign site visits is to make sure the design and development team knows who the users are and what they do and need. You cannot make promises about what will come of the information you bring back, but you can promise to bring it back and report it.

- Don't spread gossip or rumor. Users may probe you with their questions because they want to know what's going to happen to their jobs, their processes, their tasks. They want to be the first in the office or the first on the block to know about changes. They know you're doing site visits because your team or your client is considering changes or dreaming up new products. Their curiosity is understandable, but unless you've been told what to say, you have to say, "I don't really know." If users' curiosity is going to be an issue, before you go on the site visits, decide what you are going to say about impending changes. If appropriate, get direction or approval from management or marketing about what you can and cannot say when users ask about what is going to happen.

References cited in the chapter

Branaghan, Russ, Five simple principles of iterative design, *Common Ground*, 5 (3), September/ October 1995: 3,12–13.

Dray, Susan and Mrazek, Deborah, A day in the life: Studying contest across cultures, in *International User Interfaces*, edited by Elisa M. del Galdo and Jakob Nielsen, NY: John Wiley & Sons, 1996b, 242–256.

Ito, Masao and Nakakoji, Kumiyo, Impact of culture on user interface design, in *International User Interfaces*, edited by Elisa M. del Galdo and Jakob Nielsen, NY: John Wiley & Sons, 1996, 105–126.

Schriver, Karen A., *Dynamics in Document Design*, NY: John Wiley & Sons, 1997.

Tannen, Deborah, *That's Not What I Meant!: How Conversational Style Makes or Breaks Your Relations with Others*, NY: Morrow, 1986.

Wood, Larry E., The ethnographic interview in user-centered work/task analysis, in *Field Methods Casebook for Software Design*, edited by Dennis Wixon and Judith Ramey, NY: John Wiley & Sons, 1996, 35–56.

Making the transition from analysis to design

In Part 3, we concentrated on observing and interviewing effectively to ensure that the data you collect about your users is comprehensive and accurate. In Part 4 you learn how to organize and analyze your data and begin the steps to transfer your knowledge into an effective interface. We also help you see the importance of everything we cover in this book for all types of interfaces: software, hardware, documentation, and training.

Obviously, you have been analyzing your data as you collect it and have even been thinking about design ideas. That's fine; the process is really much more overlapping than it may seem from the linear presentation in a book. However, it is a good idea to understand your users, their tasks, their environments, and their problems before you immerse yourself in design. Designing prematurely can result in a commitment to a design idea that proves to be inappropriate and that will not work for the users or will not be acceptable to the users. As you observe your users, adding interview to interview and observation to observation, you ground yourself in the user perspective you need to design an effective interface.

We begin this part with a chapter on making sense of the data you have gathered. In chapter 11 we present and illustrate several techniques for organizing and analyzing the data from your site visits. The techniques that you use will depend on the type of information you have collected, the goals of your project, and the experience of your development team. In chapter 11 we show you how to take these factors into account as you develop user profiles, environmental profiles, workflow diagrams, task lists, task hierarchies, flowcharts, different types of scenarios, affinity diagrams, insight sheets, and more. You won't use all of these techniques, of course, so we help you think about which ones are most appropriate for your type of project and your role on the design team.

Although detailed guidelines for designing particular types of products are beyond the scope of this book, chapters 12 and 13 should help you make the transition from data gathering to designing. Design is a complex process that requires both creativity and a firmly grounded understanding of users, tasks, and environments. The information you have collected and your interactions with actual users in real working environments will assist you in designing a product, interface, documentation, and training that help users achieve their goals.

We begin the design process in chapter 12 by showing you how to set qualitative and quantitative usability goals for the product. Usability goals embody the values that will make users eager to work with a new product. Usability goals embody the expectations that your company or client has for users' productivity with the new product.

We also show you how you can take the notes and analyses from chapter 11 and find the objects and actions that you will need in the new interface through an analysis of the nouns and verbs in your task flows. As you consider how to name those objects and actions, we help you think about metaphors. Metaphors are the way to relate what you are putting on the screen to what the users are bringing to it. In the section on metaphors, you'll consider what they are and how they can help and also confuse users. Some of the issues we discuss include how realistic to make metaphors, what behaviors they invoke, how extensible the metaphor is, whether it always has to be a real-world object, and how important it is to maintain the integrity of a metaphor—not using it in contradictory ways.

In chapter 12 you also see how the scenarios that you gathered during the site visits can become "use scenarios," narrative accounts of how the users will perform their tasks in the new interface. We also describe and illustrate how you can create other representations of your design ideas from use scenarios, representations such as use sequences, flow diagrams, workflows, and hierarchies.

At the end of chapter 12, you learn how to develop initial graphical representations of your interface design, using storyboards and rough sketches, as well as more elaborate visualizations such as videos. This provides a transition to chapter 13 in which we describe prototyping at many levels from paper mock-ups to interactive computer-based programs that simulate most of the interaction of the actual product. We suggest very strongly that you prototype before you code.

It saves money, it provides something concrete to talk about, it allows design teams to try out alternatives easily, and it lets users get involved early and deeply.

Through the discussion in chapter 13, you understand the advantages and disadvantages of different types of prototypes and you find details on how to conduct team-based prototyping sessions, including paper prototyping sessions that involve users directly in design. Finally, we urge you to do early usability evaluations of your prototypes with actual users, and you review several techniques you can use even on partial prototypes. We show you research on the value of usability evaluations over just demonstrating prototypes to users and asking for their reactions.

Chapter 14 brings the book to a close with a discussion of how everything we have talked about applies to all parts of products, documentation, and training just as much as to screen design. We address chapter 14 to all our readers, not only to technical communicators and instructional designers who have traditionally had responsibility for documentation and training, but also to all the other members of product teams. Software and hardware communicate with users in many ways and the lines between user interface, documentation, and training are fading rapidly. We show you how many different types of communication are being built into typical software applications and discuss the reasons for them.

Site visits can tell you a great deal about how your users use and do not use different types of documentation and training. In chapter 14 you get help in planning to get that information, points to observe, and questions to ask. Then you'll find ideas about turning what you learn about documentation and training during site visits into information solutions that will work for your users. In the second part of chapter 14, we help you think about specific types of documentation and training, looking at issues such as getting the right tasks into a task-oriented manual, what users look for when they go to online help, and understanding new ideas like electronic performance support systems for integrating documentation and training even more closely into the user interface. If you are designing Web sites or computer-based or Web-based training, you find hints at the end for using the process in this book to make sure that your Web site and your Web-based training are driven by user needs and not solely by new technology.

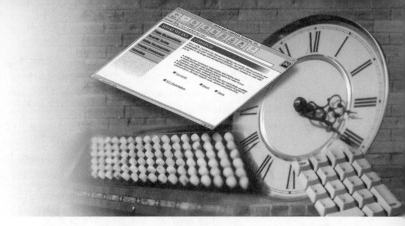

11

Analyzing and presenting the data you have collected

You have conducted your field studies, observed and interviewed your users in their working environments, and perhaps used other techniques as well. What you have now are stacks and stacks of notes, plus videotapes, audiotapes, artifacts you have collected during your visits, and the site visit reports you have written. You have also most likely been digesting your information all along, even thinking through preliminary design ideas. Now you have these questions before you:

- How are you going to make sense of all this data?

- How are you going to turn the data into useful information that you can communicate effectively to other members of the development team?

- How will you communicate with team members who have not had the opportunity to visit users?

- How are you going to turn the communications into decision making about the design of the product interface, the documentation, and the training?

The ways that you choose to analyze and present your data will depend on the richness of the data you have been able to collect, where you are in the development life cycle, the type of development effort in which you are engaged, the experience your development team has had addressing user concerns and using user-focused data, and your relationship to the team's activities. The analysis and presentation methods we discuss in this chapter accommodate a wide variety of issues during the early stage of the interface design process. At this stage, you should select methods that will advance the team's understanding and decision making most effectively. In table 11-1 we list methods which we then describe in more detail in the rest of this chapter.

Analysis method	Brief definition
Lists of users	Lists of the types of users you have seen on your site visits, including estimates of their percentage in the total user population and brief definitions of each, if necessary
Lists of environments	Lists of the types of environments you have seen on your site visits with brief definitions of each
Profiles of users	Brief narrative and/or visual descriptions of the individual users you have met
Profiles of the environments	Brief narrative and/or visual descriptions of the environments you have seen
Workflow diagrams	Drawings of the major tasks of a larger activity either performed by an individual user or by groups of users
Task sequences	Lists of tasks ordered by the sequence in which they are performed
Task hierarchies	Tasks arranged in a hierarchy to show their interrelationships, especially for tasks that are not performed in a particular sequence
User/task matrices	Matrices that illustrate the relationship between the users you have identified and the tasks they perform
Detailed task descriptions from procedural analyses	A step-by-step description from your procedural analysis of a task, including objects, actions, and decisions
Task flowcharts	Drawings of the specifics of a task, including objects, actions, and decisions

Table 11-1 Data presentation and analysis methods.

Analysis method	Brief definition
Task scenarios	Narrative descriptions of a task, ranging from stories of incidents to elaborate descriptions of how users handled a particular incident, including details of steps, actions, and objects
Affinity diagrams	Bottom-up groupings of facts and issues about users, tasks, and environments to generate design ideas
Insight sheets	Lists of issues identified through user studies and insights about them that may affect design decisions
Video- and audiotape highlights	Video or audio clips that illustrate significant observations about users and tasks
Photographs	Photographs of users and their environments that may become part of user and environment profiles
Artifact analysis	Functional descriptions of the artifacts (objects) collected from the users and that are used in the performance of tasks with implications and ideas for design of new or improved products and processes

Table 11-1 Data presentation and analysis methods. (Continued)

Obviously, you will not use all of these methods together. Select methods that best accommodate your data and the needs of your team. In the following sections, we describe each of these methods, explain how to use them, and show an example from an actual project.

As you apply the methods, we recommend that you and your development team members work together. Each of the methods, from user lists through task scenarios, requires discussion and consensus about what you have learned. You may want to try to meet together with team members in a workroom set aside for the duration of the analysis and design. You can create posters, diagrams, and other illustrations on flip chart paper and put them up on the walls. You can attach sticky notes or note cards to your flip chart diagrams. An especially felicitous work environment includes white boards which hold sticky notes well and can be drawn on with erasable markers.

If you cannot set aside a workroom, use lots of flip chart paper that you can take down and store after each design session. Make someone the designated caretaker of the team's notes. Create the various items described here and post them to a team Web site.

Methods for organizing and analyzing your data

The data that you have collected from your studies usually starts out as just that—a lot of facts needing to be synthesized and analyzed before they can lead to design decisions. In this section, we provide details about methods that have been used by many teams to organize and analyze their data. As we have said earlier, do not wait until you have all the data to begin to synthesize and analyze. Decide before you visit users which methods you might use for organizing and analyzing the data—while remaining flexible enough to add or change methods when the data cries out for a different analysis than you had planned.

Review your notes after each session with a user. Fill in places where you have used telegraphic abbreviations that you may not remember next week. Add insights and inferences—clearly marked as such. Meet with the other observer(s) to share notes and observations. Pool your notes and synthesize them into a trip report after each site visit.

If you are using affinity diagrams, you may be building your understanding as you go—adding and rearranging the sticky notes after each visit. (See affinity diagrams on page 329.)

Users and environments

The simplest tools you have for categorizing your users and their environments are lists, starting with the initial rough results of brainstorming and becoming increasingly refined as similarities and patterns are identified and anomalies registered. Lists, by their very diversity and complication, will help keep you from assuming that you are designing for some mythical "average" or "typical" user. In too many design projects, we have noted that the "typical" user often bears a considerable resemblance to the designer.

Lists often contain descriptive information that helps categorize items on the list. However, the list items may need more complete descriptions to make the details of your observations clear and memorable to your team members. These descriptions could include character matrices, user profiles, and environment profiles.

Each of these descriptive methods is described in the next sections.

User lists

You will have started your user list with your initial brainstorming about which users you want to visit. Return to your initial list and update it with new information and changes to your assumptions that you have collected during your user visits. Your list is likely to include a variety of skills, professions, job types, learning styles, and stages of use. Then organize the list into user groups with characteristics that are relevant to your design thinking at this stage. For example, in a list of users for a veterinary program, the development team had started with a simple list of possible characteristics:

- veterinarians in large and small practices

- veterinarians with and without PC experience

- veterinarians who do their own paperwork and those who have office help

After their site visits, they expanded their list of users to the following:

- veterinarians and nonprofessional office workers

- people with PC experience and new users of computers

- teenagers and senior citizens, especially since the office workers and the veterinarians cross age groups

- experts in brucellosis disease in cattle and those who rarely encountered it in their practices

- those simply entering data and those responsible for analyzing the data

- another set of users: individuals compiling the data at the U.S. Department of Agriculture

- those enthusiastic about the software and others dubious about the amount of time it would take to use

- people supervising several clerical workers and others who run the whole show by themselves

- regular users and others who would use the program infrequently

- people with disabilities or special needs

- people who spoke English as their native language and others who did not

- people in offices with many computers and people in offices with only one computer used for a variety of tasks

The user lists often start small and get larger as you visit more sites. Not all of the characteristics that you list will make their way into the interface design, but getting them all down increases your awareness of the diversity among your users. A long list of diverse groups may also lead you to undertake more field studies to clarify the differences or to investigate further the percentages of each group in your user population. For example, you are likely to make different design decisions if you learn that a high percentage of people in your user population are domain experts than if you learn they are likely to be new to the domain.

Character matrices

Your simple lists of users might then be enhanced by creating a character matrix. A character matrix includes each user you have visited in terms of characteristics you believe to be relevant to your design problem. For example, the list of veterinary users might be grouped in terms of

- length of time using PCs

- frequency of PC use

- knowledge of the subject matter

- motivation for using the software

- language skills

Not everything in your list of users has made it into the character matrix.

Take the character matrix and label each of the users according to the characteristics you've chosen. Include quantitative information if you have it, or plan to survey a larger group of users to ensure that you have a good understanding of the percentage of users according to each characteristic. Now that you know what characteristics you are interested in, your survey will be much more relevant and you will collect better data.

The example character matrix in figure 11-1 shows that a high number of the users visited are somewhat or very motivated to learn the new software you are proposing. However, at least half of the group are new or inexperienced computer users. All have some knowledge of the subject matter the software will address, and one's primary language is not English.

If you believe this group is representative of your user community as a whole, you still may want to verify the mix of characteristics by calling or sending a demographic survey to a larger number of potential users than you were able to visit. If this group is indeed representative, you may decide that the design must deal with the lack of computer experience, and the interface must be translated into Spanish.

You may find one user or a small number of users who represent a significant and potentially important or problematic user group. In that case, you may need to do more site visits to collect more information about that group. In the case illustrated in figure 11-1, there is one elderly user with little computer experience and low motivation to learn new software. Maybe you need to find out how many elderly users you are likely to have and whether they have these same characteristics.

Veterinarian characteristics	User 1	User 2	User 3	User 4
Age	45	57	36	73
Computer user	Frequent	Occasional	Never	Infrequent
Windows familiarity	Good	Good	None	None, uses a DOS machine
Subject matter expertise	Expert	Advanced beginner	Expert	Competent
Language	English	English	Spanish	English
Motivation for learning software	High	Medium	High	Low
Primary computer user at work	Yes	No	No computer users	No

Figure 11-1 Example of a character matrix.

Ginny worked with a team that decided to do site visits in one geographic area. The user profile that emerged, related to computer expertise, was quite different from the assumptions that the team originally had made. The team wondered if the people in that geographic area were different from the larger community. As a result, they decided to extend the study to another geographic area.

Environment lists

In addition to listing user groups, make lists of the environments in which you found your users working. Your lists might also include some of the key characteristics of those environments. In a study of hospital personnel using a comprehensive hospital information software system, we found the following environments:

- hospital administrative offices

- nursing stations

- patient rooms

- laboratories

- physicians' offices

- treatment rooms with low levels of light

- areas likely to have water, chemicals, or other waste present

- areas where signal interference between computers and other equipment might take place

- areas accessible to patients and visitors

The environment list led to discussions about how to accommodate users working in environments that created special problems. Certainly, you will need to make decisions about whether you will support all the environments. What percentage of your users work in each of the environments? How important is that particular environment to your market? Do you need to create special versions of your interface for a particular environment? For example, you may need to make different font size, type, and color choices for computers in the low-light treatment rooms, or you may need to create one interface that works well in both low light and regular lighting.

JoAnn found that the users' working environment did not provide easy access to PC computers. The computers were in the users' offices, not in their work areas. As a result, the users appeared reluctant to look for information on the Web or even on a CD-ROM. To be effective, the information had to be incorporated into the online help system built directly into their laboratory equipment.

Depending upon what you learn initially, you may need to go back to the special environments to conduct a more detailed investigation.

User profiles

Your list of user groups and your character matrices may be enhanced by creating detailed user profiles of representative users. The user profiles can be lists or narratives or visual descriptions of the users you have visited. You may select a few users as exemplars of particular user types. We recommend that you first enhance your descriptions with specifics from your observations and interviews of actual people you visited. Then add notes on the unique characteristics of other users in the group. Figure 11-2 shows a list of characteristics of one of the veterinarians visited.

In thinking about your design as it might affect Al, you may conclude that you need to create an interface that can be learned easily but one that takes advantage of basic computer knowledge. You may also need something that is easy to use out in the field rather than only in the office. You can take advantage of this user's expertise in the subject matter but you'll have to ensure that the terminology on the screen is used accurately. You'll have to think about the communications problems. You weren't aware that there was any place left in the United States that didn't have access to fax lines and modems. In fact, you thought that party lines went out in the 1950s. Maybe there is a way that vets like Al could send disks to the

- User 1 (Al, a pseudonym). Large animal veterinarian
- Rural Wyoming, county population about 3,500
- Al told us there are more cows than people around
- Age 45
- Doctor of veterinary medicine, specializing in large animals
- More time spent at client sites (farms and ranches) than in the office
- Prefers outdoor to indoor work in general
- Office work done mostly by assistants (local teenagers, elderly mother) but all by hand, lots of forms
- Frequent computer user, only user in the office (doesn't want anyone else to touch the computers)
- Computer used for business accounting only
- No Web access or CD-ROM available
- Has difficulty in the rural area getting additional phone lines for computers
- Told us that everyone is on party lines, which makes using modems or fax machines next to impossible
- Expert in brucellosis disease; very concerned with incidence and record keeping
- Meticulous in record keeping, both computer and paper files
- Likes to use a tape recorder to record case observations; tape recording is later transcribed
- Appears to be a hands-on learner; prefers learning by doing
- Taciturn, good listener, careful observer
- Likes the idea of having a computer system for veterinary observations
- Would like a way to send and get information from the USDA about some of the problems in his area

Figure 11-2 Example of a list-based user profile.

local USDA office on a regular schedule and also receive disks of information to be downloaded.

To enhance your user profile further, you may include a narrative or visual description. The power of narrative descriptions and pictures of users is that they tend to be more memorable to your team members than simple lists. However, if you construct lists of the type illustrated in figure 11-2, you are likely to describe the user in the process of producing the list.

Figure 11-3 illustrates a narrative user profile. This profile describes another one of the veterinarians encountered in the study, User 4, known as Harry.

> User 4, known by our team as Harry, is a 73-year-old large animal veterinarian. Harry practices in a rural community in southern Illinois, about 100 miles from the Southern Illinois University campus where he attended veterinary school. Harry has a computer in his office, but he made a special point of telling us that he doesn't use it very much. He said he really doesn't know much about this Windows stuff. His computer still has DOS.
>
> Harry knows enough about brucellosis disease, studied it in school, of course, but they don't see much of it in his area. In fact, he hasn't seen a case in 35 years, not since an outbreak that scared everyone enough to make them very careful. He really doesn't know if he'd be interested in hooking up his computer to a modem so that he could communicate with the USDA. Doesn't sound all that useful.
>
> Harry's office is handled by his two staff members, a 32-year-old woman who is the office manager and an 18-year-old man who is interested in becoming a veterinarian. The office manager has some computer experience. She uses the old DOS machine for accounting and billing. The teenager has a lot of computer experience but isn't involved in using this computer. Harry never uses the computer unless he has to.

Figure 11-3 Sample user profile in narrative form.

Harry presents a lot of problems for an interface design. He has little computer experience and none with a Windows interface. In fact, he may be reluctant to upgrade to Windows simply to use the software you are designing. You may want to consider an alternative DOS version of the interface if people like Harry represent enough of the user population. Even his office manager lacks Windows experience. It might be easier to provide information to Harry on paper and ask him to complete forms. The incidence of the disease is low today, but if you know that it may become a much more significant factor, you may want to be sure that Harry can use—and will be willing to use—your system.

User profiles like the one describing Harry can also be illustrated with a user poster. Posters are useful for communicating visually with your development team and reminding everyone that the users are real people. A user poster might include several photographs of the users and their work environments, quotes from the users that illustrate their personalities and their goals, narrative descriptions or bulleted lists of characteristics, and any other material you believe will reveal who the users are and how they are likely to respond to your system design. The user poster in figure 11-4 illustrates a visual presentation of the information gathered about Harry.

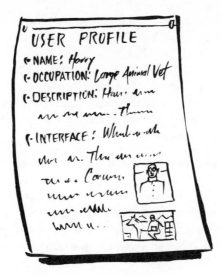

Figure 11-4 Sample poster illustration of a user.

Environment profiles

Environment profiles serve the same function as user profiles, to enhance the lists of user environments and make them more detailed and memorable for the design team. The profiles can be lists, narratives, or visual descriptions of the user environments you encountered during your site visits. Figure 11-5 describes the user environment at a mine site where computers are soon to be introduced to keep track of changes to the underground works.

> The mine site is located at 10,000 feet above sea level in the Colorado Rockies. The underground works go down 3,000 feet. At 10,000 feet, the air pressure is low, which affects the disk drives on a computer. There is insufficient air pressure to support the disk. The underground works are full of dust, blown around by the high-powered ventilation fans, creating almost the feeling of a constant gale. The noise levels are often very high because of the wind and the machinery in use. There is also the noise from the blasting going on to loosen the rock deposits.

Figure 11-5 Example of an environment profile.

As the product designer for this environment, you may want to plan for a special disk drive that will handle the low pressure problem. You may also want to find an alternative to a keyboard and mouse. The dust, dirt, and wind are likely to damage peripherals designed for office use.

As the interface designer, you may want to consider the physical difficulties faced by your users. Will it be possible to minimize the amount of time they spend at the computer? Can tasks be designed so that they have only a few steps and can be done very quickly? Can you create a highly visual screen with little need for reading? Can you allow for a lot of direct manipulation, perhaps with a touch screen or something equivalent that will hold up in the environment? The mine environment presents challenges that you would not often encounter in a regular office environment.

Profiles of office environments are also very useful to developers, especially when they illustrate the real conditions users often labor under. Real office environments are often rather messy, full of sticky notes around computers, half-height partitions, users sharing space and equipment, manuals locked away in drawers or filing cabinets. Figure 11-6 is a profile of an office environment. Figure 11-7 is a visual depiction of the same scenario.

> Rose works in a real estate office. All the agents work at individual desks in a large room. Rose has a computer on the corner of her desk. Her desk also has a telephone and a telephone number organizer—but it does not have stacks of paper. She keeps her desk clean because potential buyers come in and sit across from her. She has to have open space to see them and to show pictures, brochures, and fact sheets of properties for sale. She shares the printer and fax machine, so they are a walk away—in the back room.
>
> Rose's computer is festooned with sticky notes—telephone numbers, instructions for key tasks in the software she uses, and more, as depicted in figure 11-7. The manuals for the software got lost somewhere before the computers where delivered. No one has any software manuals so they just ask each other when they have problems.

Figure 11-6 Another example of an environment profile.

Workflows, tasks, and procedures

In this section, we present methods you can use to describe the tasks that you have observed and discussed during your site visits. You may have lots of free-form notes or notes you've taken in your Observers' Notebook, but they may be unavailable to your colleagues. They may also be difficult for you to access in note form. You need ways to recall and communicate what you've learned. You want methods that preserve the important and exciting details of your observations and create the same level of excitement and understanding among your colleagues. You know, however, that no one will be able to create a design from your notes. They need you to pull the notes together and do some analysis. At the same time,

Figure 11-7 Rose's office—an environmental profile.

you don't want to spend hours of additional time creating massive task analysis reports that no one wants to read.

In this section, we present eight methods for showing users' tasks:

- workflow diagrams
- task lists
- task sequences
- task hierarchies
- user/task matrices
- detailed task descriptions from procedural analyses
- task flowcharts
- task scenarios

Some of these methods, such as workflow diagrams, task lists, and task flowcharts may be similar to methods your team members have used before to design products and interfaces. Other methods, such as detailed task descriptions and task scenarios may appear new and different. At the end of this chapter, we discuss how to choose the best methods for your information, your design problem, and your team members.

Workflow diagrams

Many tasks are collaborative. They are performed by several people, often in different parts of an organization or even between organizations and over a period of time. Such tasks are best captured and analyzed diagrammatically using workflow diagrams. A workflow diagram is the outcome you want if you are most interested in workflow analysis. See chapters 3 and 6 for information about analyzing workflows with your users and during site visits.

Workflow diagrams help you illustrate a collaborative sequential task or set of tasks. Tasks of this type usually move through a number of steps. Information is often passed from person to person to meet the overall goal of the task. Each step in the process has users as well as goals to achieve.

Figure 11-8 illustrates another workflow example: an accounts payable function from the receipt of a vendor invoice through the payment of the invoice. It includes a parallel task of recording the payment information in the general ledger. The goal of the function, which encompasses many tasks and subtasks, is to pay the invoice as long it is properly prepared and reflects the specifications of the original purchase order.

Figure 11-8 Example of a workflow diagram of the accounts payable function.

To create such a diagram, return to your notes about the workflow you have observed. Isolate the major steps in the workflow, especially when the work moves from one user to another. Draw blocks for each major step, either by sketching the person who is doing the task and labeling the sketch or by simply labeling a box to represent the step, noting alongside or within the box who does the task and any other relevant characteristics of the task. In figure 11-8, we've chosen to illustrate the workflow by drawing sketches of the people involved and noting what they do.

The workflow diagram shows how tasks proceed from one group of users to another. It should also show how objects are altered as they are moved along. For example, the invoice that arrives from the vendor is attached to a copy of the original purchase order and to a form that lists all the payments already made against this purchase order. Copies of the invoice, the purchase order, and the account listing are sent to the responsible business manager to be signed off. Accounts payable also keeps their own file copy of the information. Even if you are going to create a paperless system where all this is scanned and dealt with electronically, the workflow diagram will show you who needs to see what information when.

If you are the interface designer, you need to understand how the information pieces (invoice, purchase order, and listing) are assembled by the payables clerk. You need to know what the clerk does with the information (forwards one copy, keeps another). You also need to find out what happens if the information is not returned by the manager according to schedule. In fact, you need to know the business rule for the schedule and how users keep track of the schedule.

By tracking the workflow of the larger task first, you avoid focusing too soon on one or more discrete parts of the task. Without understanding the whole task, you are likely to miss significant parts of the task in your interface design. As you attempt to construct your workflow diagram, you may find that you need to go back to the users to clarify points in the flow or fill in gaps in the apparent logic. The diagramming process itself helps you see where the points of confusion are.

JoAnn learned, during a study of a medical records application, that a complex sequence of events traced the movement of patient information. First the physician tape recorded notes on the patient's condition. Then the medical transcriptionist created a typed copy of the notes. Then the notes were placed in a patient file in the medical records room, ready for the physician's review and signature. Next the physician was notified that there were records that needed to be reviewed and signed. The physician had to go to the records room, review the transcript, note any changes, initial them if they were brief, and sign the record. If the changes were extensive, the physician had to notify the transcriptionist with a note to revise the text. Once the text was revised, the whole sequence of events began again until the transcript was complete, correct, and signed by the physician as shown in figure 11-9.

The first interface prototype did not take workflow into account. As a result, the physicians could not make sense of their role in the workflow. The interface design had to be completely changed to reflect the workflow much more precisely and accurately. Not until the developers visited the medical records area in nearby hospitals and understood the workflow was the interface design adequate

to support the task and clearly understandable to the transcriptionists, the
physicians, and others involved in the process.

Figure 11-9 The complex sequence of how patient information moves through a specific system.

Task lists

To design a useful product, you have to know the tasks users will do with it. A task list is almost certainly one of the outcomes of your analysis. You'll find examples of task lists and a discussion of different levels of generality—or granularity—in chapter 3. We suggest that you first do a task list at a high level of generality. Make it comprehensive and be sure to phrase the tasks in the language that users have used to describe the tasks during your observations and interviews. By using the users' language, you preserve their way of thinking about the tasks as well as the terminology they prefer. You may find, of course, that you have some of the same tasks listed more than once because users have different names for what they do. You may also have missed some tasks because user have the same names for what may turn out to be quite different tasks. By looking at your more detailed descriptions of the tasks, you should be able to eliminate duplicate tasks with different names or rename tasks that have the same name but are really different.

In the task analysis that JoAnn conducted to design the interface for a hospital patient admission system, the design team listed the following tasks:

- *recording patient demographic information, including name, address, social security number, telephone number, age, gender, religion, and more*

- *retrieving patient information (if the patient has been to the hospital before) by patient name, address, and social security number*

- *recording information about patient insurance coverage, including primary and secondary policies, employers, addresses, telephone numbers, insurance policy and group numbers, responsible parties, and so on*

- *recording information about the reason for admission, often from the physician's office rather than from the patient*

- *recording information about the particular admission, including date, time, physician, medical history, and so on, from the physician's office*

- *accessing information about the patient's room assignment (service, ward, room, and so on)*

- *creating the patient's identification bracelet*

Creating the task list involved observing and interviewing the admission clerks at the hospital as they admitted patients and as they recorded information over the telephone from the physicians' offices. The task analysis also included interviewing admissions supervisors about their roles in the process; collecting sample forms, reports, and other paperwork; interviewing hospital administrators about the business rules related to the admissions task; and observing and interviewing clerks from the physicians' offices as they made the hospital reservations for the patients. Although the admissions task centered on the work of the admissions clerk, a number of other people in several different departments performed ancillary tasks. Thus, this combined a workflow analysis with generating a task list for one part of the workflow. The analysis also included observations of the patients themselves, especially in high-stress situations like the emergency room.

In addition to making task lists yourself following your site visits, you might also want to enlist the help of your users in creating task lists. We often work with users directly in listing the tasks they perform and arranging the tasks into sequences and hierarchies. Participatory design techniques provide many ways that developers and users can work together during the design and development life cycle.

During a customer partnering, JoAnn asked the participants to come up with their own task lists as a homework assignment. At the next meeting, each participant presented his or her task list, which was then transferred to sticky notes and put up on the wall. After all the participants presented their lists, the group worked together to combine them into a single flow of actions and decisions. The combined list represented a consensus among the users. However, the variations in task performance among the users were also retained. In this way, the designers identified a primary task flow as well as individual task requirements.

Task sequences

The previous example demonstrates how a task list quickly becomes a task sequence or flow. Task sequences are often ordered lists of the sequence in which the tasks are most often performed. Creating a task sequence means talking with users about which tasks they perform first and last to reach their goals. It means talking about each separate task that makes up the flow and how each task is related to the whole. It means discovering what parts of the sequence must be performed in a particular order and which parts can be varied.

You can illustrate the task sequence as an ordered list. This list is different from the collaborative workflow diagram described earlier because we are now talking about a task sequence that is usually performed by a single user. The task sequence for this person may itself be part of a larger workflow.

Figure 11-10 illustrates a typical chronological task sequence as performed by one of the admissions clerks in the example we have been using.

As you create the task sequence, note details about the task, including time to complete the task, alternative paths to be taken under special circumstances, and other information you gathered about the task during your observations and interviews. Note differences in task performance among different users. You will use these notes to decide the main flow of the task in the new interface, the data that has to be accumulated, how significant a particular order is to successful and rapid completion of the task, what exceptions must be taken into account, what might be automated and what should continue to be performed by the users, and so on.

Task hierarchies

The interrelationships among tasks can be clarified by placing them in a hierarchical relationship to one another. A task hierarchy resembles an organization chart with the CEO at the top (the most general task) and the clerks at the bottom (the detailed tasks, often including steps and decisions). Tasks at the top of the hierarchy point more closely to the goals the user is trying to achieve, while tasks lower in the hierarchy show what activities are required to achieve the goals. For example, figure 11-11 shows the hierarchical relationship of tasks performed by hospital admissions clerks.

- Greet the patient and ask for name and social security number.

- Find the patient's folder in the collection of today's admissions folders.

- Make sure the folder contains the medical information from the patient's physician. If it does not, add a note to the file indicating the information is missing, add the note to your physician callback list, and, before the end of the day, call the physician's office to have the information faxed immediately to you.

- Complete the demographic information on the admissions form.

- Complete the insurance information on the admissions form.

- Find the patient's assigned room on the medical information form.

- Type the patient's name, social security number, and service, room, and bed number on the patient's ID bracelet.

- Put the patient's ID bracelet into the badge maker to seal.

- Attach the bracelet to the patient's wrist.

- Direct the patient to the appropriate floor and service.

- Place all the forms in the patient's folder. Call the physician's office if necessary to obtain any missing medical information.

Figure 11-10 A example of a chronological task sequence.

The various subtasks that the admitting clerk performs are not performed in any particular order, although some are clearly performed near the beginning of the shift (collecting the patient folders for the day) and others near the end of the shift (preparing the admissions report for the day). Other activities take place as the day proceeds, such as admitting patients or calling physicians' offices. The clerk also calls patients at home several days before the scheduled admission to collect basic demographic information before the patient arrives. The hierarchy makes the relationship among the tasks clearer.

A task hierarchy can be developed at a high level to analyze user goals or can be extended into lower levels to identify subtasks. Task hierarchies can also be used to show many levels of tasks in very large systems. However, when you get to the level of specific actions and decisions, you are doing what we call a procedural analysis. There are better ways of illustrating procedures, which we discuss later in the chapter.

Task hierarchies can become very complex as a more complete picture of the task environment is produced from subsequent visits. Users can be enlisted to assist in developing informal task groupings that will help in constructing hierarchies.

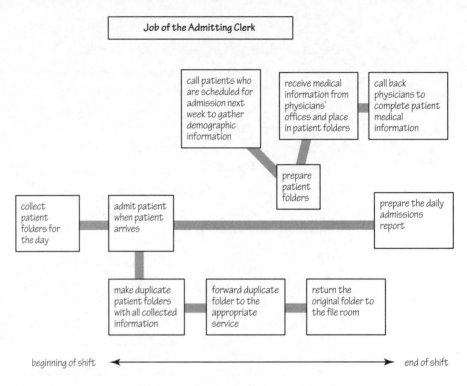

Figure 11-11 Sample task hierarchy at a high-level of detail.

A task grouping activity with users enabled JoAnn's team to provide a new task organization for the developers of the system administrator's manual for a small-business phone system. The administrators worked together to list and group all of the tasks they performed to keep the telephone system running. They included routine tasks like adding and removing users, changing passwords, changing access privileges, and so on. They split routine tasks into tasks they did to change the settings for individual phones and those they did that affected the phones throughout the system. They included maintenance tasks, some of which were performed regularly, some occasionally, and some only in response to emergencies. They also noted that one class of tasks was especially difficult to perform—establishing the time-of-day restrictions on all the phones in the system.

The users' groupings assisted the technical communicators in organizing the manual's table of contents in a way that made sense to the users, rather than organizing the information in a way that made sense to the telephony engineers or the technical communicators.

The new groupings resulted in several sections in the system administrator manual, including sections for routine tasks, regular preventive maintenance, emergency troubleshooting, and problem solving.

In interface design, the task hierarchy may influence menu and icon design as well as how the tasks are accessed and when sequences are appropriate. For example, the menu bar in a Windows application should be designed from the information in your task hierarchy.

User/task matrix

In most design cases, you will find it useful to compare your lists of tasks and task sequences to the user groups you have identified. By creating a user/task matrix, you can illustrate how user groups relate to task performance. Some user groups never perform a particular task while others perform it frequently. The user/task matrix illustrates these relationships (see figure 11-12).

Tasks	Admissions clerk	Ward clerk	Physician's office
Collect patient demographic data	Frequent	Never	Frequent
Collect patient insurance data	Frequent	Never	Frequent
Collect patient medical data	Sometimes	Frequent	Frequent
Assign patient to room and bed	Never	Frequent	Never
Make patient ID bracelet	Frequent	Sometimes	Never
Give directions to floor and room	Frequent	Sometimes	Never

Figure 11-12 User/task matrix for hospital admissions.

Notice that the user/task matrix in figure 11-12 points out considerable redundancy in the admissions task. The same information is collected by the admissions clerk that has already been collected by the physician's office. In the design of a new system that takes the entire workflow into account, this duplication of effort could be eliminated by providing a better link between the physician's office and the hospital.

Larry Marine (personal communication, 1997) points out that in many cases, developing a role/task matrix is more useful than a user/task matrix. In a role/task matrix, we look at how differently even the same person may behave in different situations. In the example in figure 11-13, some users only fit the browser role while other users may sometimes be in one role and sometimes in another.

The same individual may take on all of the roles illustrated in figure 11-13 under different circumstances. She may just browse when catalogs arrive at her home. She may be searching for an item as a birthday gift for a friend. Or she may have a specific individual item that she wants to purchase immediately. The role/task matrix makes all these relationships clearer.

Tasks	Browser	Searcher for a specific item	Buyer
Flip catalog pages and look at pictures	Frequent	Never	Never
Mark items for future reference	Frequent	Sometimes	Never
Search for a specific type of item	Sometimes	Frequent	Frequent
Compare prices and quality	Sometimes	Frequent	Sometimes
Select an item to buy	Sometimes	Frequent	Frequent
Give credit card information	Sometimes	Frequent	Frequent

Figure 11-13 User/task matrix for catalog users in different roles.

Detailed task descriptions from a procedural analysis

When you are designing a new interface, you also want to capture how the users perform the task at present. How much detail you need depends on the nature of the task and how much you plan to change what users do. You may need a lot of information to understand the details of a very complex task. If you are designing an air traffic control system, you will analyze in great detail exactly how the tasks are now being done. You need to know every piece of the process used to guide airplanes to land safely, the relationships between information and actions, the way the controllers interact with one another, and so on.

For other tasks, you may need only a basic sketch of the steps. For example, if you are designing a system that automatically creates patient ID bracelets, you don't need to know how the admissions clerk operates the plastic laminating machine. The manufacturing process will work completely differently in the new system. You will need to know when the bracelets are created as part of the larger admissions task.

A detailed task description might include a step-by-step account of the actions performed and decisions made by the users. Once you have the details, you can analyze them for your interface design. Objects defined by the users' actions may become database elements. The actions and decisions the users take may become part of the interface menus and dialog boxes. Knowing how the task is currently done by users gives you important insights into how the users think about their tasks.

You may want to write a detailed task description using action and decision steps as illustrated in figure 11-14. In this analysis, we were trying to understand how sales representatives think about the task of calling back a customer.

You might further analyze your detailed task description by summarizing the action steps, separating out the decisions and feedback, and listing the artifacts and tools used in the process.

1. Pull out the callback list and note all the callbacks scheduled for today. If I have the callbacks in a list I can sort, like a spreadsheet, I'll sort them by date.

2. Take out the file folders with the information on the customers I need to call back. I have these organized by the company name, because I often have more than one contact in a company and the contacts change.

3. Read my notes from the previous call and take a quick look at the call history if there is one. Highlight or note the things I want to mention.

4. Check the phone number on the callback list to make certain I have the right number written in. It's really easy for me to transpose numbers.

5. Place the call. Leave a voice mail message if necessary. Call again at another time of day. Don't leave too many messages, but note how many calls I placed.

6. When I actually talk to the customer, write a note for the file about the conversation, hopefully while I'm still on the phone.

7. Note any changes in address, telephone number, or contact name.

8. Put a new callback on the list with the date decided on from the conversation.

Figure 11-14 Sample of a detailed task description.

For example, this user uses a list or spreadsheet to organize callbacks, file folders organized by company, notes and telephone numbers in the file folders, and telephone numbers on the callback list, probably for ease of access. Each of these physical artifacts can be analyzed. They may become the primary interface objects in your design. The actions associated with the objects will become the actions you include in menus or dialog boxes. If you have observed users, you'll have the data for these procedural analyses from your observations and from talking with users as you did the observations.

We should point out that this well-organized description of tasks is rarely provided in such a straightforward manner by the users if you are interviewing rather than observing them. They usually talk about what they are doing in the order in which they remember. Details are usually presented out of context with the step, as they are remembered. Also users do not always perform the same tasks in the same way. They remember some of the variations out of order with their explanations of the primary task activities. The more you observe rather than interview, the more likely you'll have a thorough and accurate detailed task description.

You may also find yourself observing more than one person performing what seems like the same task. Individual users are likely to vary how they do the tasks, including the specific steps, the way they make decisions, and the variations they take into account. Your final analysis of the task is likely to be a composite of several variations, including statements made by supervisors and company officials about how the task is supposed to be performed.

Task flowcharts

Some tasks proceed through a series of decisions, actions, and alternative paths depending on unique conditions. The users often have a variety of optional ways of doing the same thing. You may want to create flowcharts of the detailed steps of tasks that show the branches for the conditional decisions and alternative paths. To create a flowchart, look for a trigger event that represents the starting point of the task for the users. Then, draw a series of boxes that represent the actions that the users take. If there are decisions to be made, use diamonds in your flowchart and represent the decision point as a question that the users must answer to proceed. Decision points often lead the users back to previous steps in the flow or divide the flow into alternative paths, depending on the answer to the question. Continue tracing the flow through actions steps and decision points until you reach what the users consider to be the end of the task.

A flowchart makes the options obvious and helps you show the steps and decisions visually. Sometimes flowcharts that capture current users' procedures get large or have many branches. They become difficult to create or analyze. You can break these complex flowcharts into sections, having an overall flowchart at the beginning and then expansions of each flowchart on succeeding pages. You may want to use flowcharts primarily for tasks that are easily diagrammed.

 Ginny did an intensive procedural analysis for a client with observations and interviews. The client wanted to understand in great detail what the user did. Ginny's report was a flowchart analysis that looked like the illustration in figure 11-15.

Creating the very messy flowcharts of real users and their tasks is very instructive. The flowcharts show how often users repeat loops in the task flow, how complicated the branching can be when users make mistakes, and how absurd some of the steps are. Messy flowcharts can be very effective in illustrating the complexity and difficulty of the way users perform their tasks.

Task flowcharts and workflow diagrams can be especially useful for communicating the details of a task to developers familiar with using flowcharts in their own work. By using a known method, you will find it easier to communicate with people who are dubious about the whole process. They may consider task scenarios, which we describe in the next section, too "touchy feely" until they get more comfortable working with user information.

Task scenarios

A "scenario" is a story. You can tell stories of different lengths and different levels of detail, and, indeed, you'll find the word "scenario" used in many different ways in the literature on user and task analysis. [See, for example, the various chapters in *Scenario-based Design* (Carroll 1995).]

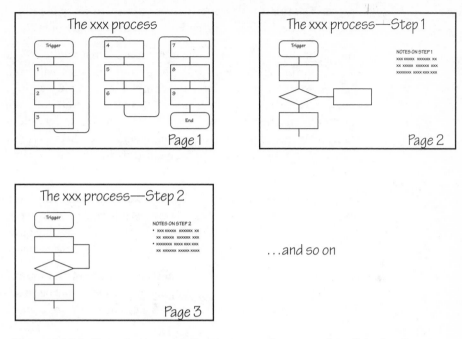

Figure 11-15 If you have a complex process and want to show it in detail, consider a multi-level flowchart like this one.

Scenarios can be about users, their work, their environments, how they do tasks, the tasks they need to do, and all combinations of these elements. Storytelling has the advantages of bringing people, places, and actions alive. It can also give you insights into the attributes of tasks you need to accommodate in your design, what users value, and what they see as aids and obstacles to accomplishing their goals. Scenarios can focus on the primary users—the people who will actually use what you develop—or the secondary users—the people who benefit by what the primary users do.

In the rest of this section, we discuss four types of scenarios that vary in their level of detail and the use the development team might make of them. We include

- **Brief scenarios.** Very brief stories that give just the facts of a real situation the primary user had to deal with, but that don't go into detail on how the user does the task.

- **Vignettes.** Brief narratives, perhaps with a visual, that give readers a high-level, broad brush view of a user, the user's environment, and the user's current way of doing something.

- **Elaborated scenarios.** Narratives with more details. Which details you focus on depend on what you want the team to take from the story.

■ **Complete task scenarios.** Narratives that carry the story through from the beginning to the end of a task or sequence of tasks.

You might also combine a profile of the user, perhaps with a picture, and a profile of the environment, perhaps with one or more pictures, with your scenarios to make the story even more vivid and complete. The more elaborated and complete scenarios can even lead into detailed task analyses and task flowcharts. Scenarios at all levels are effective ways for you to transfer your observations into memorable stories for yourself and other team members. Scenarios are often written as text, but they also may be illustrated with drawings or diagrams rather than with a lot of text.

Brief scenarios. When you watch and talk with users during site visits, you see them dealing with all types of situations. While you are there, you are also likely to hear about other situations that you did not actually see. We have found it useful to think of the story of each of these situations as a "brief scenario."

Figure 11-16 is an example of a brief scenario from observations of a travel agent. We've left out the part about arranging the airline flights because we want to concentrate on the process of renting a car. The names, of course, are made up.

> Joan Gaynor, the travel agent, takes a call from Mrs. Reed. The Reed family is going on a vacation and they want Joan to arrange for airline tickets and to reserve a rental car for them. When Joan talks about it, she says she is booking a car for the Reeds. The family includes two adults and three children: 11, 7, and 3. They need a car that will hold five and all their luggage. They need a car seat for the toddler. They want to pick up the car when they fly into the airport in Salt Lake City and drop it off at the same airport a week later just before their flight back. They want to rent from an agency that has cars at the airport so they don't have to carry their luggage. They want the cheapest rental they can get for the week with no mileage charges.

Figure 11-16 An example of a brief scenario.

A brief scenario tells you about a situation that your design will have to let the users handle. It doesn't tell you how the users do the task today. It doesn't give you any details about how to have users do the task in a new design. You may change all the ways the user does the task, but the brief scenario will still be there as a reality for users to deal with no matter how you design the product.

What a brief scenario does give you is the task itself and many of the attributes or data elements that are related to the task. It also gives you some of the customer's values, which the primary user, in this case, the travel agent, has to fulfill to meet her goal of making the customer happy. And it can give you vocabulary to use in the design.

In our example, the task for this brief scenario is what travel agents call "booking a car" and what this customer called "reserve a car for them." As you read the story of this situation, you realize that to book a car, a travel agent has to deal with many attributes, and each of these will have to be data elements in any design you develop:

- "a car big enough for five and luggage" = size of the car
- "a car seat for the toddler" = special amenities
- "fly into the airport at Salt Lake City" = city to get the car
- "drop it off at the same airport" = city to leave the car
- "a week later" = length of time for the rental
- "agency that has cars at the airport" = location of the rental agency within the city
- "cheapest rental" = price

As you gather more brief scenarios for similar situations, you will find variations on the task. For example, other brief scenarios of car rentals might involve a traveler who wants to change a reservation or cancel a reservation. You may also find which tasks are the most frequently performed.

You may find attributes that did not appear in this brief scenario and thus realize the need for other data elements. You will certainly hear about more specific instances of these attributes. For example, other brief scenarios may involve travelers who want to rent a car for two weeks, or a weekend, or from a Friday to a Tuesday. Or they may involve travelers who want to rent a car at a location other than the airport.

You also get some of the user's or secondary user's values through a brief scenario. In our example, price is very important to the Reed family. In another brief scenario, you might find that the customer wants an agency that rents a certain make of car.

Here's a way to work with brief scenarios: Write each story on a large index card. You can use one color index card for all the brief scenarios about one type of situation, such as renting a car. Try to get the story down in the words you heard from the user and secondary user. That will give you vocabulary to put into your design.

When you have a stack of cards with brief scenarios about similar situations, such as rental cars, go through them and find the verbs that indicate the tasks. Write each of those on a smaller card of some other color. Select a third color for the attributes or data elements. Find phrases in each situation that indicate one instance of any attribute, such as "car seat for the toddler." Write each on a card in your third color. Then sort the stack of attribute cards into groups that go together and that you can name. For example, you may have many different examples of special amenities that come up in brief scenarios about car rentals, such as car phone, ski rack, CD player. Some attributes will appear in every brief scenario, such as length of time for the rental. Others, like special amenities, may come up only in some brief scenarios. Figure 11-17 shows you an example of part of an analysis of renting cars based on a stack of brief scenarios.

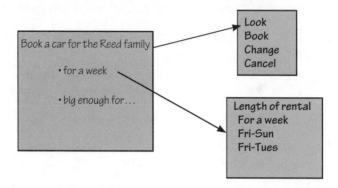

Figure 11-17 From brief scenarios you can extract both a task list and data elements with the values you need for them.

Vignettes. A vignette, like a brief scenario, is a general description of the task. In a vignette, however, one of your major goals is to capture the essence of the user's interaction with the current way of doing things.

Figure 11-18 is a vignette that describes how a catalog user interacts with the paper catalogs delivered through the mail to her house. This vignette gives you a broad picture of the catalog task but covers only part of the process. Vignettes or quick scenarios of this type give you a sense of the users and the users' activities without going into details about how the tasks are performed.

Jill creates a stack of new catalogs in a corner of her kitchen. When she is preparing dinner, she can flip through a catalog, browsing to see what's new or what's on sale or what strikes her interest. In the evening, she picks out five or six catalogs to look at while the family is watching television. She may even take a few catalogs to bed at night, keeping a small stack on her nightstand.

Generally she simply browses through the pictures, reading descriptions only if the pictures look interesting. When she finds something she might be interested in buying, she'll either dog-ear the page, draw a circle around the object, or mark the page with a sticky note. She keeps the catalogs with their marked pictures around until she is ready to make a purchase.

Figure 11-18 Example of a vignette.

As an interface designer, you can use vignettes to introduce the task to your team members. They ensure that all team members have the same basic understanding of the users, the tasks, and the environment. You can also use the vignettes, as well as the other more detailed scenarios, as the foundation for planning the flow of information and actions that will appear in the interface.

Well-written vignettes are useful for conveying the values that users attach to their activities. In the vignette of Jill and the catalogs, you begin to see how important the experience of browsing the catalogs is to Jill. She likes looking at the pictures, reading the descriptions, occasionally marking items she finds interesting. At one point during the site visit, she referred to her catalog browsing as "a relaxing, mindless thing to do." If the new online catalog system is going to attract users like Jill, the interface design has to convey the same pleasant experience. No pressure, no sense of having to make decisions, just looking at interesting pictures.

If you are the interface designer for the catalog system, you will want to preserve the feeling behind the task. You don't want to design an interface that presents only written descriptions of items.

Elaborated scenarios. At the next level of task scenarios, you can include more information about the users' situation and details about how the users perform their tasks. For example, you might take the catalog scenario further by looking at what happens when Jill tries to find a particular item. Figure 11-19 illustrates this elaborated scenario.

Jill has browsed through most of the catalogs soon after they arrive. Now she needs to get something for her father's birthday. She remembers a neat new gadget she knows her father will love. It's called a GPS for GeoPositioning System. It's somewhere in the stack of catalogs but she doesn't remember which one. She can immediately eliminate the clothing and toy catalogs, but now she has a stack of gadget catalogs. She's afraid it will take her most of the morning to find the GPS before she can order it. None of the catalogs has indexes or tables of contents. In fact, the items are arranged randomly to encourage browsers and keep people looking at everything in the catalog. Its a great technique for the catalog company, but it makes looking for an individual item very inconvenient.

Figure 11-19 Example of an elaborated scenario that reveals part of the catalog design problem.

This more elaborated scenario introduces a problem with the current design of catalogs: Users cannot easily find individual items. The scenario should suggest an extension of the catalog metaphor to the interface design team. The catalog metaphor translated into the computer design can be enhanced by a new attribute—the ability to search for an item. This scenario might lead the design team into a discussion of how to handle a search.

Complete task scenario. At a third level of task scenario, you can include even more details about the users, environments, high-level goals, and tasks, as well as detailed procedures. In figure 11-20, we analyze Jill's task of placing her catalog orders before Christmas by presenting the complete task scenario.

Jill is ready to place her critical Christmas order. She has selected gifts for eight family members from three different catalogs. She has her items marked with sticky notes on the pages and circles around the items on the pages. She also has her address list and her credit cards. She wants to use two different credit cards so she doesn't put too much money on any one card.

Jill dials the 800 number for the first catalog. She wants three items in this catalog sent to three family members at two different addresses. The customer service clerk asks her for each item by number. She identifies the first item and goes through the questions about size and color. The item she wants is in stock. She gives the clerk the name and address for this item and the message she wants on the greeting card plus the gift wrap she wants. The clerk asks her for the next item. After she gives the item number, they discuss size and color. The clerk tells her that the color she wants is out of stock in that size and will not be available until after Christmas. Jill is distressed and flips quickly through the catalog pages looking for a substitute item. The clerk suggests a similar item on another page. Jill looks at that item and decides it's OK, even though it's not exactly what she wanted. She goes through her size, color, name, address, gift wrap, and card explanations again. She and the clerk go on to the third item, which luckily is in stock.

Then the clerk asks for Jill's credit card information. She lists her card, the number, the expiration date, and her billing address. The clerk then gives her a confirmation number and they review the expected delivery dates. Jill decides to have one of the items sent by express mail. That means she and the clerk have to reopen that part of the order and discuss the mailing options.

After this transaction, Jill dials the numbers of the other two catalog companies and goes through the whole story again, with similar problems. She is unable to find a replacement for one out-of-stock item. She'll have to go back to her catalogs at a later time and review her options again. The whole ordeal has taken Jill about two hours on Saturday morning. She feels exhausted and frustrated with the replacements and the missing items. She has been standing up at her phone the whole time, her back hurts, and her Christmas shopping is still not finished.

Figure 11-20 Example of a detailed scenario for catalog shopping.

Task scenarios describe the users' world as it is currently with problems and frustrations noted. They present the design problems that you will need to account for in your interface design. They can be text oriented, as they are in the proceeding example, or illustration oriented, depending upon your particular skills with writing or drawing and the best way to present the information to others on your development team.

Later in the design process, you will move from task scenarios (narrative descriptions of the present state) to use scenarios (narrative descriptions of the future state). Use scenarios provide an effective tool for envisioning the user environment you hope to create with your new product design. However, you will find yourself returning to the task scenarios to decide if the users' goals and mental models of the tasks are preserved in the new design. You will also use the task scenarios in your usability tests.

Other methods for analyzing your data

In the previous section, you learned to take your raw observation notes and present them in ways that are easier for you and your team members to understand and recall as you try to get a complete picture of your users, their tasks, and their environments. In this section, you take the output of your presentations and reorganize it so that relationships become clearer.

Affinity diagrams

Affinity diagrams provide you with a tool for transferring ideas from your observation notes into issues to address during your design process. We recommend beginning with your notes, either hand written or typed. You can also use the same process to review transcripts of video and audiotapes if you have made these.

Here is a process for creating affinity diagrams that comes from contextual inquiry techniques described by Beabes and Flanders (1995), Holtzblatt and Beyer (1994), and Raven and Flanders (1996):

1. Review your notes, highlighting interesting observations and issues. You might use a highlighter to mark items, or you might write out a highlight list.

2. Review your lists, notes, and observations with your team members.

3. Provide each team member with a set of sticky notes or note cards and ask them to write down one issue on each sticky note. Team members can write as many notes as they choose. Each note should identify the site visit that it came from. In fact, we find it helpful to use a different color of sticky note for each site visit.

4. As team members write the notes, they stick them on a white board, cork board, or even a convenient wall. As team members post their notes, they may get new ideas and add new notes based on the notes others have produced.

5. As the notes are put in place, the team organizes the sticky notes into groupings. Anyone can move any note as many times as they wish. That's the advantage of sticky notes or note cards—they can easily be moved around. However, you might find you'll have to tape the notes down because they tend to fall off after a few hours. Just use tape that is easy to remove.

6. Create labels for the groups as they occur during the process.

7. Once the team is satisfied that the notes are adequately grouped, review each group together. Discuss the issues noted in the cards. Rearrange the cards as necessary.

Figure 11-21 illustrates how the white board might look once some of the sticky notes are in place.

Figure 11-21 Example of an affinity diagram.

Once the labels and notes are in place, use them with your team to discuss the user interface requirements that are likely to emerge. You may discover, for example, that your users are reluctant to install their own software. During your field observations, you heard over and over that your users really are unhappy about products that they have to install themselves, especially if they perceive that the installations require them to understand technical terms and make technical decisions. They expect that the dealer or consultant they hire will complete the installation for them and assist them in importing their data into the system. Although they believe they will be comfortable analyzing the data and deciding what actions to take, they are not anxious to become involved in the more technical activities of installation.

Affinity diagramming, as practiced by Wixon, Holtzblatt, and Raven in their version of contextual inquiry, is a bottom-up approach. You start, as illustrated, with the observation data and watch the issues emerge.

In a study of how system administrators expected to use an information Web site, JoAnn learned that users were frustrated whenever they spent time downloading a document only to discover it was the same document they had downloaded several weeks before. Several users mentioned during the site visits that it would be helpful if they could read a brief description of the document before they downloaded it. The current Web site provided only titles, no descriptions. They also wanted a publication date or a version number included in the brief description so that they could verify that the document contained new information.

The observation in the story was made by several users during the site visits. The accumulation of notes in the affinity diagrams produced agreement among the team members that they needed a way to date the abstracts of every downloadable document in the site.

Insight sheets

Mary Beth Raven and Alicia Flanders brought up the idea of *insight sheets* at a Usability Professionals' Association conference. An insight sheet is a piece of paper with a major insight at the top, such as "The error messages don't help users recover from errors quickly." Under that insight are listed specific examples from observations and interviews that support and explain the insight. You might also have sections on an insight sheet for implications of the insight and for design ideas that you are considering to deal with the insight.

Insight sheets can come from affinity diagrams. If the group label for a set of notes that the team has put together is an insight, you are basically transferring the label and the notes onto one sheet of paper.

You may find that developing insight sheets is a helpful technique even if you do not do affinity diagramming. Some teams do not have the space to spread out hundreds of sticky notes. Some teams just find that they are not comfortable with many small notes. Therefore some teams don't see affinity diagramming as the technique they want to use.

Here's how you might develop insight sheets when you are not doing affinity diagramming: You are likely to get insights as you review the site visit reports or other logs from observations and interviews. Every time you realize that you have an important insight, put it down as the heading on a sheet of paper, either real paper or a page in a computer file. As you find instances or specific notes that relate to that insight, put each one under the heading as one item in a bulleted list, as illustrated in figure 11-22.

Insight: Self-paced training modules may not work well with our users.

Supporting notes from the site visits:

- Users are paid only for the hours they work. Almost all are part time.
- Managers are reluctant to allow users time to do computer-based training modules during work hours because they would have to hire more staff to cover those times.
- Although users think their jobs are very important, most have other obligations (family, a second job, commitments to volunteer organizations) that mean they cannot give up time from their job for training at their own expense.
- None of the users we visited has a computer at home.
- The people who get and keep this job seem to be extroverts. They like being with people. That seems to make them good as telephone support, customer service representatives. Going off by themselves to take self-paced training removes them from the social environment and they don't want to do that.

Design ideas based on this insight:

- Make the interface do the training.
- Build the interface as an electronic performance support system.

Figure 11-22 An example of an insight sheet.

When you write insight sheets, think carefully about the way that you word the insight and the items in your bulleted list. Try not to blame the user. Also, try to be concrete enough so that the insight plus the examples in the bulleted list lead to specific ideas for designs. For example, if users make mistakes because they cannot remember which menu item to select, don't write "The users don't understand how the system works." You might write "The menu hierarchy doesn't seem to match the users' mental model."

You might also want to accumulate all of your insights (the headings on your insight sheets) into a list of major points to share with others on the team, with users, and perhaps with upper-level management. That list might be the major finding from your site visit study.

Methods of enhancing your presentations

As you and your team members work together to understand what you have learned about your users, their tasks, and their environments, you may want to create more elaborate presentations to bring your insights to others in your organization. Consider creating

- highlights of audio or videotapes that you have accumulated at user sites

- assemblages of photographs from your site visits

- collections of artifacts you have accumulated with appropriate labels so that everyone know what they represent

Each of these techniques is described briefly in the next sections.

Video- and audiotape highlights

Most development teams find it too time consuming to review the hours of video or audiotapes they took during their field studies. You may find it best to create highlight tapes of significant events or statements. You can then use the highlight tapes to bring certain events to the team's attention. Make the entire tapes available to anyone who would like to see them on their own and encourage the reviewers to make notes of significant issues that they can bring to the team discussions.

Be aware that selecting excerpts, just like any distillation of raw data, requires careful decision making. It is entirely possible to bias your team's discussion by the choices you make. If there are several different views of an issue, be certain to illustrate the differences in your excerpts.

Remember that videotapes, and audiotapes to a lesser extent, are extremely powerful in forming opinions about the interface. They can solidify a team's focus on user needs, but they can also lead a team to incorrect or ineffective decisions.

Photographs

Still photographs of users and their environments help to remind the team members that they are developing tools to be used by real people in real situations, not abstractions of typical users.

JoAnn once worked with a development team that took pictures of users during their site visits. They pinned the pictures to the same wall they were using to outline the detailed layout and organization of the interface and the underlying program. The pictures reminded them of the users they had met. They realized that the program they designed had to be usable by the real people in the photos, as illustrated in figure 11-23. Then they would have succeeded in meeting their quality and usability goals.

Figure 11-23 Photo of a user performing a task.

Photographs are also useful for showing characteristics of the users' environments. What if you saw that the users worked in cramped quarters where it was impossible to use a reference manual? Then you might decide to create a job aid that would work in the users' environment. One graphic design team created electrical drawings that could be hooked over the door of the computer cabinet. The drawings hung at eye level and were hands-free. The users could consult them as they worked.

Artifact analysis

During your site visits, you probably collected a variety of artifacts: documents, notes, sticky notes, job aids, tools, reports, input sheets, forms, and more. Create an analysis sheet that lists all the artifacts collected and indicates where they were found, what purpose they serve, what details you have found significant, and any other information you believe the team needs to take into consideration. Figure

11-24 shows a portion of an artifact list. Figure 11-25 illustrates a typical collection of artifacts from a site visit.

Artifacts from the user site visit (district representative #1):

- cheat sheet put together by the user on performing the procedure
- copies of pages on which the user has added notes and small sketches
- sample pages from a third-party manual that the user considers very helpful
- photograph of the bookcase that shields the sun coming in the window and where the user keeps his manuals
- list of all the manuals stored in the hallway

Figure 11-24 Sample of an artifact list.

Figure 11-25 Illustration of typical artifacts from a site visit.

You can then create an affinity diagram or an insight sheet from the artifact list that focuses on the information you want to take into consideration later in the process. The artifacts may become the objects or metaphors of your interface. You need to understand the attributes of these objects as they exist today. You also need to understand their limitations. As objects are translated to the computer, they may assume attributes that make them more valuable.

The team that originally thought of putting the metaphor of the check register on the computer (the original Quicken developers) collected sample check registers from their users. They watched users fill out the registers and write checks. They also learned about the mistakes users made transferring numbers from the checks to the register, the arithmetic mistakes users made subtracting each check from the previous total, the many users who never balanced their check registers at all, and so on. The computer check register they designed assumed responsibility for the arithmetic, freeing the users from the subtraction and addition task and making it more accurate.

You need to understand enough about the task artifacts to be able to translate them into the new product environment. You may be able to extend the computer functions and enhance the task in ways never before available to the users. You may even have an opportunity to eliminate tasks that the users no longer need to perform. Artifact analysis will help you do so.

Selecting the best methods for your analysis

So far in this chapter, we have shown you several ways to make sense of the information from your site visits. Clearly, you are not going to use all of them. Which methods you use will depend on whether you are designing the interface of an entirely new product, creating a new interface for a legacy product, or redesigning the interface from an earlier version of the product. In this section, we suggest how you might want to proceed in each of these situations.

Designing an entirely new product

When you are engaged in designing a completely new product from scratch, you are likely to need several methods. The methods help ensure that you are looking at your user and task data from many perspectives. Each method gives you a different insight into how the product must look and feel to satisfy user needs. You may begin with simple lists and quickly expand those lists into task scenarios. You may move from task scenarios into use scenarios that outline your vision of the users' interactions with the new interface. See chapter 12 for more on use scenarios.

You are most likely working on new designs for work your users do today. Thus you need to collect task information, including high-level and detailed descriptions of how the tasks are performed. If, however, you know that all the details of the tasks will change, you may want to limit your analysis to major steps in the process, simply in the interest of saving time. The details are most likely to change in the new interface. Remember, nevertheless, that the better you understand the details, the more likely you are to make the right decisions about how the tasks will change in the new design.

You may also be working on new design ideas that are unlike anything your users do today. If so, you may want to concentrate your analysis on constructing user profiles and understanding how users work with related products.

For a new product, you need to carefully create and analyze detailed user profiles. You don't want to overlook any of the differences in user characteristics. These differences may prove significant in establishing the scope of the new design. The choices you make about what options to include are often dictated by differences in user needs. Under such circumstances, the outliers you identify are just as important as the most common behaviors. The typical and the eccentric both help define the interface.

> *JoAnn worked on a project in which a type of software that had been used for customer data analysis by very large retail firms was being rethought to design a product for small retailers. The marketers and developers were having a difficult time rethinking the user task environment because they were so familiar with users in the large-company environment. Detailed user profiles of the small business owners, as well as rich task scenarios, enabled them to understand the essential differences in how the new users thought about analyzing their customers.*

If you are trying to get information to help design a totally new product, you might be particularly interested in the methodology called "systematic creativity" which Jean Scholtz and Anthony Salvador developed at Intel (Salvador and Scholtz 1995, Scholtz and Salvador 1998). They interview users and focus on users' goals and objectives as well as facilitators and obstacles in meeting those goals and objectives. They also gather and track product goals, which usually come from marketing. As they point out, knowing when marketing goals and users' goals support each other and when they conflict is important in making decisions about new products.

Creating a new interface for a legacy product

What if you are creating a new interface for a legacy product, especially one from a mainframe environment? You may find that you already have task lists. Your job is to redesign how the tasks are performed.

To understand how users work with the old system means you have to study their work. Perhaps your initial analysis takes place in the usability lab. Then you make site visits to better understand the users, their environments, and their corporate cultures. You may want to start with site visits. Then you'll use detailed task analysis to learn exactly how the tasks are performed and what mistakes are typical.

You may even want to use your site visits to find out if your assumptions about the users are still true. If you haven't really observed users in several years, you may be surprised. You may also learn that the groups of users have expanded considerably since your original examination of the problem.

A team was working on the redesign of the interface for a teller system used in savings and loans. They discovered that many of the developers who had worked on the mainframe system design some years before made assumptions about users that were no longer true. They assumed that tellers were mostly college graduates with business degrees. They thought that users were hired because of their educations in accounting. Visits to the savings and loans, observations of the tellers, and interviews with the supervisors and human resources department personnel revealed that tellers were most likely to be women willing to work part time. No one encountered in the site visits had a degree in accounting; they gained all their financial knowledge on the job and in their initial training. They were more likely to be hired for their customer service style and friendliness to customers than for their technical backgrounds or educational qualifications.

Many companies are replacing legacy systems at the same time that their markets have greatly expanded. More and more companies are finding that they operate in a global market, but the legacy product was built when their market was primarily local. In your analyses for design, make sure that people pay attention to global issues and to differences in user profiles, environmental profiles, and task analyses for users in different countries.

Given a legacy system, you may want to construct detailed flowcharts to review how users are actually performing tasks given the current interface, rather than how management or training assumes they are performing tasks. Such an analysis will often reveal workarounds that users have created to improve efficiency which can be incorporated into the new design.

In creating a new interface for a legacy product or redesigning the interface for an existing product, it is important to review the skills required in the new environment and analyze to what extent your users have those skills.

In one project, Ginny discovered that users had far less experience with a graphical user interface than others on the development team imagined. User profiles and brief task scenarios were instrumental in helping the team understand the users' capabilities and potential weaknesses. If users don't have the skills, planning for a smooth transition will be a necessary part of the design.

Selecting the right methods for analysis depends on team issues

The tools that you choose to turn data into information and information into decision making will depend upon a number of issues:

- the familiarity of your team members with the data, especially their direct involvement in the site visits

- the familiarity of your team members with the various communication tools typically used in user and task analysis

- the experience of your team members in working with user information to guide their decision-making process

- the willingness of your team members to address user information with serious concern

- your role on the team as either a full team member or a consultant to the developers

- the type of information you have collected

- the stage of data collection you are in, whether at the very beginning of the process or engaged in collecting details for further iterations of the design

Remember that the point of all communication of data and information is to focus the development team on understanding users and their tasks before the product is designed. With this focus you will be encouraged to believe that the product will be designed from the beginning to support the users' goals.

In many development processes, user considerations are often sublimated to functional concerns. Marketers focus on ensuring that features provided by the competition and identified by potential buyers will appear prominently in the product design. Developers focus on ensuring that the functions work as specified and deliver information to the users as efficiently as possible. Issues concerning features and functions should not by themselves be sufficient to overturn attention to the users' needs and goals. But, in many cases, once functional and feature-oriented decisions are built into the basis of the product design, it becomes difficult to change the design to account for user performance.

However, if the users' needs and goals are understood early enough in the development life cycle, the revelation that the design is not going in the right direction can lead to significant changes.

JoAnn worked on a medical records application described earlier in this chapter. Early in the development life cycle, JoAnn conducted a low-cost usability test to find out if the design of the application made sense to the users. The users were totally confused about what to do. The development team was shocked to find that what they thought was an understandable interface caused such problems. They decided that they needed to know a lot more about the users' tasks, so they scheduled visits to nearby hospitals. The next version of the interface was completely different and significantly improved. More importantly, members of the development team became devoted to early user studies and usability testing and included them as integral parts of their design and development life cycle.

When early design decisions are made without full consideration of the users, their goals, their values, and their existing ways of performing tasks, we often find that changes to the design become difficult and costly. Consequently you will find it extremely important to do as much of your user and task analysis as early as possible and to communicate your results in a way that will influence the behavior of the development team.

Jonathan Grudin (1991, 1993) in his study of the behaviors of development teams, points out that trade-offs are continually made during development, trade-offs influenced by functional requirements, ease of development, inclusion of features, efficient use of hardware and software, and attention to ease of use. Ease of use, or attention to how the users will perceive the way their goals have been implemented in the product and how their performance is supported or subverted, is often considered just one of many trade-offs. The goal of analyzing user data and communicating it effectively should be to elevate the needs of users to a higher level in the trade-off debate.

As you plan how to bring user information to your team members and help them get excited about user-centered design, consider the following scenarios:

■ You are a full-time member of the development team and your team members are already excited about user-centered design.

■ You are a part-time consultant to the development team and you must encourage them to take responsibility for the user in the design process.

■ Your team has a lot of experience working with user information.

■ Your team has experience with user information, but not with the method you want to introduce.

■ You team has little or no experience with user information or the methods of user-centered design.

You are a full-time member of the development team

As a full-time member of the development team and as the team member chiefly responsible for conducting field studies, you will have many opportunities to enhance your team members' vision of the users' goals. You can encourage everyone to take part in the site visits. You can invite everyone to participate in reviewing the data and analyzing the results. But, most importantly, you can continue to ensure that the users' perspective is taken into account as design decisions are made. You can take an active role in using several of the analysis tools at various stages of the development process, as they become more or less appropriate.

You need to take into account, of course, the team dynamics. Does your team make decisions about the interface at team meetings, working through to a consensus? Is someone in charge of arbitrating disagreements or differences of opinion about the importance of a particular user issue? Does the arbiter explain his or her decision-making process or make decisions about priorities and announce the result? Do members of the team go off on their own to implement design ideas after a team discussion? Do they bring the design ideas back to the team for review? Are individuals permitted to work in a vacuum, making all their own decisions about design and design trade-offs? Or is their work reviewed by other team members, project managers, quality assurance, or usability professionals to provide feedback and ensure that user needs are taken into account?

In the best circumstances, everyone on the team will participate in collecting the information from potential users, analyzing the information collected, and using the information to make design decisions.

You are a consultant to the development team

If you serve as a consultant to the development team, you may not take part in all the design meetings or you may be present only to advise the team members about the user information that has been collected. They have sole responsibility for deciding whether or not to take a characteristic into account or to design according to the results of a particular task analysis. In this case, you may want to institute a more formal process of analyzing study data. A series of formal steps will help to ensure that a step in the process is not eliminated or misunderstood. As a consultant, you need to introduce each analysis step and ensure that it takes place without biasing the information.

Those serving as human factors consultants often find themselves stretched very thin among all the projects they have to support. One of the ways to handle the lack of time and attention is to enlist the help of members of the design teams who are already especially sensitive to user concerns. They may want to take part in the field studies and assist in ensuring that the data is properly presented and analyzed. They may also assist in ensuring that the users' needs continue to be represented during the discussions of design trade-offs.

Your team is very experienced with a variety of methods used to communicate user information

If your team is more experienced in working with user data and is anxious to include user information in its development process, the variety of tools that you use should include almost everything available: task lists, user lists, environment lists, fully fleshed out task and use scenarios, still photos of users, videotapes of users doing their work, audiotapes of users discussing the tasks they perform, and stacks of artifacts from their workplace documenting the things they create as they work. The full range of tools will assist your team in looking at the information collected from many different perspectives.

Your team has experience with user data but not with the analysis methods you choose to use

Your team members may already be familiar with task flowcharts and task lists from their previous experience in analyzing the flow of data through a system. Systems analysis often includes similar data-capturing techniques. If you are able to present user data in a form already familiar to team members, they will be less likely to dismiss the data as overly subjective. It is important, however, to make sure they understand the differences between empirical user data—your real facts from being with users in the field—and traditional systems analysis—desk-based thinking of how "it ought to work" focusing more on the technology than on the people.

As your team gains experience considering systematic user data as part of the development process, they may become more comfortable using techniques such as affinity diagrams. As you introduce affinity diagrams, you need to emphasize the importance of sorting through the details of user information and focusing on the similarities in behavior rather than the seeming confusion and variety of differences. Those new to user studies often find themselves overwhelmed by the diversity of points of view and the inherent "messiness" of user information. Helping them see the similarities in the data, without forgetting to analyze the differences for critical insights, will help to reduce the reluctance often shown to take user information into account.

Your team has no experience considering user data

If your development team has no previous experience applying user data to their design efforts, you may need to proceed slowly to introduce the information you have collected. Your job will be made easier by the extent to which your team members have participated in the user site visits. The more personal experience they have had with users, the more likely they will bring these experiences to bear on the design process.

User profiles, brief scenarios, and photos of users will help change the mindset and focus of the development team members. You will find it useful to move quickly into the specifics of your task analysis, producing familiar artifacts such as task lists, flowcharts, and workflow diagrams.

JoAnn was working with a software development team that had never been exposed to user information before. In collecting information about the users, JoAnn's team used videotapes. At the team meetings to review the information, they showed excerpts from the videotapes to illustrate particular observations and draw conclusions about user behaviors. Several of the programmers asked to view the entire videotapes on their own and were really excited about gaining a new perspective on the users.

Unfortunately old habits prevailed. The programmers, used to working alone, used their personal interpretations of the information on the tapes to make their own design decisions. They changed portions of the interface without discussing those changes with the team.

It took a concerted effort by the usability specialist and the head of development to bring the team back around. After the redesigns were reviewed and found equally difficult to use, the team members recognized the need for a team development effort. They met to gain a clearer understand of what the users were saying, sketched design ideas, and turned them into paper prototypes for usability testing. Only after the paper tests did they redesign the interface.

In another case, the engineers used their observations during a usability test to make immediate changes to the equipment interface. Two of the engineers went back to their hotel in the evening and arrived in the morning with the interface changes completed. The changes, which had not been discussed with other team members, were not well conceived. They did not adequately take into account the underlying causes of the users' mistakes. The next set of tests using the new design resulted in a repeat of the previous problems. Not until the entire team, including the human factors professionals, sat down together to analyze the data, did the entire team arrive at a design change that solved the problem.

If your team members have had little contact with users and you have been required to do the field studies yourself, you will need to develop several methods of communicating what you have learned. It may be best, in this instance, to choose forms of data analysis that will be treated as systematic and legitimate. Task listings, task flowcharts, brief descriptions of significant user traits, descriptions of environmental issues, and other techniques that emphasize factual information may be better received by an inexperienced team than some of the techniques that depend more fully on narrative accounts, such as scenarios.

References cited in the chapter

Beabes, Minette A. and Flanders, Alicia, Experiences with using contextual inquiry to design information, *Technical Communication*, 42 (3), August 1995: 409–420.

Carroll, John M., Ed., *Scenario-Based Design: Envisioning Work and Technology in System Development*, New York: John Wiley & Sons, 1995.

Grudin, Jonathan, Obstacles to participatory design in large product development organizations, in *Participatory Design: Principles and Practices*, edited by Douglas Schuler and Aki Namioka, Hillsdale, NJ: Lawrence Erlbaum Associates, 1993, 99–119.

Grudin, Jonathan, Systematic sources of suboptimal interface design in large product development organizations, *Human-Computer Interaction*, 6 (2), 1991: 147–196.

Holtzblatt, Karen and Beyer, Hugh, Making customer-centered design work for teams, *Communications of the ACM*, 36(10), October 1993: 93–103.

Raven, Mary Elizabeth and Flanders, Alicia, Using contextual inquiry to learn about your audiences, *The Journal of Computer Documentation*, 20 (1), February 1996: 1–13.

Salvador, Anthony C. and Scholtz, Jean C., Systematic creativity in software user interface design, in *Engineering for Human-Computer Interaction*, edited by Leonard J. Bass and Claus Unger, NY: Chapman & Hall, 1995, 307–332.

Scholtz, Jean C. and Salvador, Anthony C., Systematic creativity: A bridge for the gaps in the software development process, in *User Interface Design: Bridging the Gap from User Requirements to Design*, edited by Larry E. Wood, Boca Raton, FL: CRC Press, 1998, 217–247.

Other books and articles for further reading

Jacobson, Ivar, The use-case construct in object-oriented software engineering, in *Scenario-Based Design: Envisioning Work and Technology in System Development*, edited by John M. Carroll, New York: John Wiley & Sons, 1995, 309–336.

Jonassen, David H, Hannum, Wallace H., and Tessmer, Martin, *Handbook of Task Analysis Procedures*, NY: Praeger, 1989.

Rubinstein, Richard and Hersh, Harry, *The Human Factor: Designing Computer Systems for People*, Bedford, MA: Digital Equipment Corporation, 1984.

Shneiderman, Ben, *Designing the User Interface: Strategies for Human-Computer Interaction*, 3rd ed., Reading, MA: Addison-Wesley, 1998.

Tognazzini, Bruce, *TOG on Software Design*, Reading, MA: Addison-Wesley, 1996.

Tognazzini, Bruce, *TOG on Interface*, Reading, MA: Addison-Wesley, 1992.

Wood, Larry E, Ed., *User Interface Design: Bridging the Gap from User Requirements to Design*, Boca Raton, FL: CRC Press, 1998.

12

Working toward the interface design

In chapter 11 you learned about using a variety of methods to organize and analyze the information you developed from your site visits. While you were gathering information and analyzing the results with your team members, you doubtless have been thinking about many ideas for the interface, documentation, and training that you want to design. Designing is not an activity that you can strictly schedule. Each team member thinks about design ideas every time you add new information from your user and task analysis.

The next step in the process is to take the information you have gathered and analyzed and begin the process of designing for the user. This book is not about interface design, nor about the design and development of documentation and training. You will find many books and articles to guide you through these processes in the "Other books and articles for further reading" section at the end of the chapter. We do, however, point out the basic steps that you might use to move from data gathering and analysis to design.

The process steps in this chapter are only suggestions. You and your team members need to immerse yourselves in the information, generating design ideas, prototyping, testing, and iterating the process until you meet your usability and quality goals for the product. The methods described in more detail in this chapter are detailed in table 12-1.

Interface design method	Brief definition
Qualitative usability goals and measurable objectives	Lists of the goals you need to achieve to ensure that your users find the interface usable. Quantitative measures of the goals, as needed
Objects/actions: Nouns/verbs	Lists of nouns and verbs that represent objects that you need to create and actions that you need to support
Metaphors	Conceptual models that reflect how your users will think about the new interface
Use scenarios	Brief narrative descriptions of the users, tasks, and environments as they will look in the new design
Use sequences	Ordered lists of the tasks as they will be performed by the users in the new design
Use flow diagrams	Drawings of the specifics of a task, including objects, actions, and decisions, as it will occur in the new interface
Use workflows	Drawings of the major tasks of a larger activity as they will be performed by an individual user or by groups of users
Use hierarchies	Tasks arranged in a hierarchical arrangement to show their interrelationships in the new interface
Storyboards	Scripts and illustrations that illustrate the new design in the context of users, tasks, and environments
Rough interface sketches	Preliminary and very rough sketches of screens, menus, dialog boxes, and more in preparation for paper prototyping.
Video dramatizations	Video dramatizations of the new work environment with the new product in place

Table 12-1 Interface design methods.

Designing from what you've learned

To begin your design process, first establish the qualitative and quantitative usability goals for your design. Designers often ask of iterative design processes, "When will we be finished?" The answer is, "It depends." It depends on what you are trying to achieve. If your only goal is to get the product out on schedule, you may have to stop with a single iteration of the interface design. Such a practice is not all that uncommon. Many interfaces are, and certainly appear to be, last-minute affairs, thrown together so that the users have something to interact with. They often cause other problems and have to be redone—iterated after users are unproductive and unhappy.

If, on the other, your principal goal is to ensure a usable product that your users will find pleasant and productive to use, you probably need a few more iterations. We simply do not know enough about translating the outcomes of our field studies into specific designs to arrive at an optimal design on the first attempt. There is no rule book that says user observation A equals interface object A. You can't simply follow a standard set of interface design rules from the operating system developers (Windows, UNIX, Mac, OS/2). Even if you follow all the rules and guidelines carefully, you are likely to end up with an unusable interface. We have seen many interfaces that keep very close to the guidelines but that users still find incomprehensible.

Note: Tom Dayton, Al McFarland, and Joseph Kramer have designed a process called The Bridge that provides one way to translate a task flow into GUI objects and actions and then to GUI design (see Dayton et al. 1998). Their method is only part of a larger, iterative development process. Beyer and Holtzblatt (1997) also have a systematic overall approach called Contextual Design.

To define an end to the iterative design process requires that you define a set of goals that you will achieve before you stop designing. The qualitative and quantitative usability goals should reflect the goals you observed with your users plus the limits that you want to set for your development effort. Design limits are often set by budgets and deadlines. They can also be set by market decisions. Your company may decide that you will not be able to address the usability needs of a certain group of users. For example, you may have very expert users who want shortcuts to perform their tasks. You decide that you don't have time to build in all the shortcuts when 95% of users will not need them. On the other hand, you may decide to ignore the usability requirements of very novice users in the interface design. Instead, you plan to handle their needs through training.

JoAnn's company worked on a project in which a high percentage of the users lacked basic typing skills. The initial interface design required a great deal of typing. The design was changed to allow for more "clickable" choices by adding radio buttons and check boxes. The design team decided, however, that some limited typing had to be required because the technology at the time made handwriting recognition unfeasible. Plans were made to teach basic typing skills as part of the preparatory training.

The point is to make your design decisions rationally and to realize that they are all marketing decisions. Every time you decide that a given group of users will not be accommodated in your design, you must weigh the risk that those people will choose not to buy or use your product. You must understand the potential costs of taking that risk. If the group of users that you are not accommodating is internal, you must weigh the risk of increased job turnover and increased downtime as old users learn new ways, perhaps very slowly, reluctantly, and with many errors. If you decide that many problems are training or documentation issues because you don't want to accommodate users in the interface, you must be sure that appropriate resources are given to developing the training and documentation. You must also weigh the risk of people not taking the training and not using the documentation. Although JoAnn's story shows a situation where the decision to train in basic typing skills was probably a correct one, and although it is true that you cannot always accommodate all user groups, it is always better to make the interface as obvious as possible to the users rather than to assume that training and documentation will overcome problems in the design.

Qualitative usability goals and measurable objectives

Given all the information you now have about your users, their environments, their goals, and their tasks, defining qualitative usability goals for your interface, documentation, and training should not be difficult. List the user issues you identified in your insight lists and affinity diagrams and turn them into qualitative usability goals (see figure 12-1).

Qualitative goals are derived from values the users bring to the task. You discover these values when you meet the users, watch them at work, and talk to them about their needs.

JoAnn learned that catalog users valued the telephone conversations they had when they called in to order items. They valued the seemingly personal information that the telephone clerks appeared to have about the products. The new online catalog design would fulfill their usability goals if we could preserve that personal quality.

Issue	Qualitative usability goal
Users want to be certain they are looking at all the information available about the patients.	Users are satisfied that they have access to all the information they need to make good decisions.
Users want to be able to write a prescription as quickly and easily as they can do by hand.	Users are satisfied that they can write prescriptions quickly and easily in about the same time they now take to write them by hand. They will be satisfied with the accuracy trade-off if the time condition cannot be met.
Users want to be sure they can get to all the patient information they need with ease so that they can make good diagnoses.	Users are satisfied that the patient information is easy to access and that it is organized so that it doesn't interfere with the patient's treatment.

Figure 12-1 Example of qualitative usability goals for patient information.

Measurable objectives are sometimes more difficult to derive because they must include measurements that are inherent in your users' definition of the work to be done. You may have learned, for example, that your users believe they should be able to install your software without having to call for customer assistance. However, in examining the diversity of user profiles you have collected, you have to admit that some percentage of your user population may have installation problems. You may want to create a measurable objective that reads like these (see figure 12-2).

Goal	Measurable objective
Users will find the installation process understandable and easily follow it step-by-step to achieve a successful installation.	No more than 10% of users will call customer support for help to install the product.
Users are able to connect their laptop and desktop computers together and share files between them.	Users will be able to complete the connection between their laptop and desktop computers and share 10 files in less than 20 minutes with no help.

Figure 12-2 Sample measurable objectives based on usability goals.

The quantitative measurements provide a way for you to know if you have achieved an acceptable level of usability in the users' performance with your product's interface and documentation. The measurements are derived from workplace observations and discussions with users.

Deriving quantitative measurements from workplace observations may be difficult and sometimes impossible. Often the best you can do is come close to the users' expectations. For example, the measurable objective in the example above states that users want to complete the connection in less than 20 minutes. We arrived at that objective by observations of users working with a competitive product. Users who completed the task in 20 minutes or less seemed satisfied with the efficiency of their task performance. Users who took more than 20 minutes became frustrated at the difficulty of the task. That indicated that we wanted to design so that the installation took less than 20 minutes for the great majority of users. This objective could be tested during the development process through laboratory and workplace usability tests.

List the goals that you have identified and then establish ways to measure your success at meeting them. Figure 12-3 illustrates goals and objectives we might create for the patient chart software designed to be used by physicians and other health care professionals.

Goal	Measurable objective
Users will be able to find the information they need to diagnose and treat patients.	100% of the users will be able to find patient information within three minutes.
Users will be able to order pharmaceuticals and tests for patients as quickly as they do currently.	Users will be able to place an accurate order in less than 1 minute after a 30-minute practice session.
Users will be pleased with using the patient chart software.	80% of users will rate the software at the highest level of satisfaction.

Figure 12-3 Example of usability goals and measurable objectives.

Once you define the goals for your interface, you may need to investigate further to establish the appropriate measurable objectives. The higher you set the measurements, the more difficult they may be to achieve and the more design iterations they may require. You can set your objectives low to avoid iterations but you are also more likely to have frustrated and disappointed users. For example, you can write an objective that says that only one in ten of your users will be able to install the software without assistance. An objective like this will be relatively easy to achieve and may decrease your development time and costs. However, the low level of expectations may result in significant increases in support costs and loss of potential sales because of angry customers.

The goal to keep the prescription-writing time short led to aggressive design iterations for the patient chart system. The interface included standard dosages for each drug, quick tables to indicate number of times per day or per week to administer the drug, type of administering (by mouth, intravenously, etc.), and other point-and-click items that made the details simple and fast to complete. Despite all these efforts, it remained difficult to meet the time measurements to the users' satisfaction. We had to emphasize the trade-offs of accuracy and speed of transmittal, plus the safeguard against drug interactions.

Goals that are derived from users' values help drive design iterations in the right direction. We need to work hard at preserving the values and achieving the goals while we alter the way the work is performed.

Objects/Actions: Nouns/Verbs

By this time in your analysis, you will have descriptions of the way users perform tasks to reach their goals. You may have task flows and task scenarios. You may have descriptions of the artifacts they use as they perform the tasks. These artifacts can include forms, palettes, documents, papers, lists, and more. The artifacts in your users' environment will become the objects of your interface design. Nouns in your task flows and task scenarios also lead to objects for your design; verbs in the task flows and task scenarios lead to actions for your design.

Review your task scenarios and the output of other analytical methods described in chapter 11. Underscore, circle, write sticky notes, or make lists of all the objects and all the actions that you can identify. For example, if you are designing an interface for the patient chart system, your list of objects and actions might look like the one illustrated in figure 12-4.

Your list of objects and actions will become the objects you translate onto the computer screen, the activities you place in pull-down menus and icons, the information you organize into dialog boxes, and so on.

You may want to write all of the objects onto sticky notes or white cards. Then, you can add to the cards by noting the attributes that the objects exhibit. For example, your white card listing the patient may note that the patient object has the following demographic attributes: name, address, telephone number, social security number, next of kin, and insurance coverage. All these attributes are

PATIENT CHART SYSTEM	
Objects:	Actions:
The patient	Finding the right patient chart
The patient's chart	Ordering lab tests
Patient's current and past medications	Reviewing test results
Patient's lab results	Reviewing patient demographic information
The doctor	
List of standard laboratory tests	Making treatment notes
List of prescription drugs	Investigating possible drug interactions
	Ordering drugs

Figure 12-4 Example of a list of objects and actions from the patient chart system.

related to the patient. Other attributes might be attached to the patient's chart, such as medical history, current medications, recent test results, physical condition, and so on.

The objects also have actions associated with them. The patient's chart has to be found among all the charts in the system. Then the chart must be opened by the physician and scanned for current information. The physician wants to add notes to the chart, keeping track of vital signs, results of examinations, medications prescribed, and new tests ordered.

As you record the nouns and verbs from your users' tasks and environments, you should begin to visualize the objects that you will have to account for in your interface design. The patient might become part of a patient list organized by name, physician, date of last visit, time of appointment, and so on. The list of all patients might need to be searchable if the list becomes too long to browse easily. That might suggest a search mechanism, a way to sort the list into shorter components, or a way to organize the list into the group of patients who will visit the clinic today.

As you continue listing nouns and verbs and identifying them as possible objects and actions in your interface, consider ways to shorten the lists. At early stages of the design, you will often find yourself with long lists of objects and actions. As you work through the attributes and associate actions with objects, you may find that you have some repetition. In most cases you will be able to eliminate the repetition by recognizing that some objects you have listed are attributes of other objects. For example, we first listed the patients' address and phone number as separate objects. Those objects remained until we recognized that address and phone number were better thought of as attributes of the patient rather than as independent objects.

You might be interested in the specific methodology used by Dayton and others by which they are often able to reduce the number of objects for the design by using the concept of attributes and containers. Some objects contain other objects; some objects are attributes of others (Dayton et al. 1998).

Metaphors for the interface design

By thinking about the objects and actions you must account for in the interface, organic design concepts will begin to emerge. The term *metaphor* describes the overall concept you may use to organize all the objects and actions into a coherent whole. Metaphors have contributed to the success of many graphical user interfaces: spreadsheet, documents, folders and tabs, fill-in forms of all types, paint palettes, virtual machine controls, and the check register are some of the more obvious examples. CD-ROM and Website design has introduced even more metaphors including 3-D spaces like storefronts and playrooms. For a comprehensive list of metaphors, including those associated with command-line interfaces (edit, escape, run, debug, purge, etc.), see Collins (1995).

Metaphors provide analogs from the users' real world to the virtual world you have constructed in the interface. If you are carrying over the image of a real-world object, users will assume that it operates in similar ways on the screen. For example, a user who has experience with a specific form in a paper version will bring assumptions about it to the computer-based version. If the paper version has fields that indicate how many characters are acceptable for each field, users will assume that the length of the fill-in area for a field on the screen is telling them how long the response can be. If you design each response area on the screen to be the same size, you are not matching the users' assumptions about how the form works.

If you are designing a straightforward visual representation of the users' current process, you might want to stay very close to the existing objects. For example, if users are working from paper-based forms, the form you construct in the interface could look exactly like the paper form the users are used to. The interface form might even preserve the awkward fill-in order of the paper form, especially if the users will be entering information from the paper forms completed by someone else.

In other instances, you may want to redesign the paper form to facilitate on-screen use, especially if the original form was poorly designed. For example, you might alter the metaphor but not enough to make it unfamiliar. You might preserve the attributes of the original paper form but change the way the users interact with the form in the interface.

Instead of showing the form so that it looks like the paper version, you might make the questions into a dialog box, with only one or two questions appearing on the screen at one time. If the paper form has lots of branches or has sections that only some people fill out, making it into a dialog box allows the computer to bring up only those questions that are relevant to each user based on answers to previous questions. Some of the popular programs to help you do your income tax work that way. Instead of giving you a copy of the form to fill out, they ask questions and then create the form from your answers. The metaphor has become "a dialogue" rather than "a piece of paper to be filled out." Many people are more comfortable having a dialogue than filling out a form.

Extending the functionality of the metaphor

Metaphors can also be substantially changed to take advantage of the computer environment, as long as the changes are coherent for the users. Users of graphical user interfaces have also come to expect certain behaviors from a computer version of the form that are obviously different from paper forms. The computer enhancement of the paper form should allow the users to complete the form more easily. The users could select a city from a drop-down menu or type part of the city name and have the computer complete the rest of the name and fill in the state and zip code automatically. The users might expect the computer form to format the telephone number with standard punctuation while they simply type a series of numbers.

The computer spreadsheet is a good example of an extended metaphor that works better in the interface than it ever did in manual form. Accountants using paper spreadsheets had to add the columns of numbers and print the sum in manually. The computer version of the spreadsheet calculates the sum automatically. Accountants also had to erase numbers, print in new ones, and recalculate the sums if they had to change the information. The computer version automatically recalculates once a formula is in place.

Intuit, early in the development of Quicken, their personal and business accounting program, decided to use a graphical representation of the check register as a primary metaphor for users entering the application. In the first versions of the program, the check register was nearly the first screen that appeared. Users were immediately able to understand how to use the graphical representation, since it looked almost exactly like the register they carried around with their checkbook. They could type in the name of the recipient, the date, and the amount. The program took care of the check number and the date (with some changes necessary for back dates, etc.). The users did not need any instruction to use the check register, nor did they need to consult the documentation. The interface informed them about its use.

The computer version of the patient chart became extensible in many ways in comparison to the paper version of the chart. The physician could view a graphic of the patients' vital signs over time once the information had been entered. That extension allowed for analysis of blood pressure or heart rate over long periods of time, assisting diagnoses and allowing new physicians to obtain a quick review of patient history.

The computer version of the clothing catalog preserved the attractive, four-color photographs but allowed the users to change the colors of entire items rather than just viewing color swatches at the side of the page.

Metaphors invite analogous behaviors among users

Metaphors help users think about the screen objects much as they would think about real-world objects. They attach both behaviors they understand from the analog world and behaviors they have learned to expect from the digital world. Unfortunately users transfer some behaviors from the analog world of the metaphor that end up creating problems in their use of the object in the digital world. The problems occur given the extent to which the digital metaphor "improves on" its analog. For example, word-processing software automatically calculates the width of the text column and places a typed word on the next line if it exceeds the column width. The users do not need to type a carriage return at the end of a continuing line of text as they would have to do using a manual typewriter. Nevertheless, this behavior, so well learned by users who first typed on a typewriter, often carries over inappropriately to the digital environment. The learned behavior causes users to add unnecessary carriage returns at the end of lines.

Because actions that users attach to metaphor objects are so powerful, designers must select metaphors extremely carefully. They are effective reinforcers of desired behaviors; they are just as effective reinforcers of undesired behaviors.

JoAnn worked with a team that was designing a system to be used by physicians to interact with patients and their medical records. The system displays information about the patient, including demographics and medical history. The system also allows the physician to enter new information and place orders for medications, tests, and general care. The system replaces the physical chart with its pages of handwritten notes and printouts of test results that have typically been used both in physicians' offices and in hospitals.

The dominant object in the users' environment was the traditional handwritten chart. Yet the physical chart presented many usability problems. Because all the information is entered chronologically, it becomes very difficult to trace trends. Physicians can review what happened at a particular point in time, but they have difficulty comparing information collected in the past and over time. No facility is available for charting trends. Interactions among medications are difficult to track because it is difficult to trace medication history in a handwritten chronological record.

Handwriting problems make the information less accessible as well. Poor handwriting contributes to problems in medicating patients, giving effective care, and performing tests.

Because data from tests and treatments come from a variety of sources and in many different formats, there is a high probability of misfiling. Test results never arrive, are misplaced in the wrong person's file, or are removed for review and never returned.

Selecting a metaphor for the computer application thus proved problematic. The team wanted to simulate the chart's immediate availability and ease of use for note taking. They also wanted to permit caregivers to review information that was collected during a specific visit. At the same time, they could provide a number of significant advantages by offering the ability to combine information so that trends might be evaluated, avoid the handwriting problems and their associated errors, and avoid the problems of incomplete, misplaced, or lost information.

The team chose a metaphor that was much like the physical chart, but with significant differences. The information was organized by category, with tabs along one side of the screen so that the caregivers could look at medications, laboratory tests, care descriptions, demographics, treatments, etc., by clicking from tab to tab. Within a tab, the display information was presented in reverse chronological order, with the most recent information first. The caregiver could look at current test results and scroll back to view earlier test results. The detailed results could also be made available through hypertext links to more detailed records. The information on vital signs and other time-dependent information could be presented graphically so that trends would be immediately visible. Because information from ancillary departments (pharmacy, laboratory, and so on) was connected to the same database, test results could be made immediately available in the electronic version of the chart.

The interface designer used a modification of the real object to eliminate misunderstandings and promote accuracy, completeness, and productivity for the caregivers and the patients. Yet the metaphor's departure from the original object was not sufficiently distant to cause problems in conceptualizing the information. During usability testing, the team found that after 15 or 20 minutes, physicians with no previous PC experience were able to navigate the interface and concentrate on patient care. The chart interface was clearly transparent to the work being done.

The initial implementation of the metaphor was not as successful, however, in facilitating order entry. Physicians were to use the software to order medications, treatments, and tests for their patients. In the real world, they entered their orders by writing them on prescription forms or other forms listing treatment or test options. It was clear during the task analysis that the physicians valued the ability to enter orders quickly. They were aware, however, that quickness could be a trade-off with accuracy. It was possible that someone would misread their handwriting. It was also possible that they might make a mistake in something like the proper dosage of a drug for a particular patient, or they might be unaware of another drug the patient was taking that could interact with the new prescription.

By implementing order entry inside the chart application, the team could substantially increase the speed and accuracy of the process. The team implemented check-off buttons for tests, drop-down lists of drugs and standard dosages, and standard treatment options. The system could calculate dosages by patient weight and report discrepancies and also report possible drug interactions immediately for the physicians' response. Unfortunately the design could not duplicate the speed of scrawling a note on a prescription form, at least not without forsaking the other advantages that the computer provided. The design of the interaction could be improved and speed optimized but the users' goal of nearly effortless and fast order entry could not be completely achieved.

Not all metaphors are real-world objects

A good metaphor does not have to be a perfect representation of the real-world object that it comes from. In fact, trying to make the computer-based image too realistic can detract from its use as a metaphor. Alan Cooper in *About Face* (1995) describes an interface that tries to look like storefronts on a street. It becomes more and more complicated as the designers try to maintain the metaphor until it is no longer helping the users, but hindering them.

The Windows interface that many of us know is based on a mixture of metaphors. The metaphor mix may cause some users to take a while to understand all of its features. The developers who first named the Microsoft graphical user interface "windows" may have seen it as a metaphor from house windows, but that's not a metaphor that works for many users. Most users don't see the window on the screen as having anything to do with windows in their houses. Instead, they now have two definitions of windows: the windows at home and the Windows on the computer screen. Moreover, the Windows interface itself mixes several metaphors. Windows on the computer have scroll bars. Real windows do move up and down, but what we see out of them does not change as we open the window. Scroll bars are a metaphor that does not come from house windows, but from rolls of paper. Many of us have an image of reading a roll of paper even though we probably have never actually done so. Many dialog boxes in Windows have tabs. Tabs come from neither house windows nor scrolling rolls of paper. They come from notebooks— yet another metaphor. Many dialog boxes in Windows also have "radio buttons." Some radios do have buttons that are mutually exclusive. If your radio is on AM, it cannot also be on FM. But that's yet another metaphor from another medium.

The mix of metaphors may be one reason why Windows takes a while to learn and why many novice users have difficulty with some features of Windows, such as tabs in dialog boxes. That learning curve may be an important factor in your design, especially if you have many users who are learning Windows at the same time that they are learning your application. Developers who are themselves expert Windows users need to be reminded that new users are likely to have a period of time when they are not yet comfortable with all the metaphors that are in the interface while also working with the metaphor of your application.

Over time, however, users do learn at least the most critical features of the Windows interface. Then it serves to promote expectations for future applications. Users who are familiar with the Windows look come to understand how to interact with its visual objects. They then expect to use the down arrow on the scroll bar to see what is below the current page in the window. They expect to get a dialog box when they select a menu item that has three dots after it. They expect that selecting an icon will cause an action to happen immediately. If you are designing an interface for users who use other products that have already been developed using an interface standard, being consistent with the standards allows users to take advantage of metaphors they have learned.

Maintaining the integrity of the metaphor

Once you have established the metaphor you are using, it is critical to maintain its integrity. If we look at the famous trash can metaphor used on the Apple desktop, we can get an idea of what happens when a metaphor is allowed to take on meanings that don't fit. Apple designers worked with two rules for the design of desktop objects: that each object have only one function and that they minimize the number of objects on the desktop. They chose to compromise between creating a minimum number of desktop objects and keeping one function per object when they created the trash can metaphor. They gave the trash can two functions: to delete files and folders from the desktop and to eject floppy disks. As a result, they ended up confusing new users.

The story is that Apple received more calls to customer support about this trade-off than any other aspect of the interface. Users had no trouble learning to associate the trash can with deleting something; they had a terrible time associating a trash can with ejecting a disk. Many novice users were concerned that they would destroy the contents of the disk in some way and were very reluctant to use the metaphor for its second, and seemingly irregular, function.

As you think about appropriate metaphors to use in your design, you should look at the interrelationship of tasks in the users' workflow. Some tasks, like setting the computer clock or printing a document, are independent tasks that will have their own operating metaphors that need not be tied into the overall application metaphor. That is why many designers use the preprogrammed objects like print or set clock and simply link to them from inside their application. You can link users to separate tools that still look and operate consistently on their own even though they depart from the metaphor used for the application.

On the other hand, if the tasks your design encompasses are interrelated, you will need to consider carefully their interrelationship. The metaphor will need to support the interrelationship among tasks if the interrelationship is key to helping the users achieve their goals.

Use scenarios

Once your metaphor begins to take shape, review its applicability to the tasks you have identified and the workflow and goals you need to support. Then test your early design ideas against the original task scenarios at each of the four levels described in chapter 11: the brief scenario, the vignette, the elaborated scenario, and the complete task scenario. Remember that the task scenarios are narrative descriptions of what the users are doing in their current environment. Use scenarios are narrative descriptions of how the users' goals will be achieved with a new product and interface.

To create a use scenario, return to your task scenario and review the actions and decisions that occur in the users' environment. Be certain that you understand the values that users attach to their goals and the ways they have always performed the tasks to support their goals. If you can preserve the values, you can often change the way the task is performed or present appropriate trade-offs to the users.

Next, sketch out the steps of the task scenario in the new interactive environment you want to create. Decide as you proceed which steps will be performed by the users and how the interface will support that performance. Decide which steps will entirely disappear from the users' responsibility because the system can perform them much more efficiently and effectively. For example, users need not look up a zip code if they have already typed the street address, city, and state. The system should be able to insert the correct zip code from a database. Users should not have to type in the next check number when the system already knows the previous check number in the home accounting program.

As you create the use scenario, you may want to concentrate primarily on a narrative description of the user performing the tasks. However, you may feel prepared to begin to sketch the interface or the types of interactions that you are beginning to visualize. Or you may have team members who are particularly skilled in sketching. Use their talents to provide rough preliminary sketches of the interface. Figure 12-5 illustrates a use scenario for the new patient chart system.

Dr. Morgan turns on the laptop computer in her office and logs on with her name and security password. The first screen she sees lists her patients for the day in the order of their appointments. Her first patient is Harold Hancock. She selects Harold's name and double-clicks to open his chart. She verifies that she has the correct chart by noting Harold's name and address on the first page. She selects the tab that shows her the information from his last visit, including the drugs she prescribed and the tests she ordered. She moves to the test results page and quickly scans the results of the recent tests. She also notes that Harold's vitals have just been updated by the nurse.

Dr. Morgan unplugs the laptop and carries it into the examining room, plugging it in after greeting Harold. She discusses Harold's current problems, making notes on the computer and clicking to record the results of the examination. They discuss a change in his medication, which she enters on the medications screen. A message appears on the screen, warning of a possible interaction with another drug Harold was prescribed last year. She asks him if he is still taking that drug and advises him to make sure he doesn't take it while he takes the new drug. She presses a button to send the prescription to Harold's pharmacist of choice, information that was entered into the system long before.

Meanwhile, Harold's pharmacist notes the incoming order on his computer system. He prints out the order and fills the prescription, having it ready for Harold when he arrives straight from the doctor's office. The pharmacist includes the notes about the possible interaction with a previous medication on the sheet he prints out to give Harold with the prescription.

Returning to the office scene, the doctor finishes Harold's examination and discusses his progress with him. They decide that he really needs surgery to correct the problem, and they discuss a possible schedule. Dr. Morgan tells him to get dressed and discuss the surgery schedule with the office assistant.

When Harold sits down with the assistant, they review information from the hospital about open slots in the surgery reservation system. They agree on the date and time, as the assistant records Harold's basic information in the reservation screen and submits the reservation with the relevant information about Harold to the hospital.

Figure 12-5 Example of a use scenario.

Obviously the scenario could continue through a variety of interactions in this complex workflow, including billing Harold's insurance company for the visit. This use scenario begins to set the stage for the type of interaction the designers are envisioning. It also points out some potential problems in the design. Where will Dr. Morgan put the laptop computer in the examining room so that she can easily enter notes and prescriptions? Typically she would have the handwritten chart on the desk in the room and would sit down to take notes. Will she plug in the computer at the desk? What about the data links to the patient history, new test results, and Harold's pharmacy? That means a system that includes a server, a modem connection, and appropriate wiring in the offices. How easy will it be to sell the medical office on this infrastructure?

The use scenarios can and should be extended to tell longer stories and more complex interactions with the proposed design. They should eventually include the exceptional cases that you have discovered during the task analysis and all the peculiarities inherent in your user population. They should even include cases in which you observed users making mistakes and having serious problems so that you can account for the problems in your design. If your metaphor is robust, you will be able to apply new scenarios to the metaphor without having to distort it. In fact, one important way of judging the success of a metaphor and the interaction design is that you can continue to apply new use scenarios to the base design, and they will fit with only minor modifications.

You can stop constructing scenarios at the point when the majority of new scenarios you try out are substantially the same as ones already generated. You can stop constructing scenarios when they no longer result in changes in the design of the interface. That indicates that your design has established patterns for the users' interactions that are complete and consistent.

Creating use scenarios that include documentation and training

A use scenario for documentation, including both paper and electronic forms, accounts for how the users might access documentation to support their learning and use of the interface. The interrelationship between the interface and the help system should be established in a use scenario so that the help becomes an integral part of the interface design. If you are considering adding wizards, coaches, or guides to your interface, you will want to develop detailed scenarios that focus on how these interactive objects will function. Would they serve only the needs of novice users learning to perform a function for the first few times? Would they also serve the needs of experienced users who prefer to use a set of macros to perform a complex task rather than spend the time and effort to hammer the task out in the interface. For example, the chart wizard included in Microsoft Excel enables every user, including a sophisticated user, to create a relatively complex graph quickly and easily.

Use sequences

A use scenario tells a story about the users and their proposed interactions with the new system. With a use sequence, you take part of a scenario and turn it into a sequence of steps. The steps should clearly indicate what actions the user will perform, what decisions the user must make, and what actions the system will perform for the user.

In their description of the ATM (automated teller machine) design and development, Rubenstein and Hersch (1984) suggest that task sequences in the form of task-oriented manuals be written before the software interface is designed. The manuals describe in detail how a task will be done in the new software. "Writing the manual first" enables the design team to examine the details of the new user performance, to maintain consistency among tasks in the new design, and to relate future performance with the users' current ways of performing the tasks.

In the task sequence illustrated in figure 12-6, the designers have envisioned at a high level how the user will interact with the new Web-based catalog shopping system.

Note that no details about the layout or graphic look of the page have been worked out in this example. The use sequence simply indicates what the user will be doing, step by step. The use sequence details a series of actions that the user performs on the interface objects: the graphic of all catalogs, the catalog home page and table of contents, the catalog page, and the item description.

A use sequence of this sort provides a convenient method for agreeing on the task flow for one user performing one task in the new design. All members of the development team, including users who are participating in the design process, can review the sequence and ensure that all the steps are accounted for and the user is capable of understanding and following the sequence.

During the development and review of the use sequence, designers and users inevitably bring up exceptions to the task and additional design questions. The team can either incorporate the exceptions or design ideas into the use sequence, or they can note the questions and design ideas and move onto another use sequence.

For example, in the catalog use sequence, the team may want to know if and how the user might return to the home page of the individual catalog. They may ask where else the user might want to navigate. They may consider whether or not they want to display on every page the catalog table of contents that appeared on the catalog's first page. What if the user wanted to go directly to children's clothes rather than laboriously turning all the pages until the children's section appeared?

We find it useful to write the use sequences on large sheets of flip chart paper so that everyone on the team can see how the sequences are emerging. Team members who suggest new design ideas or bring up issues with the design can write their issues and ideas on sticky notes that can be attached to the use sequence for future consideration.

1. The user arrives at the catalog shopping home page, sees a description of the catalog shopping system, and views the initial graphic of the shopping area.

2. The user decides to browse through the catalogs and clicks the Go to Catalogs button.

3. A graphic display of all the catalogs appears.

4. The user clicks on a catalog and the catalog home page appears with a graphic and a table of contents of what is in the catalog.

5. The user clicks on the Open Catalog button and sees a catalog page with the pictures of the items displayed.

6. The user clicks on the page-turn icon in the lower right corner and proceeds through the picture pages.

7. The user wants to read the description of an item, so she clicks on the item and another window opens slightly offset with a written description.

8. Buttons or icons on the secondary page indicate choices for Marking the item, Ordering the item, and More information (if any is available).

9. The user can scroll through the description, finding information on colors and sizes.

10. The user dismisses the description by clicking on the picture, which is visible behind the description.

11. The user proceeds through all the pages of the catalog. A number at the bottom of each page indicates which page the user is on and how far she has to go to get to the end of the catalog (3 of 50).

12. When the user reaches the last page, the first page appears again.

13. The user can also go back by clicking on the back page icon in the lower left corner (maybe looks like a dog-eared page).

Figure 12-6 Example of a use sequence for an online catalog system.

In relation to the use scenarios, the use sequences focus on step-by-step user actions with respect to the interface design. Use scenarios focus on the actions in context of the users' goals and environments. It is important that the design team keep the scenarios in mind and review the use sequences in the scenario context as the new design emerges.

As the number of use sequences grows, you will find that keeping them separate becomes more and more difficult except for areas of the new design that are completely separate. For example, the use sequence for the clerk's tasks may never intersect with the use sequence for the administrator's tasks. However, as you increase the number of individual use sequences, you will find many opportunities for intersecting pathways. These intersections may be better illustrated through use flow diagrams.

Use flow diagrams

Use flow diagrams emerge as the scenarios and use sequences increase in number and complexity to show how the users will take many paths through the new interface. The flow diagrams show the overall movement through the interface. Figure 12-7 illustrates the use flow diagram for the emerging design of the Web-based catalog shopping application.

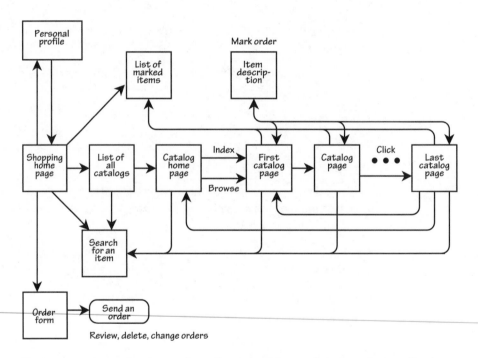

Figure 12-7 Example of a use flow diagram of the catalog shopping application.

As you can see from the catalog shopping example, the use flow diagram quickly becomes complicated, even for a very small design. You will find it necessary to create subsections of the flow diagram so that you can show the details of how the users will work with certain portions of the overall activity.

As you create and add detail to the flow diagram, you are creating the objects and actions that will become the focus of your graphic interface design. For example, the catalog shopping design at this stage has defined a number of objects, including an order form, a personal profile screen, a search mechanism, and more.

Involving the user in the development of use flow diagrams

In their method of participatory design, Dayton et al. (1998) suggest building use flow diagrams at an intensive session including user representatives to define both the current task flow and requirements for the new task flow. The users work together with interface designers, developers, and others on the development team to create the use flow diagrams for the desired application. From the diagram, the team then creates a paper prototype of the graphical screens. The paper prototype is used for an initial usability walk-through of the proposed design, referring back to the original task flow.

The customer partnering method described in chapter 6 also involves users in the analysis and design of use flow and workflow diagrams. However, JoAnn's customer partnering method involves users over a period of weeks or months in addressing current task flows, designing new use flows and workflows, and evaluating proposed interface designs.

Use workflows

The use workflow diagram is not limited to the actions of one user with one part of the interface. The diagrams can also be used to represent many users interacting with different aspects of the new design. The workflow diagram shows how the users' environment changes as the new product is introduced.

In chapter 11, we looked at the medical records application as it was being performed manually at the hospital. The manual system required a lot of physical movement by the medical records staff and the physicians to record, transcribe, review, correct, and sign the medical records. In one hospital JoAnn visited, the medical records department was in the basement, which meant the physicians had to make trips down to the basement to review and sign their medical records. In the new system design, illustrated in figure 12-8, all the interactions are done electronically.

Although the first iteration of the design indicated that the transcriptionist would still type the record from the physician's audiotape recording, the final iteration of the design introduced a voice-recognition system that virtually eliminated the need for the transcriptionist. Some physicians continued to be uncomfortable making voice annotations. The design had to allow them to receive a printout of the computer record that they could annotate by hand or by audiotape and send (by hospital mail or through the computer's audiotape system) to the medical records area.

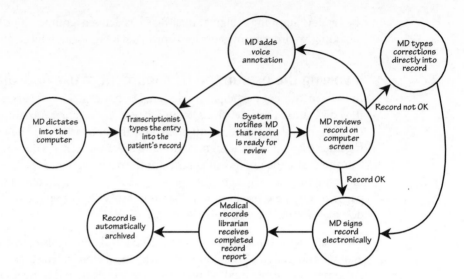

Figure 12-8 Workflow diagram of the medical records application.

Changing the workflow through process reengineering

The workflow diagram is an effective visual method for illustrating a complex set of interactions. It gives you an opportunity to trace the movement of information, objects, and actions through the work group. It also gives you an opportunity to find areas in which the workflow must be significantly modified to realize productivity gains from the introduction of new technology.

It has been a truism in traditional systems analysis that the designer looks for opportunities to optimize the information flow through the new system rather than simply "computerizing" the inefficiencies of the workplace. And certainly, introducing computers into the office environment has changed the nature of work, especially in heavily transaction-based applications such as accounting. At the same time, the limitations of technology and a lack of attention to human-computer interactions have often resulted in designs that have made the work more difficult to perform.

Workflow analysis and redesign, as well as other user-centered design methods we discuss in this chapter, can go a long way toward ensuring that design teams consider people and their interactions in the design process, whether the system is designed to be used by one person working alone or by many people working in sequence and collaboratively.

Workflow analysis and redesign should also lead to reevaluating the practice of putting new interfaces on legacy software, often in a mainframe environment. We see many GUI interfaces running on PCs that are simply rearrangements (using pull-downs, pop-ups, and dialog boxes) of the original legacy character-based screens. These PC designs perpetuate the existing workflows, and often perpetuate ineffective designs that fail to increase productivity.

> *JoAnn once taught a user-centered interface design workshop to a group of engineers who were considering redesigning a character-based, largely command-driven interface for a complex automation tool. During the workshop, the engineers viewed a videotape of a user observation/interview that illustrated the difficulty highly skilled people had with the old interface. It was only then that they were able to envision a new interface design that was not only visual, but also allowed direct manipulation of objects. The new design ideas were very radical but reflected the needs of a collaborative engineering workgroup rather than the needs of the individual designer.*
>
> *Seeing the work done in a different context than they had assumed enabled the design team to think "out of the box." Their new system design, including the graphical user interface, represented a breakthrough in their industry.*

Stories of gains in productivity are, unfortunately, not as common as they might be. But when workflow analysis is part of the redesign process, the gains can be substantial. Tom Landauer, in *The Trouble with Computers* (1995), argues that computers have not increased workers' productivity but that they could do so enormously if attention were paid to user-centered design.

Use hierarchies

Hierarchy charts are most often used to illustrate the way users currently organize their tasks into groups. As described in chapter 11, you can use them to examine how tasks and subtasks are distributed across members of a workgroup. You can also use hierarchy charts to map additional functionality that you can offer to a workgroup through a design or redesign of a computer system.

If your team has already constructed a task hierarchy showing the current division of tasks and subtasks across a workgroup, you can create a new "use hierarchy" to show how the relationship among tasks will change with the new design. If you have already used sticky notes to construct your task hierarchy, use a different color sticky note to show where new capabilities will be added to the users' task environment because of the new technology.

For example, in the catalog system design you might show how the "personal profile" functions will fit into the central browse/search design, as illustrated in figure 12-9.

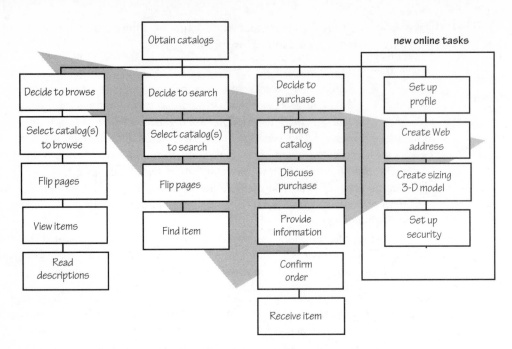

Figure 12-9 Example of a use hierarchy for the catalog shopping system.

Are "feature-rich" and "usability" both possible?

The catalog shopping example shows how new features can be incorporated into an existing interface or added to a new interface. The catalog metaphor is derived, of course, from paper catalogs and the hierarchy reflects a design that maintains the users' conceptual models of browsing and searching. However, we can extend the metaphor to include functionality that is not possible given a paper catalog. For example, users can record personal profiles that might enable them to view only those items that come in their sizes. They might be able to zoom in on the picture of the item on the catalog page to get a closer look at the fabric or turn the item around to look at the back. They might also be able to view a garment in all the colors available or try a garment on after recording basic measurements in the personal profile.

By using a combination of use scenarios and use hierarchies, the design team can add features while still maintaining the integrity of the design and ensuring that new features are integrated into known features. A comprehensive and appropriate design metaphor, derived from the users' conceptual model of the tasks, should be extensible to new functionality without substantial distortion. The design team should be able to anticipate possible distortions by testing the functionality through the methods of user-centered design.

Storyboarding and sketching

So far all the methods introduced in this chapter have depended on text descriptions and diagrammatic illustrations. Designing a visual user interface has, of course, a significant graphical component. Nothing that the designers have done so far, except for the selection of a metaphor, has led to the visual design of the computer interface. In actual practice, of course, you will find yourself fairly quickly creating rough sketches of the way the screens might be laid out.

In this section, we recommend storyboarding as a way to communicate your design ideas more visually to your user community and your design team. A storyboard combines text and graphics, moving the design process along into rough sketches of what the interface might look like. Two levels of storyboard are useful. High-level storyboards correspond to the use scenarios and workflow diagrams that show the overall flow of work for an individual or a workgroup. Detailed-level storyboards include rough sketches of screen layouts and designs that correspond to the use sequences outlined for the detailed level of task performance in the new system. The rough sketches in the storyboard are often the prelude to more fully conceived paper prototypes of the screens and controls.

Designing high-level storyboards

Storyboards are used in the context of a complete use scenario to illustrate how the new design will fit into the users' world. Figures 12-10 and 12-11 illustrate both a task scenario and a use scenario for a project involving personal banking. The storyboards illustrate the interactions of the banker and her customers and show how the new computer application will fit into the environment and correct many of the problems inherent in the existing system design.

Harriet encounters many problems with documentation, records, interactions with customers, and knowledge of the products during this scenario. The resulting new design is referred to as an embedded performance support system (EPSS). In the following use scenario, we see Harriet working through the mortgage approval process, accessing information to support decision making, and using computer-based tutorials to learn new information. New learning, decision support, and external and internal documentation are all types of user support within the context of the interface design.

The loan application interface incorporates an online help system, copies of documents and brochures, a link to the multilist real estate system that is external to the bank, a script that directs the trainee to use the correct workflow, an expert system that helps Harriet analyze the differences among the loan types, a spreadsheet for calculating what-if scenarios for the various loan types, and a videoconferencing system.

PERFORMANCE SUPPORT SYSTEMS
TASK SCENARIO

Action   Illustration

1. Harriet is a new mortgage loan officer at the state bank. She was promoted to her position two weeks ago and received two full weeks of classroom training in mortgage loans. Now she is alone on the frontline with only three feet of desk between her and her first customer.

2. Mr. and Mrs. Mitchell are a young couple applying for their first home loan. Mr. Mitchell explains the couple's house-buying plans. He mentions that this will be their first home. He also notes that he's afraid their income isn't very high and may not be sufficient.

3. Harriet assures the couple that she is sure the bank will be able to develop an appropriate plan to support their purchase. She walks across the room to the forms cabinet and obtains a copy of the basic loan form. She begins to ask questions of the Mitchell's so that she can complete the form. She writes the information on the form by hand. The mortgage loan clerk will have to type the information into the computer system later so Harriet writes slowly and carefully to ensure that her handwriting is clear.

(Scenario continues for 20 steps)

Figure 12-10 Harriet's banking task scenario.

A storyboard need not be as elaborate as the one illustrated, although it was simple to construct the drawings using clipart. You can make rough sketches of scenes in the use scenario or illustrations of human-computer interactions so that users and other reviewers understand how the new design will fit into the current work environment. They will also be able to assess more accurately how the new design might require them to change their current work environment if they want to realize the promised productivity gains.

PERFORMANCE SUPPORT SYSTEMS
USE SCENARIO

Action	Illustration

1. Harriet is a new mortgage loan officer at the state bank. She was promoted to her position two weeks ago and received two full weeks of classroom training in mortgage loans. Now she is alone on the frontline with only three feet of desk between her and her first customer.

2. Mr. and Mrs. Mitchell are a young couple applying for their first home loan. Harriet's computer screen is tuned to her mortgage support system. Harriet has already identified herself as a new loan officer to the computer system. As she glances at the initial screen, a brief message reminds her to smile and greet the customer. OK, she knows she can do this.

3. Mr. Mitchell explains the couple's house-buying plans. He mentions that this will be their first home. He also notes that he's afraid their income isn't very high and may not be sufficient.

(Scenario continues for 20 steps)

Figure 12-11 Harriet's banking use scenario.

Designing detailed-level storyboards

The type of storyboard that figures 12-10 and 12-11 illustrate does not include any significant representation of the graphic design of the screen. Storyboards, however, can be used to begin the process of screen layout and design. In the storyboard illustrated in figure 12-12, the development team has begun to construct rough screen sketches for the catalog shopping system.

Storyboards at the detailed level illustrated here provide a transition to the more detailed layouts of paper prototypes, discussed in chapter 13. The storyboard still maintains the original connection with the use scenarios and use sequences by including the users' perspective on the objects and actions to be supported in the new interface design.

Figure 12-12 Storyboard for the catalog shopping system.

Video dramatizations

On occasion, you will find it valuable to prepare a more elaborate storyboard of your new design ideas. You may have users or user managers who have a difficult time visualizing how the new design will fit into their environment or how the design will look and feel once it is complete. You may need to convince your own management or a client that your vision of the new design is worth an investment of money and time. You may want to try to excite members of a development team about a new vision of the future. In these cases, and when you have sufficient time and budget to fund the effort, you should consider a video dramatization.

Perhaps the most famous video dramatization is the one created by Apple Computer designers to present their vision of an active agent, the "Knowledge Navigator" (Dubberly and Mitch 1987). In the video, the user, a professor doing a presentation on his research, employs an agent designed into his computer to gather and present data he needs. The agent appears to be a computerized version of a person playing the role of the ultimate assistant. The agent not only does what it is asked to do but also reminds the user of needed activity and brings new information to the user for his attention.

Apple used the video to communicate with the public and its potential customers about its vision of how computers might work in the future. The video pictured an environment in which the computer became a partner in the performance of a complex series of tasks. Apple designed the video dramatization of the future computer long before developers were able to create such an agent for the Macintosh or the PC. Only in the last year have we seen similar agents (lacking the anthropomorphism) appear in Web-based systems.

Bruce Tognazzini and others at Sun Microsystems created an elaborate video dramatization to illustrate how computers might look and be used in the future. Their video presentation, called "Starfire," is described in *TOG on Software Design* (Tognazzini 1996) and is available for purchase. "Starfire" dramatizes a particular use scenario based on the needs of a team of designers bringing out a new automobile. The video presentation depicts a group of Detroit product managers, led by Julie, planning the release of a new sports car. Julie is seen in her office at her workstation, which is actually her entire desk with a huge screen encircling her and extending onto the desktop. It is the desktop interface become literal.

"Starfire" shows Julie and team members throughout the world working on the presentation she makes to management to get the "go ahead" to introduce the new car. She uses her computer system to communicate with team members, interactively collaborate on the design of her report and her presentation, communicate with her family, retrieve and edit an archived video, and search for newspaper and magazine articles that she needs to support her arguments. All of these actions are performed in the context of her desktop workstation.

Tognazzini argues that all the technology needed to create the envisioned system is available today (Tognazzini 1994, personal communication). Unfortunately the ability to create such a comprehensive and usable tool would depend on the collaboration of many development organizations, an event he considers unlikely to occur any time soon.

The "Starfire" use scenario is based on an analysis of the goals and tasks performed by a product team, particularly in the automotive industry. Producing the video dramatization first required that the video-design team create a "living" but not a "working" prototype. The prototype arose from the analysis of the users, their tasks, and their environment and the use of user-centered methods like those described in this chapter.

The Starfire video was obviously expensive to produce. However, Tognazzini argues for its effectiveness in making a design case and generating excitement about a new design possibility, "Starfire freed us to explore where the industry can be if we all work together on a common goal…." (Tognazzini 1996, 54). "Gone are hardware limitations and computer artifacts. Everything works perfectly, no matter how many times the spectator looks at the tape, and messages both subtle and explicit can move the user toward any conclusions the filmmaker had in mind. These are both the advantage and curse of video prototyping. Will you end up with a prototype of a system that can be built, or only a slick piece of propaganda?" (Tognazzini 1996, 369-370).

If you cannot afford to produce a "Starfire," you still might find dramatization useful. On occasion, both of us have "acted out" through role playing with team members how the new design might look and feel in the users' environment.

References cited in the chapter

Collins, Dave, *Designing Object-Oriented User Interfaces*, Redwood City, CA: Benjamin/ Cummings, 1995.

Cooper, Alan, *About Face: The Essentials of User Interface Design*, Foster City, CA: IDG Book Worldwide, 1995.

Dayton, Tom, McFarland, Al, and Kramer, Joseph, Bridging user needs to object oriented GUI prototype via task object design, in *User Interface Design: Bridging the Gap from User Requirements to Design*, edited by Larry E. Wood, Boca Raton, FL: CRC Press, 1998, 15-56.

Dubberly, Hugh and Mitch, Doris, *The Knowledge Navigator*, video, Apple Computer, 1987.

Landauer, Thomas, *The Trouble with Computers*, Cambridge, MA: MIT Press, 1995.

Rubinstein, Richard and Hersh, Harry, *The Human Factor: Designing Computer Systems for People*, Bedford, MA: Digital Equipment Corporation, 1984.

Tognazzini, Bruce, *TOG on Software Design*, Reading, MA: Addison-Wesley, 1996.

Wood, Larry E., The ethnographic interview in user-centered work/task analysis, in *Field Methods Casebook for Software Design*, edited by Dennis Wixon and Judith Ramey, NY: John Wiley & Sons, 1996, 35-56.

Other books and articles for further reading

Carroll, John M., Ed., *Scenario-Based Design: Envisioning Work and Technology in System Development*, New York: John Wiley & Sons, 1995.

Galitz, Wilbert O., *The Essential Guide to User Interface Design*, NY: John Wiley & Sons, 1997.

Gibbs, W. Wayt, Taking computers to task, *Scientific American*, 277 (1), July 1997: 82–89.

Howlett, Virginia, *Visual Interface Design for Windows: Effective User Interfaces for Windows 95, Windows NT and Windows 3.1*, NY: John Wiley & Sons, 1996.

Lakoff, George and Johnson, Mark, *Metaphors We Live By*, Chicago: University of Chicago Press, 1980.

Mandel, Theo, *The Elements of User Interface Design*, NY: John Wiley & Sons, 1997.

Mayhew, Deborah J., *Principles and Guidelines in Software User Interface Design*, Englewood Cliffs, NJ: Prentice-Hall, 1992.

Shneiderman, Ben, *Designing the User Interface: Strategies for Human-Computer Interaction*, 3rd ed., Reading, MA: Addison-Wesley, 1998.

Weinschenk, Susan and Yeo, Sarah C., *Guidelines for Enterprise-Wide GUI Design*, NY: John Wiley & Sons, 1995.

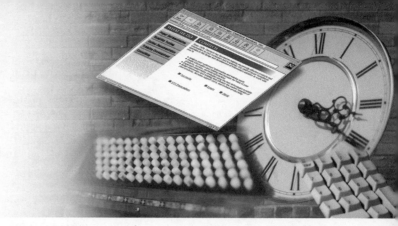

13

Prototyping the interface design

In chapter 12, we discussed how you might use your user and task analyses to begin designing the interface. One of the best ways to explore and encapsulate design ideas is through prototypes. In this chapter, we begin with background, defining prototypes and explaining why they are so useful for those of you who may not yet be doing prototyping. The two major sections that follow are about building prototypes and evaluating them. We end with a link to the rest of the development process. You'll find these topics in this chapter:

- Setting the background

    - What is a prototype?

    - What are the advantages and disadvantages of different types of prototypes?

    - Why prototype?

- Building prototypes

    - Deciding where to start

    - Starting a paper prototype

    - Prototyping as a team

- Evaluating prototypes

    - What should you look for?

- Walking through the prototype

- Usability testing the prototype

- Testing alternative designs

- Caveat: Demonstrations and reviews are *not* the same as usability testing

- Enhancing your user and task analysis during prototyping

- Helping others learn about users and tasks during prototyping

■ Continuing the process

- Iterating prototypes, completing the prototype

- Continuing user and task analysis beyond the prototype stage

Setting the background

Prototyping is a critical tool in the design of an effective interface because prototyping allows you to test your designs with the users.

What is a prototype?

A prototype is an easily changeable draft or simulation of at least part of an interface. It is similar in concept to building a foam core model or other physical mock-up of hardware. It is similar in concept to having a paper mockup of a document to show the approximate size, shape, binding, page layout, etc.

You can develop prototypes ranging from extremely low-fidelity sketches of what the interface and screen flow might look like to extremely high-fidelity interactive simulations that are essentially indistinguishable from the final product. You can use many techniques for prototyping, including creating interfaces

■ with pencil, pens, chalk, or color markers on paper, overheads, a whiteboard, or other surface

■ on paper or another flat surface using not only writing implements but also plastic objects or sticky notes in different colors and shapes representing buttons, icons, menus, fields, etc.

■ on a computer with a word processor and drawing program, printing out the screens for review and informal usability testing

■ on a computer with tools like PowerPoint or SuperCard that allow you to simulate some of the interactivity of the real product (Users can work on the computer, clicking on a picture of a button on one screen and getting whatever that button would retrieve in the real product.)

■ on the computer with tools like Macromedia Director, Toolbook, Smalltalk, or Visual Basic that give an even more realistic simulation of the way the product will work (Users can actually perform at least some tasks and get a realistic sense of the system's response, sometimes not with realistic response time but with realistic data and messages.)

You might have yet another way of prototyping that we did not mention. Also, new ways are being thought of all the time. So don't think of these examples as *the* five types of prototypes. Think of them as possibilities on a continuum from low fidelity to high fidelity. A low-fidelity prototype does not really act the way the system will. A low-fidelity prototype may not even look entirely the way the system will. It may only include sketches of where fields will be, for example. Nothing will be presented in the final fonts or colors.

Furthermore, calling all of these "prototypes" is not universally accepted. Some people call the first two examples "mock-ups" because they are only on paper. Others use the word prototype, distinguishing the medium by saying "paper prototype" and "computer-based prototype."

What are the advantages and disadvantages of different types of prototypes?

Each type of prototype has advantages and disadvantages. But don't view low fidelity versus high fidelity as an either/or choice. You'll probably want to do both. Many designers work their way through the continuum, starting with rough sketches, moving to more finished paper prototypes or to computer-drawn screen images, and then to higher-fidelity prototypes. As you think about the different types of prototypes, consider these points about their advantages and disadvantages. Also see Rudd et al. (1996) for a good discussion of many points about low-fidelity and high-fidelity prototypes.

Sketches and paper prototypes
Advantages include the following:

■ They cost little to produce.

■ They are fast and easy to create and to change.

■ They lend themselves to easy creation of alternatives.

■ They require only tools everyone knows how to use.

■ They work well to show "proof of concept" and to explore metaphors.

- They allow everyone on the team to participate in creating the prototype.

- They may encourage more suggestions because they seem more changeable.

Disadvantages include the following:

- They usually only show some of the final functionality.

- What is sketched may not be feasible in the final technology.

- Eventually they will be thrown away.

- They require a human facilitator to mimic what the computer will do.

- The paper versions may lack "face validity" to users, that is, they may not be taken seriously enough.

Low-fidelity, noninteractive, computer-drawn prototypes

Low-fidelity prototypes produced with a drawing program share most of the advantages of paper prototypes but they are not as quick or inexpensive to create. They do require knowledge of the computer tool being used to draw the screens. Therefore they are more commonly created by designers outside of working sessions with users and others. Of course, the team can meet to discuss the design and to perhaps draw some preliminary sketches. They can meet again to review and critique drafts from the designer. The actual creation of the prototype, however, is usually not done in meetings when it involves a computer-based tool.

Low-fidelity, noninteractive, computer-drawn prototypes also share most of the disadvantages of paper prototypes. They may have more face validity with users because they look more like real screens. But they have to be printed to be used in a walk-through or usability evaluation because they have no built-in functionality.

Intermediate-fidelity, computer-created prototypes

Intermediate-fidelity prototypes, produced with a tool like PowerPoint, also require knowledge of the computer tool, but many more people who take on design roles, including technical communicators, graphic artists, human factors engineers, and others are familiar with slide-making tools like PowerPoint than are familiar with programming tools like Visual Basic and Smalltalk. These intermediate-fidelity prototypes have the advantage that users can manipulate them online. They may not be as fast or cheap to create as paper prototypes, and you may want to sketch out what you want to do before moving to the computer.

High-fidelity prototypes

Advantages include the following:

- Users can work with them directly.

- They often cover more tasks or functions than low-fidelity prototypes.

- They look and feel more like the final product.

- If done in a tool that feeds directly into code, they show what is feasible in the final product.

- They can be used by marketing and sales as demonstrations of the product.

Disadvantages include the following:

- They are more expensive to build.

- They are more time-consuming to build.

- They require knowledge of a prototyping tool.

- They may raise unrealistic customer expectations of how soon they can have the product.

Why prototype?

Prototyping is an excellent strategy for several reasons. If you need to make a business case for prototyping, you might cite these four points: Prototyping saves money, is concrete, fosters alternatives and iterations, and allows users to be actively involved at the design stage.

Prototyping saves money

Most software groups use prototyping because of the great cost savings. The earlier in the process you find problems, the less those problems cost to fix. Pressman (1992) estimates that the cost of change is 1.5 to 6 times greater during development than during design and 60 to 100 times greater after product release. Making changes in the prototype is much cheaper than making them in a coded product. The new cost-beneficial philosophy is "code only once."

Prototyping is concrete

With a prototype, you are putting design ideas down in black and white or even vivid colors. Instead of talking in the abstract, everyone on the team can show each other what they mean by "having buttons for these functions" or "creating icons that users understand." Team members from different areas, for example, a software engineer and a marketing manager, who may have different meanings for similar words, may find it easier to talk about the product with a prototype in front of them. Moreover, a prototype can be shared with users, customers, developers, managers, and others who are not on the design team. Miscommunication about what is going to be in the product and how it will work is less likely with a concrete example than when you only have written specifications.

Prototyping fosters alternatives and iterations

The whole point of a prototype, whether drawn on paper or created with a computer-based tool, is that change is easy. With prototyping, you can try out different alternatives, including wildly different concepts, metaphors, or approaches to an application. With prototyping, you can also rapidly iterate a design. You can let users try out something, find the weaknesses in it, change it, and let users try out the changed version, all within a few days.

A note of caution: Rapid iteration can be great. During design sessions or design reviews, changing as new ideas come up and as the team walks through the design you are building is certainly appropriate. However, once a design has reached a certain level of stability, be wary of churning. Don't jump to conclusions and change the design for every user who comes to evaluate the system. Iterate thoughtfully. Keep a log of changes and the rationale for the changes. Wait to see three or more users work with the prototype before you change it. Make sure that changes maintain the interface's coherence and consistency. Consider how changes that you make in one place affect other screens and other tasks.

Prototyping allows users to be actively involved at the design stage

One of the most exciting aspects of prototyping is the way that it lets users be involved early and deeply in designing a product. If you do the design by yourself or if you work as a team but cannot involve users on the team, you should have users evaluate the prototype before you go on to coding. Without a prototype, many users find it difficult to picture what the product will be like. Without a prototype, users have nothing to work with until late in development when it is often impossible to change the product.

If you can work with users as you prototype, they can participate fully in design sessions, especially if you do paper prototyping. One of the rationales for paper prototyping is the democratization of the process, because the only tools needed for design are ones we all know how to use. As Muller says (1993, 227), "there are no issues of users having to explain their desires to an analyst (who 'owns' the prototyping technology), or of users fearing embarrassment (through lack of ease with the technology), and therefore refusing to try out their ideas."

Note that we are not saying that users should do the design by themselves. What they contribute is their perspective as users. If you work on a prototype as a team, others must also be there to contribute their perspectives. Developers who know what is and is not feasible in the technology that will be used for the final product also have critical information to contribute. Marketing representatives and business analysts may have the perspective of the company's goals to contribute. And, of course, interface designers, human factors specialists, technical communicators, and graphic artists all have skills to bring to developing workable designs. In team design sessions, it is the synergy of the group that produces a design that may incorporate ideas from all the participants.

Building prototypes

Once your team has decided that prototyping should be part of your design process, you need to determine how to begin the prototyping process.

Deciding where to start

Depending on your situation, your primary concerns may be any of the following:

- the flow of screens for major tasks

- the overall metaphor and how it will be carried out

- the screen layout of the basic task screen

- screen layouts for all the screens

- alternative metaphors or other alternative design ideas

The general wisdom in the field is to start with the most critical and frequent task. You cannot do everything at once, and if you allow yourself to think of every variation and minor task from the beginning, you may be unable to move ahead. We agree with that advice, but also caution you to remember that the minor tasks and variations on the tasks, as well as the peripheral tasks that connect your application to other parts of a workflow, must eventually be part of the product. They should eventually be part of the prototype.

Starting a paper prototype

You may be a lone designer, or you may be working on a team and the team may or may not include users. Whichever situation you work in, you or the team are likely to start by sketching ideas on paper. In this section we give you some tips for getting started. We remind you that this book has been about gathering data for design, analyzing it, and using it as you design. Creating good designs is an extremely complex topic that takes us beyond the scope of this book. For good references on design, see the "Other books and articles for further reading" section at the end of chapter 12.

ßetting up a grid

A grid is a set of imaginary lines on the screen that divides the screen into specific areas to hold different design elements. Figure 13-1 shows an example of a grid for a typical Windows-based application.

Setting up a grid can help you make your screens consistent and coherent, which is a very important aspect of making products usable. Start with paper that is the correct size for the area of the interface, for example, the size and shape of a screen on a 13-inch monitor. Draw lines to indicate different areas on the screen that will be present on all screens, such as menu bars, tool bars, scroll bars, etc.

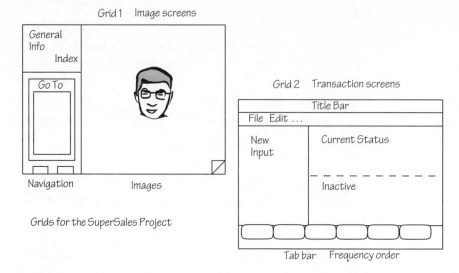

Figure 13-1 Using a grid helps you maintain consistency and coherence across screens.

Also set up a grid for the open space of the screen. The grid can be very light lines that indicate where on the screen dialog boxes, message boxes, and the main objects and buttons that link to other screens will appear, especially if they are repeated from screen to screen. You can also set up grids for where elements will go inside dialog boxes, message boxes, and other parts of the interface. Once you have set up the grid, you can photocopy it so that you have lots of paper with the grid on it to work with.

When you set up a grid, you are helping yourself and other designers stay consistent. Consistency is one of the keys to a successful interface. For example, once users learn where to go to find the buttons on a Web page that link to other parts of the Web site, they can get to those buttons quickly. If you put the buttons on the top on one page, on the bottom on another page, on the side on a third page, you confuse users and make them take time to hunt around for the buttons.

If several designers are working on an interface, setting up a grid and deciding on issues like where the buttons will be is absolutely critical. Otherwise, each designer may make a different choice. That can lead to unnecessary arguments among designers and grief for users. Even if you are designing by yourself, setting up a grid is a useful technique. It's just too easy to get caught up in the screen you are working on and forget the decisions you made for the screen you designed a few days ago.

You may need different grids for different types of screens, such as main windows, dialog boxes, message boxes, etc. Work to keep them consistent with each other as much as possible.

Don't fill in all the details at first

If you are primarily trying to figure out what will go on each screen and where it will go, you don't need to worry at first about carefully writing every field label or message and drawing every icon. When graphic artists do rough sketches, they just use shapes or squiggly lines to indicate where different elements will go and approximately how much space they will take up. Later, of course, you'll need to indicate exactly which field label, icon, or button goes where, and exactly how long each response space will be. But you can treat those as two different stages in the progression of your paper prototype, as shown in figure 13-2.

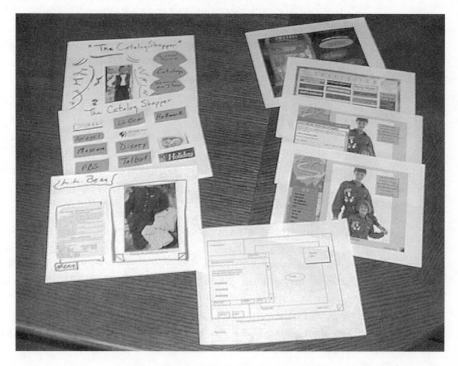

Figure 13-2 For rough sketches, you can use lines and shapes without being specific about the words or pictures. This picture shows rough sketches on the left and more finished views on the right, the second stage of creating prototypes.

Make neat copies to show to others

Start with rough sketches to iron out issues of what should go on which screen, where to place objects on the screen, etc. Don't be afraid to erase, redo, or throw out paper. When you're pretty sure you've got the screens laid out, however, make clean, neat copies to show to users, managers, and others. Unless you have some real reason to share all the stages you went through, you only need to show them the design you want them to try out or react to. Making neat copies will get your design better attention and look more professional.

Prototyping as a team

Prototyping does not have to be a team effort. Circumstances may dictate that you must do the design by yourself. Even if you are working by yourself, you might still want to read some parts of this section, especially the ideas about what to prepare (tools to use in paper prototyping) and about communicating the design to others. You can probably adapt and use them even for the situation where you are the lone designer.

If you can work with others as a team, however, you may find it very useful and stimulating. Prototyping, particularly paper prototyping, works very well as a team effort. The group dynamic can enhance creativity. The shared experience can contribute to all the members having a better understanding of each other's needs and constraints. Team-based paper prototyping leads to buy-in and shared ownership, at least for those who participate, that may facilitate acceptance of the product down the road. A prototype that better meets users' needs may emerge from the team effort.

Team-based paper prototyping is an outgrowth of the Scandinavian work on participatory design (Ehn 1989, 1993). We note that our ideas on team-based paper prototyping have been strongly influenced by the methodologies that stem from CARD (Muller et al., 1995; Tuder et al., 1993), PICTIVE (Muller 1991, 1992, 1993, 1996), and The Bridge (Dayton et al. 1998) as well as by others who have shared case studies of their work. See the case studies in Wood (1998) as examples.

We also note that both Muller and Dayton et al. see their methodologies as more than design tools. Muller sees PICTIVE as a technique that may be useful at several points within software development. He says that it "may be used for early requirements gathering and analysis… It may be used for design work… It may also serve a conflict resolution role" (Muller 1993, 215). Dayton et al. use The Bridge as a coherent methodology for "1. expressing user requirements as task flows, 2. mapping task flows to task objects, and 3. mapping task objects to GUI objects" (Dayton et al. 1998, 20).

What do you need to prepare?

You might want to use some of the ideas in this section even if you are designing by yourself. A typical kit for a paper prototyping session might include paper that is cut to the right shape to represent the area of the interface, colored pens, colored markers, index cards, pads of sticky notes (like Post-it notes) in different colors and sizes, tape that is easy to remove, erasers, scissors, ruler, and pre-designed pieces that are relevant to the project.

Some notes on these items:

■ The basic interface area might be a computer screen, but it could also be the faceplate of a telephone, fax machine, controller, or other device. Make the paper version mimic the correct shape of the overall interface area.

- You could just work with pencil and paper, but it's more fun to add color and to have pieces that represent interface elements such as menu bars, fields, icons, etc.

- When selecting pens and markers, think about who will be looking at the design through what medium. Pens that make thin, light lines may not show up well on a videotape if that is how you are going to show the design to others. Markers that are too thick may not let you draw as many lines in a space as you would actually get in the design.

- Some people are allergic to some types of markers. You might want to have pens available in case someone is allergic.

- You might want to have at least some sticky notes that are precut into relevant sizes and shapes for menus, icons, fields, field labels, message boxes, etc.

- Muller (1993) has used plastic pieces as well as paper pieces, including icons prepared in advance.

If you are working as a team, you also need a conference room or other space to work in where the team can spread out and have a flat surface to work on.

Who participates in a team-based session?
A team-based paper-prototyping session, like all group activities, needs a skilled facilitator. The usability specialist might take that role. However, the facilitator must be seen as a neutral party by all participants. So, if issues of usability are likely to be controversial or meet with resistance from others on the team, someone else should facilitate.

Because everyone gets to do hands-on work in constructing the prototype, you need to keep the team to five or six people. Relevant roles include facilitator, user, usability specialist, interface designer, human factors specialist, developer, systems engineer, or other technology specialist. You may want two or three users who represent different parts of the user community or people at different stages of use. One person may fill the roles of usability specialist, interface designer, and human factors specialist. The technology specialist needs to be someone who knows what can and cannot be done in the technology that will be used to build the product. You may also need a business analyst and/or a marketing specialist who knows about changes in business processes that the company wants to incorporate into the new design. A technical communicator may be an important member of the team both because the essence of an interface is communication and because a major part of design may be decisions on types of documentation to include (help, messages, just-in-time training aids, etc.) and where on the screens they should appear.

How do you communicate to others what you've done?
Some teams videotape the results with commentary by the people who were doing the design. Some teams videotape the entire session. If you do that, you may need to put microphones in strategic places in the room, and you may need to try to keep everyone from talking at once. Some teams mount the resulting paper prototypes on walls for others to review and comment on.

You can also use a set-aside space to put up your paper prototypes. Karat and Bennett (1991) introduced the idea of a design room, a room dedicated to the team working on a project. The team uses all four walls for keeping project information in view. In Karat and Bennett's design room, one wall is for requirements, one for product objectives, one for design constraints, and one for design abstractions. Many teams that use affinity diagramming have adopted the idea of a dedicated design room.

The relevance of a design room for prototyping, especially for showing paper prototypes, is obvious. Even if you are a lone designer, your office or the hallway outside of it might become your "design room." Kevin Simpson describes the technique of using what he calls a "user interface war room," which he defines as "an affectionate way of describing a room dedicated to the purpose of getting ideas to flow freely, putting them up on paper, discussing them, and ending up with paper prototypes of a system" (Simpson 1998, 252). Judy Ramey (personal communication, 1997) describes how students designing Web sites put up their design sketches on the walls of their cubicles and how everyone was invited to (indeed expected to) look at everyone else's designs and comment on them by placing sticky notes on the paper prototypes.

You can share the emerging design in a public space even when you cannot have a dedicated room. Rantzler describes a project in which the design was actually conducted in the hallway outside one of the designer's rooms. As he says, "This approach of taking the work out in the open had several advantages." The advantages he lists are "unlimited workspace, high visibility, instant feedback, and quick test runs" (Rantzler 1998, 174). Rantzler's case study is reminiscent of the way that Gould and his colleagues developed and tested messaging kiosks for the Los Angeles Olympics (Gould 1987).

Evaluating prototypes

What should you look for?
When you have users try out prototypes, consider how well the prototype is working for users on dimensions like these. Does the prototype

- convey a consistent conceptual model?

- match the users' mental model?

- match the user's way of working?

- use the users' words?

- cover the tasks that users expect to be able to do with the product?

- work for all the scenarios (situations) that users say occur?

- streamline tasks for the user?

- help users make the transition from what they've been doing before?

- divide the work well between the computer and the user?

- provide messages where and when the user needs them?

- maintain consistency in the look and feel across screens?

- maintain consistency in where buttons, icons, and other navigation tools are across screens?

- maintain consistency in the vocabulary used across screens?

In appendix C, we give you a more thorough checklist that you can use when evaluating prototypes.

Walking through the prototype

In a walk-through, you and others take a brief scenario (a story of a situation that the product must allow users to accomplish—see figure 11-16 and the discussion there) or a use scenario or a use flow (your vision of how a user will accomplish a given task with the new version of the product—see the discussion in chapter 12) and go through the design step by step. You are looking for any potential problems users may have, such as places where the design is not logical or may mislead users, steps that cannot be done in the new design, or processes that require too many steps. You are seeing if users will be able to accomplish the task at all and, if so, whether they will be able to accomplish it easily and quickly. Although you aren't yet measuring the design against your usability goals for it, you should have them in mind as you walk through the design with several scenarios.

Most teams incorporate informal walk-throughs by the team members as part of prototyping design sessions. In fact, you can do walk-throughs at many points in the design to be sure that the emerging design is going to work. Even if you are designing by yourself without a team, you should walk through the design with several real scenarios to make sure you haven't left anything out.

If you are designing by yourself, you should invite others (others in your own group, others who will work on other aspects of the product such as technical communicators, trainers, usability specialists, business analysts, and, of course, users) to walk through the design, too. Just as it is impossible to proofread your own writing after a while because your mind fills in words you didn't even type, it is impossible to see all the problems in your own design. You know how it is meant to work so you cannot imagine that someone will choose a different path or misread a label.

A walk-through by anyone other than users, however, is only the first evaluation technique to use. It is not sufficient. To know how well the emerging design is going to work for users, you must have users try it out. If users were part of the design team, you must have other users try it out. The users on the design team, like the lone designer in the previous paragraph, know too much about the design. They may not be able to predict how other users will work with the product, what pathways other users will select, or what words other users will find incomprehensible.

Usability testing the prototype

Whether or not you involve users in creating the prototypes, you definitely should have users evaluate them. We strongly recommend that you do real usability evaluations (informal usability testing) rather than just demonstrating to users what the product will do and asking for their subjective feedback.

To us, you are doing usability testing any time you have representative users or potential users attempt to do realistic tasks with a version of the product while someone watches, listens, takes notes, and asks questions. You do not need a formal usability lab to do usability testing. You can use a conference room, an office, or the user's site. You do not need a high-fidelity prototype. You can use paper and have a human play the role of the computer. You do not need a complete prototype. You can get useful information about specific issues, such as whether the icons are meaningful or whether users can find what they need in a Web site, even with only part of the prototype developed. For more on what a usability test is and how to plan, conduct, and make sense of a usability test, see Dumas and Redish (1993) or Rubin (1994).

You can do usability evaluations of paper prototypes

Rudd et al. (1996, 78) point out that typically "[u]sers do not exercise a low-fidelity prototype to get a first-hand feel of how it operates; rather low-fidelity prototypes are demonstrated by someone skilled at operating the prototype." They list "limited usefulness for usability tests" as a disadvantage of low-fidelity prototypes. It is true, as they say, that when users work with low-fidelity prototypes, a human facilitator must play the role of the computer. However, in our experience, you can do very informative usability evaluations in that mode, and you get more useful information than you do by having users watch a scripted demonstration and give their opinions of it.

For the usability evaluation of a paper prototype, you are the computer, as figure 13-3 shows.

Figure 13-3 You can have users work with a paper prototype just as they would work with the interface in any other usability test.

You put the first screen the user would see in front of the user and ask, "What would you do?" If the user stops after the first action, you ask, "And what would you do next?" If the user gives a general answer, you probe for the exact action the user would take. For example, if you put a data entry screen in front of the user and say, "The cursor is here in this field," the user might say, "Okay. I type the last name in here and then move to the next field." You would then ask, "How would you move to the next field?" If you need to probe further, you might ask, "Would you press a key? Would you use the mouse? Would you do something else?" If the user says, "a key," you probe further with, "Which key would you press?"

Probing like this while users are working with a prototype gives you a much better sense of how successful the product will be than showing the user how it is going to work and getting reactions to your demonstration. You also get much greater insights into users' knowledge and mental models than you can possibly get from questionnaires and interviews.

You don't need a complete prototype to get useful information

You can do usability evaluations with only menus, with only a few functions developed, or with only some choices working. Of course, you won't learn about functions that aren't yet in the prototype, but you do get the high-level knowledge you need early on to feel comfortable that you are on the right track with the overall flow, the metaphor, the vocabulary, the icons, and whatever else is in the prototype. We describe usability evaluations like this and what you can learn from them in more detail later in this chapter in the section on enhancing your user and task analysis during prototyping.

Testing alternative designs

Rapid, iterative prototyping with usability testing is a great way to test out alternative designs. Instead of arguing about which approach is better, let the users decide by trying both.

> *Ginny and her colleagues worked with a group that was not sure which of two approaches would work best for a particular application. The designers mocked up both approaches for the same major tasks and made color prints of the prototype screens. They had users come to work with both prototypes in a typical comparative usability test using a human facilitator to change screens for users. The users talked out loud, explaining what they would do at each step, what they would type in each field, what they would expect to happen next with each choice they made. After they worked with both, the users were asked which they liked and why, but that subjective discussion came only after they had tried both approaches themselves. The team felt the information was more useful and valid than what they would have gotten by just showing the two approaches to the users and asking only for opinions. Based on what the users did and on the details of their explanations in the debriefing, the team incorporated some features of each approach in the final design.*

Note: To be fair to both designs, you should counterbalance the order in which you have users work with the designs. That is, if you have two designs, participant 1 uses design 1 first and then, perhaps after a break, does the same or a similar task with design 2. Participant 2 starts with design 2. Participant 3 starts with design 1, and so on. That way, both designs have an equal chance of benefiting from the user having practiced with the task before using that design.

When all participants use both designs, you have what experimental psychologists call a "within-subjects" study. You could also have participant 1 only use design 1; participant 2 only use design 2, and so on. That would be a "between-subjects" study. In a "between-subjects" study, you have to assign users to the "design 1" or "design 2" groups so that overall the users in both groups have similar user profiles. The problem is that you won't usually have enough participants in a prototype evaluation to feel comfortable that the users in the two groups are well matched. Therefore we recommend that whenever possible you evaluate alternative designs with a within-subjects study in which all participants use both designs.

Caveat: Demonstrations and reviews are not the same as usability testing

The reactions you get from demonstrating a product to users and asking them how well it will work for them may not be at all predictive of what happens when the users actually try to work with the product.

Looking good is not the same as being useful and usable
We have both heard of numerous cases where users said, "Oh, that looks great," and then rejected the product when it got to their desks.

> *The users of one product were initially very enthusiastic about the new version of the product they were getting. When it was demonstrated to them, they were very impressed by the flashy graphics, the very artistic icons, the ways that the marketing representative who was demonstrating it showed them it would help them do their major task. They caught the marketers' and developers' excitement and were looking forward to switching to the new version.*
>
> *When they got it and tried to use it, however, the situation changed dramatically. Yes, they could use it to do the basic task that had been covered in the demonstration. But when they went beyond that, they found that the new version didn't let them do many of the other tasks they performed regularly. In particular, it wasn't well integrated with other applications that they used. Also, the new version was much slower than the product it was replacing and speed was important to these users. Within days in some places and weeks in other places, most of the users had stopped using the new version and had gone back to the old one.*
>
> *In this case, the user and task analysis had not been thorough enough. Moreover, the designers had gotten caught up in creating a stunning interface for the part that users see when they start the product and had paid less attention to the human factors details of how users would do anything beyond the basic version of the basic task. The users' positive reactions to being shown the new interface lulled the designers into thinking they had done enough.*

Users may not be able to predict the problems they will have
Real use on the job or in the home is what counts, not reactions to a show-and-tell demonstration. Users cannot easily predict the problems they will have in real use just by looking at the interface or reviewing it.

An interesting research study by Heather Desurvire and colleagues made this point very clearly (Desurvire 1994). Desurvire conducted a usability test of a product that indicated the product had 25 usability problems. She also had three groups of people do a heuristic evaluation of the same product. A heuristic evaluation is a review in which the reviewers have a set of guidelines (the heuristics) against which they are considering the product. For this study, Desurvire used 10 heuristics adapted from a list suggested by Nielsen and Molich (1990), such as "Speak the user's language" and "Minimize memory load."

The heuristic evaluations were done by three usability specialists, the three software engineers who designed the product, and three users. The types of users who did the heuristic evaluation were similar to the types of users who participated in the usability test.

Each heuristic evaluator was told to predict the problems that users were likely to have with the product. Taking the 25 problems found in the usability test as the baseline (100%), Desurvire and her colleagues calculated the percentage of those problems that each group of heuristic evaluators identified. Figure 13-4 shows the results. The users who reviewed the product predicted only 2 of the 25 problems that actually occurred in the usability test.

Method	Percent of problems found	Number of problems
Occurred in the usability test	(100%)	25
Heuristic evaluations		
1. Experts	44%	11
2. Software Engineers	16%	4
3. Non-experts (users)	8%	2

Figure 13-4 Users who reviewed the product predicted only 2 of 25 problems that people like themselves had when they used the product (Desurvire 1994, 184; reprinted by permission of John Wiley & Sons, Inc.).

Moreover, all of the heuristic evaluations found lots of minor problems compared to the severity of the problems found in the usability test. Figure 13-5 shows the number of problems identified in each method classified by severity. Users predicted only 1 of the 17 errors that caused task failure. Even the experts predicted only 5 of the 17 most serious errors found in the usability test.

Don't rely on demonstrating the design to users or asking for reviews as the primary way of involving users in prototyping a product. Get them more actively involved through participatory prototyping and through usability evaluations in which they actually try to complete tasks with the prototype.

	Problem severity code		
Method	Minor annoyance or confusion	Problem caused error	Problem caused task failure
Occurred in the usability test	5	3	17
Found in heuristic evaluations:			
1. Experts	80%	67%	29%
2. Software engineers	40%	0%	12%
3. Nonexperts (users)	20%	0%	6%

Figure 13-5 Usability tests tend to uncover severe problems. Heuristic evaluations and other review techniques tend to uncover more minor problems (Desurvire 1994, 185; reprinted by permission of John Wiley & Sons, Inc.).

Enhancing your user and task analysis during prototyping

If you are this far in the book, we assume you have done or are trying to do user and task analysis by getting out to users' sites. If you have done, or are planning to do site visits, you may be concerned about how few users you were able to see and talk to. But learning about users and tasks doesn't stop with the predesign data gathering and analysis. You should think of all the usability activities you do throughout design and development as opportunities to learn more about users, their goals, their values, their tasks, their concerns.

If the product is being developed for a very specific and very small user group, you may, of course, be working with the same people at all stages of the process. If you are engaging in customer partnering or have a user advisory group, you may also work with the same people over time. But most product development teams bring in different users for different activities.

Typically, for design sessions and for evaluating prototypes, you select people who have not participated in previous usability activities, such as site visits. If you have a few users come to help with design, you almost certainly want other users to evaluate the design through usability testing. Therefore, involving users in prototyping adds to the number of different users you work with and learn about.

Although each individual usability activity (site visits, participatory design, evaluations of the first prototype, evaluations of a further iteration of the prototype, etc.) typically involves only a limited number of users, over all the usability activities those numbers add up. By the time the product is ready for release, you may have observed, listened to, and talked with 40, 50, or more users.

Adding to your user analysis

During the site visits, you were probably observing users doing what they are already comfortable with and knowledgeable about. Watching users work with a prototype may give you *more* information about users' skills, learning styles, and working styles than you got during site visits. You may now be watching users who are being challenged by new interfaces and new operating systems, where before you saw them only with their old interfaces and old operating systems. You may want to take that information into account in redesigning the prototype.

Ginny was conducting usability evaluations of a prototype for users who were going to move from a DOS-based legacy system to a graphical user interface. One of the major questions the client had about the users was how comfortable and knowledgeable they were likely to be with Windows. The users' responses to a questionnaire showed that many of the users had Windows-based computers and rated themselves as very comfortable with and very knowledgeable about Windows.

However, when these users began to use the prototype, which was a fairly robust high-fidelity interactive prototype on the computer, it became obvious that many of the users had only a very rudimentary knowledge of Windows. Some knew how to select consecutive rows in a database only by dragging the mouse down the list; they didn't know about shift-click. Some did not recognize the tabs in a multitabbed dialog box. Some did not notice or know what to do with a horizontal scroll bar across the bottom of the screen.

These gaps in their knowledge of Windows were serious. Because the one way they knew to select consecutive items was not implemented in the prototype, some users concluded that they had to work on one item at a time. That made the product seem incredibly inefficient, and was definitely not the way the designers had meant them to work. On one screen, a critical field that users had to fill out required scrolling horizontally to the right, but some users didn't even realize the field existed, didn't fill it out, and got an error message. When the designers saw the users having these problems, they changed the interface to better match what users really knew rather than the users' self-ratings.

We can speculate on why many users in this example rated themselves so high in terms of comfort with and knowledge about Windows when there was so much about Windows that they did not know. One possibility is that they use Windows regularly but in very limited ways. They use a word processor, but only to send simple letters. They exchange e-mail with others in the office. They use Windows as a pass-through to access the legacy program. They know what they do every day and they are comfortable doing what they do. They know what they know, and they do not know about all the aspects of Windows that they don't use.

Site visits for this project taught the development team a great deal about the users' current processes, mental models, and vocabulary. But the site visits didn't show what users did *not* know about Windows. That came out only when users started to work with the prototype. Prototyping added information to the user analysis.

Adding to your task analysis
Evaluating prototypes with users is also an opportunity to expand the task analysis you did during the predesign site visits. In the prototypes, at different stages, you can concentrate on specific aspects of task analysis, such as navigation schemes and hierarchies, and processes that you evaluate through scenarios.

Testing navigation schemes and hierarchies. One type of task analysis you can do at the early design stage is to get help from users in building the navigation scheme and hierarchy for the product. Navigation (getting to where you need to be) is a critical aspect of almost all interfaces, including software products, telephone menu systems, print manuals, online help, and Web sites. After all, a product (including software, other devices, documentation, etc.) is usable only if users can

- find what they need

- understand what they find

- use what they understand appropriately to achieve their goals

The "finding" part is immensely important. If users can't find the Web page they need, it doesn't matter how well designed it is. It doesn't matter how much functionality you've built into the voice mail system if the functions remain hidden because users cannot find their way through the menus.

You can have users evaluate a prototype that includes only the proposed menu structure and/or icons. For example, to find out if a proposed set of icons is meaningful to users, you can use various versions of something you might call the "icon game." Here are a few variations on this theme. The one you use will depend on your goals:

- Give users a page with all the icons and have them tell you what each means.

- Give users more context: draw the frame of an empty screen on the page, line the icons up as if they were a toolbar on the screen, put the screen name on top, and now ask them to name each icon.

- Give users a page with icons in one column and a list of names in the other and see if they can match the icons to the names. Then ask them what they think each one does. (Users may be able to name it and yet misunderstand what will happen if they select it.)

- After doing either of the first two techniques in this list, show users the tooltips with each icon and let them react to the tooltips, telling you which icons make more sense now that they have read the tooltip and which still seem unrelated to the name. Then do other parts of the usability evaluation. Come back and give users the icons again without the tooltips and see which they remember.

■ Have them try to do scenarios with the icons as the way to move through the product.

Even with just menus, just icons, or menus and icons, you can still do scenario-based usability evaluations. The issue you are addressing is how well users will be able to navigate. You, as the computer, tell them what they will get with each choice that they make and show them the next set of menus or icons, even if you don't have any of the other parts of the screens ready. Give the user an actual scenario as in any usability test, like the example in figure 13-6.

> **AN EXAMPLE OF A SCENARIO:**
>
> You have just put a bulleted list into your document by selecting the style, "bullet," from a style list. You look at the list in the document and decide that you would rather have a different symbol for the bullet at the beginning of each item in the list. Tell me what you would do to change what the bullet looks like for all the lists in your document.

Figure 13-6 An example of a scenario that you can use just to test a menu hierarchy.

Note: You can do similar usability evaluations of how easily users will navigate in documentation before you actually write anything. If you outline print documents or create a map of your online help system before you write, which you should, you are creating the table of contents. That's one of the primary navigation tools for users. Give users a realistic scenario and ask them to tell you where they would look to get the information to do the tasks in that scenario.

Prototyping processes through scenarios. If you have more of the prototype developed than just menus, icons, tables of contents, and other navigation tools, you can learn even more about the tasks users do, how they do them, and how well your emerging design is likely to work for the users. Basically, as in any usability evaluation, you give the users a realistic scenario of a real task and watch and listen as they attempt to do the task with the prototype.

If the trigger for the task is data they would be getting on a particular form or other document, you can have examples ready for them to use. Or you can ask them to bring a file of the data they would get to begin the task. If their own data is too sensitive, you can ask them to create a file for the purposes of the usability evaluation. With a paper prototype, you can have them actually write on the paper if they would normally type in information, or you can just have them tell you what they would put in each field.

In each usability evaluation, you are likely to be observing several users you did not see in the site visits. Each of them brings you new perspectives on the same tasks you watched users doing during the site visits. You may also discover new scenarios and new tasks that you didn't happen to see in any of the site visits. Evaluating prototypes can add to your task analysis. Debriefing users after they do the tasks can also enhance your user analysis by helping you understand the users.

You might also consider doing usability evaluations of prototypes in different geographic areas. When you were planning the site visits, you almost certainly had to trade off getting as broad a view of users, tasks, and environments as possible with issues of time and costs. If you take your prototype to more users in more areas, each series of usability evaluations in the prototype stage adds to your understanding of users and their tasks.

Helping others learn about users and tasks during prototyping

In earlier chapters we discussed the importance of communicating what you've learned during site visits so that other designers, developers, technical communicators, marketing specialists, and managers understand more about the users, their tasks, and their working environments. We've given you lots of tips and techniques for sharing information with others through videotapes, still pictures, scenarios, storyboards, etc.

Participatory prototyping and usability evaluations during prototyping are also opportunities to bring these other people into the process. You can have a few others in the actual sessions with the users, but the real advantage if you do usability evaluations of prototypes at the development site is that you can invite others to observe and take notes from another room. With usability evaluations of prototypes, more developers, technical communicators, trainers, and managers may get to see real users doing real tasks with the emerging design. For many, this may be their first exposure to users trying to work with the product. Waiting for formal usability tests later would not serve the same purpose. You want them to see the users trying to work with the product while changes are still easy to make.

If you have a usability laboratory, it can be used for prototyping sessions or usability evaluations with observers behind a one-way glass. If you don't have a usability laboratory, you can use two conference rooms, as shown in figure 13-7. Do the session in one with videotaping equipment. Take a feed from the video camera to a monitor in the other room. Whether you are videotaping both prototype and user or only the prototype and not the people, be sure that all the voices are coming through to the other monitor.

Figure 13-7 You can have observers in another room with a monitor showing what is happening in the usability evaluation.

Getting observers to take notes

It helps to get the observers involved by asking them to take notes. One idea is to lay large sheets of white paper on the table—flip chart paper works well. Give observers pads of sticky notes in different colors. Set up a color scheme, such as yellow = notes about the user, blue = notes about the prototype. Tell the observers to write down any insights they have while watching and listening. Let them put their sticky notes onto the large sheets of paper. You can then collect the large sheets of paper with the sticky notes attached. You can put them up on the walls around the observers' room so that people who come to observe the second participant can see what others had to say while observing the first participant. (You may find that it helps to tape them down onto the large sheet of paper so they don't fall off.) You can type up what's on the sticky notes and add it to your log for the session.

It helps to do a little training with observers or at least to put a short instruction sheet in the observers' room. The most important items on that instruction sheet would be these:

- Try to capture the user's behavior or facts about the user or the prototype. A note such as "user selected the edit icon before selecting the record he wanted to edit" is more instructive than a note such as "user doesn't understand how Windows works."

- Try to concentrate on specific observations; don't redesign now. Now is the time to see what is happening and to identify problems. We have to be clear about the problems before we redesign.

Other ideas for successful observations:

- Let lots of people know about the sessions. Send e-mail inviting them. Tell them the schedule. Tell them a little about the users who are coming and about what you will be doing.

- Personally invite any special people who should observe, even for a short time, such as high-level managers.

- Have a sign-in sheet so you know who was there.

- Have pens available to go with the sticky notes.

- Put out candy. Word will get around and people will come.

- If you are concerned that some observers may jump to inappropriate conclusions while watching, try to have a team member as an observer to monitor what is happening in the observation room. Have that person handle any inappropriate remarks on the spot or alert someone who can better handle the situation outside of the observation room.

Handling inappropriate reactions

For many people, the first exposure to a real user working with a prototype or product is a shock. They cannot believe that someone could be having that much trouble with something that they or their colleagues or the people who work for them have developed. Out of their shock may come inappropriate reactions, including:

- **Defensiveness,** shown by comments such as "Where did they find such a stupid user?" "That user isn't representative." "You're doing the test all wrong." "We need to find smarter users." "If they can't do this, they don't deserve to work here."

- **Despair,** shown by comments such as "Let's kill the project. It can't be fixed." "How could the programmers (or help writers) be so stupid?"

- **Rush to redesign,** shown by comments such as "Okay. We can fix that one. We'll just do…" (and so on, with the idea of separate fixes for each problem that they see instead of waiting to see all the users, analyzing all the problems, and then making consistent and coherent design decisions).

■ **Solve it in training or documentation**, shown by comments such as "Training (documentation) is going to have to see this. They're the people who have to make it work now."

If a usability specialist is sitting in the observation room and taking notes as an observer along with the programmers, writers, or managers who are seeing their first usability evaluations, the usability specialist can temper some of these inappropriate reactions. Depending on the reaction, the usability specialist might engage the observer in a discussion, including:

■ reminding the observer how the participants were recruited and what qualifications the particular user has to be a participant

■ pointing out that users are "reality." If the product is for public sale, and the company does not want to sell its products to people like this user, that's a marketing decision they can make—but it might not be a wise one. If the product is for inhouse users, and the observer thinks this user is too stupid for the product, will all users like this one be fired? Where will the company find other users to hire who will not have trouble with the product?

■ arranging for the observer to see other test participants. When observers see four or five users stumble in the same place in a program, they often change their reaction from "stupid user" to "stupid program." That's not usually a productive reaction either. The usability specialist needs to deal with that reaction as well.

■ countering arguments to kill programs by cautioning observers not to jump to conclusions based on seeing just one person or just a few minutes of an evaluation

■ cautioning observers that they can't be sure what needs to be fixed until they see how many people have trouble at that point and understand what the problem is really all about

■ pointing out that quick fixes might just be band-aids on a situation that needs a well thought out, consistent, and coherent solution and that design meetings will follow the usability evaluations

■ reminding observers that not all users get to training or read documentation and considering how to make the interface more intuitive is the better goal to strive for

Continuing the process

Creating a first set of prototypes is not the end of the process. To get the design right, to produce a product that users will find easy to learn and use, requires continuing prototyping. An initial prototype reveals some problems; subsequent prototypes reveal additional problems.

Iterating prototypes, completing the prototype

Prototyping allows rapid changes based on user input. Typical usability evaluations of early prototypes involve three to six users for each round of evaluation. Don't make changes after each user unless it is obvious that the change is necessary. That user may be the only one who ever has the problem. Three to six people should usually be enough for you to feel confident about the changes that are needed.

Although you may start working with users on a prototype with nothing or very little developed, and we urge you to do usability evaluations on partially developed prototypes, you should also complete the prototype and test it with users before coding the product. You can get a very good idea of how the overall metaphor and flow work by doing a partial prototype that handles the major tasks. However, as you expand the prototype to the lower-level screens, to secondary functions, to less common scenarios, you may find that you want to tweak the metaphor, change the menu structure, move some icons, or change some of the style. Because consistency is critical, you should consider all the aspects of the design before you code any. The features that you consider peripheral may turn out to be very important to users.

In one product, the designers and developers paid a lot of attention to the main screen and the main workflow that accounted for the basic part of the task that the users did regularly. However, they didn't spend as much time on other aspects of the product, such as importing, exporting, and printing. To the designers and developers, those were not the major parts of the application they were creating. When the product got to users, however, the users were unhappy. They could not easily figure out how to generate their reports. The menu options leading to printing didn't make much sense to the users. The printing process required several steps that users didn't think were necessary. They couldn't preview their data to see if they had selected the right report.

This example gives us three lessons.

First, in a user and task analysis, it is vital to capture the connections between the application you are working on and other applications that people use. It is also vital to consider all the outputs that users generate from the application, not just the work they do in the application.

Second, tasks that do not seem critical to designers and developers may in fact be frequent and critical to users. Site visits earlier in the project might have led these designers to a better appreciation of how important importing, exporting, and printing were to these users.

Third, although it is right to start prototyping by considering the most frequent and critical tasks, you cannot stop there. You have to eventually carry the prototype and the usability evaluations down to all the common tasks and all the parts of the application.

Continuing user and task analysis beyond prototyping

Sometimes project directors see the value of site visits and user input to design but then think usability assessment should stop during the product development. They think users should then wait for what they often call "user acceptance testing" or "beta testing." That's not a good idea.

This attitude seems to be based on the belief that once everything is specified, coding just carries out the specification. But implementing specifications is never trivial. Invariably issues arise that require changing or deviating from the specification. If the goal is a product that works for users, those changes and deviations need to be based on the user and task analysis, and they need to be evaluated by having users try out the emerging product.

Although you can—and should—put usability goals and use scenarios into a specification, you cannot specify exactly how real people are going to react to or use anything you create. Usability goals are what you want the implementation to achieve. You cannot know what the implementation achieves unless you test. Use scenarios are the development team's view of how users ought to work in the new system. Just because you wrote the use scenario for a task doesn't mean users will do the task that way. Usability goals and use scenarios are good ideas, but they do not do away with the need to test with users.

Every detail that the developers create to implement a specification can set off a wrong assumption on the users' part or confuse or otherwise derail the users. The only way to know what users do when presented with the implementation is to watch them try to work with it.

The attitude of "we can't do any more usability; now we have to just code it," is often driven by the project manager's total focus on schedule and cost. Nothing can interrupt or interfere with coding. We appreciate the importance of schedule and budget. However, if users reject the product in the end, getting it out on time and meeting the budget may turn out to be poor measures of success. Issues that come up during coding should be reviewed for usability, using all the data from your earlier user and task analysis. They should also be tested with users.

References cited in the chapter

Dayton, Tom, McFarland, Al, and Kramer, Joseph, Bridging user needs to object oriented GUI prototype via task object design, in *User Interface Design: Bridging the Gap from User Requirements to Design*, edited by Larry E. Wood, Boca Raton, FL: CRC Press, 1998, 15-56.

Desurvire, Heather W., Faster; cheaper!! Are usability inspection methods as effective as empirical testing?, in *Usability Inspection Methods*, edited by Jakob Nielsen and Robert L. Mack, NY: John Wiley & Sons, 1994, 173-202.

Dumas, Joseph S. and Redish, Janice C., *A Practical Guide to Usability Testing*, Greenwich, CT: Ablex, 1993.

Ehn, Pelle, Scandinavian design: On participation and skill, in *Participatory Design: Principles and Practices*, edited by Douglas Schuler and Aki Namioka, Hillsdale, NJ: Lawrence Erlbaum Associates, 1993, 41-77.

Ehn, Pelle, *Work-Oriented Design of Computer Artifacts*, Hillsdale, NJ: Lawrence Erlbaum Associates, 1989.

Gould, John D., Boies, Stephen J., Levy, Stephen, Richards, John T., and Schoonard, Jim, The 1984 Olympic messaging system — A test of behavioral principles of system design, *Communications of the ACM*, 30, 1987: 758-769.

Karat, John and Bennett, John L., Working within the design process: Supporting effective and efficient design, *Designing Interaction: Psychology at the Human-Computer Interface*, edited by John M. Carroll, Cambridge: Cambridge University Press, 1991, 269-285.

Muller, Michael J., PICTIVE: Democratizing the dynamics of the design session, in *Participatory Design: Principles and Practices*, edited by Douglas Schuler and Aki Namioka, Hillsdale, NJ: Lawrence Erlbaum Associates, 1993, 211-237.

Muller, Michael J., Retrospective on a year of participatory design using the PICTIVE technique, *Proceedings of CHI'92*, Monterey, CA, ACM, 1992: 455-462.

Muller, Michael J., PICTIVE—An exploration in participatory design, *Proceedings of CHI'91*, New Orleans, LA, ACM, 1991: 225-231.

Muller, Michael J., and Carr, Rebecca, Using the CARD and PICTIVE participatory design methods for collaborative analysis, in *Field Methods Casebook for Software Design*, edited by Dennis Wixon and Judith Ramey, NY: John Wiley & Sons, 1996, 17-34.

Muller, Michael J., Tudor, Leslie G., Wildman, Daniel M., White, Ellen A., Root, Robert W., Dayton, Tom, Carr, Rebecca, Diekmann, Barbara, and Dykstra-Erickson, Elizabeth, Bifocal tools for scenarios and representations in participatory activities with users, in *Scenario-Based Design*, edited by John M. Carroll, NY: John Wiley & Sons, 1995, 135-163.

Nielsen, Jakob and Molich, Rudy, Heuristic evaluation of user interfaces, *Proceedings of the ACM SIGCHI Conference*, Seattle, WA, 1990: 249-256.

Pressman, Roger S., *Software Engineering: A Practitioner's Approach*, NY: McGraw-Hill, 1992.

Rantzer, Martin, Mind the gap: Surviving the dangers of user interface design, in *User Interface Design: Bridging the Gap from User Requirements to Design*, edited by Larry E. Wood, Boca Raton, FL: CRC Press, 1998, 153-185.

Rubin, Jeffrey, *Handbook of Usability Testing*, NY: John Wiley & Sons, 1994.

Rudd, Jim, Stern, Kenneth R., and Isensee, Scott, Low vs. high fidelity prototyping debate, *Interactions*, 3 (1), January 1996: 76-85.

Simpson, Kevin T., The UI war room and design prism: A user interface design approach from multiple perspectives, in *User Interface Design: Bridging the Gap from User Requirements to Design*, edited by Larry E. Wood, Boca Raton, FL: CRC Press, 1998, 249-280.

Tudor, Leslie G., Muller, Michael J., Dayton, Tom, and Root, Robert W., A participatory design technique for high-level task analysis, critique, and redesign: The CARD method, *Proceedings of the Human Factors and Ergonomics Society*, Seattle, WA, 1993: 295-299.

Wood, Larry E, ed., *User Interface Design: Bridging the Gap from User Requirements to Design*, Boca Raton, FL: CRC Press, 1998.

Other books and articles for further reading

Nielsen, Jakob and Mack, Robert L., Eds., *Usability Inspection Methods*, NY: John Wiley & Sons, 1994.

Schuler, Douglas and Namioka, Aki, Eds., *Participatory Design: Principles and Practices*, Hillsdale, NJ: Lawrence Erlbaum Associates, 1993.

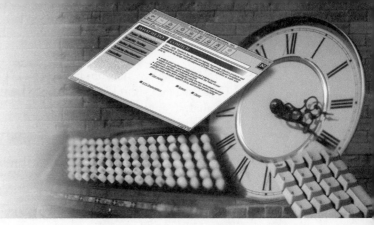

14

User and task analysis for documentation and training

User and task analysis is as critical for documentation and training as it is for any other part of any product. It has always been clear to us that the basic guidelines for effective communication apply equally to both "the stuff on the screen" and "the stuff on paper." The specifics of how you might implement a guideline differ, but the principles are the same: understand the users, understand what the users want to do, use the users' language, make the layout help people find what they need quickly, and so on. And the process for getting there is also exactly the same.

If you are responsible for documentation or training, you must realize that all information and instructional materials have users, tasks, and interfaces just as other products and parts of products do. So this chapter is relevant to you no matter what type of documentation or training you are designing.

If you are not directly responsible for what you think of as documents or training materials, this chapter is still relevant to you because all software and hardware products communicate with users in many ways. Today, much of the documentation and training is in the interface. The lines between documentation, training, and interface have blurred so much that old distinctions are no longer meaningful. Planning and designing how the product will communicate is an essential part of planning any product.

So no matter what your background or your role on a design team, we think you'll learn a lot by thinking about documentation and training and how user and task analysis applies to them.

In this chapter, we cover the following questions:

- What types of documents and training materials need user and task analysis?

- What counts as documentation and training in a software application?

- Why are there so many types of communication in software?

- Who should prepare documentation and training materials?

- Why should you do user and task analysis for documentation and training?

- What might you do during site visits if your focus is documentation or training?

- What can you do with the information you gather during site visits?

- How do you move from decisions to prototypes?

- User's manuals: Why is organizing by users' tasks so important?

- Getting started manuals: What is minimalism?

- Online help: What do people want to know?

- On the screen: What is an electronic performance support system?

- What about the Web?

- What about computer-based and Web-based training?

What types of documents and training materials need user and task analysis?

All of them, including

- manuals, quick reference cards, job aids—any other informational or instructional materials that are part of a software or hardware package

- context-sensitive help or tutorials linked to a software or hardware product

- any type of Web site

- documents or training materials that users access online, even if they are not about using or learning a software application or a piece of hardware—for example, an online benefits handbook, online forms, computer-based training for any type of work

- a document that is itself the entire product even if a computer is not involved at all—for example, a printed benefits handbook, paper forms, or a government regulation

- training materials to be used apart from any other product, such as instructor-led training on any topic

Complaints abound in the popular press about the uselessness of most manuals. When you tell people that you design and write documentation for products, they are quick to tell you their stories of personal frustration. But documentation doesn't have to be frustrating; it can be truly helpful if we understand how users learn from and use print and online information. You can get some help from research in cognitive psychology, document design, and instructional design (see, for example, Carroll 1990; Redish 1993; Schriver 1997; Wright 1987).

You can get some help from other practitioners who have distilled this research into good advice on how to create successful documentation and training. (See, for example, Boggan et al. 1996; Brockmann 1990; Clark 1987; Gery 1991; Hackos and Stevens 1997; Horton 1994; Price and Korman 1993.)

But to that general background information and general advice, you must add the specifics of understanding *your* users, their work, and the ways that they use documentation and training. To make your documentation and training work for your users requires direct experience with those users. Just as we cannot guess or intuit what will make a particular interface usable with a particular group of users, we cannot sit in our cubicles and guess what accompanying information and training will be effective.

What counts as documentation or training in a software application?

Graphical user interfaces and direct manipulation of objects on the screen, as well as the ability of computers to monitor and respond to user actions and requests, have vastly expanded the opportunities for computer-delivered information and training. We are no longer restricted to a printed user's manual. Help doesn't have to be a static display. We can embed words and pictures, tooltips or balloon help, messages, wizards, cue cards, coaches, even an embedded performance support system in the interface itself.

All of these communication tools provide information or instruction or both. Figure 14-1 shows how software products today communicate with and help users do their work.

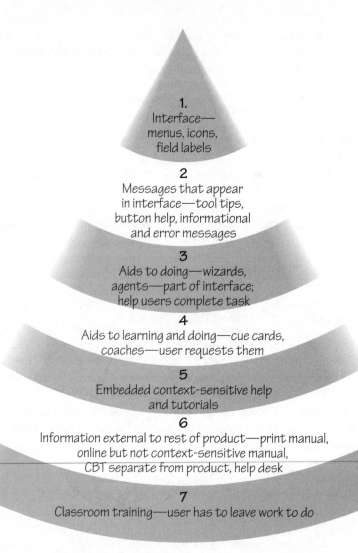

Figure 14-1 Software products include information and instruction at many levels.

We draw figure 14-1 as a series of concentric circles to show distance from the center of activity—the interface. In the first circle are the words, graphics, and layout that every user sees—the user interface that you have been focusing on throughout this book. The interface is itself a form of information. It consists, as all information does, of words and graphics as well as screen or page design (layout, typography, color, etc.).

In the next circle is additional information that comes as part of the interface but that is not automatically there when the user opens the application. This information is meant to help users quickly move ahead with a task. By the click of a mouse button, they can get tooltips or bubble or balloon help, brief messages that may be just enough information to continue the task. The addition of a question-mark cursor enables users to get more information, either to explain "what is…" or "how to…" or how to recover from a problem.

The third circle represents some of the new ways that have recently been developed to walk users through tasks, such as wizards and agents. These are meant to help users do the task immediately. In some cases, users can actively choose whether to see this documentation. In other cases, the designer, recognizing the needs of the majority of users, has decided to aid the users in their task performance by embedding the software task in an information-rich context. For example, sometimes designers make wizards available to users who choose to use them, but in other instances, often for installation or other infrequently performed tasks, the designer provides a wizard as the only way to do the tasks.

The fourth circle includes some new and special types of instructional aids, sometimes called "just-in-time training aids," such as cue cards or coaches. These are meant to help users learn while doing. As you proceed outward to the fifth, sixth, and seventh circles, the help, documentation, and training materials and other learning and reference opportunities become more indirect, always initiated by the users, and less and less closely attached to the software. But they are all documentation or training.

The goal of software is to support users' performance. Everything mentioned in figure 14-1 is a way to support users' performance. All of these types of support must be designed as integral parts of the interface rather than added as an afterthought. That means that decisions on which of them to include, what roles they will play, and how to design each of them are part of your early design decisions. To make those design decisions, you need to address the learning and reference needs of your users during your site visits. User and task analysis, directed at informational and instructional requirements rather than functional requirements, is necessary to create everything from the primary interface through all the circles in figure 14-1.

Why are there so many types of communication in software?

You may ask why we need so many different ways of supporting users: menus as well as icons; tooltips that users can choose to open or to ignore; wizards, cue cards, coaches, and intelligent assistants that can be turned on or turned off; and so on. The answer lies in your user analysis.

If you observe and talk with users or if you survey users, you will almost certainly find that your users have a wide range of working styles and learning styles. You will find people who prefer the keyboard and people who prefer the mouse. You will find people who learn best through words, people who learn best through pictures, and people who learn best through touch. You will find risk takers—people who like to learn by trial and error through playing with the product—and non-risk takers—people who want clear instructions to follow so they don't make mistakes. Even the same person may follow different working styles in different circumstances, for example, in low stress versus high stress situations.

In an earlier article (Redish 1995), Ginny suggests that one of the reasons that software products include so many ways of accomplishing the same task is that developers have to meet the needs of an ever-expanding and diverse user population. In another article (Redish 1998), she suggests that documents such as minimalist manuals must also pay attention to the diversity of users' working and learning styles.

If, in site visits, you pay attention to how users work with documentation and training materials, you are likely to find some who actually read the manual before starting, others who skim through the documentation, others who don't open it until they are in trouble, and still others who pride themselves on not removing the shrink wrap. You'll find some users who go to online help for every situation, others who dip into it when they are really stuck, and others who are reluctant ever to go to help. You'll find some who want to work through a tutorial by themselves; others who opt for classroom instruction, sometimes even at their own expense; and others who want to learn only as they are working.

Software has to include many ways of communicating with users in order to communicate effectively with *all* users. It has to offer support for users with different working and learning styles. It also has to offer support for users who are at different stages of use. Novices may make the most use of the more hand-holding and directive types of information and instruction. Advanced beginners may rely on some of the built-in aids to accomplish tasks quickly. Competent and expert performers may look for quick information about new areas but prefer for the most part to have information and instruction out of the way while they are working.

The many ways of communicating that we show in the concentric circles of figure 14-1 are attempts to meet the needs of a broad range of users. If you are not sure that you have that broad a range of users for the product you are designing, go out on site visits and watch how your users and potential users work and learn. Our guess is that you will in fact find much more diversity than you have assumed.

Who should prepare documentation and training materials?

As you see how much communication takes place in most software products, it becomes obvious that people whose professional specialty is communicating with users have a vital role to play on project teams. People whose professional specialty is documentation may be called document designers, technical communicators, information developers, information product engineers, and other similar titles. People whose professional specialty is training may be called instructional systems designers, learning products engineers, multimedia specialists, trainers, and other similar titles.

Both documentation and training specialists can bring critical skills and knowledge to early design work. In Rantzler's Delta method (Rantzler 1996, 1998), for example, technical communicators are critical members of design teams along with system designers and usability engineers. As he says, "[t]he technical communicator plays an important role, deciding what information should be included in the system and finding an appropriate structure for the user interface, system services, and enabling information. The technical communicator should also (together with the usability engineer) act as a link between the designers and the users since he or she often has both training and experience in how to explain complicated technical issues to inexperienced users" (Rantzler 1998, 157).

Programmers should not have to add responsibility for documentation and training materials to their already overburdened plates. They should not be writing manuals or help. They should not be developing tutorials. They should not be writing Web pages. They should not be writing messages. They should also be relying on the professional expertise of documentation and training specialists for help with all the words and graphics and screen design in the interface, for help in general with making sure that all aspects of the product will communicate effectively with users.

Why should you do user and task analysis for documentation and training?

If you are a technical communicator or instructional designer reading this chapter, you'll see that we've just argued strongly for your having a major role in early design activities. You also have to be proactive about taking that role. Successful documentation and training is planned from the beginning of the project and is based on understanding the actual users of the product, the tasks they need to do, the words they use for those tasks, and the ways they search for information.

When users cannot find what they need in a manual or in online help, we have to wonder why the information they need is not there. If it is there, we have to wonder why they cannot find it. The only answer we can imagine is that no one worked with the users to understand what information they look for or the way they search.

Documenting the product isn't good enough

Many technical communicators and instructional designers know how important interactions with users are and are frustrated at being unable to work directly with users. Others, however, have been content to wait until late in a project to be invited to develop documentation and training as ancillary materials.

They have, unfortunately, been content to document only what the product does from the product's point of view. Even when they write task-oriented manuals, they may be relying on developers, business analysts, or others to give them lists of tasks. And those task lists are all too often derived from product functionality.

The key to successful documentation is not to document the product but to give users the information they need to successfully do their work with the product. The difference is the focus—users accomplishing their work rather than functions being used.

Just "thinking" about the audience isn't good enough

If you are a technical communicator whose education has focused on practice as well as theory in document design and usability, you may well be aware of the need to do the type of user and task analysis that this book is all about. But if you are a technical communicator whose education is in more traditional English composition or literature, you may be used to doing audience analysis by sitting at your desk and thinking about who your readers might be. The traditional concept of "audience invoked" or "audience imagined" may work for writing an essay. However, it does not work for writing successful manuals or online help.

An essay is usually read from beginning to end, but people don't generally read manuals or browse through help files. They search for specific pieces of information.

You need to know how users search—what words they look up in indexes and keyword searches and how they define the tasks they look for in tables of contents. You cannot learn their words and their task names by sitting at your desk or by relying on developers or analysts to tell you.

Developing training materials just from the product isn't enough

If you are an instructional designer, you may see yourself in a similar position. Analyzing users and their needs is an important part of traditional instructional systems design. Instructional designers are supposed to (1) figure out what people need to know to use a product successfully and then (2) go and find out what most people now know and don't know that is important for using the product successfully. Their goal is then to develop training that builds on what users already know and bridges the gap between that and what the users need to know.

That type of "gap analysis" is an important part of the process of developing successful instructional materials. Unfortunately it isn't actually done through site visits with users nearly as often as it should be. The information that instructional designers rely on may be superficial statements of user characteristics from marketing or development or another department. Sometimes instructional materials aren't based on anything specific about users. The instruction just focuses on teaching the new product without any attempt to understand what users already know, what is truly relevant for users, how users are likely to work with either the product or the instructional materials, the vocabulary that would be meaningful to users, or the types of mistakes that users will make.

Moreover, in the traditional training department, instructional designers wait until all the decisions have been made about how users will work with the product, that is, until after the design is done. But if they were involved in projects earlier, instructional designers, like technical communicators, could contribute a great deal to designing a product that will, in fact, require less separate training later. To do that, instructional designers, like technical communicators, need to get out and see how users are working today, that is, to do site visits for user and task analysis.

What might you do during site visits if your focus is documentation or training?

Here are five areas that you might be interested in exploring during site visits to get information for documentation and training. (We have tried to provide broad coverage of issues with these five, but there are certainly other areas to explore, observations to make, questions to ask. This list is by no means exhaustive. Nor do we mean to imply that every site visit must cover all these areas.)

1. How much documentation or training is needed for different tasks? What tasks do people think they should have to learn about? What tasks would make them go to a manual or online help? What tasks do people think they should be able to do without any learning at all?

2. How do your users use (or not use) documentation and training now? If your project is a Web site, how do your users work with other Web sites that are like yours?

3. What are your users' experiences with training, expectations about training, motivation to do different types of training? What incentives would make these users participate in training?

4. Who does which tasks? What might that mean for dividing up information into different pieces of documentation and training materials?

5. Are there special user groups? Should you think about creating specific types of documentation or training for different groups of users?

Let's examine each of these a bit more deeply.

How much documentation or training is needed for different tasks?

Many years ago, Patricia Wright and colleagues (Wright et al. 1982) did a study that showed that consumers have very definite ideas about how much they should have to read in different situations. Even though the study was done with individual questionnaires and not through group discussion, there was a high level of agreement among the participants. For example, the consumers in that study agreed that a TV should not need instructions. You take it out of the box, plug it in, and turn it on. For other products, they agreed that more instructions would be necessary.

As you watch and listen to users in your site visits, you may get a good sense of which users in which situations want what type of documentation and when they don't want to have to deal with documentation at all.

How do your users use (or not use) documentation now?

You might be interested in how people now get information, why they make the choices they make, and what problems they have with current documentation. When you are observing users, you might plan to be especially observant about when and why they do go to documentation, and just as important, when and why they do not go to documentation but need help. You might find out how they get that help.

Here are several lists of questions that might be relevant for site visits. You might answer some of them through your observations. You might need to ask users to get some of the answers. When asking outside the context of an observation, evaluate the answers carefully. Remember that users' self-reports are not as accurate as behavior that you watch. Also, be conscious of how you ask the questions. Don't lead the user to give you a particular answer. (See chapter 10 for more on asking questions in a neutral manner.) You can use what you learn from these questions to decide what to put on paper and what to put online, how to structure online help, and what words to use not only in manuals and help but directly in the interface for icons and menus.

Where are the documents or training or Web site? How accessible are they?
If you are interested in paper documents:

- Are user's manuals available to the users?

- Where are the user's manuals kept?

- If they are not near the users, why not?

- Does the user you are observing or interviewing even know that manuals exist?

- Does the user believe that he or she has access to the manuals?

- Are the manuals really where someone tells you they are? (Are they lost? Do they disappear because someone borrows them and no one knows who has them?)

- Do users want paper documents when the information is only available online? Why?

If you are interested in Web-based documents:

- Does the user have Web access?

- What speed is that access?

- Is it fast enough to satisfy the user?

- Does the user open the Web document while keeping other work open? If not, why not?

How do people use them?
We've put the word "manual" in these questions. You can substitute "help," "tutorial," "CBT," "Web," or whatever you are interested in for the word "manual" in each of these questions.

- Does the user ever go to the manual? Why? Why not?

- When does the user go to the manual?

- How does the user look for information? Through the table of contents? The index (keyword search)? By flipping pages (browsing help or the Web)? By full string search? By remembering a URL? By putting keywords into a Web search engine?

- What words is the user searching with?

- Does the user find relevant information? Why? Why not?

- Does the user understand what she or he finds? Why? Why not?

- Is it helpful? Why? Why not?

The user trying to program the VCR whom we've mentioned in earlier stories started out by trial and error, looking for buttons on the machine. He didn't even look for the manual until he gave up on finding the solution himself. He opened the manual, went to the table of contents, found a heading he thought was relevant, jumped directly to that page, got one useful hint from what he saw there (that he had to get a menu to come up on the television screen), turned to the machine to try to work with that hint, and put the manual down. When that hint didn't immediately solve the problem, he looked once more at the manual and then went back to trial and error. Only after several minutes did he remember by himself (not from the manual) that he needed to set the TV to channel 3 in order to work on anything to do with the VCR.

Other observations have shown that lots of users work the way this VCR user does—jumping into the middle of the manual to do a specific task. The writer of the manual, however, seems to have assumed that the user will read all the pages before that task. The manual may have had an instruction on an earlier page to set the TV to channel 3, but that didn't help this user work with the documentation. A reminder on the page the user looked at, the page with instructions for "setting up the VCR to record a program later," would have saved this user many minutes of unproductive work.

Have users developed their own documentation and training?

As you observe, pay attention to indications that the user has personal versions of documentation for tasks or parts of tasks.

- Has the user created personal documentation?

- If so, what does it look like?

- Is it a printout from the product's documentation?

- Is it something the user actually wrote?

- What topics are in it?

- Is part of the documentation a translation of material from the product documentation?

- If so, what words is this user using?

- Why did the users create this documentation?

- How did the users create it?

Documents that users have created for themselves are often very useful artifacts. If it is not too large or difficult to copy, ask if the user is willing to share the self-created documentation with you. Don't push, however, if the user is reluctant; in that case, just take notes. If you can get a copy, you'll be seeing at least one user's version of what is important, of an organization that works for that user, of vocabulary that is more meaningful to that user than what was in the original.

You might put sticky notes on your copy after the visit to remind yourself why the user chose that topic or felt the need to redo the documentation. It may be a signal of problems with the software or hardware, not just with the documentation.

In a series of site visits, the observers noticed that many users had their own "cheat sheets" of the same set of information. Some had a printout from the help system; others had written the information on paper or an index card. Some had it tacked to cork boards above their computers. One had it pasted on a pullout shelf of her desk. Several kept it handy in a top drawer. The fact that so many users had made the same decision to get that information down on paper and put it where they could find it told the observers that (1) it was important information, (2) it was difficult to remember, and (3) it was not easy to get online while doing the task. When asked about the self-created documentation, users explained that it contained the codes for the many possible variations of the same task. In the system the users had, it was up to the user to enter the correct code for the variation of the task being done. Ironically, the computer always had enough information by the time this code was needed to know which variation of the task the user wanted to do, but it hadn't been programmed to use that information. Observing users' personal documentation revealed a problem for which the best solution was fixing the software.

What are users' experiences with training?

You may be particularly interested in issues related to training materials. With each question, you may well want to probe for reasons and values. For example, if you ask about classroom training, the user may be willing to go if it is free but not if it costs money or may be willing to go if it is on company time but not if it is on personal time. Those reasons and values may be critical for you to know. In some cases, probing for a specific incident of use will get you the most useful information:

■ Did the user get training?

■ What type of training (classroom, short demonstration, computer-based training)?

■ How useful did the user think the training was?

■ Would the user go to a class about your application? Why? Why not?

■ Would the user work with stand-alone computer-based training? Why? Why not?

■ Has the user ever worked with the built-in training aids in other products? When? How was the experience?

Who does which tasks?

Getting a task list, really gathering users' tasks in their words, is as critical for documentation and training as it is for any other part of the product. To create a task-oriented manual, you have to know what tasks to include, how users group tasks, how they talk about what they do, and so on.

You may also want to focus on whether different types of users do different tasks. For example, you may think that administrators do a certain set of tasks and clerks do another. One of the objectives of your site visits may be to confirm or challenge assumptions about who does which tasks because that information leads directly to decisions about organizing documentation and training.

Are there special user groups?

As you observe and talk to users at different stages of use, in different jobs or roles, you should be thinking about whether there are any special groups within the user population for whom you may want to do something special in the documentation or training. For example, if you are trying to get people who now use a competitor's product to switch to your new product, you might consider creating a booklet or a special help system for those transfer users. They already know the tasks they want to do, they just need to know how to do it your way. Your booklet or help system would have to be based on a contrastive analysis; you would have to know how users work in the competitor's system.

What can you do with the information you gather during site visits?

Many of the techniques for analyzing data that we covered in chapter 11 apply to documentation and training as well as other parts of the product. You might want to enhance your user profiles with information on how each user does and does not use documentation and each user's attitudes toward and use of training materials. You might want to add to your environmental profiles information about where you found the documentation and how different types of documentation and training would or would not fit into the physical, cultural, and social environment. You might have insight sheets that specifically focus on issues related to documentation and training. Certainly you will want to develop task lists, group tasks into sequences and hierarchies, and consider how to provide support to users to accomplish the work implied in those task lists.

All of that information should be useful to answer these three questions which are among the early design decisions that every project team must consider. We discuss each in the sections that follow.

- How will you meet different users' information and training needs in different situations?

- How can you use your task lists to make decisions on modular documentation and training?

- What should go in print and what should go online?

Meeting different information and training needs

As you analyze the notes from your site visits, you might build a matrix of specific users, specific situations, comments, and proposed documentation and training solutions. Figure 14-2 is an example of part of such a matrix. A matrix like this can help you with some of the critical early design decisions, such as how much documentation and training to build directly into the interface.

User types for Product A	Tasks	Comments	Proposed information solutions
Typical user (working at home on personal computer)	Install software on personal computer	Most users do not want to deal with installation; want computer to do it	Installation wizard; no documentation; words and questions in wizard in clear language
Experienced user transferring from older version of same program	Same tasks as did before but new steps	Wants to be up and running quickly; no interest in tutorial	Quick reference card explaining differences; include old words in new online help system; include help topic of "What's new in this version?"
Experienced user transferring from our competitor's program	Same tasks as did before	Knows what wants to do; just wants to know how to do it our way; have to capture this user quickly or may go back to old software	Small booklet directed at this audience with just what they need to know to transfer; special online help for them; put words from the other product in our help search function
New user who is also a novice at the work and who is fearful of getting in and playing around; likes to work through tutorial	A list of specific tasks that these new users would be likely to do in the first few times with the product would go here	Is not sure of process to follow, but knows goals; doesn't want to be overwhelmed; fearful; but willing to use tutorial	Short (5 minute) tutorial; very friendly; clear vocabulary; short sentences; graphics; show overall process; how to do basic steps
New user who is also a novice at the work but who has no patience for tutorial that is not the user's own work	The same list of specific tasks that these new users would be likely to do in the first few times with the product would go here	Same knowledge, but not fearful; wants to do own work immediately	Cue cards, coach, to lead through doing task once

Figure 14-2 Part of a matrix to capture specific documentation and training issues and proposed solutions.

Using task lists to decide on modular documentation and training

Many companies that put out complex products with many user groups find that trying to capture everything for everyone in one large manual serves no one well. The sheer size of the manual may overwhelm users who then call for support instead of opening the book. Because finding what they need in a document that tries to be all things for all users is much more difficult than in a smaller document, users may give up on it. Moreover, there is no need to burden users with information about tasks that they cannot or will not do. Instead of one large manual, try modular documentation with different pieces for different users.

Modules can be based on who will do the work, on when it will be done, or on what users will need as they go through different stages of use. Figure 14-3 illustrates the documentation for a large product where one group in a company is going to set up and configure the server for the system and then administer and maintain it; end users are going to have to get up to speed quickly and then want information for doing their tasks; and transfer users and more competent users just need quick reminders.

In chapter 11 we showed you how a user/task matrix can make it clear who does what. When you have decided who will do what tasks in the new product you are developing, you can use the same type of user/task matrix to make decisions on documentation. For example, looking at the user/task matrix in figure 14-4, you can quickly see that the system administrator of the office telephone system is going to be doing a different set of tasks than the telephone users. (Note that we have only included a few of many tasks for each user group. A complete task list in this matrix would be much longer.)

With a user/task matrix like this, you would probably decide to develop two separate manuals so that telephone users will not be burdened with information that they don't need. Separating the information would make each manual smaller and the information in each manual easier to locate.

Of course, the system administrators are also telephone users. But they probably see that as two distinct roles and would expect to have different information sources when they are being system administrators and when they are being telephone users.

Thinking about documentation in terms of a user/task matrix isn't only about print manuals. It's also about online help, training materials, messages, how a Web site is organized, etc.

Deciding what to put in print and what to put online

This question invariably comes up in developing strategies for documentation and training in product design, and it is an important issue to consider early in product design. The answer, of course, is "it depends." As Bill Horton (1994, 4)

Figure 14-3 Breaking information into modules for different users is a cost-effective solution that helps everyone.

Tasks	System administrator	Telephone user
Print reports of usage	Frequent	Never
Add phones to system	Sometimes	Never
Change privileges for an extension	Sometimes	Never
Set personal voice mail message	Never	Frequent
Transfer someone to another extension	Never	Sometimes
Connect two outside calls together to have a three-way conversation	Never	Sometimes

Figure 14-4 A user/task matrix can help you make good decisions on documentation.

writes, "There are no absolute rules for what should and should not go online. The capabilities of systems and the needs of users vary so widely that such rules are of little use." And what it depends on, of course, is the specific users, their specific work, and their specific environments. To make wise decisions for your product, you must have good information about your users, their work, and their environments. The information you need can only come from the types of site visits this book is all about.

In many companies, decisions about print versus online documentation are driven primarily by policy decisions rather than users' needs. That is, a decision will be made to put everything online because it seems like the less expensive choice or because it is "the way to do it today." Budget is important. Being seen by consumers as having the latest and greatest is important. But decisions made for such policy reasons alone may backfire if you don't understand your users well enough.

Paper may be necessary. We have all heard stories about computer companies that put out products with no paper documentation only to have to go back and write the manuals because users clamored for them. If users call for help because they can't or won't use the online information, all the cost benefit from not printing documentation may be lost.

On the other hand, online may be necessary. We don't want you to read the previous paragraph and say, "so we should do paper documentation." If you put everything on paper and your users don't get the paper manuals because their companies buy a site license with one copy of the documentation, your support costs may by huge. What we are saying is that cost-effective decisions require knowing what will work for your users in their situations.

In a study of users of laboratory equipment, JoAnn found that users kept asking for quick reference cards that could be attached to the machine and pulled out when necessary. Many users remembered when the same type of equipment had a pull-out shelf under the machine with a card in it. The company apparently abandoned doing that some years ago, but no one seemed to remember why. Providing the information that goes with the lab machines on computers doesn't work for these users. The computers are in their offices, not in the labs next to the lab equipment.

As you work on decisions about providing the right solutions to users' needs for information and instruction, consider both the messages and the media. In her book with Dawn Stevens (Hackos and Stevens 1997), JoAnn points out that the way information is structured and the way it is distributed are two separate considerations. For example, you can have a book structure (paragraphs of text, an author's voice and point of view), or you can have a help structure (task specific, numbered steps, usually no distinctive voice). Each of these structures can be distributed on paper or online.

Also remember that books and help aren't the only structures you can use. You can have a form structure, and that too can be on paper or online. You can have dialogs, as in many embedded performance support systems. You can have checklists, as in cue cards. You can have tables and lists that are incorporated into book structures or help structures, both on paper and online. You can have dynamic structures with animation as part of books, help, or forms, and although you may think of dynamic structures only as part of online documentation, they needn't be. Just think of the pop-up books that are popular with children. Even hardware is not limited to paper or online information.

> *Ginny keeps the user manual for her fax machine next to the machine, but she seldom has to open it. The physical machine was designed with space for a quick reference card that is glued to a portion of the face of the machine. It is always there and it can be read even while the user is doing a task with the machine. The task that Ginny does most often, other than faxing, is putting in new rolls of paper. Most of the process is made obvious by the physical contours of the machine, but there's one metal bar that probably trips up a lot of users. Instead of making people experiment or go to the manual, the designers put an instruction right on the metal bar. It says, "Pass the paper under this guide." Those are the types of solutions you think of when you watch users working. But they have to be decided on early enough to be part of the physical design of the hardware.*

How do you move from decisions to prototypes?

Once you have decisions on the ways you are going to support users' performance with information and instructions, you need to capture those decisions in an information plan and content specifications. The information plan provides the overall picture of all the solutions. The content specifications provide the detailed picture of each solution (what will be in the cue cards, in each type of help, in each manual, in each tutorial, etc.).

Creating a successful information plan

A successful information plan presents the strategies that you have decided to use to help users with information and training. The foundation of the information plan is what you learned in your user and task analysis. In the background section of the information plan, you should have four summaries:

- the characteristics of the product
- the characteristics of the users
- the tasks users are likely to perform
- the environments they are likely to work in

All but the first of these come directly from your user and task analysis. They form the basis for your decisions on strategy that are recorded in the next section of the information plan.

The heart of your information plan should be the design implications and media choices that you draw from your user and task analysis. In the section on design implications, you explain what types of information and training you intend to develop and how they will meet the needs you uncovered in your site visits. In the section on media choices, you explain what media (paper, online, Web-based, labels, quick reference cards, classroom training, computer-based training, and so on) you will use, how you will use each, and why they are the most appropriate choices to meet your users' needs.

Once you have outlined your strategy for supporting your users, in the rest of the information plan you describe the resources (people, schedule, equipment, tools, budget) you will need to accomplish the information plan. [See Hackos (1994) for more details about developing information plans.]

Creating successful content specifications

Once you have established your documentation and training strategy through your information plan, you are ready to outline in detail how the documentation and training will be organized. We urge you to write content specifications or detailed training designs for each part of the strategy in your information plan. The format may vary with the medium. You may have a detailed annotated outline of a users' manual. You may have a storyboard and detailed design document for a computer-based, multimedia training. You may have an outline of the modules for classroom training. You may have a map of an online help system with a list of topics. What all of these specification documents share is that they show and explain in some detail how each will be organized to meet the users' needs.

JoAnn's team prepared a content specification for a manual for the administrator of a small business phone system. The specification carefully outlined how the tasks would be structured to meet the users' needs. They had learned that the users thought about their tasks in three major parts: tasks done to change the settings on individual telephones, tasks done to change the settings on the telephone system as a whole, and tasks done to set night restrictions systemwide. They decided to organize the administrator's manual in the same way, starting with the simpler individual phones, and moving on to the systemwide changes, and then to night restrictions.

Within the individual sections, however, the team decided on another organizational structure. The administrators could make many different changes to individual phones, such as turning on or off the music on hold, restricting a phone to local calls only, allowing conference calls or call waiting, and so on. However, in observations of administrators performing these tasks, the team learned that the administrators didn't do the tasks in any particular sequence. The tasks were done infrequently, whenever someone moved an office or needed a feature. As a result, the team decided to organize the individual phone tasks alphabetically in that section of the manual. This random order made it easier for the users to look up and complete any task in any order. In addition, each task module contained all of the information needed to perform the task, with no cross-references to other sections or assumptions about remembering earlier information in the book.

This story shows how the users' ways of performing the tasks directly influenced the technical communicators' plans for organizing and writing the manual. The content specification included the detailed outline and the rationale for it.

In addition to a detailed outline and rationale, you should also include the requirements of the media. For example, the content specification of a paper-based manual might include information about the page size, binding, and cover design. The content specification for online help or computer-based training might name the software tool to be used. The content specification for classroom training might include information about audio-visual and other equipment that will be needed in the classroom.

Also remember that design does not mean only physical design; it includes all aspects of design from organization to writing style to page design. It includes everything that will affect how the users use and respond to the information and training.

To help you think about the decisions that would go into information plans and content specifications, we focus the rest of the chapter on specific issues related to different types of documentation and training both on paper and online.

User's manuals: Why is organizing by users' tasks so important?

People use software and hardware to accomplish goals. The primary support they need is information and instructions for doing the tasks that are necessary to accomplish those goals. When users turn to support materials, they are most often looking for information to help them either figure out what tasks to do to or how to do those tasks.

Matching documents to users who are *reading to do*

Tom Sticht and his colleagues, while studying soldiers working with military manuals, had a revealing insight about documents (Sticht 1985): namely that writers often have an incorrect assumption about how people use documents. Document users can either be *reading to learn* or *reading to do*. In school, students are reading to learn; they are expected to work through a textbook, reading coherent prose and remembering it for later. In the workplace, almost all people almost all the time are reading to do. They use documents to make immediate decisions or take immediate actions. They do not read even short documents like memos, and certainly not manuals or other support material, from beginning to end. They skim, they skip, they jump to a specific place, grab what they need, and get out as quickly as possible.

So, most people, most of the time, who need support while using software or hardware are using documentation for quick reference. Like all generalizations, there are exceptions to this statement. In some situations, some users want conceptual information that is background to using a new type of product. Such situations are however much rarer than many developers, and many writers, would like to believe; and even in those situations, busy readers are looking for information that can be grabbed in small chunks, absorbed quickly, and easily located after the typical interruptions of their work lives.

Building useful navigation tools into workplace documents

If a document is meant for reference, with the expectation that users are trying to get immediately to just the place they need, navigation in the document becomes critical. Navigation on paper or online is accomplished primarily through the headings of sections or titles of help topics, which become the table of contents or contents list, and through the index or keywords in a search function. If the entries in the table of contents and the index don't match the words that users bring to them, the users may not find what they need or may be frustrated by the time and number of tries it takes to find something relevant.

Making sure the tasks are in users' words

If users come wanting to do tasks, organizing a manual or help system by tasks is the right approach. The question that Ginny has been asking lately (Redish 1997, 1998) is "whose tasks are being included in the documentation?" Most technical communicators and instructional designers are developing task-oriented material, but far too often the tasks focus on what the system can do and not on the work users are trying to accomplish.

If you write about "using the insert menu," you are organizing by functionality even though that's a task-oriented heading. It does not match a task that users come to the product wanting to accomplish. They may want instructions on "numbering the pages in a document" or "adding a footnote to a document" without realizing that either of those tasks are accomplished by using the insert menu. When you write about "working with the such-and-such tool," you are organizing by functionality. That's the product's solution, not the user's goal.

Figure 14-5 gives you an example of the difference between the user's point of view and the product's. If users come wanting "to get a sharper image," but the manual only has a heading for "Using the Resolution Tool," users may not realize that's where they need to go. The table of contents should have the heading "getting a sharper image." The text can then say, "to sharpen the image, you use the resolution tool."

Figure 14-5 Documentation needs to start from the user's view of a task and then link the product's solution to that in the text.

Why do so many "task-oriented" manuals focus on the product's solutions instead of the users' goals? The answer is probably that technical communicators are getting their information by using the product or by getting task lists from developers, marketers, or analysts rather than through site visits with users. Only by going out and seeing what users are trying to accomplish can you make the match between the users' view of the world and what the product is offering.

Getting started manuals: What is minimalism?

Making matches to the users' view of the world is especially important in the users' first encounters with a product. That's what tutorials and getting started guides are all about. Ginny coined a term, *reading to learn to do*, for the way that users work with these documents (Redish 1988). These documents are hybrids of the two main types of reading: We want users to learn about the product but users do not want to spend time studying as they would with a textbook. They want to get right in and accomplish work.

In the 1980s, Jack Carroll and colleagues at IBM's Watson Research Center studied users as they first learned new software. Carroll found that users do not want to read. Users jump the gun to act as soon as they see anything that looks like instructions. They want to do real work and look for information that matches the tasks they are trying to do. They make hypotheses about what went wrong when they make errors and act on their own hypotheses even when the information on the screen is telling them something else. That research, its implications, and Carroll's solution, which he calls "minimalism," are summarized in *The Nurnberg Funnel* (Carroll 1990). For an update on minimalism, see Carroll (1998).

Most people think that "minimalism" is about making documentation shorter. That's really only a consequence of the more important parts of the minimalist approach. Minimalism is mostly about focusing documentation on users doing tasks. It's about understanding users and what they know well enough to be able to leave out information that most users already know. It's about understanding the errors that users are likely to make so that part of the little information you give people is how to avoid or recover from problems. It's about getting people actively engaged in what they are doing by encouraging them to try things (Carroll 1998; Van der Meij and Carroll 1995; Carroll and Van der Meij 1996).

Minimalism is an effective documentation strategy when done well, as Carroll and others have shown. For two examples, see JoAnn's chapter in the book on minimalism (Hackos 1998) and an earlier study by Hans van der Meij (Van der Meij 1992). Doing minimalism well only happens through understanding the specific users of a product, the specific tasks they want to do, the errors they are likely to make, and the words they use to understand the tasks. In other words, it requires user and task analysis and then iterative interactions with users through drafts and revisions. But those are, in fact, the keys to successful documentation of any type, print or online, getting started or using, for software or for hardware.

Online help: What do people want to know?

By online help, we mean information embedded in and accessible from an application. We mean the type of help that people usually go to while they are working under pressure to complete a task. Although users could browse help screens at leisure, that's not the typical mode of use. Typical online help today is context sensitive, that is, what users get depends on where in the product they are when they select help. And typical online help is linked hypertext, which means that users can jump to a topic from a contents list, from a keyword search list, sometimes from a full-text search, and often from another, related topic.

So what should online help include? Just as with a user's manual, most of the time, users go to help because they don't know what to do or they don't know how to do it. The most common user's question is "How do I do X?" X may be a general goal:

"I want to fax something with this fax software. What do I do first?" X may be a specific task: "I want to send a cover sheet with my fax. How do I get one on my screen and fill it out?" (See figure 14-6.)

Figure 14-6 Users most often want help on procedures. They also come with their own words.

Users seldom go to help to ask "How does this system work?" or to ask "What is this?" The only time they want to know "What is this?" is if they are looking at an icon on the screen or see a word they don't know in a menu or message. Help for that is best given in tooltips or bubble or balloon help, although the definitions should also be available through search words and a contents section on "What is…?" or "What does … do?"

The help topics that users want most are procedural. And again, the only way to know what procedures to put into help, what titles to give them, and how to word them is to do user and task analysis. If the help titles are the names of system functions, like "Using the Resolution Tool," users will have an even harder time finding what they need than they typically do with paper documents. At least with paper, they can flip the pages and more easily scan through topics if they can't find what they need directly.

Users also want their own words in the help because that's what they go looking for. Online help has an advantage over paper in that you can have as many words as you want in the search function. The length of the search list (which is in fact the index) isn't apparent and thus doesn't overwhelm users. You may also want to include in help and in the search list information about something users might look up even if it isn't part of the product.

Ginny was watching users working with the prototype of the new version of a product. The company had done some process reengineering while upgrading the software and wanted to see how obvious the new process could be made through the software.

Although the company knew a lot about the old process, the help for the new software originally focused just on describing the new screens and the new way of doing things. At one point in the process, most of the users helping to evaluate the prototype expected to be working with a certain form. Because that form had been completely dropped from the new process, it wasn't mentioned anywhere in the new system. But the users didn't know that. Of course, one solution could have been to assume that everyone would go through training and learn the change. But another much less expensive solution was to put the old form name into the help system and write a help screen that explained that it wasn't needed anymore.

The key as always is understanding your users, the knowledge and expectations they bring, the tasks they are used to doing, the tasks they will now be doing, and the words they use. With that knowledge, you can put information into help that matches what your users are looking for.

On the screen: What is an embedded performance support system?

The philosophy of an embedded performance support system (EPSS) is to support the user who is doing work with just what the user needs as the user needs it in the course of doing that work. The foundation of EPSS is performance-centered design, which is another view of what we have been calling user-centered design. When Gloria Gery, who is usually referred to as the originator of EPSS, contrasts traditional design with performance-centered design, her first two activities are task analysis, including analyzing cognitive tasks and verbal interactions, and contextual inquiry, including analyzing the entire work context (Gery 1997a). These are exactly the activities that we have stressed throughout this book.

A performance support system does not have to be entirely embedded in the computer system. Everything in the concentric circles of figure 14-1 could be components of a performance support system—if they are coordinated and focused on helping the user do the job. If the pieces are separate constructs, created from a data-centric or system-centric point of view, not planned together, and not all focused on the user's work, they will not form a successful performance support system. The key, as both of us have been teaching for many years, is that everything the users get must work together to do one thing—help the users accomplish their work.

Categorizing support by its distance from the work

What Gery has brought to the table in promoting EPSS is the notion that the best support is most closely linked to the users' work (Gery 1991). Gery divides support into three categories:

- external, that is, manuals, classroom training, stand-alone computer-based training, help desks, and other resources that are not connected to the interface; these are in the outer two circles (6 and 7) of figure 14-1.

- extrinsic or linked, that is, online help, cue cards, coaches, and other aids that are connected to the interface but called up as separate entities; these are the middle circles (4 and 5) of figure 14-1.

- intrinsic or embedded, that is, part of the interface, such as menus, icons, screens, dialogs, wizards, and agents; these are the first three circles (1, 2, and 3) of figure 14-1.

Gery says that the goal in performance-centered design is that 80% of the support should be intrinsic to the application, available through the interface, and so tightly integrated that the user cannot distinguish between support and interface. What an EPSS does is push us to meld interface and support so that the application supports the work directly.

Striving to bring support directly into the interface

Designers have in fact been bringing more support into the interface as graphical user interfaces have made it easier to do. Once upon a time, users had to go to paper manuals to see the list of options for a field. Later they could find the options online in help, but the help took over the entire screen, so they had to remember or write down the option they wanted and then go back to the data screen to enter it. Today, they can have a pull-down list and can select the option as part of the interface. That's a form of EPSS. Users just see it as part of the work; they don't even think of it as support.

The focus of work on EPSS has been not just to move support like field options into the interface, but to turn what has more traditionally been documentation and training into interface. At first the examples were to make what might have been a set of manuals and workbooks into online tools and templates that were suggested by the application and made available at the moment they were needed.

Making application and support a seamless whole

More recently, work on EPSS has been to embed the performance support so deeply into the software that it is seamless. As Barry Raybould (1996) writes, "In an embedded [E]PSS, a software application becomes the EPSS. There is no distinction between the performance support system and the software application. The software interface is designed in such a way that it provides the necessary guidance through the work tasks and delivers the appropriate information and advice when, where, and how the worker needs it."

For example, an application with an EPSS would present the process to the user step by step, would provide advice if needed at each step, and would include contingency messages, such as telling customer service representatives as soon as they enter a certain zip code that delivery to that zip code requires an extra day. An application with an EPSS might provide all sorts of analytical and information tools to a clerk who is trying to help a client make a decision about benefits in the context of the client's particular benefits package. Based on information in the computer about the client's package, the application would suggest questions for the clerk to ask and provide ideas of what to recommend based on the answers from the client (Gery 1997b).

To create an application with that much support built in requires

- a deep understanding of the work

- a deep understanding of the users and their need for knowledge at specific points in the process

- a knowledge base of the contingency rules and of the questions users have and the answers they need and of when in the work those questions arise

- close collaboration between support designer and software designer

The benefits of considering the work as a whole and thus building support into the interface design are (1) being able to eliminate much of the traditional documentation and training and (2) having users be able to work efficiently and productively immediately. User and task analysis are vital components of that type of interface design.

What about the Web?

The Web is a medium, not a structure. You can have books on the Web. You can have help on the Web. You can have forms on the Web. You can have software applications on the Web. Just like books and help and forms and software in any medium, every Web site and every Web page has users who are doing tasks in a particular environment. And every Web site and Web page has an interface. So everything we've been saying in this book applies to Web design and development.

Some people are not sure whether Web sites are software or documentation. As we said at the beginning of the chapter, in some sense it doesn't matter, because the issues in interface design and document design are the same: who are the users, what do they come to the site to do, how do they use the site to meet their goals, how do they navigate, what words do they use when they search, how does the layout help or hinder them in accomplishing their goals.

When we are asked to get involved in Web development projects, we both often feel as if we have "deja vu all over again." We're back where we were years ago in software and documentation projects. It is the technology of the Web that gets people excited, and everyone defers to the technology experts who may know little about the users, the company's purposes in having a Web site, how people will use the Web site, or the skills needed to create a usable navigation system and interface.

Web site design and development need exactly the same combination of skills as any other design and development project: usability specialists to do user and task analysis and iterative usability evaluations, document design and technical communication specialists to create useful layouts and provide clear writing, graphic artists because it is a very visual medium, subject matter specialists to check that the content is accurate, and technology specialists (developers) if more elaborate programming than HTML scripting is required. In fact, because so many Web sites are primarily information, documentation, training, or forms, skills in document design, technical communication, instructional design, or training are of paramount importance.

Web site design and development also need exactly the same process as any other type of document or application. Too many Web sites are developed the way that documents used to be written, that is, with attention only to the information and not to the users. Both research and experience have long shown us that successful documents require planning, analysis, organization, and careful thought about content before writing. Figure 14-7 is Ginny's model of the process of preparing successful documents.

We often hear that the time scale of Web development projects is so rapid that there is no time for planning, analysis, or evaluation. Our answer is that you can't afford not to at least think about who will use it; whether they will be browsing, searching, filling out forms, or using it in other ways; how they will navigate through it; what words will work for them; and so on. You can do user and task analysis before you design. You can go out and watch users working with the Web with other similar sites before you build yours. You can watch them work with similar information in other media. You can find out about the environment in which they work and the technology they have.

Here are just two Web design situations and the questions to think about. What similar questions should you be asking for your Web project?

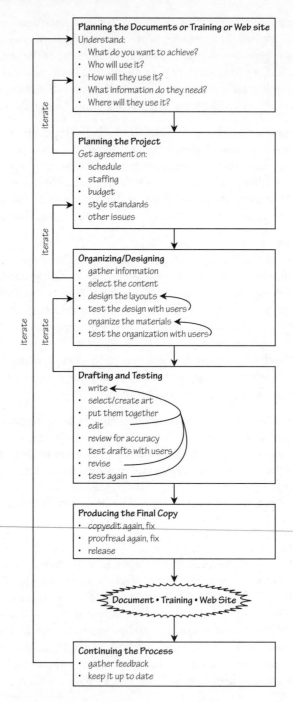

Figure 14-7 Process model of creating successful documents applies just as much to Web sites as to any document (developed by Redish).

- If you are making what used to be embedded help files into an intranet, have you considered users who telecommute? Will what used to be available on their own hard disks now be available only over a modem? Will the company pay to have dedicated phone lines installed in their homes and give them extremely high-speed modems? If not, will they stop using the help, and what will be the consequences?

- If you are planning to deliver a Web-based application to customers, have you found out whether customers in the market niche you are targeting have Web access? Do you know what types of computers they have? What speed their modems are? What browsers they use? Are you assuming the customers will upgrade their systems to match the technology you are using for your Web application? Does past experience indicate that this is a valid assumption in your market?

You can have users help you develop navigation hierarchies using the techniques described in chapter 13, such as card sorting, icon recognition testing, and usability evaluations when you have only the headings and navigation buttons with no other content. You can do rapid iterative evaluations with Web sites on the Web itself. You can even reach users globally on the Web.

There is a great deal you can do to focus on users and usability with the Web. You just have to do it.

What about computer-based and Web-based training?

Much interactive multimedia training that has been delivered through CD-ROM is moving onto the Internet or onto intranets. CD-ROM has the advantage of providing an inexpensive delivery mechanism that can be rich in video, audio, animation, and interactivity to enhance the learners' experience. Web-based training provides ease of access to training but does not yet have the bandwidth to enable the richness of media or interactivity now provided on CD-ROM. Much of the promise of Web-based training will have to wait for improvements in technology.

In either case, however, instructional designers must be careful to balance an understanding of what will be effective in addressing the learners' need against what will be the most clever use of the new technology. Too often we find computer- and Web-based training that contains all the latest technical tricks but fails to take into account the learning needs of the users.

User and task analysis, the front-end analysis of traditional instructional design, should not be neglected just because we can deliver an exciting special effect. As in any other software development activity, without a clear understanding of users' needs and learning styles, all we will end up with is clever programming. It seems as if many organizations choose to ignore everything they know about instructional design when they are offered glitz.

To develop sound instruction, whether delivered in the classroom or electronically, we must first know who our users are, what tasks they need to learn to perform, and what environments will make learning and doing a challenge. With these foundations in place, we will be able to produce training opportunities that will please both the learner and the learner's organization.

Summary

Throughout this chapter and throughout this book, we have emphasized the importance of using interfaces, documentation, and training to enhance human performance and productivity. If products are easy to use and reasonable to learn, people are happier about using them in their jobs and in their homes. Well-designed products make people feel productive—make people feel that they can get something done in a reasonable amount of time with a reasonable amount of effort. The product not only doesn't get in the way, it actually enhances the quality of the task and supports the values that the users bring to the task. People get something done, and they might actually have fun doing it.

Not only does good design make work and home more pleasant, even in the midst of constantly changing technology, it is also good for business. When companies find that software and hardware products work well for employees, they gain in terms of increased productivity, fewer mistakes, less training, and less reliance on various means of support.

To achieve this quality of design requires a user-centric point of view. It means that we as designers get out into the users' world and appreciate what it is like to be one of them. It means that we as designers become excellent observers, good at probing for more understanding and listening actively to what users are trying to tell us about themselves. It means developing considerable empathy for users and understanding what it must feel like to use products that don't make sense.

Good design happens when we include users in the design process: through visiting them where they work and live, encouraging them to participate in interactive design sessions, and working with them through an iterative design process.

References cited in the chapter

Boggan, Scott, Farkas, David, and Welinske, Joe, *Developing Online Help for Windows 95*, Boston, MA: International Thompson Computer Press, 1996.

Brockman, R. John, *Writing Better Computer User Documentation: From Paper to Hypertext,* version 2.0, NY: John Wiley & Sons, 1990.

Carroll, John M., Ed., *Minimalism Since the Nurnberg Funnel,* Cambride, MA: MIT Press in cooperation with the Society for Technical Communication, 1998.

Carroll, John M., *The Nurnberg Funnel: Designing Minimalist Instruction for Practical Computer Skill,* Cambridge, MA: MIT Press, 1990.

Carroll, John M. and Van der Meij, Hans, Ten misconceptions about minimalism, *IEEE transactions on Professional Communication,* June 1996: 72–86.

Clark, Ruth Colvin, *Developing Technical Training,* Reading, MA: Addison-Wesley, 1989.

Gery, Gloria, Traditional vs. performance centered design, available at www.epss.com/lb/artonlin/articles/gg1.htm, 1997a.

Gery, Gloria, Beyond the usual suspects: Defining impacts of performance support, *Proceedings of the Softbank's Interactive'97 Conference & Expo,* 1, Denver, CO, June 1997b: 235–240.

Gery, Gloria, *Electronic Performance Support Systems,* Tolland: MA: Gery Performance Press, 1991.

Hackos, JoAnn T., Choosing a minimalist approach for expert users, in *Minimalism Since the Nurnberg Funnel,* edited by John M. Carroll, Cambridge, MA: MIT Press in cooperation with the Society for Technical Communication, 1998, 149–178.

Hackos, JoAnn T., *Managing your Documentation Projects,* NY: John Wiley & Sons, 1994.

Hackos, JoAnn T. and Stevens, Dawn M., *Standards for Online Communication,* NY: John Wiley & Sons, 1997.

Horton, William K., *Designing & Writing Online Documentation: Hypermedia for Self-Supporting Products,* 2nd ed., NY: John Wiley & Sons, 1994.

Price, Jonathan and Korman, Henry, *How to Communicate Technical Information: A Handbook of Software and Hardware Documentation,* Redwood City, CA: Benjamin/Cummings, 1993.

Rantzer, Martin, Mind the gap: Surviving the dangers of user interface design, in *User Interface Design: Bridging the Gap from User Requirements to Design,* edited by Larry E. Wood, Boca Raton, FL: CRC Press, 1998, 153–185.

Rantzer, Martin, The Delta method—A way to introduce usability, in *Field Methods Casebook for Software Design,* edited by Dennis Wixon and Judith Ramey, NY: John Wiley & Sons, 1996, 91–112.

Raybould, Barry, Two flavors of EPSS, *Technical & Skills Training,* February/March 1996, excerpt available on the Web at www.goparagon.com/pt07003.htm.

Redish, Janice C., Minimalism in technical communication: Some issues to consider, in *Minimalism Since the Nurnberg Funnel,* edited by John M. Carroll, Cambridge, MA: MIT Press in cooperation with the Society for Technical Communication, 1998, 219–245.)

Redish, Janice C., Applying research to practice: Helping users find what they need, available on the Web at www2.ari.net/redish, 1997.

Redish, Janice C., Are we really entering a post-usability era?, *The Journal of Computer Documentation*, March 1995: 18–24.

Redish, Janice C., Understanding readers, in *Techniques for Technical Communicators*, edited by Carol M. Barnum and Saul Carliner, NY: Macmillan, 1993, 14–41.

Redish, Janice C., Reading to learn to do, *The Technical Writing Teacher*, xv (3), Fall 1988: 223–233. Reprinted in *IEEE Transactions on Professional Communication*, 32 (4), December 1989: 289–293.

Schriver, Karen A., *Dynamics in Document Design*, NY: John Wiley & Sons, 1997.

Sticht, Tom, Understanding readers and their uses of texts, in *Designing Usable Texts*, edited by Thomas M. Duffy and Robert Waller, Orlando, FL: Academic Press, 1985

Van der Meij, Hans, A critical assessment of the Minimalist approach to documentation, *Proceedings of the SIGDOC Conference*, NY, ACM, 1992: 7–17.

Van der Meij, Hans and Carroll, John M., Principles and heuristics for designing minimalist instruction, *Technical Communication: Journal of the Society for Technical Communication*, 42 (2), May 1995: 243–261.

Wright, Patricia, Writing technical information, in *Review of Research in Education*, 14, edited by E. Z. Rothkopf, Washington, DC: American Educational Research Association, 1987, 327–385.

Wright, Patricia, Creighton, P., and Threlfall, S. M., Some factors determining when instructions will be read, *Ergonomics*, 25 (3), 1982: 225–237.

Other books and articles for further reading

Bain, Steve and Gray, Dan, *Looking Good Online: The Ultimate Resource for Creating Effective Web Designs*, Research Triangle Park, NC: Ventana Communications Group, 1996.

Gagne, Robert M., Briggs, Leslie J. Briggs, and Wagner, Walter W., *Principles of Instructional Design*, Fort Worth, TX: Holt Rinehart & Winston, 1988.

Horton, William K., *The Icon Book: Visual Symbols for Computer Systems and Documentation*, NY: John Wiley & Sons, 1994.

Horton, William, Taylor, Lee, Ignacio, Arthur, and Hoft, Nancy L., *The Web Page Design Cookbook: All the Ingredients You Need to Create 5-Star Web Pages*, NY: John Wiley & Sons, 1996.

Morris, Mary, *Web Page Design: A Different Multimedia*, Upper Saddle River: NJ: Prentice Hall, 1996.

Pfaffenberger, Bryan, *The Elements of Hypertext Style*, Boston: MA: AP Professional, 1997.

Sano, Darrell, *Designing Large-Scale Web Sites: A Visual Design Methodology*, NY: John Wiley & Sons, 1996.

Zemke, Ron and Kramlinger, Tom, *Figuring Things Out: A Trainer's Guide to Needs and Task Analysis*, Reading, MA: Addison-Wesley, 1982.

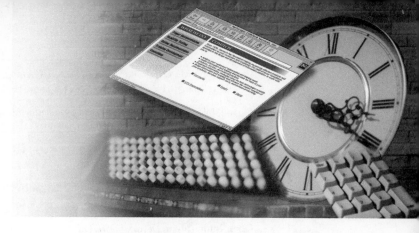

Bibliography

Andrews, Deborah C., *International Dimensions of Technical Communication,* Arlington, VA: Society for Technical Communication, 1996.

Bain, Steve and Gray, Dan, *Looking Good Online: The Ultimate Resource for Creating Effective Web Designs,* Research Triangle Park, NC: Ventana Communications Group, 1996.

Beabes, Minette A. and Flanders, Alicia, Experiences with using contextual inquiry to design information, *Technical Communication,* 42 (3), August 1995: 409–420.

Benyon, David, The role of task analysis in systems design, *Interacting with Computers,* 4 (1), April 1992: 102–123.

Beyer, Hugh and Holtzblatt, Karen, *Contextual Design: Defining Customer-Centered Systems,* San Francisco: Morgan Kaufmann Publishers, 1997.

Bias, Randolph G. and Mayhew, Deborah J., Eds., *Cost-Justifying Usability,* San Diego, CA: Academic Press, 1994.

Boggan, Scott, Farkas, David, and Welinske, Joe, *Developing Online Help for Windows 95,* Boston: International Thompson Computer Press, 1996.

Branaghan, Russ, Five simple principles of iterative design, *Common Ground,* 5 (3), September/ October 1995: 3,12–13.

Brockman, R. John, *Writing Better Computer User Documentation: From Paper to Hypertext,* version 2.0, New York: John Wiley & Sons, 1990.

Butler, Mary Beth and Tahir, Marie, Bringing the users' work to us: Usability roundtables of Lotus Development, in *Field Methods Casebook for Software Design,* edited by Dennis Wixon and Judith Ramey, New York: John Wiley & Sons, 1996, 249–267.

Carroll, John M., Ed., *Minimalism Since the Nurnberg Funnel,* Cambridge, MA: MIT Press in cooperation with the Society for Technical Communication, 1998.

Carroll, John M., Ed., *Scenario-Based Design: Envisioning Work and Technology in System Development*, New York: John Wiley & Sons, 1995.

Carroll, John M., *The Nurnberg Funnel: Designing Minimalist Instruction for Practical Computer Skill*, Cambridge, MA: MIT Press, 1990.

Carroll, John M., Ed., *Interfacing Thought: Cognitive Aspects of Human-Computer Interaction*, Cambridge, MA: MIT Press, 1987.

Carroll, John M. and Van der Meij, Hans, Ten misconceptions about minimalism, *IEEE transactions on Professional Communication*, June 1996: 72–86.

Clark, Ruth Colvin, *Developing Technical Training*, Reading, MA: Addison-Wesley, 1989.

Collins, Dave, *Designing Object-Oriented User Interfaces*, Redwood City, CA: Benjamin/Cummings, 1995.

Cooper, Alan, *About Face: The Essentials of User Interface Design*, Foster City, CA: IDG Book Worldwide, 1995.

Dayton, Tom, McFarland, Al, and Kramer, Joseph, Bridging user needs to object oriented GUI prototype via task object design, in *User Interface Design: Bridging the Gap from User Requirements to Design*, edited by Larry E. Wood, Boca Raton, FL: CRC Press, 1998, 15–56.

Del Galdo, Elisa M. and Nielsen, Jakob, Eds., *International User Interfaces*, New York: John Wiley & Sons, 1996.

Desurvire, Heather W., Faster; cheaper!! Are usability inspection methods as effective as empirical testing?, in *Usability Inspection Methods*, edited by Jakob Nielsen and Robert L. Mack, New York: John Wiley & Sons, 1994, 173–202.

Diaper, Dan and Addison, Mark, Task analysis and systems analysis for software development, *Interacting with Computers*, 4 (1), April 1992: 124–139.

Dray, Susan and Mrazek, Deborah, A day in the life of a family: An international ethnographic study, in *Field Methods Casebook for Software Design*, edited by Dennis Wixon and Judith Ramey, New York: John Wiley & Sons, 1996a, 145–156.

Dray, Susan and Mrazek, Deborah, A day in the life: Studying context across cultures, in *International User Interfaces*, edited by Elisa M. del Galdo and Jakob Nielsen, New York: John Wiley & Sons, 1996b, 242–256.

Dreyfus, Hubert L. and Dreyfus, Stuart E., *Minds over Machines*, New York: Macmillan, 1986.

Dubberly, Hugh and Doris, Mitch, *The Knowledge Navigator*, video, Apple Computer, 1987.

Dumas, Joseph S. and Redish, Janice C., *A Practical Guide to Usability Testing*, Greenwich, CT: Ablex, 1993.

Ehn, Pelle, Scandinavian design: On participation and skill, in *Participatory Design: Principles and Practices*, edited by Douglas Schuler and Aki Namioka, Hillsdale, NJ: Lawrence Erlbaum Associates, 1993, 41–77.

Ehn, Pelle, *Work-Oriented Design of Computer Artifacts*, Hillsdale, NJ: Lawrence Erlbaum Associates, 1989.

Ellison, Matthew, Help in the UK, *Proceedings of the WinHelp 97 Conference*, Seattle, WA, 1997.

Fisher, Phil and Sless, David, Information design methods and productivity in the insurance industry, *Information Design Journal*, 6(2), 1990: 103–129.

Flanagan, John C., The critical incident technique, *Psychological Bulletin*, 51 (4), 1954: 327–358.

Forslund, Charlene J., Analyzing pictorial messages across cultures, in *International Dimensions of Technical Communication*, edited by Deborah C. Andrews, Arlington, VA: Society for Technical Communication, 1996, 45–58

Gagne, Robert M., Briggs, Leslie J., and Wagner, Walter W., *Principles of Instructional Design*, Fort Worth, TX: Holt, Rinehart, & Winston, 1988.

Galitz, Wilbert O., *The Essential Guide to User Interface Design*, New York: John Wiley & Sons, 1997.

Gery, Gloria, Traditional vs. performance centered design, available at www.epss.com/lb/artonlin/articles/gg1.htm, 1997a.

Gery, Gloria, Beyond the usual suspects: Defining impacts of performance support, *Proceedings of the Softbank's Interactive'97 Conference & Expo*, 1, Denver, CO, June 1997b: 235–240.

Gery, Gloria, *Electronic Performance Support Systems*, Tolland, MA: Gery Performance Press, 1991.

Gibbs, W. Wayt, Taking computers to task, *Scientific American*, 277 (1), July 1997: 82–89.

Gould, John D., Boies, Stephen J., Levy, Stephen, Richards, John T., and Schoonard, Jim, The 1984 Olympic messaging system — A test of behavioral principles of system design, *Communications of the ACM*, 30, 1987, 758–769.

Grudin, Jonathan, Obstacles to participatory design in large product development organizations, in *Participatory Design: Principles and Practices*, edited by Douglas Schuler and Aki Namioka, Hillsdale, NJ: Lawrence Erlbaum Associates, 1993, 99–119.

Grudin, Jonathan, Systematic sources of suboptimal interface design in large product development organizations, *Human-Computer Interaction*, 6 (2), 1991: 147–196.

Hackos, JoAnn T., Choosing a minimalist approach for expert users, in *Minimalism Since the Nurnberg Funnel*, edited by John M. Carroll, Cambridge, MA: MIT Press in cooperation with the Society for Technical Communication, 1998, 149–178.

Hackos, JoAnn T., Finding out what users need and giving it to them: A case-study at Federal Express, *Technical Communication*, 42 (2), 1995: 322–327.

Hackos, JoAnn T., *Managing your Documentation Projects*, New York: John Wiley & Sons, 1994.

Hackos, JoAnn T., Elser, Arthur, and Hammar, Molly, Customer partnering: Data gathering for complex on-line documentation, *IEEE Transactions on Professional Communication*, 40 (2), June 1997, 102–110.

Hackos, JoAnn T. and Stevens, Dawn M., *Standards for Online Communications*, New York: John Wiley & Sons, 1997.

Hiser Group, *The Element Tool Kit*, Prahan, Victoria, Australia, 1997.

Hoft, Nancy, *International Technical Information*, New York: John Wiley & Sons, 1995.

Holtzblatt, Karen and Beyer, Hugh, Contextual design, principles and practice, in *Field Methods Casebook for Software Design*, edited by Dennis Wixon and Judith Ramey, New York: John Wiley & Sons, 1996, 301–333.

Holtzblatt, Karen and Beyer, Hugh, Making customer-centered design work for teams, *Communications of the ACM*, 36(10), October 1993: 93–103.

Holtzblatt, Karen and Jones, Sandra, Contextual inquiry: A participatory technique for system design, in *Participatory Design: Principles and Practices*, edited by Douglas Schuler and Aki Namioka, Hillsdale, NJ: Lawrence Erlbaum Associates, 1993, 177–210.

Horton, William K., *Designing & Writing Online Documentation: Hypermedia for Self-Supporting Products*, 2nd ed., New York: John Wiley & Sons, 1994.

Horton, William K., *The Icon Book: Visual Symbols for Computer Systems and Documentation*, New York: John Wiley & Sons, 1994.

Horton, William, Taylor, Lee, Ignacio, Arthur, and Hoft, Nancy L., *The Web Page Design Cookbook: All the Ingredients You Need to Create 5-Star Web Pages*, New York: John Wiley & Sons, 1996.

Howlett, Virginia, *Visual Interface Design for Windows: Effective User Interfaces for Windows 95, Windows NT and Windows 3.1*, New York: John Wiley & Sons, 1996.

Ito, Masao and Nakakoji, Kumiyo, Impact of culture on user interface design, in *International User Interfaces*, edited by Elisa M. del Galdo and Jakob Nielsen, New York: John Wiley & Sons, 1996, 105–126.

Jacobson, Ivar, The use-case construct in object-oriented software engineering, in *Scenario-Based Design: Envisioning Work and Technology in System Development*, edited by John M. Carroll, New York: John Wiley & Sons, 1995, 309–336.

Jonassen, David H, Hannum, Wallace H., and Tessmer, Martin, *Handbook of Task Analysis Procedures*, New York: Praeger, 1989.

Jones, Scott, Kennelly, Cynthia, Mueller, Claudia, Sweezy, Marcia, Thomas, Bill, and Velez, Lydia, *Developing International User Information*, Bedford, MA: Digital Equipment Corporation, 1992.

Juhl, Diane, Using field-oriented design techniques to develop consumer software products, in *Field Methods Casebook for Software Design*, edited by Dennis Wixon and Judith Ramey, New York: John Wiley & Sons, 1996, 215–228.

Karat, John and Bennett, John L., Working within the design process: Supporting effective and efficient design, in *Designing Interaction: Psychology at the Human-Computer Interface*, edited by John M. Carroll, Cambridge, MA: Cambridge University Press, 1991, 269–285.

Katel, Peter, Bordering on chaos, *Wired Magazine*, July 1997: 98–107.

Kirwan, Barry and Ainsworth, Les K., *A Guide to Task Analysis*, London: Taylor & Francis, 1992.

Lakoff, George and Johnson, Mark, *Metaphors We Live By*, Chicago: University of Chicago Press, 1980.

Landauer, Thomas, *The Trouble with Computers*, Cambridge, MA: MIT Press, 1995.

Mandel, Theo, *The Elements of User Interface Design,* New York: John Wiley & Sons, 1997.

Mayhew, Deborah J., *Principles and Guidelines in Software User Interface Design*, Englewood Cliffs, NJ: Prentice-Hall, 1992.

Means, Barbara, Cognitive task analysis as a basis for instructional design, in *Cognitive Science Foundations of Instruction*, edited by Mitchell Rabinowitz, Hillsdale, NJ: Lawrence Erlbaum Associates, 1993, 97–118.

Mirel, Barbara, Minimalism for complex tasks, in *Minimalism Since the Nurnberg Funnel*, edited by John M. Carroll, Cambridge, MA: MIT Press in cooperation with the Society for Technical Communication, 1998.

Mitropoulos-Rundus, David and Muszak, Jerry, Criteria for determining if consumer "in-home" usability testing is feasible for your product, *Common Ground*, 7 (1), January 1997a: 10–12.

Mitropoulos-Rundus, David and Muszak, Jerry, How to design and conduct a consumer in-home usability test, *Common Ground*, 7 (2), April 1997b: 1, 8–14, 19.

Moore, Geoffrey, *Crossing the Chasm: Marketing and Selling High-Tech Products to Mainstream Customers*, New York: Harper Business, 1995.

Morris, Mary, *Web Page Design: A Different Multimedia*, Upper Saddle River: NJ: Prentice-Hall, 1996.

Muller, Michael J., PICTIVE: Democratizing the dynamics of the design session, in *Participatory Design: Principles and Practices*, edited by Douglas Schuler and Aki Namioka, Hillsdale, NJ: Lawrence Erlbaum Associates, 1993, 211–237.

Muller, Michael J., Retrospective on a year of participatory design using the PICTIVE technique, *Proceedings of CHI'92*, Monterey, CA, ACM, 1992: 455–462.

Muller, Michael J., PICTIVE - An exploration in participatory design, *Proceedings of CHI'91*, New Orleans, LA, ACM, 1991: 225–231.

Muller, Michael J., and Carr, Rebecca, Using the CARD and PICTIVE participatory design methods for collaborative analysis, in *Field Methods Casebook for Software Design*, edited by Dennis Wixon and Judith Ramey, New York: John Wiley & Sons, 1996, 17–34.

Muller, Michael J., Carr, Rebecca, Ashworth, Catherine, Diekmann, Barbara, Wharton, Cathleen, Eickstaedt, Cherie, and Clonts, Joan, Telephone operators as knowledge workers: Consultants who meet customer needs, *Proceedings of CHI'95*, Denver, CO, ACM, 1995: 130–137.

Muller, Michael J., and Kuhn, Sarah, Eds., Special issue on participatory design, *Communications of the ACM*, 36 (4), June 1993.

Muller, Michael J., Tudor, Leslie G., Wildman, Daniel M., White, Ellen A., Root, Robert W., Dayton, Tom, Carr, Rebecca, Diekmann, Barbara, and Dykstra-Erickson, Elizabeth, Bifocal tools for scenarios and representations in participatory activities with users, in *Scenario-Based Design*, edited by John M. Carroll, New York: John Wiley & Sons, 1995, 135–163.

Nielsen, Jakob, *Usability Engineering*, San Diego, CA: Academic Press, 1993.

Nielsen, Jakob and Mack, Robert L., Eds., *Usability Inspection Methods*, New York: John Wiley & Sons, 1994.

Nielsen, Jakob and Molich, Rudy, Heuristic evaluation of user interfaces, *Proceedings of the ACM SIGCHI Conference*, Seattle, WA, 1990: 249–256.

Norman, Donald A., *The Design of Everyday Things*, NY: Doubleday, 1988 (originally published as *The Psychology of Everyday Things*, NY: Basic Books).

Pfaffenberger, Bryan, *The Elements of Hypertext Style*, Boston: AP Professional, 1997.

Prail, Amanda, Suggestions on collecting observational data, *Common Ground*, 1 (2), 1991: 3–4.

Pressman, Roger S., *Software Engineering: A Practitioner's Approach*, New York: McGraw-Hill, 1992.

Price, Jonathan and Korman, Henry, *How to Communicate Technical Information: A Handbook of Software and Hardware Documentation*, Redwood City, CA: Benjamin/Cummings, 1993.

Ramey, Judith, Rowberg, Alan H., and Robinson, Carol, Adaption of an Ethnographic Method for investigation of the task domain in diagnostic radiology, in *Field Methods Casebook for Software Design*, edited by Dennis Wixon and Judith Ramey, New York: John Wiley & Sons, 1996, 1–15.

Rantzer, Martin, Mind the gap: Surviving the dangers of user interface design, in *User Interface Design: Bridging the Gap from User Requirements to Design*, edited by Larry E. Wood, Boca Raton, FL: CRC Press, 1998, 153–185.

Rantzer, Martin, The delta method - A way to introduce usability, in *Field Methods Casebook for Software Design*, edited by Dennis Wixon and Judith Ramey, New York: John Wiley & Sons, 1996, 91–112.

Raven, Mary Elizabeth and Flanders, Alicia, Using contextual inquiry to learn about your audiences, **The Journal of Computer Documentation*, 20 (1), February 1996: 1–13.

Raybould, Barry, Two flavors of EPSS, *Technical & Skills Training*, February/March 1996, excerpt available on the Web at www.goparagon.com/pt07003.htm.

Redish, Janice C., Minimalism in technical communication: Some issues to consider, in *Minimalism Since the Nurnberg Funnel*, edited by John M. Carroll, Cambridge, MA: MIT Press in cooperation with the Society for Technical Communication, 1998, 219–245.

Redish, Janice C., Applying research to practice: Helping users find what they need, available on the Web at www2.ari.net/redish, 1997.

Redish, Janice C., Are we really entering a post-usability era?, **The Journal of Computer Documentation*, March 1995: 18–24.

Redish, Janice C., Understanding readers, in *Techniques for Technical Communicators*, edited by Carol M. Barnum and Saul Carliner, New York: Macmillan, 1993, 14–41.

Redish, Janice C., Reading to learn to do, *The Technical Writing Teacher*, xv (3), Fall 1988: 223–233. Reprinted in *IEEE Transactions on Professional Communication*, 32 (4), December 1989: 289–293.

Redish, Janice C. and James, Janice, Going to the users: How to set up, conduct, and use a user and task analysis for (re)designing a major computer system, *Proceedings of the Fifth Annual Conference UPA '96*, Dallas, TX, Usability Professionals' Association, 1996.

Redish, Janice C. and Ramey, Judith A., Special section: Measuring the value added by professional technical communicators, *Technical Communication*, 42(1), February 1995, 23–83.

Rubin, Jeffrey, *Handbook of Usability Testing*, New York: John Wiley & Sons, 1994.

Rubinstein, Richard and Hersh, Harry, *The Human Factor: Designing Computer Systems for People*, Bedford, MA: Digital Equipment Corporation, 1984.

Rudd, Jim, Stern, Kenneth R., and Isensee, Scott, Low vs. high fidelity prototyping debate, *Interactions*, 3 (1), January 1996: 76–85.

Salvador, Anthony C. and Scholtz, Jean C., Systematic creativity in software user interface design, in *Engineering for Human-Computer Interaction*, edited by Leonard J. Bass and Claus Unger, New York: Chapman & Hall, 1995, 307–332.

Sano, Darrell, *Designing Large-Scale Web Sites: A Visual Design Methodology*, New York: John Wiley & Sons, 1996.

Scholtz, Jean C. and Salvador, Anthony C., Systematic creativity: A bridge for the gaps in the software development process, in *User Interface Design: Bridging the Gap from User Requirements to Design*, edited by Larry E. Wood, Boca Raton, FL: CRC Press, 1998, 217–247.

Schriver, Karen A., *Dynamics in Document Design*, New York: John Wiley & Sons, 1997.

Schriver, Karen A., Plain language through protocol-aided revision, in *Plain Language: Principles and Practice*, edited by Erwin R. Steinberg, Detroit, MI: Wayne State University Press, 1991, 148–172.

Schuler, Douglas and Namioka, Aki, Eds., *Participatory Design: Principles and Practices*, Hillsdale, NJ: Lawrence Erlbaum Associates, 1993.

Shneiderman, Ben, *Designing the User Interface: Strategies for Human-Computer Interaction*, 3rd ed., Reading, MA: Addison-Wesley, 1998.

Simon, Herbert A., *Administrative Behavior*, NY: The Free Press, 3rd edition, 1976.

Simpson, Kevin T., The UI war room and design prism: A user interface design approach from multiple perspectives, in *User Interface Design: Bridging the Gap from User Requirements to Design*, edited by Larry E. Wood, Boca Raton, FL: CRC Press, 1998, 249–280.

Stevens, Albert L. and Gentner, Dedre, Eds., *Mental Models*, Hillsdale, NJ: Lawrence Erlbaum Associates, 1983.

Sticht, Tom, Understanding readers and their uses of texts, in *Designing Usable Texts*, edited by Thomas M. Duffy and Robert Waller, Orlando, FL: Academic Press, 1985.

Tannen, Deborah, *That's Not What I Meant!: How Conversational Style Makes or Breaks Your Relations with Others*, New York: Morrow, 1986.

Tognazzini, Bruce, *TOG on Software Design*, Reading, MA: Addison-Wesley, 1996.

Tognazzini, Bruce, *TOG on Interface*, Reading, MA: Addison-Wesley, 1992.

Tudor, Leslie G., Muller, Michael J., Dayton, Tom, and Root, Robert W., A participatory design technique for high-level task analysis, critique, and redesign: The CARD method, *Proceedings of the Human Factors and Ergonomics Society*, Seattle, WA, 1993: 295–299.

Van der Meij, Hans, A critical assessment of the Minimalist approach to documentation, *Proceedings of the SIGDOC Conference*, New York, ACM, 1992: 7–17.

Van der Meij, Hans and Carroll, John M., Principles and heuristics for designing minimalist instruction, *Technical Communication: Journal of the Society for Technical Communication*, 42 (2), May 1995, 243–261.

Virzi, Robert, Refining the test phase of usability evaluation: How many subjects is enough, *Human Factors*, 34(4), August 1992, 457–468.

Weinschenk, Susan and Yeo, Sarah C., *Guidelines for Enterprise-Wide GUI Design*, New York: John Wiley & Sons, 1995.

Whiteside, John, Bennett, John, and Holtzblatt, Karen, Usability engineering: Our experience and evaluation, in *Handbook of Human Computer Interaction*, edited by Martin Helander, New York: Elsevier Science, 1988, 791–817.

Wixon, Dennis and Jones, Sandy, Usability for fun and profit: A case study of the design of DEC rally version 2, in *Human-Computer Interface Design: Success Stories, Emerging Methods, and Real-World Context*, edited by Marianne Rudisill, Clayton Lewis, Peter B. Polson, Timothy D. McKay, San Francisco: Morgan Kaufmann Publishers, 1996, 3–35.

Wixon, Dennis, Pietras, Christine M., Huntwork, Paul K., and Muzzey, Douglas W., Changing the rules: A pragmatic approach to product development, in *Field Methods Casebook for Software Design*, edited by Dennis Wixon and Judith Ramey, New York: John Wiley & Sons, 1996, 57–89.

Wixon, Dennis and Ramey, Judith, Eds., *Field Methods Casebook for Software Design*, New York: John Wiley & Sons, 1996.

Wood, Larry E., Ed., *User Interface Design: Bridging the Gap from User Requirements to Design*, Boca Raton, FL: CRC Press, 1998.

Wood, Larry E., The ethnographic interview in user-centered work/task analysis, in *Field Methods Casebook for Software Design*, edited by Dennis Wixon and Judith Ramey, New York: John Wiley & Sons, 1996, 35–56.

Wright, Patricia, Writing technical information, *Review of Research in Education*, 14, edited by E. Z. Rothkopf, Washington, DC: American Educational Research Association, 1987, 327–385.

Wright, Patricia, Creighton, P., and Threlfall, S. M., Some factors determining when instructions will be read, *Ergonomics*, 25 (3), 1982: 225–237.

Zemke, Ron and Kramlinger, Tom, *Figuring Things Out: A Trainer's Guide to Needs and Task Analysis*, Reading, MA: Addison-Wesley, 1982.

APPENDIX A

Template for a site visit plan

Brief introductory paragraph. What is the study about? Include the name of the study or product or project. Include other key points for an executive who might read only this paragraph.

Issues and objectives

Issues
List the questions you want to be able to answer after this study.

Objectives
State what you hope to accomplish with the study. Consider what you want to do with the results of the study—design a new software system, revise an existing system, reduce calls for help, reduce product returns to retail stores, increase productivity of users, etc.

You may want to list only issues or only objectives or both.

Participants

- State how many people you intend to visit in the study. Summarize why you have chosen this number of participants. The details of your participant selection appear below.

- List the characteristics they will all have in common.

- List the characteristics you will vary and the rationale for each. Some examples might be experience on the job (novice, advanced beginners, experts), experience with technology, size of business, or other factors.

- Use a table to show how you will define each group with each variable. (For example, to measure that someone is a novice at the job, you might say "less than one year of experience.")

- Put a number in each cell to represent how many people with that combination of characteristics you want as participants.

Matrix for selecting participants

	Variable one		
Variable two	Define group 1 in variable 1	Define group 2 in variable 1	Define group 3 in variable 1
Define group 1 in variable 2			
Define group 2 in variable 2			
Define group 3 in variable 2			

Locations

- State how many geographic areas you will include in the study.

- If you have chosen them, list them and why you chose them.

- If you have not yet chosen them, list the criteria you will use to choose.

- State how many participants you will visit in each location.

- List any restrictions, concerns, or special features about the locations.

Schedule for the field study project

■ Give the overall time frame of the study. State any constraints on completion (end of fiscal year, prior to a phase review on the project).

■ Give times for major phases and activities during the study. You might include a schedule table or a Gantt chart with dates and milestones.

■ Show these activities (unless they are not relevant to your study):

- finish site visit plan
- organize teams
- select locations
- prepare screening questionnaire
- prepare introductory letter
- prepare demographic questionnaire
- recruit participants
- prepare release forms
- prepare confidentiality agreement
- decide on techniques and activities for each visit
- decide on data collection methods
- arrange for equipment (video, audio, still camera, paper, etc.)
- develop checklists for teams to use when preparing to go to site
- prepare all materials for teams to use on site (observer's notebook)
- make travel arrangements
- train teams
- conduct site visits and write trip reports
- write thank you letters
- analyze data
- prepare report or presentation
- deliver report or presentation

■ Include a calendar schedule that can be filled in as sites are identified and teams are assigned to specific site visits; include travel time on the calendar schedule.

Recruiting

- Name the person(s) or group that will do the recruiting.

- List any help that other people or groups will give. Be explicit about the help so that responsibilities and dependencies are clear.

- Include the screening questionnaire or notes on requirements for the screening questionnaire if it still needs to be developed. When it is developed, it becomes part of the site visit plan.

Data collection techniques and schedule for each site visit

- List the techniques you will use during each visit; if some users of the site visit plan are not familiar with the techniques, you might include brief descriptions.

- List each activity that teams will do on each visit in the order in which you expect them to happen. For each activity, name the technique(s) that the teams will use.

- You might include a schedule of what will happen when in each visit.

Schedule for each site visit:

Time	Activity/data collection technique
_____	Greet manager, review plan for visit
_____	_____
_____	_____
_____	_____
_____	_____
_____	_____
_____	Pack up all equipment and papers
_____	Thank participant(s) and manager, give out gifts, leave

- You might also match activities to issues and objectives so that you show why teams will do each activity and so you are sure that you are gathering information for each issue and objective.

How activities map to issues and objectives:

Issue or objective	Activity/data collection technique
Issue 1	
Objective 1	

Teams

- If the people who will conduct the site visits have been selected, name them.

- If decisions have not been made, explain how they will be selected and paired up.

- Explain the responsibilities of teams, including specifically who will do what and when.

- Explain how teams will be trained.

Materials

- If materials have been developed, list them.

■ If materials still need to be developed, you might use a table like this.

Materials to be developed	Person responsible	Date ready	Reviewer
Screening questionnaire			
Letter of introduction			
Schedule for teams			
Demographic questionnaire			
Release forms			
Observers notebook with:			
Goals and objectives			
Schedule for each visit			
List of activities with guidelines			
Interview protocols for each role			
Copies of forms			
Artifact log			
Site visit report template			

Media

■ List the media you will use.

■ For each medium (video, audio, still camera, paper, laptop), list what part of the visit or which activities it will be used for.

■ List any restrictions, concerns, or special features related to each medium.

■ Indicate who will be responsible for arranging for each medium, knowing how to use it, making sure all the parts of it are ready for each site visit, unpacking and setting it up at the sites, and taking it down and repacking it at the sites.

Data analysis and reporting

■ List the data analysis techniques you will use for each type of data collected or for each activity during the site visit.

■ Give keys to success for each.

How data analysis maps to data collected:

Activity/data collection technique	Analysis techniques to be used

■ Give plans for presenting the data, including audiences, formats, and dates.

Appendixes

■ Include samples of all materials, such as the screening questionnaire, introductory letter, interview protocols, and other parts of the observer's notebook.

■ Include checklists. One checklist you should definitely have is a list of everything that you must have on the site visit. Use the checklist every time a team goes out.

The following is a fairly comprehensive checklist from which you can select what your teams will need.

Check	Supply to be taken
_____	Audio recorder
_____	Cassettes for recorder
_____	Batteries for recorder
_____	Microphone(s), if speaker will be far from audio or video recorder
_____	Extra batteries for microphones; long cords if microphone needs to be plugged in
_____	Laptop with cords and extra battery
_____	Diskettes for backing up files
_____	Small flip top notebooks
_____	Pencils, pens
_____	Portable printer with cords and cable

Check	Supply to be taken
_____	Paper for the portable printer
_____	Folder for each site visit
_____	Copy of letter of introduction that went to that site
_____	Demographic questionnaires that participants have already filled out
_____	Blank demographic questionnaire for any participant lacking a filled out one
_____	Release form for each participant at site (and extras)
_____	Supplies for process flow: poster paper, colored markers, color sticky notes
_____	Observers' notebook with interview protocols for each participant
_____	Other lists, questionnaires, forms, scenarios, props for planned activities
_____	Artifact log (could be a file on the laptop)
_____	Folder to put artifacts in
_____	Still camera
_____	Film for camera
_____	Batteries for camera
_____	Video camera (scan converter, lab in a box or lab in a bag)
_____	Tapes for the video camera (make sure they are the correct speed)
_____	Batteries for the video camera
_____	Power strip
_____	Extension cord
_____	Plugs for type of outlets

APPENDIX B

Resources

The following companies sell equipment for audio and videotaping at user sites and in usability labs. The authors do not endorse any of the companies. They are listed here for your information.

Norm Wilcox Associates, Inc.
Portable usability labs and data logging software
4574 Timbery Court
Jefferson, MD 21755
Phone: 1-888-A-LAB-2-GO
or phone: 301-473-8124
E-mail: alab2go@aol.com

Systems Integration Group
Networked usability, real time remote testing, recording, and distribution
1184-A W. Corporate Dr.
Arlington, TX 76006
Phone: 817-649-0088
Fax: 817-633-5920

Triangle Research Collaborative, Inc.
Multimedia research tools for the professional
100 Park Offices, Suite 115
Research Triangle Park (RTP), NC 27709-2167
Phone: 800-467-9093 or 919-549-9093
Fax: 919-549-0493
E-mail: 73227.3714@compuserve.com

Usability Systems, Inc.
Solutions for creating usable products
1150 Alpha Drive, Suite 100
Alpharetta, GA 30201
Phone: 770-475-4210
E-mail: ed@usablity systems.com
Web: http://www.usabilitylabs.com

APPENDIX C

Guidelines for user-interface design

These guidelines represent a composite of information acquired over the past several years from Apple, Microsoft, Motif (X Windows), and OS/2. We tried to develop guidelines that were standard across platforms rather than platform-specific guidelines. The list is intended to be comprehensive but not exhaustive. You will need to consult the specific guidelines for the platforms you are working with.

You may also want to consult the general guidelines in reviewing your design that are provided by Jakob Nielsen in *Usability Engineering*. See the Bibliography for the details.

Remember that these guidelines must be taken in the context of the rest of the book. Just following guidelines for interface design will not be sufficient to achieve usability. You can produce an interface that follows all the guidelines and still is not fit for your users, their goals and tasks, and their environments. As you review the guidelines and decide how to implement them, keep your users in mind. Remember that you may need to make exceptions to these general guidelines to fit the specific needs of your users. You will also need to test your implementation with your users doing their tasks in their environments.

Menus

These guidelines help designers make choices about the design of interface menus.

Menu bar

- Have you selected which menu items are going to be standard (remain across all applications) items on the menu bar?

- Have you determined which menu items in the menu bar are application specific?

- Do you use constant menu titles and keep the placement of those titles in the menu bar constant?

- Is the menu bar visible at all times?

Menu behavior

- Does your application allow users to see all options at any time and to choose any available option at any time?

- Does your design allow users to view the menu without making a selection?

- Does your application highlight the selected command?

- Are unavailable menu options dimmed out?

- Is the menu hidden but the menu title highlighted while the operation runs?

- Does your application provide the user with feedback while an operation runs?

Menu elements

- Are menu item names chosen according to function, verbs for commands and adjectives for attributes?

- Are item names the word(s) users have for the action?

- Are the menu items grouped logically, based on function and frequency of use?

- Does your application use standard menu dividers to provide stability for the user and to make the items easy to locate?

Characters and text styles in menus

■ Does your design use a standard character to indicate the menu item that is in effect?

■ Does your application distinguish clearly between mutually exclusive attributes (only one item can be in effect at a time) and accumulating (nonexclusive) attribute groups (any number can be in effect at the same time)?

■ Does your application use a standard character to indicate which menu items employ dialog boxes or other input devices to obtain more information from the user before the command executes?

■ Does your design use a standard character and an icon to alert users that an application needs attention, for example, when a command has been interrupted?

■ Are keyboard equivalents used appropriately; for example, are there keyboard equivalents for most, if not all, menu items, especially the most important or most frequently used?

■ Are mnemonic characters used for menu items to accommodate users who do not have a mouse?

■ Do you use a standard text style for menu items to ensure consistency in font choices, capitalization, and other related style issues?

Toggled menu items

■ For toggled menu items, do you provide two different items describing opposite states when possible?

■ If you are using a single toggled menu item and changing its name to indicate opposite states, are the names of the commands unambiguous?

■ Are toggled menu items set off with menu dividers?

Scrolling menus

■ Do you use a symbol to indicate which menus are scrolling menus?

Hierarchical menus

■ Are hierarchical menus used only when there is no space left in the menu bar?

■ Do hierarchical menus, when used, provide a set of attributes rather than commands?

■ Do you use a standard character to indicate which menu is a hierarchical menu?

■ Do you use only one level down in a hierarchical menu?

Pop-up menus

■ Are pop-up menus used to present a list of choices from which the user can make only one selection?

■ Are the selections presented in the pop-up menus appropriate? For example, do you avoid presenting lists of commands in the pop-up menus?

■ Do you make the pop-up menus appear as one object by using the same fonts and keeping the same widths for the closed and open states of the menus?

■ Do you use a standard character to show the current selection? Is the current selection visible in the menu after it closes?

■ When appropriate, are type-in pop-up menus available for users to type a choice not already displayed in a list or to make a selection more quickly?

Tear-off menus and palettes

■ Does your application highlight or outline the current selection in tear-off menus?

■ Does only one copy of a tear-off menu appear on the desktop at a time?

■ Does your application highlight or outline the current selection in a palette?

■ If you include a palette as part of your window, is the palette located so that it does not conflict with the standard window controls?

Windows

These guidelines help designers make choices about the design of interface windows.

Window controls

■ Does your application provide structural components (title bar, size box, close box, zoom box, scroll bars) with which the user controls the window?

- Are the use and location of window controls the same across all applications?

- If you are designing for a color screen, do you use color to enhance the appearance of the window controls?

Utility windows

- Does your application use utility windows to provide users with additional tools or controls that affect the active window?

- Do you use utility windows to present controls only when you cannot use a dialog box or make additions to the window frame?

- Can users open more than one utility window at a time?

- Do the utility windows float on top of the document window?

- Is the utility window hidden when the corresponding application is in the background?

Active windows

- Do you display important information first in windows?

- Are the windows uncluttered and do they maintain a good appearance at different bit depths, if necessary?

- Does your application allow only one active window (the one the user is currently working in) at a time?

- Does the active window appear at the front of the screen, and is it visually distinct from inactive windows? For example, are the window controls missing from all but the active window?

- Does your design require users to activate a window and then act again to make a selection?

Opening windows

- Does your application provide a variety of ways for users to open windows?

- When the user opens a new document window, do you insert a title in the title bar, for example, "untitled"?

- Is it clear that the title you insert for a new document is intended to be a temporary title?

- When a user opens an existing document, does the document name appear as the window title?

Window display order

- Does your application display different types of windows in a specified order? For example, do document windows always appear closest to the desktop while dialog boxes appear on top of the document window?

- Have you thought carefully about the users' need to move from one window to another? When users need to move frequently between active windows, avoid using modal dialog boxes.

Window position

- Do you have a standard state for a window, that is, set values for the initial size and position of a window?

- If the user changes the standard state of a window, do you save this information so that when the document is reopened the window is the same size and in the same position as the user previously selected?

- Do you use the same size and position on the screen for all new document windows?

- Does your application position subsequent new document windows so that the title of the preceding window remains visible?

- When a document is reopened, is the user-specified window size adjusted to fit the size of the monitor (if it is different than the one previously used)?

- Do dialog boxes and alert boxes open on the screen where the user is working?

Window closures

- Does your application provide a variety of ways for users to close windows?

- When a document window closes, does an alert box appear to give users the option to save the changes they made to the document?

- Are there visible effects when a window closes? For example, does it seem to retreat to an icon?

Window movements

- Is there only one method of moving a window? Is the method the same across all applications?

- Does your application provide visible effects when users move a window, for example, a dotted outline of the window that moves with the pointer?

■ Does your application restrict users from moving a window to a position from which they cannot reposition it, for example, off the screen?

Window size changes

■ Does your application have a minimum and maximum window size based on the physical size of the display?

■ Is there only one method of changing the size of a window? Is the method the same across all applications?

■ Is there one corner of the window that is unmovable and from which the window grows or shrinks?

■ Does your application provide a visible effect of changing the window size, for example, a dotted outline that follows the pointer?

■ Does changing the window size affect only the amount of the document that is visible in the window?

Scrolling in windows

■ Does your application provide both horizontal and vertical scroll bars on a window?

■ Does a scroll box show users their location in the document relative to the whole document?

■ Do users have a choice of how to scroll through a document, for example, by clicking a scroll arrow, clicking the scroll box, or using function keys?

■ Does each method of scrolling a document move the contents of the document by a unique and specific unit (one line or one full window)?

■ Can the user drag the scroll box to quickly move in the document?

■ Does your application provide automatic scrolling when appropriate, for example, when the user enters new information at the edge of the window?

■ When you use automatic scrolling, do you move the document only as much as necessary?

Zoom box

■ Can users toggle between the standard state of a window and one that they have defined (user state) by using a zoom box?

Split windows

- Does your application provide a control that allows users to split a window?
- Can users split a window by dragging the control (split bar) to the location in the scroll bar where they want split windows to appear?
- Does your application provide visual feedback for users when they drag the split bar, for example, an outline of the split line that follows the pointer?
- Are the location of the split line and the content of the split windows saved when the document closes?
- Is the split bar easy to remove?

Dialog boxes

These guidelines help designers make choices about the design of dialog boxes and fill-in forms. Dialog can be modeless, that is, the application can continue whether or not the user responds to the box. Modal dialog boxes require the user to respond before the application can continue.

Appearance

- Have you standardized the appearance of the various types of dialog boxes?
- Do you customize colored dialog boxes using the default window color table to ensure consistency when users change colors?
- Does each dialog box use the standard system font size, for example, 12 point?
- Do you visually separate buttons that could cause data loss, for example, Save and Don't Save?

Movable modeless dialog boxes

- Can the user interact dynamically with all movable modeless dialog boxes?
- Do you use movable modeless dialog boxes whenever possible to allow users to perform tasks that can be performed in any order?
- Do you use movable modeless dialog boxes so that users can keep certain command accesses open and available?
- Does each movable modeless dialog box contain a title or text explaining which command or what circumstance triggered its appearance?

■ Does each movable modeless dialog box contain a close box, a title, and at least one button?

■ Does your application display movable modeless dialog boxes with logical preset values for the user to confirm?

■ Does your application display each movable modeless dialog box until the user explicitly closes it using a close control?

■ When you display a movable modeless dialog box, do you disable menu bar choices containing commands that are invalid in the current context?

■ Does your application restore menu items after the movable modeless dialog box closes?

■ Does your application give users immediate feedback by updating controls such as checkboxes and radio buttons?

■ Are the actions of your movable modeless dialog boxes consistent with user expectations about the results of their actions?

■ In what order do you check user input? Does your application provide appropriate feedback so that users know when their choices will take effect?

■ Should your application provide a dialog box enabling users to add new commands created with macros?

■ Should your application provide samples in dialog boxes showing changes that are not immediately displayed in the application?

Movable modal dialog boxes

■ Does your application use movable modal dialog boxes to complete actions begun with menu commands, for example, when it needs more information from the user?

■ Do your movable modal dialog boxes suspend actions in the same application so that the user must respond before continuing in the same application?

■ Can users switch to another application before responding to the movable modal dialog box?

■ Do your movable modal dialog boxes allow the user to use context-appropriate commands on the menu bar?

■ Do you distinguish movable modal dialog boxes from movable modeless dialog boxes by not including a close box, but by requiring users to click a button to respond?

- Are your modal dialog boxes movable to avoid obscuring information from users?

- Do you use movable modal dialog boxes to display the status of long-running operations executing in the background?

Modal dialog boxes

- Do you use modal dialog boxes when your application needs information from the user before it can continue?

- Does your application require the user to respond to modal dialog boxes before performing any other actions using the application?

- Do you use modal dialog boxes rarely, and for tasks that the users perform infrequently?

- Does your application display only one, or at most two, modal dialog boxes at one time, for example, an alert box displayed when a file might be overwritten?

- Does the second modal dialog box obscure as little of the first box as possible to give the user context for addressing the second box?

- Does resolving the second box also dismiss the first box and does canceling the second box leave the first box displayed so that the user can make alternative choices?

- Should help menus and edit menu items remain active when the modal dialog box displays?

Alert boxes (note, caution, stop)

- Do your alert boxes look like and behave like modal dialog boxes, of which they are a subset?

- Have you divided alert messages into categories, for example, nonthreatening notes, advanced warning of potential data loss or danger, or notification that an action cannot be completed because it is impossible in the current context?

- Should you provide an appropriate icon to represent each type of alert modal dialog box?

- Do your alert messages tell users what went wrong, why it went wrong, and what they can do about it?

Navigation/control

- Can the user navigate through the elements contained in dialog boxes by clicking the fields?

- Can the user navigate through the elements contained in dialog boxes by tabbing from field to field?

- Can the user move backward through the elements contained in dialog boxes by combining shift and tab?

- Can the user scroll one-by-one through displayed lists in dialog boxes using arrow keys?

- Can the user select list items in dialog boxes by typing the initial letters of list items?

- Does your application indicate which element in the dialog box is currently accepting input from the keyboard? For example, does that element contain a blinking insertion point or a selected text range?

- Does your application use the name of the document or application so that users can make decisions about one of several documents or applications that may be in use?

- Does your application have standard file dialog boxes that show a file's position in relation to the disk it is stored on?

Controls

These guidelines help designers make choices about the design of the graphical objects users manipulate in windows and dialog boxes. Using controls, users cause instant action, cause audible results, modify future actions, select choices, or assign parameters in a range.

Buttons

- Is each button sized to fit the name it surrounds?

- Does your application provide visual feedback when a user makes a selection, such as visually highlighting (inverting) a button?

- Does your application provide appropriate visual feedback even when a user activates buttons or fields from the keyboard or other input device?

- When a user presses the escape key, the command-period combination, or another escape sequence, do you invert the cancel button?

- Does your application respond to input from a mouse or pencil by tracking the location of the cursor and inverting the buttons only when the cursor encounters them?

- Does the location of the cursor when the mouse button is released determine the application's response? For example, does the application respond only if the cursor is on a button when the mouse button is released?

- Do you use an additional border to indicate default buttons?

- Do the Enter and Return buttons trigger the same action as if the user clicked the default button?

- If it is not potentially dangerous, is the default button the button users are most likely to select?

- Do you avoid using a designated default button if the Return key is used in editable text fields?

- Do you use an ellipsis in a button name if the button displays a dialog box requiring more information, not mere confirmation?

- Do your Cancel buttons allow users to dismiss an operation they started, with no side effects, or to undo changes done by the dialog box?

- Do your Done buttons maintain changes indicated in the dialog box and then close the box?

- Do boxes containing Done omit the Cancel button if returning the user to the original setup would be unreasonable?

- Do your Stop buttons halt a process midstream and allow for possible side effects?

- Do your OK buttons accept the changes, close the dialog box, and apply the settings made in the box?

- If you use Apply buttons, do you always accompany them with Cancel buttons to avoid confusing the meanings of OK and Cancel?

- Do you provide "hot" areas for selecting small or thin objects to avoid requiring extraordinary hand-eye coordination?

Radio buttons

- Should you use radio buttons to indicate related choices that are not necessarily opposite?

- Does your application turn off other selections when a radio button is clicked, since only one choice in the group is valid at one time?

- Do you indicate which button is active?

- Have you listed at least two choices in each group? Have you limited the choices to not more than seven or eight?

- Is each group visually separated, for example, with a dotted line?

- Does each group have a few words or a phrase to describe the choices?

- Are the radio buttons individually labeled or labeled at each end of a range?

- Can users click either the button or the label?

- Do you maintain the same labels, not changing content by context?

On/off choices

- Does your application label options that can be turned on or off?

- Can users click to activate or deactivate the option?

- Do the labels clearly indicate two opposite states?

- Have you grouped options into logical groups and visually separated the groups?

- Is each option independent of the other options in the group, that is, can any number in each group be on or off at any time?

- Does the application provide visual feedback indicating whether the options are activated or deactivated, such as a check or an x in a square?

- Do you use these types of choices to enable users to explicitly choose operations other than the normal operations?

- If labels are ambiguous, have you considered using radio-button-type choices instead?

Sliders

- Do you represent ranges of values, magnitude, or position using sliders?

- Do your sliders indicate the current value?

- Should your slider allow the user to control the current value?

- Should your slider represent digital or analog information?

- Do you use meaningful labels for sliders?

- Are you improperly representing the relative position of the visible portion of a document or list with a slider when you should be using a scrolling list and scroll bar instead?

Spin boxes or little arrows

- Does your application need to enable the user to increase or decrease values in a series by selecting one of two arrows pointing in opposite directions?

- Can the user choose to bypass the arrows and type numeric or textual values directly into the display box?

- Do the units of value depend on context?

- Can the user change the value by one unit by clicking on an arrow?

- Can the user press the arrow to continue changing the value until the mouse button is released?

- Do you highlight the arrows when they are clicked or pressed to give the user feedback?

Directory graphics

- Will users have a graphical representation of the directory and file organization?

Text entry fields

- Is the level of text editing capabilities you design for text entry fields compatible with full text editing capabilities?

- When entering text in fields, can users access the undo, cut, copy, paste, and clear options in the edit menu?

- Within text fields, can users delete text, double-click a word to select it, select a substring in the field and replace it, or select a whole field and type new text?

- When does your application perform edit checks? For example, if the only appropriate value in a field is a string of digits, do you display an alert box when the user types a nondigit?

- Should your application perform an edit check as soon as the user clicks outside the field or selects Return, Enter, or Tab?

Scrolling lists

- Does clicking an item in the list select it?

- Do you allow users to select more than one item by holding down the shift key and clicking additional choices?

- Can users scroll through the list without making any selections?

- If you must shorten item names to include them in a scrolling list, do you eliminate text in the middle to preserve the version numbers users often add to the ends of names?

- When users type ahead in the selection box and you move the list to the word, do you accept the users' keystrokes sequentially as part of the same word?

Keyboard input

- Does your application assign the same default functions to the two Enter keys on a typical PC keyboard?

- Does your application follow the general principles for arrow keys and PC navigation keys, such as ensuring that Ctrl plus a navigation key moves the cursor by a larger unit than the unmodified key?

- Does the Tab key navigate through the fields of a dialog box and wrap to the first field?

- What keyboard techniques can users employ to switch focus to other open windows?

Icons

These guidelines help designers make choices about icons, if used. Icons can be used in an application to help users manipulate objects, to save space, and to facilitate international use.

Do you need icons?

- Does your application require icons to facilitate direct manipulation, save space, or encourage international use?

- Do you avoid using icons when the information would be more clearly conveyed using text, for example, in error messages?

- Do you include text with the icon and provide the users the opportunity to see the icon only or the icon and text together?

- If you use icons, are they well-designed, legible, and consistent?

- Do you provide tool tips or balloon help for each icon? Does the tool tip include the menu name for the icon? Does the tool tip provide additional information?

Which icons? How many?

- Which parts of your application could be more clearly represented with icons instead of text?

- Does your application need to represent concrete and familiar items for users, such as tools?

- Do you need basic icons to represent documents, templates, database elements, PICT files, extensions, preferences, or editions?

- Can you limit the number of different icons to 12 to 20?

What do they look like?

- Have you designed the icons in a standard size (30- by 60-pixels)?

- Do you avoid gratuitously cute icons?

- Have you used straight lines and 45-degree angles wherever possible to avoid jagged edges?

- Have you adjusted the ragged edges using pixels of neutral colors on the outline (anti-aliasing)? If so, did you do so sparingly so that icons do not appear blurry or out of focus, causing some people to question the quality of their eyesight or the monitor display?

- Are your icons visually distinct and as much as possible like the objects they represent?

- Can you make your icons less confusing by avoiding the use of text and insignificant detail within the icon itself?

- If you use drop shadows to indicate light source, are the shadows consistently oriented throughout the interface?

- If users may be viewing your application on various monitors or different computers, do your icons appear consistent, for example, in 4-bit color for black-and-white monitors, and in 8-bit, 16-bit, or 32-bit color for color monitors?

- If you are representing actions, does the icon have a label?

Have you tested the icons?

- Do icons look right and convey the expected messages to users?

- Do you need to create a set of different sizes of the same icon, ot color versions, to convey the same idea on color monitors or in the parts of your application such as lists, menus, windows, or dialog boxes?

- Should users be enabled to choose whether they manipulate icons or activate menu commands in your application?

- Do you provide visual feedback when a user selects an icon, such as inverting black-and-white pixels or darkening colors?

- Does the selected icon appear significantly different, for example, do you avoid coloring icons half black and half white or with large areas of 50 percent gray, which would provide little change when inverted?

- Should you test icons or sets of icons on the various backgrounds on which they are likely to appear?

- Do you maintain a consistent meaning for each icon, since people expect different shapes to have different meanings and may infer a difference where none was intended?

- Can you test your icons on your target audience to make sure the icons are understandable to the user and sets are comprehended as being the same icon?

- Will you need a graphic arts designer to design or review your icons?

Do you expect this application to be used internationally?

- If your application will be used internationally, and since international computers are not limited to EGA and VGA standards, do your icons maintain their aesthetic appeal in various resolutions and screen aspect ratios?

- If your application is destined for worldwide use, do you avoid humor since humor typically does not translate well?

- Do your icons display images that will be recognizable in other cultures?

Color

These guidelines help designers make choices about colors, if used.

Can you use color and how much can you use?

- Will users of your application be using color-compatible computers and monitors?

- Does your use of color enhance meaning and help users focus on their work rather than drawing attention to the interface itself?

■ What is the minimal color capability of the computers and monitors on which your application is designed to run?

■ Will some users be using your application on black-and-white monitors, or, conversely, do the tasks completed with your application require full-color vision on a color monitor?

■ If you are creating training or tutorial materials, should you use color to lead a user through a lesson?

Which colors?

■ Have you optimized your design to the type of display most often used? For example, if users only have access to 4-bit color and black and white, do you use a 4-bit color palette?

■ Is your use of colors consistent with the way users may already be using colors in their work? For example, if you are writing an interface for street traffic controllers, do not choose orange, purple, and blue for the traffic light icons.

■ Would the use of colors help users categorize anything in their work?

■ Should you enable users to customize their work by enabling them to select a small number of colors, such as four to seven, and later change both the colors selected and the number of colors selected?

How do they look?

■ Will users be able to change the colors? If so, will the ones you choose be compatible? If users change colors, will that change the meaning conveyed by the colors?

■ Will your design have to accommodate various resolutions and screen aspect ratios, since international computers are not limited to EGA or VGA standards?

■ Do you use color redundantly to communicate important information to people with color-deficient vision, avoiding troublesome colors, particularly reds and greens?

■ Do you also provide other visual clues when you use color, such as text labels, shape, location or position, pattern, sound, or highlighting?

Testing

■ You will need to know how the computer numerically handles hue, saturation, and brightness values, but does your interface insulate novice users from unnecessary technical information and allow the user to use colors in the ways with which they are familiar?

■ How do users, both novice and expert, need to use colors or need colors represented to them?

■ Did you know that since light blue is difficult to distinguish, you should avoid using it unless you need a color that is unobtrusive, such as for backgrounds or grid lines?

■ Did you know that color in small objects is difficult for the human eye to distinguish? If you are conveying significant information with colors in small areas, you should select highly or obviously contrasting colors.

Behavior

These guidelines help designers make choices about the computer's response to the user.

User expectations

■ Does your application provide feedback in response to commands and signal task completion or duration for long operations?

■ Does your application consistently follow the conventions for click, press, drag, and double-click?

■ Does your application fulfill user expectations for selecting and completing tasks with text, arrays, or graphics, as necessary?

■ Does your application clearly define what actions occur when objects or icons are dragged and dropped?

Usability

■ Since some users have difficulty double- or triple-clicking, do you reserve these for shortcuts such as opening files and selecting words, at the same time designing other ways to perform the same task?

■ If your application only uses single- and double-clicking, does the application do nothing when the user triple-clicks by mistake? If your application only uses single-, double-, and triple-clicking, does the application do nothing when the user clicks four times by mistake?

■ Does your application "time out" on commands only when necessary, and only after allowing users a humanly appropriate amount of time to continue, for example, 1 minute?

- Do you provide drop-down lists of options so that the users do not have to remember what to enter in a field?

- Can users save or quit any time except within modal dialog boxes?

- Is the widest possible range of activities available to users at any time?

- If yours is not a music application, will users with hearing problems be able to use it? For example, do you accompany audible cues with visible cues and enable the user to choose visual cues instead of auditory signals?

- Have you avoided the use of Alt or Option key combinations if you expect your application to be used internationally, or if the system reserves Alt key combinations for its own use?

- Does your application minimize high-speed flashing on the monitor, which can cause seizures in some individuals?

- Do you minimize the number of screen colors to reduce flashing when a screen's color table is updated during screen redrawing?

- Are you protecting users by allowing them to undo actions? Can they undo a sequence of actions or only undo the last action taken?

- Are you protecting users by providing confirmation messages for potentially disastrous actions?

Pointers and selecting

- Should your application accept input from a mouse and other currently available input devices such as pointers, image scanners, and bar code scanners, as well as input from a keyboard, since some users may require or prefer keyboard input?

- Do users achieve the same results from pressing and holding a mouse or pointer button and clicking it, except in well-defined areas such as scroll bars and spin boxes?

- Should you enable users to double-drag (drag and drop) graphics or text within or between windows?

- Can users expect to use standard selection techniques throughout your application to make single, multiple, contiguous, or disjointed selections?

- Should your application enable users to use margin selection to select large areas of text or arrays with a single click?

- Should your application enable users to select graphical objects?

- Does your application differentiate between selection and manipulation, for example, visually changing the pointer or object while the mouse is in the button-down position and maintaining the feedback until the release transition?

■ Can users cancel selections or adjust selections in either direction?

■ Do you have keyboard techniques for making the types of selections available with a mouse or other pointer?

■ Does your application need to indicate hot spots or zones by changing the pointer shape when it is over the zone?

■ Does your application use a cursor, highlighting, or a dotted box to indicate where typed text or other user input will appear (where the interface focus is)?

■ Can users move selected objects without additionally selecting special borders or handles?

Text editing

■ Does your application avoid putting deleted text in the clipboard?

■ Whenever text is deleted, does the application close the gap?

■ Have you considered what kinds of spaces users will want when they cut and paste?

■ Does your application provide static progress indicators, such as a pointer of some kind, for tasks longer than 2 or 3 seconds and less than 5 seconds? Can users switch to another task while they are waiting?

■ If tasks will take longer than 5 seconds and prevent access to the window, does the application provide a dynamic progress indicator that is unmistakable and obvious (for example, graphical indicators, percentage-complete messages, elapsed-time messages, or progress indicators for subtasks)?

Language

These guidelines help designers make choices about language.

Fonts

■ Is your systemwide font at least 12 points in size, and is the type legible on the screen in all other sizes you use? Some newer fonts designed specifically for on-screen viewing may be legible in smaller sizes.

■ Do you use a sans serif font for most screen displays?

- Do you use bold fonts for control labels in dialogs so labels remain legible when dimmed to show unavailability?

- Do you have consistent rules for positions of control labels?

- Do you use consistent capitalization throughout the text used in the application?

- Do you avoid displaying words in all caps?

- Do your messages suggest correct actions and even avoid the word error to avoid blaming the user?

Translations

- Will your application be translated?

- To facilitate translations, for example, if you expect your application to be used internationally, do you store interface text as resources in the resource file rather than including it as source code for the application (title bar titles, menu names, menu items, control labels, list items, messages)?

- If you expect to translate text, have you limited English text to about one-half of the available space in limited places like status bars, since you can expect some translations to increase text volume by 30 to 100 percent?

- Have you avoided having your readers extract information based on text position alone in menus, dialog boxes, or windows, since translators may have to move text?

- Did you know that shortcut combinations such as Alt-hyphen may not translate well, since international keyboards may not be labeled with the same punctuation, or the punctuation may only be available using the Alt key?

- Have you avoided using text in icons, especially if your application will be translated?

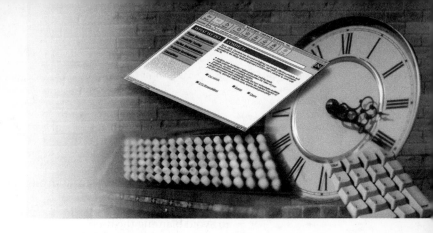

Index